Myth and the Making of History

SUNY series in Chinese Philosophy and Culture
———————
Roger T. Ames, editor

Myth and the Making of History

Narrating Early China with Sarah Allan

Edited by
CONSTANCE A. COOK,
CHRISTOPHER J. FOSTER,
and SUSAN BLADER

Associate Editor
AMY MATTHEWSON

Cover Credit: From *Old Pines* 歲寒圖 (2023). Six images from a folding album. Ink on rice paper.
© Wang Mansheng 2023

Published by State University of New York Press, Albany

© 2024 State University of New York

All rights reserved

Printed in the United States of America

No part of this book may be used or reproduced in any manner whatsoever without written permission. No part of this book may be stored in a retrieval system or transmitted in any form or by any means including electronic, electrostatic, magnetic tape, mechanical, photocopying, recording, or otherwise without the prior permission in writing of the publisher.

For information, contact State University of New York Press, Albany, NY
www.sunypress.edu

Library of Congress Cataloging-in-Publication Data

Names: Cook, Constance A., editor. | Foster, Christopher J., editor. | Blader, Susan, editor.
Title: Myth and the making of history : narrating early China with Sarah Allan / edited by Constance A. Cook, Christopher J. Foster, and Susan Blader.
Description: Albany : State University of New York Press, [2024] | Series: SUNY series in Chinese Philosophy and Culture | Includes bibliographical references and index.
Identifiers: ISBN 9781438497686 (hardcover : alk. paper) | ISBN 9781438497709 (ebook)
Further information is available at the Library of Congress.

10 9 8 7 6 5 4 3 2 1

To Sarah Allan

Photo of Sarah Allan by C. A. Cook, Yantai, China, 2014.

Contents

Preface ix

Acknowledgments xv

1. The Place of Yi Yin in the Shang Pantheon 1
   Zhu Fenghan

2. Cao E, the Filial Water Goddess: Gender and Text in the Promotion of a Two-Thousand-Year-Old Cult 25
   Robin D. S. Yates

3. An Examination of Commentaries to *Analects* 7.14, "Confucius Listened to the Shao Performance in Qi" 53
   Wang Yunfei

4. Xia-Shang-Zhou Chronology Project and Archaeological Research on the Xia Dynasty 77
   Li Boqian

5. Formation of the "Nine Provinces" according to the Tribute Payments Recorded in Oracle-Bone and Bronze Inscriptions 89
   Shen Jianhua

6. The Tsinghua University *Yue Gong qi shi* Manuscript and Township Administration in the State of Yue during the Spring and Autumn Period 121
   Wang Jinfeng

7. Marriage and Social Networks in Zhou China: Reflections on the Rules Governing Female Names in Bronze Inscriptions   145
   Li Feng

8. The Faces of Cao Gui: Fact and Meaning in Warring States and Early Han Historiography   171
   Andrew Meyer

9. Historical Narratives in Early Chinese Classics: The Case of the "Great King Leaving Bin" in Transmitted Texts and the Bamboo Slips of the *Zhou xun*   197
   Cui Xiaojiao

10. Rebuilding King Wen: Paratext as Intellectual Biography in the *Yi Zhou shu* Preface   215
    Paul Nicholas Vogt

11. Forging a "Meta-tradition": The Distinctive Philosophy of the *Huainanzi*   239
    Harold D. Roth

Afterword   267
   Harold D. Roth

List of Contributors   271

Index   273

Preface

The advent of scientific archaeology and the discovery of oracle bones more than one hundred years ago opened up the field of early China studies in dramatic ways. The constant unveiling of new archaeological discoveries, including inscriptions and manuscripts, has forced scholars of early China to broaden the scope of their research beyond the traditional sources of our received corpus. At the same time, novel theoretical approaches and methodologies have been brought to bear alongside this wave of new data. The field has been bursting with innovation and recalibration ever since.

There has been no scholar more attuned to these developments than Sarah Allan. Over the past fifty years, she has published pathbreaking scholarship on early China. Utilizing both received texts and archaeological discoveries as her sources, she has helped mold early Chinese studies with pioneering research on a remarkable range of topics and time periods—from the Neolithic up through the Han—in disciplines as varied as paleography and conceptual metaphor theory.

Myth and the Making of History is part of a three-book series, with *Bone, Bronze, and Bamboo* and *Metaphor and Meaning*, that celebrates Allan and the integral role she has played in the immense growth and development of early China as a field. Scholars throughout the world, who have collaborated with her as mentors, colleagues, and students, were invited to contribute essays in her honor, which we have compiled into these three books. While the range of specialist essays presented here testifies to the expanding boundaries of the study of early China, we believe that, as with Allan's scholarship from the very beginning, there is a compelling and overlapping concern: to understand early China on its own terms. Whether through uncovering the root metaphors of the culture, articulating the interplay between myth and history, or examining newly discovered artifacts, Allan has sought to detach from our modern vantage, to enter into the minds of the ancient peoples of China, understand how they thought, and discern how they communicated those ideas.

∾

"But what is history and what is myth?" It is a question, asked by Sarah Allan, that succinctly articulates one of the longstanding concerns of her scholarship: the complex interplay between myth and history in early China.[1] Understanding this interplay between myth and history motivated Allan's first published article, "The Identities of Taigong Wang in Zhou and Han Literature," and found fruitful expression in her initial book, *The Heir and the Sage*.[2] Using structuralism as a tool, Allan in *The Heir and the Sage* demonstrates how the "historic" model of government advocated by sage kings who ruled in distant antiquity served "to mediate an inherent social conflict—a conflict between the interests of kingship and those of community" that was felt at the time when these legends were being told.[3] In this sense, history, like myth, was a structured narrative that served to ameliorate conflict in the present.

In her subsequent book, *The Shape of the Turtle: Myth, Art, and Cosmos in Early China*, Allan was among the first scholars to challenge the existence of a Xia dynasty.[4] One of her crucial insights is how Shang myths were historicized by the Zhou for political legitimation: "The legend of Yao's abdication to Shun was a transformation of a Shang myth in which the high lord, *di* 帝, appointed the first Shang ruler . . . (while) the Xia were originally the mythical inverse of the Shang . . . [but] transformed into the story of an historical dynasty at the beginning of the Zhou."[5] Here myth transforms into history.

Myth and the Making of History presses upon the oft permeable boundary between the past and the stories we tell about it. Each chapter adopts unique lenses by which to contemplate Allan's question, "What is history and what is myth?" When brought together, the book engages in a broad and interdisciplinary dialogue on the topic, among which readers will discern both harmonizing and discordant voices. Yet overarching themes emerge. *Myth and the Making of History* begins with chapters concerned with mythologization. How do myths arise, what imbues them with potency, and how are myths themselves historically contingent? Zhu Fenghan examines the figure of Yi Yin 伊尹, whom Sarah Allan has also studied in depth.[6] In Warring States literature, Yi Yin is often depicted as a "founding minister," who was once a lowly cook or personal servant but then was raised up to become minister by the first ruler of Shang, Cheng Tang 成湯, after recognizing Yi Yin's great merits.[7] Through the close reading of unearthed oracle-bone inscriptions, Zhu looks to the prior mythologization of Yi Yin that already took place during the late Shang period. Zhu details the logic behind Yi Yin's inclusion in the Shang pantheon as a "naturalized" human spirit, despite lacking blood ties to the Shang royal family. Intriguingly, this early religious treatment of Yi Yin could bear fruitful connections to Allan's interpretation of the much later and exceptional portrayal of Yi Yin as a shaman in the Warring States manuscript *Chi jiu zhi ji Tang zhi wu* 赤鳩之集湯之屋, among the Tsinghua University collection.[8]

Whereas Zhu pursues a largely synchronic analysis of Shang mythological logic, Robin D. S. Yates conducts a diachronic survey of a two-thousand-year-old local Shaoxing 紹興 cult to Cao E 曹娥. Various factors contributed to the growth and longevity of this cult, from Cao E's veneration as a moral paragon of filial piety and ascension as a tidal deity, to even the intrigue that arose over an Eastern Han stele inscription bearing her legend. Yates reveals not only how these facets of the Cao E myth became irrevocably intertwined, but also how the nature of the cult shifted in certain historical moments, bringing one aspect of the myth to the fore over others. The versatility of the Cao E myth, in this regard, accounts for the resilience of the cult, which survives to the present.

In *Lunyu* 論語 (Analects) 7.14, Confucius is said to have lost his appetite upon hearing a performance of the Shao 韶 musical piece in Qi—but was Confucius overwhelmed by the beauty of the piece, or appalled by the ritual impropriety of its performance? Wang Yunfei charts the diachronic ebb and flow between these two interpretative positions, from the Han to the Qing, explaining the evolution of their debates and why a given theory found favor in each dynasty. Wang's chapter highlights the influential role played by commentarial traditions in shaping imaginations of the past, showing how later thinkers exploited the brevity and ambiguous wording of this *Lunyu* anecdote, molding Confucius's deeds to fit the cultural narratives of their own day.

The next series of chapters in *Myth and the Making of History* search for historicity, wrestling with the methodological question of how to learn what actually happened in the past, in the face of mythological invention and the losses wrought by time. As a point of convergence, each chapter relies heavily on archaeological data and unearthed manuscripts as a foil against which received traditions may be reconsidered. The Xia-Shang-Zhou

Chronology Project, which ran from 1996 to 2000, was a massive research program that ambitiously aimed to clarify the absolute chronology of ancient China's first dynasties.⁹ Li Boqian, who participated in the project, critically evaluates the role of archaeology within this initiative, especially for determining the existence of a Xia dynasty, one of the most controversial issues of Chinese history and, as noted before, a topic of great interest to Sarah Allan.¹⁰

For scholars interested in reconstructing the details of sociopolitical systems of ancient states, unearthed paleographic sources offer an exciting new purview to sort through layers of myth and anecdote for historical foundations. Shen Jianhua compares the "Nine Provinces" (*jiu zhou* 九州) model, most famously forwarded by the received *Yu gong* 禹貢 (Tribute of Yu) chapter of the *Shangshu* 尚書 (Venerated Documents), to records found in Shang oracle-bone inscriptions. Noticing a correlation in place names, regional products, and ideological commitments, Shen argues that the Nine Provinces model derives from the Shang tributary system and its corresponding worldview. Similarly, Wang Jinfeng conducts a close reading of the Tsinghua University Warring States bamboo-slip manuscript *Yue Gong qi shi* 越公其事 (May the Lord of Yue Attend), which narrates how the coastal state of Yue 越 grew powerful and defeated their archrivals, the Wu 吳, during the late Spring and Autumn period. Wang analyzes how the text describes units of territorial administration, to extract from a later anecdotal history the earlier political organization of townships and cities in Yue.

The making of history, in multiple senses, is at stake with the chapter by Li Feng. Li analyzes how Zhou scribes presented the titles and names of women among inscriptions on bronze vessels. He argues that these naming conventions reflected sociopolitical hierarchy, and as such reinforced social order by defining marriage relations between states and lineages. This was a making of history by the Zhou scribes, who employed language to fashion the remembrance of women in Zhou society and, further, manage how marriage demarcated state and lineage relations thereafter. Yet Li's chapter also engages in a sustained methodological debate with the scholar Wu Zhenfeng 吳鎮烽, over whether and how to excavate historical rules from the complex datasets encountered in research on early China. In this regard, Li addresses the modern making of history, weighing the objectives and possibilities of history as an academic discipline today.

Li's reflections bridge aptly to the next series of chapters in *Myth and the Making of History*, which concern the nature of history writing in early China. Andrew Meyer follows Sarah Allan's use of the theoretical model developed by Claude Lévi-Strauss for the analysis of prehistoric mythology and extends the model further, by applying it to narratives about a figure from historical times, Cao Gui 曹劌, the Spring and Autumn period knight. In doing so, Meyer offers fresh insights into the nature of early Chinese historiography itself, depicting history writing as a bricolage of fact and meaning, where an "anxiety of interpretation" is offset by the productivity of "fertile versatility." This dynamic also finds beautiful display in Cui Xiaojiao's study of anecdotes about Zhou founder kings "leaving Bin," which features ideologically charged variations in different textual traditions. Cui considers both received works, such as the *Shijing* 詩經 (Classic of Poetry), and newly discovered manuscripts, like the Peking University *Zhou xun* 周馴 (Zhou Instructions), and reveals a plasticity to history which opened the past to manipulation for later political purposes.

Yet, as Meyer foreshadows, with the potent versatility of early Chinese historiography, and its attendant interpretative anxieties, control over historical narratives often meant subsuming (rather than denying outright) texts with diverse, dissonant, or even conflicting accounts of the past. The final chapters of *Myth and the Making of History* delve into this process, detailing the strategies adopted by certain textual corpora to incorporate and explain diverse elements as part of a single overarching tradition. Paul Nicholas Vogt investigates how the Han preface to the *Yi Zhou shu* 遺周書 (Remnant Zhou Documents) sought to bring order to the "King Wen (周文王) cycle" of texts in this collection. By constructing an intellectual biography for King Wen, the *Yi Zhou shu* preface contextualizes, and thereby legitimizes, the diverse or even conflicting legacies surrounding the legendary Zhou founder. King Wen's life journey, with the growth and contradiction attested by personhood itself, resonates with the growth and contradiction apparent in the figure of King Wen manifest within the texts. In another Han period compilation, the *Huainanzi* 淮南子 (Master of Huainan), a different approach is taken to synthesize intellectual diversity. Harold D. Roth details how this syncretic text establishes a "meta-tradition," by subsuming divergent earlier traditions within a cosmological vision and self-cultivation program known as "techniques of the way" (*daoshu* 道術).

Myth and the Making of History does not—indeed cannot—provide a clear answer to the question, "What is history and what is myth?" The chapters herein demonstrate, as has Sarah Allan's masterful work, the profound entanglement of history and myth, of the past and of the stories we tell about it. Each shapes the other, weaving together an even grander narrative, one that extols the richness of our human experience. In reflecting upon the purpose of history, R. G. Collingwood once mused that "history is for human self-knowledge . . . the only clue to what man can do is what man has done."[11] What Allan's scholarship reminds us, as do the chapters found here in *Myth and the Making of History*, is that what has been done was only made possible by dreaming of what could be.

—Constance A. Cook, Christopher J. Foster, and Susan Blader

Notes

1. Sarah Allan, *The Heir and the Sage: Dynastic Legend in Early China* (San Francisco: Chinese Materials Center, 1981), ix. See also her revised and expanded edition, published by State University of New York Press in 2017.

2. Sarah Allan, "The Identities of Taigong Wang in Zhou and Han Literature," *Monumenta Serica* 30 (1972–1973): 57–99, based on her prior 1969 MA thesis.

3. Allan, *The Heir and the Sage*, ix–x; and also her further discussion in the 2017 edition, especially 8.

4. Sarah Allan, *The Shape of the Turtle: Myth, Art, and Cosmos in Early China* (Albany: State University of New York Press, 1991).

5. Allan, *The Shape of the Turtle*, 17–18.

6. For Allan's recent work on Yi Yin, see, for example, "'When Red Pigeons Gathered on Tang's House': A Warring States Period Tale of Shamanic Possession and Building Construction Set at the Turn of the Xia and Shang Dynasties," *Journal of the Royal Asiatic Society* (2015): 1–20.

7. On Allan's understanding of the "founding minister" trope and her survey of these portrayals of Yi Yin, see especially "'When Red Pigeons Gathered on Tang's House,'" 9–12.

8. Allan, "'When Red Pigeons Gathered on Tang's House,'" 13–20. Yi Yin features prominently in several Warring States period bamboo-slip manuscripts in the Tsinghua University collection. In the partner volumes to *Myth and the Making of History*, Shirley Chan (in *Metaphor and Meaning*) and Zhao Pingan 趙平安 and Wang Tingbin 王挺斌 (in *Bone, Bronze, and Bamboo*) discuss these manuscripts from diverse methodological perspectives.

9. Li Xueqin, Sarah Allan (trans.), "The Xia-Shang-Zhou Chronology Project: Methodology and Results," *Journal of East Asian Archaeology* 4 (2002): 321–333.

10. In addition to *The Shape of the Turtle*, see also her: "The Myth of the Xia Dynasty," *Journal of the Royal Asiatic Society of Great Britain and Ireland* 2 (1984): 242–256; and "Erlitou and the Formation of Chinese Civilization: Toward a New Paradigm," *Journal of Asian Studies* 66, no. 2 (2007): 461–496.

11. R. G. Collingwood, *The Idea of History* (Oxford: Oxford University Press, 1994), 10.

Acknowledgments

We would like to express our most heartfelt appreciation to our colleagues for their enthusiastic engagement with this project, their insightful scholarly outputs, and their extraordinary patience. We are certain that, as a result of their care and attention, the essays in the three books—*Myth and the Making of History: Narrating Early China with Sarah Allan*; *Bone, Bronze, and Bamboo: Unearthing Early China with Sarah Allan*; and *Metaphor and Meaning: Thinking Through Early China with Sarah Allan*—will be welcomed by scholars and students in the China field, as well as by individuals interested or involved in the study of any ancient civilization.

These three books could never have been brought to completion without the editing expertise of four colleagues. Gail Patten[1] did the first complete editing and compilation of the pieces. The editorial and computer expertise of Ehud Z. Benor[2] was indispensable in creating the template required by SUNY Press to unify the formatting of each chapter. William N. French III,[3] at an exceptionally busy and stressful time, took on the huge task of finalizing *Metaphor and Meaning*, for which we are immensely grateful. Amy Matthewson[4] beautifully finalized both *Myth and the Making of History* and *Bone, Bronze, and Bamboo*. We also wish to express our gratitude to James Peltz[5] for his support of this massive project, and to the two anonymous reviewers of *Myth and the Making of History*, who offered much helpful advice.

Our thanks go to Lehigh University for providing Constance A. Cook[6] with research funding as part of her position as an NEH Distinguished Professor. The project began when Cook was an active member of the Institute for Advanced Study in Princeton, New Jersey, whose support is much appreciated. Christopher J. Foster[7] is grateful for the support he received from Pembroke College, University of Oxford, when Stanley Ho Junior Research Fellow; and from the British Academy and SOAS University of London, during his British Academy Postdoctoral Fellowship.

Finally, Connie and Chris both wish to acknowledge the profound contribution of Susan Blader,[8] who conceived of the project as a felicitous tribute to Sarah, nurtured it constantly, and ensured—through all manner of trials and tribulations—that it grew to adulthood.

Notes

1. Administrator, Department of History, Dartmouth College, retired.
2. Emeritus, Department of Religion, Dartmouth College.
3. PhD ABD, Chinese History, East Asian Languages and Civilizations, Harvard University; Dartmouth '08.
4. PhD, History, SOAS University of London.
5. Associate Director and Editor in Chief at State University of New York Press.
6. Professor and Chair, Modern Languages and Literatures, Lehigh University.
7. PhD Chinese History, East Asian Languages and Civilizations, Harvard University; Dartmouth College '06.
8. Associate Professor Emerita, Asian and Middle Eastern Languages and Literatures, Dartmouth College.

1

The Place of Yi Yin in the Shang Pantheon

ZHU FENGHAN

TRANSLATED BY CHRISTOPHER J. FOSTER

In her book *The Heir and the Sage: Dynastic Legend in Early China*, Sarah Allan discusses the figure of Yi Yin 伊尹: "Yi Yin, the founding minister of Tang and the regent of Tang's grandson Tai Jia according to the traditional texts, receives sacrifices and influences natural phenomena in the same manner as the ancestors of the Shang kings, though he has no cyclical name and was clearly not an ancestor."[1] Elsewhere, when analyzing the relationship between Yi Yin and Tai Jia 太甲, she notes that the "Yin benji" 殷本紀 chapter of the *Shiji* 史記 describes Yi Yin as voluntarily returning the rule back to Tai Jia. Yet, in the *Guben zhushu jinian* 古本竹書紀年, Yi Yin did not bestow the rule on Tai Jia, rather Tai Jia killed Yi Yin. Allan remarks: "I do not see why the account of Yi Yin and Tai Jia's struggle in the *Guben Zhushu Jinian* need . . . be taken as more historical than other early accounts."[2] She thus questions the reliability of the *Guben zhushu jinian* on this event. Allan points out that when Yi Yin replaces Tai Jia, this "is a confirmation of the right of virtue over heredity," but he ultimately returns the rule back to Tai Jia "[because of] Tai Jia's right by heredity," and, in doing so, "he

---

This chapter was produced as part of the PRC Ministry of Education–sponsored Paleography and Chinese Civilization Inheritance and Development Program 古文字與中華文明傳承發展工程.

voluntarily subordinates his power and right to rule by virtue to the heir's hereditary right to the throne."³

Although our historical records offer differing accounts of Yi Yin's heritage and how he became Cheng Tang's 成湯 assistant, it is clear that he did not belong to the Shang 商 royal family through lineal descent. The *Lüshi chunqiu* 呂氏春秋 chapter "Benwei" 本味 narrates a myth about Yi Yin's birth, claiming that one day a daughter of Youshen 有侁 was out picking mulberries and found the infant Yi Yin in a hollow mulberry tree. This was because "his mother resided by Yi River" 其母居伊水之上, and, when the town flooded, her body transformed into a hollow mulberry tree.⁴ Thus, Yi Yin's tribal name, Yi 伊, is taken from the Yi River 伊水, despite the fact that he was raised by the Youshen tribe. The word written *shen* 侁 in the name Youshen is sometimes also written as *shen* 莘. The "Benwei" chapter moreover claims that Yi Yin joined Cheng Tang when he came with Youshen as an attendant for her marriage to Tang; the "Yin benji" also claims this.⁵ Thus, we know that the Youshen tribe was once connected to the Shang royal lineage through marriage. In light of this, Yi Yin belongs to the "Shang people" in the broader sense of this term (namely, as a clan group based on lineal descent but also including extra-lineal members who belonged to tribes attached to the clan via marriage and in other ways).

The appearance of Yi Yin in the Shang royal sacrificial records on late Shang oracle-bone inscriptions (hereafter OBI), show that the *Guben zhushu jinian* claim that Yi Yin was killed by Tai Jia is false. Scholars noticed this contradiction early on, and Allan is undoubtedly correct to question the historicity of the *Guben zhushu jinian* account.⁶

A proverb given in *Zuo zhuan* 左傳, "Duke Xi" 僖公, year ten, states: "Spirits do not relish sacrifices from those not of their kind; and the people do not offer sacrifices to those not of their clan" (神不歆非類民不祀非族).⁷ That this was indeed the guiding principle behind sacrificial practices in early China is substantiated by our extant data. Yet Yi Yin, who was neither a Shang ancestral king, nor even related to the Shang by lineal descent, still received sacrifices from Shang royalty. The reason for this must be because, as our historical records document, Yi Yin once aided Cheng Tang in defeating the Xia 夏; and he, moreover, helped rectify Tai Jia's behavior. Therefore, he was regarded as one of the founding fathers of the Shang dynasty. An anecdote about an official named Zhan Qin 展禽, recorded in the *Guoyu* 國語 "Lu yu, shang" 魯語上 is often raised to interpret this phenomenon, because it concerns a similar case where a nonblood relative received sacrifices.⁸ At the time of Duke Xi of Lu 魯僖公, a seabird (named

Yuanju 爰居) perched outside the eastern gate of Lu for three days, and the minister Zang Wenzhong 臧文仲, who was in charge of the government then, directed people from the domain to offer sacrifices to it. Zhan Qin thought that this was improper, so he explained:

> Sacrifices are important ceremonies (that order) the state. One must therefore be careful in establishing sacrifices, as they constitute a canon (of activities regulating) our state. Now, without reason, you have added to this canon (of sacrificial procedures), which is inappropriate for a good ruler. When the sage kings (first) established sacrifices, they sacrificed to those who brought order to the people, who died in service (to the realm), who labored to found our state, who were able to manage great disasters, and who guarded against great perils. Anything not of this sort was not included in our canon of sacrifices.
>
> 夫祀, 國之大節也, 故慎制祀以為國典, 今無故而加典, 非政之宜也. 夫聖王之制祀也, 法施於民則祀之, 以死勤事則祀之, 以勞定國則祀之. 能禦大災則祀之, 能捍大患則祀之. 非是族也, 不在祀典.

What this anecdote proves is that, during the Pre-Qin period, in addition to offering sacrifices to blood relatives, sacrifices could be made to figures who served the domain and its people in an extraordinary fashion. This rule is also recorded in the *Liji* 禮記 chapter "Jifa" 祭法, which will later be discussed further.

In fact, in addition to sacrificing to meritorious figures like the ancestral spirits and Yi Yin, the Shang also offered sacrifices to nature spirits, such as the Fang 方 (lit., regions) and Tu 土 (She 社; lit., altars of the soil), as well as entities whom we have yet to fully identify, such as X 𡆥. As Yi Yin was a spirit not tied to the Shang royal clan via lineal descent, what do Shang OBI tell us about his sacrifices?

Yi Yin's Day-Name (*riming* 日名)

Among the extant divination inscriptions from Yinxu 殷墟, none from the Bin 賓 diviner group of Wu Ding's reign include sacrifices to Yi Yin. The inscriptions that do mention Yi Yin belong to a nonroyal set of OBI (*fei wang buci* 非王卜辭), specifically, Yi 1 (乙一), dated to approximately the mid–Wu Ding 武丁 reign, and Li 1 (歷一), dated to the late Wu Ding reign.[9] It therefore appears that the absence of Yi Yin in Bin group inscriptions was not necessarily because Yi Yin was precluded from sacrifices during Wu Ding's reign, or that Yi Yin was only belatedly incorporated into sacrificial ceremonies. Rather, this absence may relate to the institutional roles performed by the Bin diviner group; for instance, they may not have overseen matters in which Yi Yin was supplicated via divination.

An analysis of inscriptions with content related to Yi Yin sacrifices reveals that these sacrifices mostly fell on *ding* 丁 days. Consider, for instance:[10]

Crack-making on a . . . *mao* day by Zi, on the coming *ding* day we will perform the *rong*-rite with four *lao*-sacrifices . . . Yi Yin.

卯子卜，來丁酯四牢. . . . 伊尹 (HJ 21573, Yi 1, fig. 1.1:1)

Crack-making on a *guichou* day by Zi, on the coming *ding* day we will perform the *rong*-rite, Yi Yin arrives.

癸丑子卜，來丁酯，伊尹至 (HJ 21574, Yi 1, fig. 1.1:2)

Crack-making on a *xinhai* day, Yi Yin arrives, use one ox.

辛亥卜，至伊尹用一牛 (HJ 21575, fig. 1.1:3)

Crack-making on a *yisi* day . . . Yi Yin . . . on the *dingwei* day . . . use this.

乙巳卜，. . . 伊尹 . . . 于丁未 . . . 茲用 (HJ 32792, Li 1)

On the coming day *dinghai* offer a *sui*-rite to Yi . . .

于來日丁亥又歲伊 . . . (HJ 32795, Li 1, fig. 1.1:4)

On a *guihai* day, it was divined: Should we offer a report to Yi Yin, let us on this present *dingmao* day perform the *rong*-rite with three oxen. Use this.

癸亥貞，其又㞢于伊尹，叀今丁卯酯三牛，茲用 (TN 1122 partial, Li 2)

The Place of Yi Yin in the Shang Pantheon | 5

Crack-making on a *jiazi* day, offer (sacrifices) to Yi Yin, (on the) *dingmao* day.

甲子卜，又于伊尹，丁卯 (HJ 32785, Li 1, figure 1.1:5)

Crack-making on a *yisi* day . . . Yi Yin . . . on the *dingwei* day.

乙巳卜 . . . 伊尹 . . . 于丁未 (HJ 32793, Li 2)

To Yi, let it be the *dingyou* day.

于伊，叀丁酉 (HJ 32550, Li 2, figure 1.1:6)

On the coming *dinghai* day, offer the *sui*-rite to Yi.

于來丁亥又歲伊 (HJ 32746, Li 2, fig. 1.1:7)

Figure 1.1. Oracle-Bone Inscriptions on Sacrificing to Yi Yin on *Ding* Days (1). Source: Guo Moruo 郭沫若, ed., Hu Houxuan 胡厚宣, comp., *Jiaguwen heji* 甲骨文合集, 13 vols. (Beijing: Zhonghua, 1978–1982).

In OBI that divine about sacrificial matters, the day on which the divination occurred is not necessarily the same day on which a given spirit should receive sacrifices. The inscriptions listed here, however, clearly divine whether Yi Yin should be sacrificed to on *ding* days.[11] The name Yi 伊 (with only a single character) has long been regarded as an abbreviation for Yi Yin. Qiu Xigui 裘錫圭 suspects: "When the character *yi* 伊 appears in this way, it stands for the two characters *yi yin* 伊尹." This is quite likely the case.[12]

Scholars have also noted the following set of inscriptions:[13]

On a *jiayin* day, it was divined: Yi (receives) *sui*-rites, coinciding with a Bao Ding day.

On a *jiayin* day it was divined: Yi (receives) *sui*-rites, coinciding with a Da Ding day.

甲寅貞, 伊歲, 苐 (遘) 報丁日

甲寅貞, 伊歲, 苐 (遘) 大丁日 (TN 1110, Li 2, fig. 1.2:1)

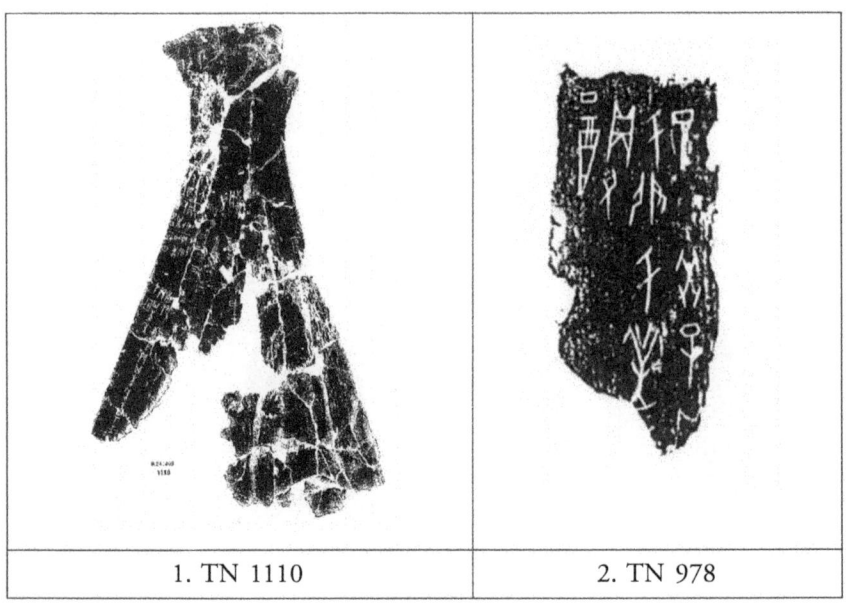

| 1. TN 1110 | 2. TN 978 |

Figure 1.2. Oracle-Bone Inscriptions on Sacrificing to Yi Yin on *Ding* Days (2). *Source*: Zhongguo shehui kexueyuan kaogu yanjiusuo 中國社會科學院考古研究所, ed., *Xiaotun nandi jiagu* 小屯南地甲骨, 3 vols. (Beijing: Zhonghua, 1980–1983).

The days on which *sui*-rites were performed for Yi Yin fall on the same day when sacrifices were offered to Bao Ding 報丁 and Da Ding 大丁, which were clearly also *ding* days.

From the previously listed oracle-bone inscriptions, we may surmise that, by the late Shang period, the Shang kings mainly believed that sacrifices to Yi Yin ought to be conducted on *ding* days. Examples from other inscriptions show that, when the recipient of sacrifices is a human spirit, the day they receive sacrifices corresponds to what is then their "day-name" (*riming* 日名). If this holds true for Yi Yin as well, then it is possible that his day-name was Ding. In fact, in the following inscription, the name Yi Ding 伊丁 appears:

On a *dingyou* day it was divined: Offer (sacrifices) to Yi Ding.

丁酉貞，又于伊丁 (TN 978, Li.2, fig. 1.2:2)

The character *ding* 丁 in the name Yi Ding is read by some scholars as *beng* 祊, the name of a sacrifice,[14] but as HJ 32785 (quoted earlier) reveals, the grammar of this line allows for the name of the sacrifice's recipient to follow after the phrase "offer (sacrifices) to" (*you yu* 又于). This would mean that the term Yi Ding 伊丁 is a name and that *ding* is potentially the day-name granted to Yi Yin. Of course, this inscription (TN 978) may also be read as: "On the *dingyou* day it was divined: Offer (sacrifices) to Yi, (on a) *ding* day." In other words, it is feasible that a break is implied between the name Yi and the word *ding*. This reading also parallels the structure of HJ 32785, which says: "Offer (sacrifices) to Yi Yin, (on a) *dingmao* day." If this is the case, TN 978 would then state that "on the *dingyou* day it was divined whether or not to offer (sacrifices) to Yi on a *ding* day."[15] Note, however, that this divination took place on a *dingyou* day, a *ding* day already. Grammatically speaking, we would therefore expect the diviner to ask whether or not "today" (*jin ri* 今日) or a "coming *ding* day" (*lai ding* 來丁) was appropriate for the sacrifice, making the general question of "on a *ding* day" seem somewhat out of place in the context of this line.

Since Yi Yin appears to have been granted a day-name, sacrificing to him accords fully with Shang religious custom. He was incorporated into the sacrificial canon as a human spirit with the day-name of Ding. This also agrees with our previous discussion about Yi Yin's heritage, as his tribe was originally part of the "Shang" clan group. Sacrifices to Yi Yin, therefore, rightfully belonged within the Shang cultural sphere.

Yi Yin in Relation to the Former Lords (*xiangong* 先公) and High Ancestors (*gaozu* 高祖)

Earlier scholarship on OBI and Shang history refers to Da Yi 大乙 (Cheng Tang) and the Shang rulers who followed after him as the "Former Kings" (*xianwang* 先王). The royal lineage for this period of Shang history is well known and is without major complications. The ancestors prior to Da Yi to whom the Shang kings sacrificed, as seen in OBI, are customarily called the "Former Lords" (*xiangong* 先公).[16] The Former Lords include six kings, from Shang Jia 上甲 to Shi Gui 示癸, who are thought to belong to the royal family through lineal descent. These six figures are included in the Zhou sacrificial calendar and received sacrificial offerings in the same fashion as Da Yi and the latter Former Kings.[17] The circumstances surrounding the Former Lords who came before Shang Jia are more complex, with Nao 夒 and Wang Hai 王亥 all regarded as "High Ancestors" (*gaozu* 高祖) by the Shang people; He 河 and Yue 嶽 enjoyed a similar status.[18] He (lit., "river") and Yue (lit., "mountain") were originally the names of nature spirits, but in OBI they are strongly anthropomorphized, a phenomenon common in ancient China.[19] Yi Yin once assisted Da Yi (Cheng Tang), so we might expect that sacrifices to Yi Yin would resemble those to the Former Kings; however, the OBI reveal that the status Yi Yin enjoyed in the Shang pantheon was more akin to that of the Former Lords and High Ancestors. For example:

> Crack-making on the *guimao* day, offer a *hui*-prayer for rain to Shi Ren.
> To Shang Jia offer a *hui*-prayer for rain.
> Crack-making on the *guimao* day, let it be Yi who drinks.

> 癸卯卜, 桒雨于示壬
> 于上甲桒雨
> 癸卯卜, 叀伊酓 (HJ 32344 partial, Li 2, fig. 1.3:1)

> (Crack-making) on the *guisi* day, offer (sacrifices) to Yi Yin with five oxen.
> Crack-making on the *guisi* day, offer (sacrifices) to X, use this.
> Crack-making on the *guisi* day, offer (sacrifices) to He, do not use this.
> Crack-making on the *guisi* day, offer (sacrifices) to Wang Hai.

癸巳, 又于伊尹牛五
癸巳卜, 又于㞢, 兹用
癸巳卜, 又于河, 不用
癸巳卜, 又于王亥 (HJ 34240 partial, Li 2, fig.1.3:2)

Crack-making on the *renzi* day, offer (sacrifices) to Yi Yin.
Crack-making on the *renzi* day, offer (sacrifices) to Yue.
. . . Should we . . . royal house.

壬子卜, 又于伊尹
壬子卜, 又于岳.
. . . 其 . . . 王家 (HJ 34192 partial, Li 2)

On the *bingyin* day, it was divined: Offer (sacrifices) to X, perform a *liao*-burning rite with minor slaves, splitting open an ox. Use this. It did not rain.

On the *bingyin* day, it was divined: Offer X *sui*-rite to Yi Yin with two *lao*-sacrifices.

丙寅貞, 又于㞢, 燎小宰, 卯牛, 兹用. 不雨
丙寅貞, 又彳歲于伊尹二牢 (TN 1062 partial, Li 2)

On the *yisi* day, it was divined: Should we offer a *hui*-prayer for grain to Yi or perform an *yi*-rite?

On the *renzi* day, it was divined: Should we offer a *hui*-prayer for grain to He or perform a *liao*-burning rite with three minor slaves, drowning three?

乙巳貞, 其秦禾于伊, 宜
壬子貞, 其秦禾於河, 燎三小宰, 沈三 (TN 93 partial, Li 2, fig. 1.3:3)

In the previously listed inscriptions, diviners ask about which spirits they should sacrifice to when giving *hui*-prayers for rain and for growing grains but do not discuss the specific days these sacrifices should be held. Yi Yin features together with the Former Lords of the Shang in these divi-

| 1. HJ 32344 | 2. HJ 34240 | 3. TN 93 |

Figure 1.3. Oracle-Bone Inscriptions with *Hui*-Prayers for Rain and Grain Directed Jointly to Yi Yin and the Former Lords. *Source*: 1 and 2: Guo Moruo 郭沫若, ed., Hu Houxuan 胡厚宣, comp., *Jiaguwen heji* 甲骨文合集, 13 vols. (Beijing: Zhonghua, 1978–1982); 3: Zhongguo shehui kexueyuan kaogu yanjiusuo 中國社會科學院考古研究所, ed., *Xiaotun nandi jiagu* 小屯南地甲骨, 3 vols. (Beijing: Zhonghua, 1980–1983).

nations. This does not imply that each spirit would have received sacrifices on the same day; it shows only that, in the minds of the Shang people when supplicating their ancestors for aid, Yi Yin possessed similar powers to those held by these Former Lords.

The appellation Yi Shi 伊奭 is also seen in these oracle-bone inscriptions:

On the *bingyin* day, it was divined: Let us on the *dingmao* day perform a *rong*-rite to X.

On the *bingyin* day, it was divined: On the *gengwu* day perform a *rong*-rite to X.

On the *dingmao* day, it was divined: On the *gengwu* day perform a *rong*-rite and *liao*-burning rite to X.

On the *gengwu* day, perform a *liao*-burning rite to Yue, following which it will rain.

On the *renshen* day, it was divined: Offer a *hui*-prayer for grain to Nao.

On the *renshen* day, it was divined: Offer a *hui*-prayer for grain to He.

On the *renshen day*, perform a *gang*-rite to Yi Shi (or Yi's consort).

It will rain. Today it rained.

丙寅貞，叀丁卯酚于 𢓊,
丙寅貞，于庚午酚于 𢓊,
丁卯貞，于庚午酚尞于 𢓊,
庚午燎于岳，又從才雨.
壬申貞，秦禾于夒.
壬申貞，秦禾于河.
壬申，剛 (剛) 于伊奭.
隹其雨.
今日雨. (HJ 33273, Li 2, fig. 1.4)

The name Huang Shi 黃奭 appears in the oracle-bone inscriptions as well, where Huang likely refers to Huang Yin 黃尹.[20] Opinions differ on how to interpret the character transcribed here as *shi* 奭.[21] Yet, whenever *shi* is found in a name other than that of Yi Shi or Huang Shi, it is always for a female consort of a Former Lord or Former King, and never for a male figure. Consorts of the Former Lords (and Former Kings), however, do not directly receive sacrificial offerings; nor are there divinations directed jointly to both them and the Former Lords. Therefore, if Yi Shi does ultimately refer to Yi Yin's consort, and she possesses the same powers as a Former Lord, then this must derive from the special status of Yi Yin. When inscriptions entreat Yi Yin to enact his powers, for the most part they do not also entreat those Former Kings who follow after the Former Lords. Thus, even though Yi Yin is of the same generation as Tang, he (and his consort, should Yi Shi in fact be female) occupied a special status in the Shang pantheon, akin to that of the spirits of the Former Lords. This was likely the result of the mythologization of Yi Yin's image among the Shang people, several genera-

12 | Zhu Fenghan

Figure 1.4. Oracle-Bone Inscriptions Related to Yi Shi (HJ 33273). *Source*: Guo Moruo 郭沫若, ed., Hu Houxuan 胡厚宣, comp., *Jiaguwen heji* 甲骨文合集, 13 vols. (Beijing: Zhonghua, 1978–1982).

tions after Tang's rule. What this proves is that Yi Yin's elevated status was not just a construction of the Zhou but began with the Shang themselves.

Yi Yin's Powers as a Spirit

Sarah Allan mentions, in the quotation given at the beginning of this chapter, how Yi Yin was able to influence natural phenomena. From our inscriptional evidence, this was indeed the case. See for instance the following inscriptions, relating to Yi Yin's powers as a spirit:

Do not offer a *hui*-prayer to Yi Yin, no rain.

弜桒于伊尹, 亡 (無) 雨. (HJ 27656, Unnamed, fig. 1.5:1)

Yi Yin . . . provided a torrential rain.

伊尹 . . . 又 (有) 大雨. (HJ 27657, Unnamed)

Crack-making on the *guimao* day, offer a *hui*-prayer for rain to Shi Ren.
To Shang Jia offer a *hui*-prayer for rain.
Crack-making on the *guimao* day, let it be Yi who drinks.
Let it be at the settlement where the king drinks.
Let it be Yi who drinks.

癸卯卜, 秦雨于示壬.
于上甲秦雨.
癸卯卜, 叀伊酓.
叀邑王酓.
叀伊酓. (HJ 32344, Li 2)

On the *bingyin* day, it was divined: Perform a *liao*-burning rite with three minor slaves, splitting open an ox . . . to . . .
On the *bingyin* day, it was divined: Offer X *sui*-rite to Yi Yin with two minor slaves.
Crack-making on the *wuchen* day, this evening it will rain.
This evening it will not rain.

丙寅貞, 燎三小宰, 卯牛 . . . 于 . . .
丙寅貞, 又彳歲于伊尹二宰
戊辰卜, 及今夕雨
弗及今夕雨 (HJ 33273 partial, Li 2)

In the two previous sets of inscriptions, we can discern from the context of the consecutive lines that the purpose of allowing Yi Yin to drink 酓 and of offering a *sui*-rite 歲 to Yi Yin with two minor slaves was to bring about rain.

Crack-making on the *dingwei* day, Yi will bring harmful rains.

丁未卜, 惟伊蚩雨 (HJ 32881, Li 2, fig. 1.5:2)

On the *yisi* day it was divined: Should we offer a *hui*-prayer for grain to Yi, perform an *yi*-rite.

On the *renzi* day it was divined: Should we offer a *hui*-prayer for grain to He, perform a *liao*-burning rite with three minor slaves, drowning three.

乙巳貞，其燊禾于伊，宜。
壬子貞，其燊禾于河，燎三小宰，沈三 (TN 93, Li.2, fig. 1.5:3)

It is Yi [Shi] who will pacify the winds.
. . . Yi [Shi] who will pacify the winds.

其寧風伊[爽]
. . . 寧風伊爽 (HJ 30259, Unnamed, fig. 1.5:4)

From these OBI, we find that Yi Yin can influence the weather and, in particular, is in charge of rains and pacifying winds. Since rainfall is obviously closely related to agricultural harvest, the Shang Kings "offer

| 1. HJ 27656 | 2. HJ 32881 | 3. TN 93 | 4. HJ 30259 |

Figure 1.5. Oracle-Bone Inscriptions Related to Yi Yin's Powers as a Spirit. *Source*: 1, 2, and 4: Guo Moruo 郭沫若, ed., Hu Houxuan 胡厚宣, comp., *Jiaguwen heji* 甲骨文合集, 13 vols. (Beijing: Zhonghua, 1978–1982); 3: Zhongguo shehui kexueyuan kaogu yanjiusuo 中國社會科學院考古研究所, ed., *Xiaotun nandi jiagu* 小屯南地甲骨, 3 vols. (Beijing: Zhonghua, 1980–1983).

hui-prayers for grain" (*hui he* 耒禾) to Yi Yin, while the Former Lords also commonly received "*hui*-prayers for the harvest" (*hui nian* 耒年, namely *hui*-prayers for grain). Beyond having powers over natural phenomena, Yi Yin does not hold sway over human affairs, which is a power possessed by the spirits of the Shang High Ancestors. In other inscriptions, Shang kings submit *gai* 勾 requests or offer *hui* prayers to He and Wang Hai to aid them in defeating enemies; they also report on the king's affairs to Wang Hai and Shang Jia; and they perform *yu* 禦 sacrifices to Shang Jia when the king requires help. At times, High Ancestor Nao and Wang Hai may even have brought about calamities for the king personally or the Shang state.[22] We do not see Yi Yin commanding any of these types of powers. Although Yi Yin was a human spirit, the Shang people modeled his image after that of a pure nature spirit, which is to say, they transformed him into a nature spirit, so that he had powers to rival those of Tu (She; the altars of soil) or X 豸. This is the reverse of what was seen before, with He and Yue.

Yi Yin was worshipped by the Shang people and received sacrifices from them for generations, because of his outstanding service in the founding of the Shang dynasty. Yet, as a spirit, his influence over the Shang people was primarily affected through powers over natural phenomena. This may be perhaps due to the fact that Yi Yin was not a lineal ancestor of the Shang kings. In the minds of the Shang kings, figures like Yi Yin were more properly classified as spirits who oversaw the entire Shang clan group, while the spirits of the High Ancestors, because of their inherited blood ties, ought to possess more formidable and expansive abilities to meddle in the royal human affairs and political domain.

It should be noted however that, among the OBI mentioning Yi Yin, there are a few rare examples that are directed jointly to both Yi Yin and the Former Kings. Because these inscriptions include only short, abbreviated sentences, their meaning is uncertain; therefore, we cannot ascertain whether they attest to Yi Yin's possessing powers over human affairs:

> Crack-making on the *guichou* day, offer (sacrifices) to Yi Yin.
> Crack-making on the *dingsi* day, offer (sacrifices) to the Ten Deities, Yi and the Nine.

> 癸丑卜，又于伊尹．
> 丁巳卜，又于十立，伊又九 (HJ 32786, Li 1)

Crack-making on the *guiyou* day, offer (sacrifices) to Yi and the Five Ancestors.

癸酉卜, 又伊五示. (HJ 32722)

Crack-making on the *renxu* day, offer *sui*-rites to Yi and the Twenty-three Ancestors. Use this.

壬戌卜, 又歲于伊廿示又三. 茲用 (HJ 34123, Li.1)

These inscriptions discuss sacrifices to Yi Yin offered in conjunction with those given to various numbers of *shi* 示 ("altars, ancestors") and are examples of the rite of "assembling the ancestral tablets" (*jihe shenzhu* 集合神主).[23] Scholars have argued that, in cases such as these, the ancestral tablets are for various Former Kings. But, as previously discussed, in the OBI we do not yet have divinations clearly entreating Yi Yin to use his powers alongside those of the Former Kings, only with the Former Lords and High Ancestors.

In the following inscriptions however, there is some indication that Yi Yin could appear in divinations directed jointly to the Former Kings:

Do not manage affairs, let it be X . . .
Do not call upon the Great Ancestors.
On the *gengchen* day, it was divined: On the *xinsi* day the king commands X.
On the *gengchen* day, it was divined: The king on the *dinghai* day commands X.
. . . X . . . Great . . .

弜立事, 叀圉 . . .
弜禹大示
庚辰貞, 辛巳王令圉.
庚辰貞, 王于丁亥令圉.
. . . 圉 . . . 大 . . . . (HJ 32849, Li 2)

On the *gengchen* day, it was divined: X selects the Great Ancestors.
On the *xinsi* day, it was divined: Select Yi and the Ancestors.
Do not select Yi and the Ancestors.

庚辰貞，🈳以大示．
辛巳貞，以伊示．
弜以伊示．(HJ 32847, Li 2, figure 1.6:1)

On the *gengchen* day, it was divined: The king on the *dinghai* day commands X.
Let it be the Ancestral Father who is selected.
On the *xinsi* day, it was divined: Select Yi and the Ancestors.
Do not select Yi and the Ancestors.

庚辰貞，王于丁亥令🈳．
叀父示以
辛巳貞，以伊示
弜以伊示．(HJ 32848, Li 2, figure 1.6:2)

This set of inscriptions first records divinations that occurred on the *gengchen* day. They inquire whether the king should command X 🈳 to manage affairs on a *xinsi* day or on a *dinghai* day, and, moreover, whether that person should then call upon the *da shi* 大示 (Great Ancestors) and select *yi shi* 伊示 (Yi and the Ancestors, i.e., Yi Yin and other ancestors) for sacrifices, or if he should select *fu shi* 父示 (his Father Ancestor, or, perhaps

| 1. HJ 32847 | 2. HJ 32848 |

Figure 1.6. Oracle-Bone Inscriptions Directed Jointly to Yi Yin and the Former Kings. *Source*: Guo Moruo 郭沫若, ed., Hu Houxuan 胡厚宣, comp., *Jiaguwen heji* 甲骨文合集, 13 vols. (Beijing: Zhonghua, 1978–1982).

Father and Ancestors) for sacrifices instead. The meaning of the phrase *yi shi* 以示 is uncertain, but, judging from the context, it may involve X 筥 "selecting" which ancestral tablets to involve in the sacrifices.[24] Among those ancestral tablets that X 筥 could "select," the "Great Ancestors" held the loftiest positions, while his "Father Ancestor" would refer to that Former King most recently connected to the current ruler. A pair of positive and negative charges follows suggesting uncertainty over whether Yi Yin should be selected. It is difficult to tell from the inscriptions what affairs, precisely, X 筥 was asked to manage, or what sort of aid he sought by selecting certain spirits for supplication. Thus, it remains uncertain whether Yi Yin possessed the power of a Former King to meddle in human affairs.

The Procedures for Sacrificing to Yi Yin

Although Yi Yin was often the subject of divination and sacrifice along with the Former Lords in the Shang pantheon—and already treated like a "naturalized" human spirit—the procedures for offering him sacrifices differed from both. The sacrifices used for nature spirits, like Tu (Soil) and Fang (Regions), and for the spirits of the Former Lords, like He, Nao, and Wang Hai (which were perhaps part of the lineage rites), include most importantly the *liao* 燎-burning rite, followed by the *rong* 酚 rite, the *you* 出 rite, and perhaps also the X 刁 rite, and the *mao* 卯 rite. Yi Yin, however, was never offered a *liao*-burning rite. For this sacrifice, firewood is piled together and set ablaze, and an animal is then cast into the fire, with the smoke rising up to the spirits for their gratification. The Warring States period *Zhou li* 周禮 record for "Da Zongbo" 大宗伯 notes that the *yin*-burning rite (*yinsi* 禋祀) was offered in sacrifice to the heavenly spirits.[25] The Shang did not sacrifice to Heaven 天, nor did they sacrifice to Shangdi 上帝, but they used the *liao*-burning rite to sacrifice to the Former Lords and High Ancestors (and also to Former Kings), which suggests that they thought these spirits were active in the sky and could receive sacrifices there, shedding light on Shang beliefs about where the ancestral spirits resided. That Yi Yin's spirit did not receive *liao*-burning rites, may be because, according to Shang religious beliefs, Yi Yin was not located in the same place as the Shang High Ancestors and Former Kings.

The Shang often sacrificed to the spirits of the High Ancestors, such as Nao, Wang Hai, He, and Yue, on a *xin* 辛 day. This was not necessarily their day-name but only the specific day on which sacrifices to these spirits were established. The word *xin* 辛 in our classical sources was associated with autumn harvests, and one of the main reasons for sacrificing to the spirits of the High Ancestors was to pray for a bountiful harvest.²⁶ The reason for sacrificing to Yi Yin, in fact, was mainly to pray for good weather, in order to obtain a bountiful harvest. Yet the day Yi Yin was usually sacrificed to differs from that of the Former Lords, as it was not on a *xin* day but on a *ding* 丁 day. Yi Yin, moreover, was likely also granted a day-name. Thus, it appears, from the perspective of the sacrificial calendar, that in the Shang pantheon, important differences still remained between Yi Yin and both the Former Lords and High Ancestors.

In summary, through an analysis of how Yi Yin was offered sacrifices, it appears that because Yi Yin was classified as an extra-lineage spirit in the Shang sacrificial canon and not related to the Shang royal family via blood ties, he therefore was still distinguished from the Shang High Ancestors.

Conclusions

Based on the previous discussion, the following conclusions may be drawn:

1. The sacrificial records to Yi Yin on the Yinxu OBI prove that Yi Yin assisted Cheng Tang and served meritoriously as a subject of the Shang dynasty. It also shows that the account in the *Guben zhushu jinian*, claiming that Yi Yin was killed by Tai Jia, has no historical basis.

2. The inscriptions mention that sacrifices to Yi Yin were often conducted on *ding* 丁 days, revealing that Yi Yin, as a human spirit, quite possibly had a day-name of Ding.

3. Although Yi Yin was a contemporary of Cheng Tang, he often appears in divinations about "offering *hui*-prayers for rain" or "offering *hui*-prayers for the harvest" that were directed jointly toward him and the Shang High Ancestors. This shows that Yi Yin held a lofty status among the Shang pantheon, through a process of deification that began in the generations following his service to Cheng Tang but before the Zhou era.

4. According to the extant OBI, Yi Yin's powers as a spirit primarily concerned natural phenomena. In sacrificing to

Yi Yin, the Shang people mainly sought his aid in bringing about bountiful harvests with good weather. Yi Yin thus provides an example of how human spirits were also deified into nature spirits.

5. We do not yet have proof among the OBI that Yi Yin, as a spirit, was also able to meddle in human affairs. Moreover, there are differences between how and when Yi Yin and the spirits of the High Ancestors received sacrifices. Thus, even though Yi Yin possessed powers over natural phenomena, which were similar or the same as those held by the High Ancestors, yet, in the Shang pantheon, he still occupied a different place than the spirits of the High Ancestors or Former Kings, quite possibly because he was not related to the royal family by blood.

This analysis of Yi Yin's place in the Shang pantheon allows us to better understand how spirits were classified in Shang religious thought. There appear to be two major types of spirits, based on whether they held lineal descent from the royal family. The first type included the High Ancestors, Former Lords, and Former Kings, who were all part of the Shang clan with blood ties to the Shang kings. These spirits received sacrifices according to the sacrificial canon for members of the Shang house and royal family. The other type is like Yi Yin. These spirits did not have blood ties to the royal family, but they were common objects of devotion to the clan group, which constituted a number of different tribal lineages, of which the Shang people were but one. Spirits of this type, like Yi Yin, would have received sacrifices from both their specific lineage members as well as from those outside their lineage. That Yi Yin was eligible for inclusion among the Shang sacrificial canon (as understood through the OBI) therefore does not overturn the maxim: "Spirits do not relish sacrifices from those not of their kind; and the people do not offer sacrifices to those not of their clan" (神不歆非類; 民不祀非族) (*Zuo zhuan*, Duke Xi, year ten). Rather, as outlined earlier, there are multiple different layers to what constitutes one's "kind" and "clan."

Notes

1. Sarah Allan, *The Heir and the Sage: Dynastic Legend in Early China* (San Francisco: Chinese Materials Center, 1981), 79.

2. Allan, *The Heir and the Sage*, 97 n. 22; Fan Xiangyong 范祥雍, *Guben zhushu jinian jijiao dingbu* 古本竹書紀年輯校訂補 (Shanghai: Shanghai renmin, 1962), 18.

3. Allan, *The Heir and the Sage*, 96 and 100.

4. Lü Buwei 呂不韋 (Qin), Gao You 高誘 (Han), *Lüshi chunqiu* 呂氏春秋, *Zhuzi baijia congshu* 諸子百家叢書 (Shanghai: Shanghai guji, 1989), 14.102 ("Xiaoxing lan er, Ben wei" 孝行覽二, 本味).

5. *Shiji* 史記 (Beijing: Zhonghua, 2014), 3.122.

6. Zhang Yongshan 張永山, "Cong buci zhong de Yi Yin kan 'min bu ji fei zu'" 從卜辭中的伊尹看"民不祭非族," in *Guwenzi yanjiu* 古文字研究 22 (Beijing: Zhonghua, 2002), 1–5; Xiao Liangqiong 蕭良瓊, "Buci zhong de Yi Yin he Yi Yin fang Tai Jia" 卜辭中的伊尹和伊尹放太甲, in *Guwenzi yanjiu* 21 (Beijing: Zhonghua, 2001), 14–23.

7. Stephen Durrant, Wai-yee Li, and David Schaberg, trans., *Zuo Tradition; Zuozhuan* 左傳 vol. 1 (Seattle: University of Washington Press, 2016), 300–301.

8. *Guo yu* 國語 (Shanghai: Shanghai guji, 1978), 165–171 ("Lu yu shang" 魯語上 9).

9. The Yi 1 "nonroyal set of OBI" (*fei wang buci* 非王卜辭) refer to those inscriptions compiled in the seventh volume of the *Jiaguwen heji* 甲骨文合集 (see n. 10), placed under the type "Yi 1 乙一"; these divinations were not performed under the patronage of the king but conducted on behalf of another individual instead.

10. HJ refers to: Guo Moruo 郭沫若, ed., Hu Houxuan 胡厚宣, comp., *Jiaguwen heji* 甲骨文合集, 13 vols. (Beijing: Zhonghua, 1978–1982). TN refers to: Zhongguo shehui kexueyuan kaogu yanjiusuo 中國社會科學院考古研究所, ed., *Xiaotun nandi jiagu* 小屯南地甲骨, 3 vols. (Beijing: Zhonghua, 1980–1983). Following the serial number, the name of the diviner group and subcategory are also given.

11. Scholars have argued that, since some OBI concerning sacrifices to Yi Yin conducted their divinations on days other than *ding*, "therefore we cannot assert that Yi Yin received sacrifices on a *ding* day" (因此不能將伊尹的祭日定于丁日) (Xiao Liangqiong, "Buci zhong de Yi Yin," 17). The day when the divination is performed may only be the day when one asks whether it is permissible to sacrifice to a given spirit, rather than being the day of sacrifice itself.

12. Qiu Xigui 裘錫圭, *Jiagu wenzi kaoshi* (*xu*) 甲骨文字考釋 (續), in *Qiu Xigui xueshu wenji* 裘錫圭學術文集, vol. 1 (Shanghai: Fudan daxue, 2012), 193.

13. Zhang Yongshan 張永山, "Cong buci zhong de Yi Yin kan 'min bu si fei zu'" 從卜辭中的伊尹看"民不祀非族," *Guwenzi yanjiu* 古文字研究 22 (2000): 1–5.

14. Xiao Liangqiong, "Buci zhong de Yi Yin," 18.

15. TN 3033 writes: "Crack-making on a *guihai* day, offer (sacrifices) to *yi yin ding*, let the offering be today" (癸亥卜, 又于伊尹丁, 叀今日又). Some scholars again interpret the *ding* of *yi yin ding* 伊尹丁 as *beng* (see n. 14). Retaining *ding* here (as opposed to *beng*) is still possible however, as the phrase "offer (sacrifices) to *yi yin ding*" could be read: "Offer sacrifices to Yi Yin on a *ding* day." The key

point is that, following this line, the diviner asks about "letting the offering be held today" (叀今日又), which is to say, whether or not they should change the date of the sacrifice to the day that this divination was made (a *guihai* day). The main concern of this divination then is if it is appropriate to change the sacrificial schedule by moving sacrifices to Yi Yin from a *ding* day (in this instance probably a *dingchou* 丁丑 day) forward to a *guihai* day (the present day). The phrase *yi yin ding* could also be read together as a single appellation, Yi Yin Ding with the *ding* taken as Yi Yin's day-name.

16. Wang Guowei 王國維, "Yin buci zhong suojian Xian Gong Xian Wang kao" 殷卜辭中所見先公先王考, in *Guantang jilin* 觀堂集林 (Beijing: Zhonghua, 1959), vol. 2, 437–438.

17. See for instance: Wang Yuxin 王宇信 and Yang Shengnan 楊升南, eds., *Jiaguxue yibai nian* 甲骨學一百年 (Beijing: Shehui kexue wenxian, 1999), ch. 11, sec. 1, 437.

18. For an example of the phrase High Ancestor He 高祖河, see HJ 32028; for High Ancestor Nao 高祖夒, see HJ 30398; and for High Ancestor Wang Hai 高祖王亥 (who is also called High Ancestor Hai 高祖亥), see HJ 30447. There are no instances to date of Yue 岳 titled as a High Ancestor. Yue is, however, often sacrificed alongside He and Nao (for instance, HJ 10076). In the oracle-bone inscriptions, we also see an Ancestral Temple to Yue 岳宗 (HJ 30290), thus it's likely Yue was in fact a Shang High Ancestor.

19. For more on the "humanization of nature spirits," as well as the "naturalization of human spirits," please refer to my previous article: Zhu Fenghan 朱鳳瀚, "Shang Zhou shiqi de tianshen chongbai" 商周時期的天神崇拜, *Zhongguo shehui kexue* 中國社會科學 1993.4: 191–211.

20. The name Huang Yin adds *yin* 尹 to a tribal name, similar to Yi Yin; Huang Yin is also included among the Shang sacrificial canon. But the inscriptions on which Huang Yin is mentioned are from the Bin diviner group. His powers, and how he receives sacrificial offerings, do not completely overlap with Yi Yin's. Moreover, there is also the following inscription, documenting how the Shang king was concerned about sacrifices conducted by the Huang clan: "It is divined: Call for the many sons of Huang to offer *you*-rites with oxen (in sacrifice) to Huang Yin" (貞，呼黃多子㞢牛于黃尹, HJ 3255 recto). This indicates that the Huang clan may have been a family lineage among the Shang people.

21. Zhang Zhenglang 張政烺 initially transcribed this character as *qiu* 臾 instead and read it as *qiu* 仇 based on the phonetic, in the sense of "companion" (*pei* 匹). Zhang moreover argued that, in the appellations Yi Qiu 伊臾 and Huang Qiu 黃臾, the term *qiu* was equivalent to *yin* 尹 ("aide"), as this "presumably claimed that an important minister of the state served as a companion to the ruler" (蓋謂國之重臣與王為匹耦也). See his: "'Qiu' zi shuo" '臾'字說," in *Zhang Zhenglang wenji—jiaguwen jinwen yu Shang Zhou shi yanjiu* 張政烺文集．甲骨文金文與商周史研究 (Beijing: Zhonghua, 2012), 7–8. Zhang later changed his reading to *jiu* 舅

("uncle"), with Yi Qiu 伊爽 standing for Uncle Yi (Yi Jiu 伊舅). He believed that this was because Tang married a daughter of the Youshen 有莘 tribe. If Yi Yin was a son of the Youshen tribe, but instead abandoned his hereditary right to lead that tribe by merging them with the Shang as a single state, then he would have been regarded as an "uncle." See: "Shi 'ta shi': lun buci zhong meiyou canshen" 釋 "它示"—論卜辭中沒有蠱神, in *Zhang Zhenglang wenji*, 43.

22. Zhu Fenghan, "Shangren zhushen zhi quanneng yu qi leixing" 商人諸神之權能與其類型, in *Jinxin ji—Zhang Zhenglang xiansheng bashi qingshou lunwenji* 盡心集—張政烺先生八十慶壽論文集 (Beijing: Zhongguo shehui kexue, 1996), 59.

23. Further examples of inscriptions where Yi Yin is mentioned together with "assembled spirits" include:

> On the *dinghai* day, it was divined: The Many Ning (sons) brought libations to offer (in sacrifices) to Yi Yin and the Nine Ancestors; use this.
>
> 丁亥貞，多宁以鬯又伊尹⿱示，兹用。(TN 2567, Li 1)

> On the *yiyou* day, it was divined: Offer a *sui*-rite to Yi and the Nine Ancestors.
>
> 乙酉貞，又歲于伊⿱示 (HJ 33329, Li 1)

The character before *shi* 示 in both of these inscriptions could be an orthographic variant of *yi* 一 ("one"). The graph before *shi* might be *gui* 龜 ("turtle"), used as a loan for *jiu* 九 ("nine"). *Gui* 龜 is classified in the *jian* initial and *zhi* final group (*jian mu zhi bu* 見母之部), and *jiu* 九 is classified in the *jian* initial and *you* final group (*jian mu you bu* 見母幽部). Since *zhi* 之 and *you* 幽 are open syllables (*yinsheng* 陰聲) in a *pangzhuan* 旁轉 relationship, *gui* 龜 could be read as *jiu* 九.

24. *Yi* 以 is classified in the *yu* initial and *zhi* final group (*yu mu zhi bu* 喻母之部) and *si* 祀 is classified in the *xie* initial and *zhi* final group (*xie mu zhi bu* 邪母之部). The *yu* 喻 initial is a dorsal consonant, while the *xie* 邪 initial is a dental consonant. In Old Chinese dentals were read like dorsals, thus the word *yi* 以 perhaps had the same pronunciation as *si* 祀. Whether this interpretation holds for the present set of inscriptions, however, requires further investigation.

25. Zheng Xuan 鄭玄 (Han), Jia Gongyan 賈公彥 (Tang), *Zhou li zhushu* 周禮註疏, *Shisan jing zhushu* 十三經注疏 (Beijing: Beijing daxue, 2000), 18.530 ("Da Zongbo" 大宗伯).

26. See Zhu Fenghan, "Tan Yinxu buci zhong Xian Gong de jiri" 談殷墟卜辭中先公的祭日, *Nankai daxue xuebao* 南開大學學報 2001, supplement: 96.

2

Cao E, the Filial Water Goddess

Gender and Text in the Promotion of a
Two-Thousand-Year-Old Cult

Robin D. S. Yates

Introduction

The study of goddesses in the Chinese tradition has expanded quite dramatically in the last few decades, but the emphasis has been, for the most part, on goddesses who had an empire-wide or at least regional or transregional following.[1] Many of them also have had close connections with the Daoist or Buddhist traditions, such as the Queen Mother of the West, Mazu, the Lady of Linshui, and Guan Yin, among a number of others.[2] The scholarship has been successful in explaining the roles of these female

---

This chapter was first presented as a paper at the International Forum on Gender and Religion in China: A Dialogue between Texts and Contexts, Chinese University of Hong Kong, December 18–19, 2015, and a revised version was presented at the Department of East Asian Studies Colloquium, Tel Aviv University, Israel, May 24, 2016. I am grateful to all the comments and suggestions for improvement that members of both audiences gave me. I am delighted and honored to offer this chapter as a small contribution to the festschrift honoring my *tongxue* Professor Sarah Allan, who has done so much through her academic career to promote the study of myth and legend in early China, as well as excavated and recovered texts.

deities in what was and is recognized as a deeply patriarchal society, even though now much has been learned to debunk the idea that this society was "Confucian" from the beginning and that it was unchanging from the late Warring States or early imperial times down to the twentieth century. The cracks and fissures in the May 4th narrative of Chinese history and its critique of imperial society and ideology have been explored and, in many cases, completely shattered, perhaps no more so than in the history as it relates to women and gender. Furthermore, a rich body of scholarship has also revealed the development of the cult of female chastity, its promotion by the state authorities, and its naturalization and embodiment by women from all levels of society.[3] This chapter will focus on a much narrower subject: the development of the cult of a local water goddess who was promoted by the state and by male literati, and who had a close connection with one of the fundamental ethical principles of Confucian ideology, filial piety. Despite this narrow focus, I shall still not be able to cover all the elements of the story within the scope of this short chapter. And, I would like to add one more disclaimer: I have never visited the temple of my subject and, thus, many of my remarks will certainly need to be revised in the light of an onsite inspection of the layout, structure, and decoration of the present buildings.

Cao E 曹娥 and Her Temple

Decades ago, the German American—later University of California, Berkeley—sociologist and folklore expert Wolfram Eberhard identified the story of Cao E 曹娥 as belonging to a cycle of myths centered on Shanyin 山陰, also known as Kuaiji or Guiji 會稽, whose central place was and still is the city of Shaoxing 紹興, the former capital of the Yue Kingdom 越國 of the Warring States period. The myths all concerned drowned persons who later became objects of cult. These myths and related cycles, concerning drowned corpses that floated upstream and became worshipped, were typical of a broad swath of cultures throughout central and southern China from Sichuan to the south and east coast.[4] Eberhard identified the cult of Wu Zixu 伍子胥 and of Cao E as being typical of the latter variety, noting that the worship of the deities usually took place on the fifth day of the fifth month.

The cult of Cao E, one of the few local cults that has survived from antiquity to the present day, commemorates the suicide of a young girl whose shaman father drowned while greeting the spirit of the Hangzhou Bay tide, Wu Zixu 伍子胥. Traditional scholarship has identified two strains within the Cao E legend, both of which were promoted by officials and literati from the Later Han dynasty to the end of the nineteenth century. The first was that she was an example of supreme filial piety, giving up her life in mourning when she was unable to retrieve the body of her father. The second, related strand was the story of the stele inscription that was written shortly after Cao E's death and marked her tomb. This story has many interesting twists to it with a wide assortment of individuals involved, including the greatest of all Chinese calligraphers, the famous Wang Xizhi 王羲之 (ca. 321–379). This chapter will briefly review the history of these two strands,[5] but it will add a third component that appears to have been forgotten with the emphasis on the first two. I will argue that, equally important, was the figure of Cao E as a local water (tide) deity and that this deity was inextricably linked with one of the central virtues of the Confucian tradition, filial piety,[6] as well as with court politics, notably in the Northern Song dynasty. The tying together of these various strands may help explain how and why the cult lasted from antiquity down to the present day, when the "mother temple" is proclaimed as the "Number One Temple of Jiangnan" (*Jiangnan diyi miao* 江南第一廟), although, of course, other temples also claim this title.

I will draw my evidence primarily from the sources cited by Shen Zhili's 沈志禮 (late 17th-century) temple gazetteer, *Cao jiang xiaonü miaozhi* 曹江孝女廟誌 (preface dated 1678), of which two exemplars have been republished,[7] as well as from those preserved in Hu Fengdan's 胡鳳丹 late nineteenth-century river gazetteer, *Cao E jiangzhi* 曹娥江志.[8] The first source draws on material extending as far back as the southern Song dynasty, as it preserves as its first preface one dated 1259, which was composed by Zhao Ruji 趙汝躓, a member of the Song imperial family and a figure at the late Southern Song court of Lizong 理宗 (r. 1226–1264).[9] The second preface was written by Wang Yu 王鈺 and dated to the fourth year of the Zhengtong 正統 reign period of the Ming dynasty, 1439, while the third preface was composed by Zhu Wanli 諸萬里, a native of Shanyin and dated 1619, the second to last year of the Ming Wanli Emperor's 明萬曆 reign.

Both of these gazetteers were based on earlier exemplars and principally record large numbers of literary compositions that were produced over the centuries by male literati, apparently lifting them from the *Cao jiang shiji* 曹江詩集, whose preface was composed by Lu Yuanchong 魯元寵, dated to the fifteenth day of the second month of the *xinmao* 辛卯 year of the Qing Shunzhi 順治 Emperor, 1651.[10] Most of these poems in various genres are on three themes: the first, on the celebration of Cao E's filial piety; the second, on crossing the river that bears her name; and the third, on the stele and/or inscription(s) erected in her honor. The two editors and, presumably, also the editor of the *Cao jiang shiji* from whom they derived many of the poems, did not include the writings of women on Cao E, probably because these writings were not available to them. Some of these poems by women are now available online through the Ming Qing Women's Writings website.[11]

First, it is important to recognize the location of the river in which Cao E allegedly drowned herself. It flows to the east of Shaoxing from south to north, debouching directly into the Hangzhou Bay, whose main river is, of course, the Qiantang River that flows into the sea southwest of Hangzhou City. The Cao E River had a number of names in ancient times as well as for portions of its course, such as the Wu River 舞江, and would have felt the full force of the tidal bore of the Hangzhou Bay before a barrier was built across its mouth in the last few years.[12] Crossing the river in premodern times, especially toward the mouth, risked encountering the tidal bore and was a dangerous undertaking, although over the centuries the bore was reduced in force due to the deposition of silt coming out of the Yellow and Yangzi Rivers to the north, creating the so-called Yuyao Salient to the east of the mouth. The massive deposition of silt affected the tides coming into the Hangzhou Bay.[13] In fact, the Cao E temple was built precisely at the spot where the tide reached the furthest inland and then turned back to the ocean[14] and a number of high tidal floods are recorded to have broken down the dikes and bridges along the river and inundated the farmland ruining the crops growing along the banks on either side.[15] In the Song, the now-lost *Kuaiji zhi* 會稽志, fragments of which are preserved in the surviving portions of the early Ming *Yongle dadian* 永樂大典, record under Shangyu County 上虞縣 that a big tide could support large boats of five hundred–*dàn* 石 capacity, while a small tide could support vessels of two hundred–*dàn* capacity.[16] Further, a sluice gate (*doumen* 鬥門) was built by the famous literatus and politician Zeng Gongliang 曾公亮 (999–1078) when he served as the local magistrate,[17] and this, too, would have reduced the force of the tidal bore and the danger of crossing the river.[18]

The Origin of the Cult

Apart from the stele inscription to be discussed later, the earliest written evidence for the story of Cao E concerns a fourteen-year-old unmarried girl committing suicide by throwing herself in the river when she was unable to retrieve the body of her dead shaman father, Cao Xu 曹盱,[19] after he drowned during the course of performing a dance ritual to welcome the spirit of the incoming tide (i.e., that of Wu Zixu) on the fifth day of the fifth month.[20] It is to be found in the *Kuaiji dianlu* 會稽典錄 by Yu Yu 虞預, a native of Yuyao who lived in the Eastern Jin period.[21] The exact wording of the original text is not so evident, as it has come down to us only in fragments that were later reconstituted.[22] However, the earliest citations in the Tang compendium *Yiwen leiju* 藝文類聚, compiled by Ouyang Xun 歐陽詢 (557–651),[23] and the first quotation in the *Taiping yulan* 太平御覽, compiled under the auspices of Li Fang 李昉 (925–996),[24] start with the words *Nüzi Cao E zhe* 女子曹娥者 (The woman Cao E), whereas later versions change the beginning to read *Xiaonü* 孝女, "The filial woman [Cao E]," the reading in the second quotation in the *Taiping yulan*.[25] Exactly when this change was effected is not clear, but it was early, as it appears in Fan Ye's 范曄 (398–445) biography of Cao E in his *Hou Han shu* 後漢書, which later became the locus classicus for Cao E's story.[26] According to the early Tang commentary by Li Xian 李賢 on the *Hou Han shu* biography, another version was recorded in Xiang Yuan's 項原 *Lienü houzhuan* 列女後傳, again with slightly different wording, but this work is not extant.[27] Clearly, as Li Xiaohong 李小紅 has recently argued, Cao Xu was a shaman, and if the story about Cao E has any historical truth—which may be doubted—as a daughter in a shaman's family, she was probably being trained to be a shaman herself.[28] The *Hou Han shu* biography continues by declaring that in the second year of the Han'an period (143 CE), her father died and she wandered the banks, weeping and wailing, while looking for her father's body, and committed suicide seventeen days later. Later, over the course of the centuries, the story of Cao E's death was further elaborated—for example, it was said that her body miraculously reappeared five days after her suicide embracing her father's corpse (fig. 2.1).[29]

In the first year of the Yuanjia 元嘉 reign period of Emperor Huan 桓帝 (151 CE), the local magistrate Du Shang 度尚 moved her grave to the south side of the river and had a memorial stele erected in her honor.[30] This stele and its wording form the second strand of the Cao E legend. There is no scholarship that ventures to explain why Du Shang decided on this initiative during one of the earliest appointments of his career, which later proved to be very impressive.[31] However, a glance at the political situation at the time may help to explain it. The court was dominated by the infamous regent Liang Ji 梁冀 and the powerful clique around the empress dowager who were supported by the eunuchs, while the Pure Crit-

Figure 2.1. "Fushi chushui" 負屍出水, *Cao jiang xiaonü miaozhi*, 47.

ics were in a vicious struggle with them for control of the court. Du, who was apparently being patronized by a powerful high eunuch Hou Ba, may have chosen to honor Cao E in response to an edict that was issued not in the first year of the Yuanjia reign period (151 CE), as reported in the biography, but four years later in the first year of the Yongshou 永壽 reign period (155 CE), for the *Hou Han shu* records that in this year, an edict ordered that commanderies and counties were to search and fish out of the water all the corpses and bones of those who had died by drowning and to give them a proper burial.[32] Needless to say, in the Yin-Yang and Five Phase thinking of the time, the female was associated with water and there were many portents and natural anomalies, such as epidemics, reported in these years and interpreted for political purposes.[33] Overabundant rains and floods were attributed by the Pure Critics to the excesses of the female and eunuch influence over the court. Whatever the year of the inscription was, by promoting Cao E's self-sacrifice and filiality, Du Shang astutely aimed to enhance his political credentials with the members of the local elite, as well as with the Pure Critics faction at the capital of Luoyang, together with the reigning Emperor Huan, who was trying to expel the Liang Ji clique; he eventually succeeded in 159 CE.

The story recounting the composition of the stele has strong elements of fable about it and the various versions of the inscription have gone into calligraphic lore and history. They have been studied extensively and I will not dwell on them here.[34] In one early account,[35] Du Shang invited a scholar by the name of Wei Lang 魏郎 (or, Gentleman Wei) to compose and write out the inscription, but he was incapable. While drinking at a banquet, Du asked Handan Chun 邯鄲淳, his disciple (or, in another version, his nephew—i.e., sister's son), to take on the task.[36] Being youthful and of unusual talent, Handan took up the brush and completed it without making a single mistake. Wei Lang sighed in astonishment and snapped his own brush.

Whether or not the story of the creation of the memorial stele to Cao E is historically accurate (there are textual variants in the inscription and the historicity of the story has been challenged), gradually more legends grew up around it. For example, China's most famous calligrapher, Wang Xizhi, is supposed to have copied out Handan's inscription (fig. 2.2).[37]

Another was that Cai Yong 蔡邕 (133–192), the most eminent calligrapher of his day,[38] wrote a cryptic eight-graph inscription on the back of the stele such that Cao Cao 曹操 (155–220), when he passed by and examined the writing, had a hard time interpreting it, unlike his assistant, Yang Xiu 楊修, who deciphered the riddle on the spot.[39] But, of course, although Cai Yong did write the memorial inscription for Magistrate Du Shang and was known for writing directly on stones, he wrote no such thing for Cao E and Cao Cao never managed to travel south of the Yangzi River.[40]

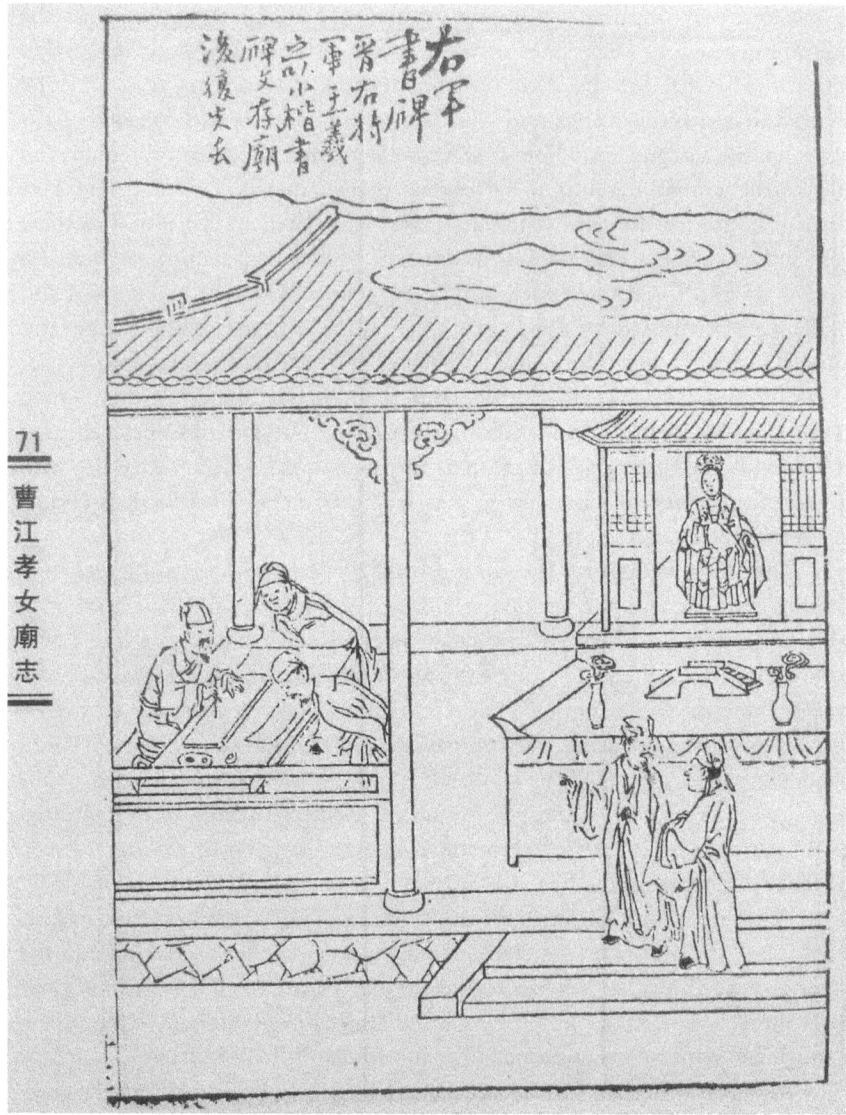

Figure 2.2. "Youjun shubei" 右軍書碑, *Cao jiang xiaonü miaozhi*, 71.

The Initial Development of the Cao E Cult

As is evident from the story presented here, in the Later Han dynasty the tidal bore in the Cao E River was associated with the spirit of Wu Zixu, not with that of the unmarried girl Cao E, at least among male elite writers. David Johnson, in reviewing the sources of the *Wu Zixu bianwen* 伍子胥變文, remarked on the Cao E story as follows:

> Leaving aside the extremely interesting question whether Ts'ao O (Cao E) was venerated from the beginning as a paragon of filial piety, or whether we have here a case of a local cult figure being "recruited" for the cause of Confucian orthodoxy, it is clear that in the mid-second century A.D. a cult which associated Wu Tzu-hsü (Wu Zixu) with a great wave on a river was well established on a river in the vicinity of the Hangchow (Hangzhou) Bay.[41]

When did the cult to Cao E begin? Was there a primordial cult to her in this region as a water deity, as implied by Eberhard, or did the cult develop after the second half of the Han dynasty, perhaps as a result of the intervention of the local magistrate, Du Shang, who instigated the setting up of the memorial stele to her? It is clear from the story quoted earlier that he had her grave moved, so there was a grave; there is no mention of her father's tomb, which, given the importance of the family in Han times, might well have been more important than that of his daughter. And there is no mention of a mother, either, who may have died by the time that Du Shang came to office. There is no family cemetery, which was common in areas further north in Shandong, for example the Wu Liang shrines.[42] If there was a cult to her prior to Du Shang, we have no surviving sources to reconstruct it. Thus it seems that the contours of the cult, as they appear later in history, where Cao E is represented as a paragon of filiality and as a tide deity, developed under the impetus of Du Shang's establishment of the stele. This is regardless of whether the local population were worshipping Cao E in some form earlier in time, or whether the river was called "Cao E" in the local Yue language, and this was then taken later as the name of a young girl, with the story elaborated upon from Han times on. It is also to be noted that Du did not establish a temple in her honor, either: he moved her grave and set up a stele—that was all.[43] There was no apparent institutionalization of a cult to her memory.

As Keith Knapp has recently shown, selfless offspring, both sons and daughters, became an important trope in writings from the late Han through the period of division, although the forms of filiality were gendered. He explains:

When we look at tales of women who refused to marry in order to nurture either their parents or in-laws, the female sacrifice is much greater. To complete reverent care, these women abandon any hope of a happy future by refusing to remarry. Unlike filial sons, who suffer only temporary deprivations, filial daughters who forego the opportunity to have descendants (sic) deprive themselves of contentment forever—both in this world and the next. Childless filial daughters-in-law who vow never to remarry do the same. Even widows with children have little to look forward to, since their relatives will constantly pester them to remarry. In short, unlike filial sons, it is never enough for a filial daughter to merely exhibit exemplary filial piety by depriving herself of good food or clothing, or by engaging in demeaning acts. This could be one aspect of her filiality, but she had to make an even greater sacrifice to gain recognition for her virtue.[44]

And he goes on to comment on the Cao E story that it "indicates that the parent's lifeless body is worth more than her life. Significantly, this type of anecdote always concerns one's biological parent, rather than an in-law. These tales thereby intimate that for a woman, natal kin were still more important to her than in-laws."[45]

Throughout the period of division and into the early Tang, there are no surviving traces of a cult to Cao E. However, the river began to be called by her name, as can be seen from the title of an essay by the child prodigy and later well-known author of the Liang dynasty, Liu Xiaochuo 劉孝綽 (481–589).[46] In the Tang two references call it either the Cao River 曹江 or (possibly) the "River of Filial Piety" (*Xiao jiang* 孝江): Xiao Yingshi 蕭穎士 (717–768), wrote a poem with the title "Autumn Dawn over the Cao River" (*Cao jiang qiushu* 曹江秋曙),[47] and the later prolific monk poet Guan Xiu 貫休 (832–912) wrote a poem titled "Crossing the River of Filial Piety" (*Du Xiao jiang* 渡孝江).[48] In this period, the stele still survived, as can be seen from its mention in Li Daoyuan's 酈道元 *Shuijing zhu* 水經注,[49] while the early court poet, Song Zhiwen 宋之問, who was forced to commit suicide in 712 CE,[50] lamented Cao E's fate in several poems.[51] In the next generation, the famous poet Li Bo (Bai) 李白 (701–762) also records a recluse laughing (*xiao* 笑) when the latter read the inscription.[52]

During the course of the Tang dynasty, however, two new developments occurred, although when they took place or if they took place earlier is, in our present state of knowledge, unknown. First, by the ninth century, a temple was constructed in Cao E's honor, but who authorized or paid for the construction and where it was located are unknown. Most likely, it was close to the stele and the tomb of Cao E, which the stele marked. However, and secondly, the stele had fallen down. These two developments can be seen in poems by Zhang Xiaobiao 章孝標 (791–873; *jinshi* 819), "The Cao E Temple" 曹娥廟,[53] and by Zhao Gu/Jia 趙嘏 (fl. 9th c.) in a poem titled "On the Cao E Temple" 題曹娥廟.[54] This latter poem only refers to the tomb, the stele, and the writing on it, not the temple itself, and the author mentions, significantly, that the stele had fallen over. One might wonder whether this was the result of the age of the stele, by this time about seven hundred years old, or whether it was the result of damage during the infamous Huichang persecution that took place in 845 CE, although it is generally recognized that it was Buddhist and other "foreign" religious institutions that felt the full force of the authorities in this episode, not Daoist or other local establishments.[55]

The Cao E Cult in the Song Dynasty

The fortunes of the cult and the temple dramatically improved in the late Northern Song dynasty as a result of political activity at the capital, Kaifeng, and the contours of these changes can be partially reconstructed from the traces left in the two gazetteers and other sources. Cao E was also sufficiently well known among the populace as to be included as one of the paragons of filial piety depicted in a set of twenty-four tiles.[56]

First, in the tenth year of the Xining 熙寧 reign period of Song emperor Shenzong 宋神宗 (1077 CE), the magistrate of Kuaiji County, Dong Kai 董楷, introduced the statue of a second filial figure to be placed alongside that of Cao E, who evidently now had her own statue, in her temple.[57] This was Zhu E 朱娥. According to the texts preserved in *juan* 9 of the *Cao jiang xiaonü miaozhi*, at a bare ten years old, Zhu E died from multiple knife wounds inflicted on her by a relative in the second year of the Zhiping 治平 reign period (1065 CE) of Emperor Yingzong 宋英宗. Her grandmother, who was raising her, got into a vicious argument with the relative and he brought out a knife. Young Zhu E's throat was slit when she tried to protect her grandmother.[58]

Then, a more substantial temple was built. Five rooms of the main hall were constructed in the eighth year of the Yuanyou 元祐 reign period of Song emperor Zhezong 宋哲宗 (1093 CE), but under whose supervision, at whose suggestion, and who funded the project is not stated (fig. 2.3).[59]

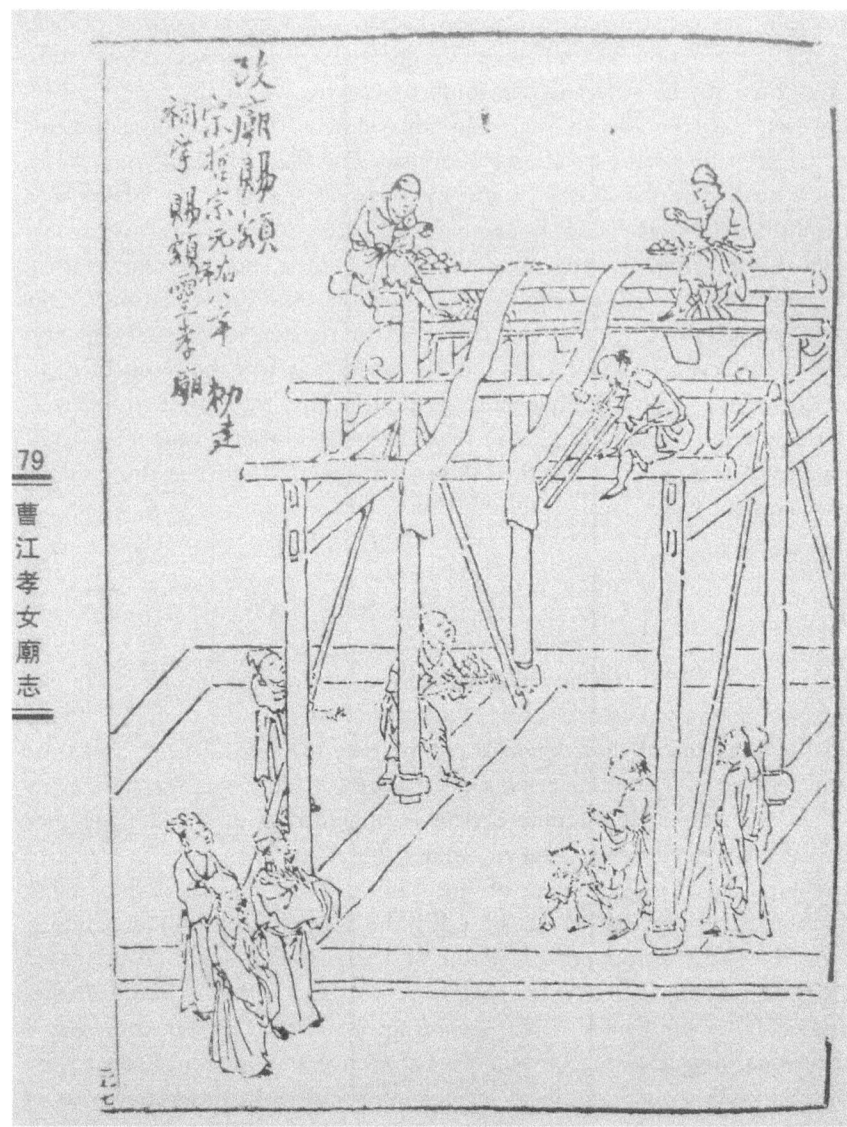

Figure 2.3. "Gaimiao ci'e" 改廟賜額, *Cao jiang xiaonü miaozhi*, 79.

However, significantly, it was in this same year that Cai Bian 蔡卞 (1048–1117), a famous calligrapher, rewrote the inscription for the Cao E stele in running script, apparently in the first month (fig. 2.4).[60] This stele is still extant and a rubbing is preserved in the National Library, Beijing.[61]

Figure 2.4. "Chongshu Han bei" 重書漢碑, *Cao jiang xiaonü miaozhi*, 81.

The two events, the rebuilding and enlargement of the temple and Cai Bian's inscription, must have been connected, the stele being placed in the newly renovated temple, where it stands today. At the time, Cai Bian was the reformist statesman's Wang Anshi's 王安石 (1021–1086) son-in-law and the younger brother of the infamous Cai Jing 蔡京 (1046–1126), who was the leader of the reformist faction and proponent of the New Policies after Wang's death. Thus, the Cao E temple must have been receiving the patronage of the Cais and the reformist faction in some fashion. Indeed, there was extreme factionalism at the court in this year and preceding years, as the ageing Empress Dowager Xuanren 皇太后宣仁 was presiding as regent over the government while the young Zhezong 哲宗 was yet to reach maturity. While the reformist faction had been purged, the conservative antireform faction fractured in bitter infighting. When the Empress Dowager Xuanren died in the ninth month of this year (1093 CE), Zhezong was free to bring back the New Policies and purge the conservative opposition.[62]

Equally important, in the fourth year of the Daguan 大觀 reign period of Song emperor Huizong 宋徽宗 (1110 CE), a delegation from the Korean kingdom of Goryeo bringing tribute prayed to the tide and received a response, and, as a direct consequence, for the first time Cao E was honored by the imperial court on the twenty-eighth day of the eighth month of the same year with a title, "Lingxiao furen" 靈孝夫人 (Spiritually Efficacious Filial Lady (fig. 2.5)).[63]

The words "Chici Lingxiao miao" 敕賜靈孝廟 (Imperially Bestowed Spiritually Efficacious Temple) were inscribed on a placard (*ebian* 額匾) and proudly hung over the main gate of the temple, demonstrating that the temple's status was confirmed and conferred by imperial grace.[64] This placard was one of the first of many that were inscribed for the temple during the course of the imperial period by famous and not-so-famous calligraphers and literati, such as the late Ming poet and loyalist Chen Zilong 陳子龍 (1608–1647), the painter Chen Hongshou 陳洪綬 (1599–1652), and the famous calligrapher Ni Yuanlu 倪元璐 (ca. 1593–1644; *jinshi* 1621), a Hanlin scholar and local from Shangyu who loyally committed suicide rather than accept Qing rule.[65] These usually four-graph inscriptions gave "face" to the temple, announcing, even to the barely literate, its authority and asserting the efficacy of its deities,[66] in addition to proclaiming their various moral and ethical characteristics.[67]

Although the first words of the introduction to the imperial order (*chi* 敕) for the Daguan bestowal are lost as a result of a lacuna in the text of the *Cao jiang xiaonü miaozhi*, it is clear that she was prayed to as a tide deity for safe passage on the river (祈潮濟江), the result of her filial devotion to her father. This grant of a title would have resulted in Cao E's name being included in the official register of sacrifices kept by the Court of Imperial Sacrifices and the local officials would have been obliged to go twice a year

Figure 2.5. "Gaoli yemiao" 高麗謁廟, *Cao jiang xiaonü miaozhi*, 87.

in the spring and autumn to perform rituals and do obeisance to her. This would undoubtedly have enhanced her prestige not only among the local populace but also among the literati and local elite.[68] In this year, 1110 CE, there was more factional fighting in the court and, after a comet was sighted in the fifth month, Cai Jing, who had previously been dismissed as chief councilor, was forced to move out of Kaifeng and was transferred to reside in Hangzhou.⁶⁹ Thus, Cai Jing was close to the site where this delegation successfully prayed to Cao E.

Still in Huizong's reign, in the fifth year of the Zhenghe 政和 reign period (1115 CE), another Goryeo embassy passed by the Cao E temple, this time bringing women for Huizong's harem. They petitioned the goddess to improve the women's appearances, stayed overnight in the temple, and by the next day, a miracle had happened: as a result of their prayers, the women had indeed transformed into beauties. When they entered the imperial court and were granted an audience, by good fortune, the goddess Cao E was granted an increase to her title, the imperial order being issued on the seventeenth day of the eleventh month of that year. She was now to be known as "Lingxiao Zhaoshun furen" 靈孝昭順夫人 (Spiritually Efficacious, Filial, Radiant, and Compliant Lady).⁷⁰ However, the *Song Yuan zizhi tongjian* 宋元資治通鑒 only records for this month that five students from Goryeo entered the Imperial University.⁷¹ Most likely, they were part of the same delegation (fig. 2.5).

During this time period, Cai Jing was back in power and Huizong's spending on pleasures, such as his gardens, and on religious patronage was growing ever more reckless.⁷² Furthermore, the granting of titles to Cao E was part of a much larger trend of granting honors to deities in the late eleventh and early twelfth centuries that was carefully analyzed by Valerie Hansen some twenty-five years ago.⁷³ She demonstrates that only bureaucrats were allowed to forward petitions for the granting of titles to deities on the basis of miracles,⁷⁴ and thus it is most likely that officials affiliated with the New Policies, including the Cai brothers, were involved in the promotion of the Cao E cult, probably in collusion with members of the local elite and the populace.

The Cao E cult continued to flourish in the Southern Song, probably helped by the fact that the court had relocated to Lin'an, the modern Hangzhou city just north across the bay. In Xiaozong's reign (1163–1189), the imperial Prince of Wei 王子魏王, who was on his way to Mingzhou 明州 (Ningbo) to rule on law cases, prayed for safe passage over the tide and was also responded to by the goddess.⁷⁵ But for the next elevation in the goddess's status it is recorded that the local elite, the populace, and the officials petitioned to increase her title by two more characters and, on the fifteenth day of the sixth month of the sixth year of the Chunyou 淳祐 reign period of Emperor Lizong (1246 CE), she was granted that of "Lingxiao

Zhaoshun Chunyi furen" 靈孝昭順純懿夫人 (Spiritually Efficacious, Filial, Radiant and Compliant, Pure and Virtuous Lady) and another placard was inscribed and hung over the second gate into the temple with the words "Chici Lingxiao Zhaoshun Chunyi furen zhi miao" 敕賜靈孝昭順純懿夫人之廟 (Imperially Bestowed Temple of the Spiritually Efficacious, Filial, Radiant and Compliant, Pure and Virtuous Lady). The calligraphy was in the hand of Grand Councilor Zheng Qingzhi 丞相鄭清之.[76] At the same time her divine father was enfeoffed as "Heying hou" 和應侯 (Harmonious and Respondent Marquis) and her divine mother, who was being recognized for the first time, was enfeoffed as "Qingshan furen" 慶善夫人 (Lady Who Enjoys the Excellent). Presumably on this occasion, Cao E had performed another miracle, as this was required by the law code of the Qingyuan 慶元 era (1195–1200),[77] but no record of the occurrence has survived: the grant of the title merely reiterates the goddess's suicide on the drowning of her father "to bring benevolence to completion" (chengren 成仁), something that was hard even for literati gentlemen (shijunzi 士君子) to do, and that she was a model for filial piety through a hundred generations.[78] The edict granting the titles reveals that by this time a township or settlement had developed in the vicinity of the temple bearing the goddess's name, Cao E Township 曹娥鎮. As the prolific poet Lu You 陸遊 (1125–1210) composed a poem with the title "E jiang shi" 娥江市 (E River Market),[79] it is quite likely that a market had developed near the temple and where the river was normally crossed, and the township grew round both the temple and the market.

Finally, the Southern Song local gazetteer Baoqing Kuaiji xuzhi 寶慶會稽續志, in describing the temple, proclaims that "the divine spirituality [of the goddess] was unusually resplendent and manifest; those coming and going prayed for/to the tide to cross the river; [she was] as trustworthy as shadow and echo." This work was republished in the fifth year of the Ming Zhengde 正德 reign period (1510 CE) and is the last mention of Cao E as a tide deity.[80]

The Cao E Cult in Later Times

The support for the temple apparently continued after the Mongols established the Yuan dynasty, but there is little substantial information apart from the fact that in the second year of the Zhiyuan 至元 reign period, probably that of Toghon Temür (temple name Huizong 惠宗), who was bestowed with the posthumous name Shundi 順帝 by the Ming Hongwu Emperor 明

弘武 after his seizure of the throne, that is, 1336 CE, the temple hall and buildings were restored by the Prefect Gongcheng (or, by Yin Gongcheng 尹宮誠).[81] The Yuan also continued the Song practice of bestowing titles on deities, and thus shortly after the restoration of the temple, in the fifth year of the same reign period (1339 CE), Cao E received another elevation in status. Henceforth she was to be known as "Xiaonü Cao E Huigan Lingxiao Zhaoshun Chunyi furen" 孝女曹娥慧感靈孝昭順純懿夫人 (The Filial Daughter Cao E, the Intelligently Responsive, Spiritually Efficacious, Filial, Radiant and Compliant, Pure and Virtuous Lady).

In the eighth year of the Hongwu period in the early Ming (1375 CE), Cao E was endorsed by imperial edict to receive official sacrifices as the "Filial Daughter Cao E." A eulogy (*lei* 誄) was composed on this occasion by one of Hongwu's most trusted generals, Liu Ji 劉基 (1311–1375), an expert in gunpowder technology but also a poet and literatus.[82] He also composed a *jueju* 絕句 poem titled "Making Obeisance in the Temple of Cao E" 拜曹娥廟.[83] Another early Ming literatus and official also endorsed Cao E by composing a poem titled "On Crossing the Cao E River" 過曹娥江, the first two lines of which read: "E took filial piety as the basis; The river therefore took the name from E" (娥以孝為本; 江因娥得名).[84] This was Fang Xiaoru 方孝孺 (1357–1402), who later famously challenged Zhu Di 朱棣, the Yongle 永樂 Emperor's (r. 1403–1424) usurpation of the throne, and died an extremely unpleasant death and was proscribed for most of the rest of the Ming dynasty. Thus, Cao E received the patronage of men who reached the summit of political power in the early Ming. As a result, the cult continued to receive official sponsorship throughout the Ming and Qing dynasties, with Ming and Qing local officials continuing to make offerings to her in the spring and autumn. The temple was repaired and expanded, and wealthy locals also acted as patrons, while the occasional supernatural story is also recorded.[85]

What is most evident, however, from the increasingly numerous poems composed by male literati famous or otherwise unknown from the Song through the Qing dynasties, on the subject of Cao E—either on the temple, on the inscription, or on the river—as well as from the numerous placards that were inscribed and erected in the temple in her honor, is that Cao E's role as water or tide deity receded rapidly from the male literati consciousness. What the male literati lauded was Cao E's devotion to her father and her self-sacrifice, and her embodiment of what was becoming the prime moral virtue for women, filiality. I have not discovered to date any mention of her in the context of chastity, even though this form of moral and ethical behavior was becoming increasingly prominent as a female virtue. This trend was reinforced in the fourth year of the Jiajing 嘉靖 Emperor's reign (1525 CE), when the governor of the province, Nan Daji 南大吉, repaired and enlarged the temple in order to install in the east and west side buildings the tablets of all the exemplary women from the commandery throughout history (*tongjun lidai lienü* 通郡歷代烈女) and to have offerings made to them in spring and autumn. However, later, when and why is not stated, this was deemed not convenient and they were removed and the sacrifices were discontinued.[86] Nevertheless, the effort to reinforce the ethical dimensions of the cult was repeated in the *dingsi* 丁巳 year of the Ming Wanli Emperor (1617 CE), when Zhu Wanli, the local literatus from Shanyin mentioned earlier, successfully petitioned to include his paternal aunt from five generations back, the filial woman Zhu E 諸娥, in the Cao E temple.[87]

Brief Conclusion

In this chapter, I have tried to demonstrate that the two-thousand-year-old cult to Cao E, which is still flourishing today, survived due to numerous factors. First, it is not clear when the cult began: it may have existed in antiquity before the Later Han story of the filial fourteen-year-old daughter drowning herself while looking for her shaman father's body. Next, the story of the inscription on the stele commemorating her filial devotion played an important part in its enduring popularity, but I have not had the time or the space to cover it here. Third, I have argued that Cao E, in addition to being a paragon of filiality, was also a tide goddess, and I have demonstrated that the official support of the Northern and Southern Song imperial court played a crucial role in confirming and enhancing the deity's power. This official support was continued throughout the imperial period and was assisted by local officials and local elites who helped to maintain and expand the temple buildings. The addition of two other paragons of filiality to the temple, and, perhaps, the lessening of the dangers of the tide on the river due to changing environmental factors, assisted in turning the cult away from the tide, which was one of its two earlier elements, toward an almost exclusive focus on filiality. Finally, the enormous textual production of male literati, writing poems in various genres on the themes of the temple, the stele inscription, and the river, as well as the actions of calligraphers and literati who inscribed placards honoring the deity, played an equally essential role in enhancing the deity's reputation. The mixture of both official and male literati support continued into the twentieth century, as can be seen today in the placard written by nationalist leader Chiang Kai-shek (1887–1975) still gracing the temple. And, it seems, the moral influence of the temple affected the ideas and practices of the local population: they have developed a reputation for filiality, which still is manifest today.[88] The extent to which these ideas and practices of the local population affected the development and focus of the cult through the course of history, which they must have done, has yet to be determined.

Notes

1. For an overview, see Alan Kam-leung Chan, "Goddesses in Chinese Religion," in *Goddesses in Religions and Modern Debate*, ed. Larry W. Hurtado (Atlanta: Scholars, 1990), 9–81. I would like to thank my PhD student, Cai Danni 蔡丹妮, for her research assistance in preparing this chapter, and Grace S. Fong for correcting some errors in the interpretation of the poems. All remaining faults are my own responsibility.

2. The bibliography in Western languages is vast: The Queen Mother of the West (Xiwangmu 西王母) has been studied in the West notably by Suzanne Elizabeth Cahill, *Transcendence & Divine Passion: The Queen Mother of the West in Medieval China* (Stanford: Stanford University Press, 1993); for Mazu, see P. Steven Sangren, "History and the Rhetoric of Legitimacy: The Ma Tsu Cult of Taiwan," *Comparative Studies in Society and History* 30, no. 4 (1988): 674–697; for the Lady of Linshui, see Brigitte Baptandier, *The Lady of Linshui: A Chinese Female Cult* (Stanford: Stanford University Press, 2008); for Guanyin, see Chün-fang Yü, *Kuan-Yin: The Chinese Transformation of Avalokitesvara* (New York: Columbia University Press, 2001). See also Catherine Despeux and Livia Kohn, *Women in Daoism* (Cambridge: Three Pines Press, 2003).

3. In English, the most recent contributions to this wonderful outpouring of scholarship are: Beverly Bossler, *Courtesans, Concubines, and the Cult of Female Fidelity: Gender and Social Change in China, 1000–1400* (Cambridge: Harvard University Asia Center, 2012), and Weijing Lu, *True to Her Word: The Faithful Maiden Cult in Late Imperial China* (Stanford: Stanford University, 2008).

4. Wolfram Eberhard, *The Local Cultures of South and East China* (Leiden: Brill, 1968), 392–394; cf. 38, 76.

5. Timothy Wai Keung Chan has published detailed research on the early stages of the story and I will not repeat his findings here. See his article "Searching for the Bodies of the Drowned: A Folk Tradition of Early China Recovered," *Journal of the American Oriental Society* 129, no. 3 (2009): 385–401.

6. For a collection of essays analyzing the various aspects of filial piety, see *Filial Piety in Chinese Thought and History*, ed. Alan K. L. Chan and Sor-hoon Tan (London: Routledge Curzon, 2004).

7. The first exemplar is the *Cao jiang xiaonü miaozhi* 曹江孝女廟, preface by Wu Xingzuo 吳興祚, dated twenty-seventh year of the Kangxi Emperor 清康熙 (1678), *keben* 刻本 printed by the Shendetang 慎德堂, reprint edition of the copy held by the Shanghai Library, *Siku quanshu cunmu congshu* 四庫全書存目叢書, series 2, "Shi bu" 史部, "Zhuan ji" 傳記, vol. 87. The second has been republished in the *Zhongguo cimu zhi congkan* 中國祠墓志叢刊, chief eds. Wu Ping 吳平 and Zhang Zhi 張智 (Yangzhou: Guangling, 2004), with a preface by the renowned scholar Ruan Yuan 阮元 (1764–1849) and compiled by Jin Tingdong 金廷棟, reprint dated 1882. The latter version reproduces a set of stone illustrations said to have been carved and placed on the walls of the temple. These have been the subject of a recent study by Gilbert Chen, "A Confucian Iconography of Cao E (Maiden Cao): Narrative Illustrations of a Female Deity in Late Imperial China," *Nan Nü: Men, Women and Gender in China* 18, no. 1 (2016): 84–114. Chen seems unaware of the third source, Hu Fengdan's river gazetteer.

8. Reprinted in Ma Ning 馬寧, ed., *Zhongguo shuili zhi congkan* 中國水利志叢刊 (Yangzhou: Guangling, 2006), vol. 70.

9. For a fascinating study of the Song imperial clan, see John W. Chaffee, *Branches of Heaven: A History of the Imperial Clan of Sung China* (Cambridge: Harvard University Asia Center, 1999).

10. Hu Fengdan lists the sources of his work in *juan* 2.12a–13b under the title "Shu mu" 書目. It seems as though the *Cao jiang xiaonü miaozhi* was based on the similarly titled work composed by Zhu Wanli dated 1619, which Hu found cited in the *Zhejiang tongzhi* 浙江通志, a gazetteer that I have not seen. Zhu Wanli's work does not seem to be extant, but he probably composed it as part of his effort to have his ancestor enshrined in the Cao E temple (see later discussion). Hu also lists a second work with the same title as having been composed by two literati from Shangyu, Yin Wei 印偉 (also written Hui 繪) and Zhang E 張噩, dated Kangxi 1667, with Shen Zhili's preface, also cited in the *Zhejiang tongzhi*. How this work differed from Shen Zhili's collection is unclear. It may have been the same. Hu also lists by dynasty the numerous other works from which he cites (*Cao E jiang zhi yinyong shumu* 曹娥江志引用書目 1a–4a) and throughout he carefully records after each citation the source of the quotation. I have not been able to determine whether the *Cao jiang shiji* is still extant.

11. Ming Qing Women's Writings: http://digital.library.mcgill.ca/mingqing/.

12. For the history of the construction, see (last accessed January 20, 2019): http://slwm.mwr.gov.cn/wllm/rhal/n01/201807/t20180718_1043152.html

13. Mark Elvin and Su Ninghu, "Action at a Distance: The Influence of the Yellow River on Hangzhou Bay since A.D. 1000," in *Sediments of Time: Environment and Society in Chinese History*, ed. Mark Elvin and Liu Ts'ui-jung (Cambridge:

Cambridge University, 1999), 344–407. The effects of the Yellow River on the Hangzhou Bay were especially pronounced when the Yellow River flowed out south of the Shandong Peninsula, combining with the Huai River, from 1194 to 1855.

14. *Cao jiang xiaonü miaozhi*, 1.3b (87–445).

15. *Guangxu Shangyu xianzhi jiaoxu* 光緒上虞縣志校續, eds. Chu Jiazao 儲家藻 and Xu Zhijing 徐致靖, in *Zhongguo difangzhi jicheng: Zhejiang fuxianzhi ji* 中國地方志集成：浙江府縣志輯 42 (Shanghai: Jiangsu guji, Shanghai shudian, and Ba-Shu, 1993), "Xiangyi" 祥異, j.42.15b–23a.

16. Ma Rong 馬榮 et al., eds., *Yongle dadian fangzhi jiyi* 永樂大典方志輯佚 (Beijing: Zhonghua, 2004), ce 2, 910.

17. *Shaoxing fuzhi* 紹興府志, "Shuili zhi er" 水利志二, compiled by Xiao Lianggan 蕭良榦, ed. Zhang Yuanbian 張元 and Sun Kuang 孫鑛, Ming Wanli 15 (1587) reprinted from the copy held in the Zhejiang Library, in Shaoxing congshu bianji weiyuanhui 紹興叢書編輯委員會, ed., *Shaoxing congshu* 紹興叢書 (Beijing: Zhonghua shuju, 2006), vol. 1, j.17.17a, 827. Zeng served as magistrate in the Tiansheng 天聖 reign period (1023–1032), according to the *Shaoxing fuzhi*, compiled by Li Hengte 李亨特, ed. Ping Shu 平恕 and Xu Song 徐崧, Qing Qianlong 乾隆 57 (1792), photographic reprint in: Fenghuang chubanshe 鳳凰出版社, ed., *Zhongguo difang zhi jicheng: Xingzhi ji: Zhejiang* 中國地方志集成 省志輯 浙江 (Nanjing: Fenghuang, 2010), j.27.10a, 611.

18. *Yongle dadian fangzhi jiyi* "Shaoxing fu; Kuaiji zhi; Kuaiji xianzhi" 紹興府; 會稽志; 會稽縣志, 883 (taken from ce 49, *juan* 2526, 9). The *Cao jiang xiaonü miaozhi*, j.1.1b, in its first subsection *Jun zhi* 郡誌, states that, although the tides on the Cao E River were less than those on the Qiantang 錢塘, the shifting sandbars had a tendency to trap and sink boats and as a result the river was called the "Iron-faced Cao E" 鐵面曹娥.

19. Timothy Chan, in "Searching for the Bodies of the Drowned," reads the graph of the father's name as Yu.

20. The dance was said to be a whirling (*posha* 婆娑) one, which probably induced a trance.

21. He also composed a history of the Jin dynasty, *Jin shu* 晉書, in more than forty *juan*, which is no longer extant.

22. The reconstructed work is to be found in the *Congshu jicheng xubian* 叢書集成續編 "Shi bu" 史部 ce 28 (Shanghai: Shanghai shudian, 1994), 1007–1039, a reprint of the *Siming congshu* 四明叢書 (Zhang shi 張氏: Zhang Shouyong 張壽鏞) Yueyuan kanben edition 約園刊本; Cao E's biography is found in j.B.20b–21a, 1031–1032.

23. "Suishi Zhong 歲時中," in Ouyang Xun 歐陽詢 (557–651), ed., *Yiwen leiju* 藝文類聚, vol. 4 (Shanghai: Shanghai guji, 1982), 74–75.

24. Li Fang 李昉 (925–996), ed., *Taiping yulan* 太平御覽 (Beijing: Zhonghua, 1985 [1960]), j.31.4a 147.

25. *Taiping yulan*, 415.5a, 1916.

26. Fan Ye 范曄 (398–445), *Hou Han shu* 後漢書 (Beijing: Zhonghua, 1965), "Lienü zhuan" 列女傳 84, j.74 2794–2795.

27. One version of the story is that Cao E threw her father's clothes (*yi* 衣) into the river chanting that where they sank, his body would be found; another is that she threw a melon (*gua* 瓜) into the water. Timothy Chan argues that the correct medium for seeking the body was a melon. A third alternative is *zhao* 爪 "claw," which perhaps might be understood as "nails," since nails were considered to be substitutes for the human body and were offered in sacrifice in early times as a body substitute, a possibility that Chan ignores. All the versions of the story that I have consulted, including that in the *Shishuo xinyu* 世說新語 (see Richard B. Mather, trans., *Shih-Shuo Hsin-yü: A New Account of Tales of the World by Liu I-ch'ing with Commentary by Liu Chün* [Ann Arbor: Center for Chinese Studies, University of Michigan, 2002], ch. 11 "Quick Perception" "Jie wu" 捷悟, 293–294), the *Jing-Chu suishi ji* 荊楚歲時記 (see Ian Chapman, trans., in Wendy Swartz et al., eds., *Early Medieval China: A Sourcebook* [New York: Columbia University Press, 2014], 479), and in Yue Shi's 樂史 *Taiping huanyu ji* 太平寰宇記 ("Jiangnan dongdao" 江南東道 8, "Yuezhou" 越州 [Beijing: Zhonghua, 2007], ce 4 j.96 1935), also say that Cao Xu drowned when he *su* 泝 "faced upstream" during his ritual. The graph may be an error for *qi* 祈 "pray," especially at the spring sacrifice for a good harvest. Wolfram Eberhard (*The Local Cultures of South and East China*, 397) notes that the water festivals, including the dragon boat festivals that were held on the same day (5th day of the 5th month), were "designed to bring fertility." For other textual variants, see the notes gathered by Shi Zhimian 施之勉, *Hou Han shu jijie bu* 後漢書集解補 (Taibei: Zhongguo wenhua daxue, 1982), ce 3, 1313–1314. The story is still being told today, see: Zhongguo minjian wenxue jicheng quanguo bianji weiyuanhui 中國民間文學集成全國編輯委員會 and Zhongguo minjian wenxue jicheng Zhejiang juan bianji weiyuanhui 中國民間文學集成浙江卷編輯委員會, eds., *Zhongguo minjian gushi jicheng: Zhejiang juan* 中國民間故事集成: 浙江卷 (Beijing: Zhongguo ISBN zhongxin, 1997), no. 352, 432–433.

28. Li Xiaohong 李小紅, "Dong-Han xiaonü Cao E yuan wei 'wunü' kaolun" 東漢孝女曹娥原為 "巫女" 論, *Zhejiang shehui kexue* 浙江社會科學 2009.5: 70–75.

29. *Cao jiang xiaonü miaozhi*, j.2.2b: 87–449. The number of days that it took for the father's body to be found varied according to the different sources. See Timothy Chan, "Searching for the Bodies of the Drowned."

30. As mentioned earlier, the river flows from north to south. However, after Shangyu County it bends and flows northwest, so the tomb may have been located along this stretch of the river. However, currently, and since the Song dynasty, the tomb and temple have been located south of Shangyu on the west bank of the river.

31. For Du Shang's biography, see *Hou Han shu* 38, j.28 1284–1287, and Rafe de Crespigny, *A Biographical Dictionary of Later Han to the Three Kingdoms (23–220 AD)* (Leiden: Brill, 2007), 182–83.

32. *Hou Han shu* 7.301. The text reads: 詔被水死流失屍骸者, 令郡縣鉤求收葬.
33. See, for example, Rafe de Crespigny, *Portents of Protest in the Later Han Dynasty: The Memorials of Hsiang K'ai to Emperor Huan* (Canberra: Australian National University, 1976).
34. See, for example, Liu Yibing 劉亦冰, "Juemiao haoci *Cao E bei*" 絕妙好辭 "曹娥碑," *Shaoxing wenli xueyuan xuebao* 紹興文理學院學報 22 (2002) 4: 11–14, 43; Zhang Pengfei 張鵬飛, "Han xiaonü Cao E bei kao" 漢孝女曹娥碑考, *Shaoxing wenli xueyuan xuebao* 34 (2014) 5: 10–13; Li Zhen 李珍, "Cao E bei mi tanwei" 曹娥碑謎探微, *Dang'an* 檔案 2015.2: 45–48.
35. *Kuaiji dianlu* in *Congshu jicheng xubian* 叢書集成續編, 28, 1031–1032. *Kuaiji dianlu* in *Congshu jicheng xubian* 28, 1031–1032.
36. There is much scholarly debate about Handan Chun's authorship of the inscription: it may have been composed by another man by the name of Handan Zili 邯鄲子禮. See Timothy Wai Keung Chan, "A Young Lady on Yellow Pongee Silk," chapter 2 of his monograph *Considering the End: Mortality in Early Medieval Chinese Poetic Representation* (Leiden: Brill, 2012), 41–64.
37. See, for example, the poem by Jiang Hongzhen 江鴻禎, "Wang Youjun shu *Cao E bei* taben ge" 王右軍書曹娥碑榻本歌, in Yun Zhu 惲珠, ed., *Guochao guixiu zhengshi ji* 國朝閨秀正始集, Qing Daoguang 道光11 (1831), *keben* 刻本 printed by Hongxiangguan 紅香館, online at Ming Qing Women's Writings, http://digital.library.mcgill.ca/mingqing/. It was fashionable in both the Tang and later Southern Song dynasties to copy out Wang Xizhi's calligraphy and many works were falsely attributed to him. See Qianshen Bai, "Chinese Letters: Private Words Made Public," in *The Embodied Image: Chinese Calligraphy from the John B. Elliott Collection*, ed. Robert E. Harrist Jr. and Wen C. Fong (Princeton, NJ: Art Museum, Princeton University, 1999), 383–384. For the attribution to Wang Xizhi of a copy of Handan Chun's (or Handan Zili's) inscription, see Cao Xuequan (1574–1647), "Tianxia Mingsheng Zhi" 天下名勝誌, in *Cao jiang xiaonü miaozhi* j.1.3b.
38. Robert E. Harrist Jr., *The Landscape of Words: Stone Inscriptions from Early and Medieval China* (Seattle: University of Washington Press, 2008), 232, calls Cai Yong "the leading author of inscriptions and the foremost calligrapher of the Eastern Han."
39. *Cao jiang xiaonü miaozhi*, j.2.4ab 87–450, citing the *Yu lin* 語林; Mather, *Shih-Shuo Hsin-Yü*, 293–94; *Taiping huanyu ji*, 96.1935. For riddles as a form of divination in China, see Tiziana Lippiello, "Interpreting Written Riddles: A Typical Chinese Way of Divination," in *Linked Faiths: Essays on Chinese Religions and Traditional Culture in Honour of Kristofer Schipper*, ed. Jan A. M. de Meyer and Peter M. Englefriet (Leiden: Brill, 2000), 41–52.
40. In fact, Cao Cao so admired Handan Chun's calligraphy that he is said to have had his children study Handan's models. See Wang Yuchi, "Striving for Perfection amid Social Upheavals: Calligraphy during the Wei, Jin, Southern, and Northern Dynasties," in *Chinese Calligraphy*, ed. and trans. Wang Youfen (New Haven: Yale University and Foreign Languages, 2008), 135.

41. David Johnson, "The Wu Tzu-hsü *Pien-wen* and Its Sources: Part II," *Harvard Journal of Asiatic Studies* 40, no. 2 (1980): 475.

42. Wu Hung, *The Wu Liang Shrine: The Ideology of Early Chinese Pictorial Art* (Stanford: Stanford University Press, 1989); Cary Y. Liu, Michael Nylan, and Anthony Barbieri-Low, *Recarving China's Past: Art, Archaeology and Architecture of the "Wu Family Shrines"* (New Haven: Yale University Press, 2005).

43. The *Cao E jiangzhi*, 1.7a, claims that Du did, but there is no evidence to support this assertion. See later discussion.

44. Keith N. Knapp, *Selfless Offspring: Filial Children and Social Order in Medieval China* (Honolulu: University of Hawai'i Press, 2005), 176.

45. Knapp, *Selfless Offspring*, 176.

46. *Cao jiang xiaonü miaozhi*, j.5.1ab. Liu's collected works were lost but were reconstructed by Zhang Pu 張溥 (1602–1641) as *Liu Mishu ji* 劉秘書集, 1879 edition republished in the *Han Wei Liuchao baisan mingjia ji* 漢魏六朝百三家集, vol. 4 (Yangzhou: Jiangsu Guangling guji, 1990); for his biography, see Yao Silian 姚思廉 (d. 637), *Liang shu* 梁書 (Beijing: Zhonghua, 1973), j.33.479–484.

47. *Cao jiang xiaonü miaozhi*, j.5.2ab.

48. *Cao jiang xiaonü miaozhi*, j.5.2b. This poem is given the alternative title of "Cao E bei" 曹娥碑 (On the Cao E Stele) in Lu Yongfeng 陸永峰, ed., *Chanyue ji jiaozhu* 禪月集校注 (Chengdu: Ba-Shu, 2006), 484–485, and the *Quan Tang shi* 全唐詩 (Beijing: Zhonghua, 1985), ce 23, j.837, 9432–9433. The stele is certainly mentioned in the first line of the poem, but it is impossible to tell whether Guan Xiu had actually had the opportunity to read the inscription on this occasion. Further research is necessary to determine the original title of the poem. As previously mentioned, the citations of poetry in the *Cao jiang xiaonü miaozhi* seem to be based on an early Qing work, while the *Quan Tang shi*, compiled at the command of the Kangxi Emperor, was published in 1707 and based on the earlier late-Ming compendium *Tang yin tongqian* 唐音統籤 edited by Hu Zhenheng 胡震亨 (1569–1645), reprinted in the *Gugong zhenben congkan* 故宮珍本叢刊 (Haikou: Hainan, 2000), vols. 595–608. The least one can say is that there were two alternative titles to this poem in imperial times.

49. In Yang Shoujing 楊守敬 and Xiong Huizhen 熊會貞, eds., *Xuxiu siku quanshu* 續修四庫全書 (Shanghai: Shanghai guji, 1995), "Shi Bu" 史部, "Dili Lei" 地理類, vol. 727, "Zhejiang" 浙江, j.40.50b–51a, 755–756.

50. Stephen Owen, *The Great Age of Chinese Poetry: The High T'ang* (New Haven: Yale University Press, 1981), 11. On Song Zhiwen's court poetry, see also his *The Poetry of the Early T'ang* (New Haven: Yale University Press, 1977), passim.

51. *Cao E jiangzhi*, j.4.1ab.

52. "Song Wang Wu shanren Weiwan huan Wangwu" 送王屋山人魏萬還王屋 in Li Bai 李白 (701–762), Qu Tuiyuan 瞿蛻園, and Zhu Jincheng 朱金城, *Li Bo ji jiaozhu* 李白集校注, vol. 4 (Shanghai: Shanghai guji, 1980), ce 3, 957: "He laughed when he read the Cao E inscription, and deeply intoned the words on yellow pongee" (笑讀曹娥碑; 沉吟黃絹語). The words "yellow pongee" appear in the

eight-word inscription supposedly written on the back of the stele by Cai Yong (see previous discussion). The *Cao E jiangzhi*, j.8.1a, records the name of the addressee of this poem as Huang 黃, rather than Wang 王. The *Cao E jiangzhi*, 4b–5a, and the *Cao jiang xiaonü miaozhi*, 5.3b–4a, both record a poem mourning Cao E by Zhou Tan 周曇, the former recording that he lived in the Tang, the latter in the Song. It is not known when this poet lived. This work is part of a huge collection of poems on historical figures that survive in a Song edition. See Zhao Wangqin 趙望秦, *Song ben Zhou Tan Yongshi shi yanjiu* 宋本周曇"詠史詩"研究 (Beijing: Zhongguo shehui kexue, 2005), 177. It is unlikely that Zhou visited the Cao E River: he took his inspiration from the Cao E biography in the *Hou Han shu*.

53. *Cao jiang xiaonü miaozhi*, j.5.2b–3a; this poem does not appear in *juan* 506 of the *Quan Tang shi* 全唐詩, ce 15, 5748–5760, which is devoted to his poetry. See also Sun Yingkui 孫映逵, ed., *Tang caizi zhuan jiaozhu* 唐才子傳校注 (Beijing: Zhongguo shehui kexue, 1991), no. 159, 590–592.

54. He passed the *jinshi* ("presented scholar" 進士) examination in Huichang 會昌 2 (842).

55. Kenneth S. Ch'en, "The Economic Background of the Hui-ch'ang Suppression of Buddhism," *Harvard Journal of Asiatic Studies* 19 (1956): 67–105.

56. Feng Hejun 馮賀軍, "Bei-Song ershisi xiao zhuandiao (liu): Cai Shun shisang yu Cao E toujiang" 北宋二十四孝磚雕(六): 蔡順拾桑與曹娥投江, *Zijin cheng* 紫禁城 2010.6: 99.

57. *Cao jiang xiaonü miaozhi*, j.1.4b. There is some doubt about the date when this event took place, as well as the magistrate's name. Dong Kai appears in a list of magistrates of Kuaiji County as holding office in the Duanping 端平 reign period of Emperor Lizong 宋理宗 (1234–1236), see *Shaoxing fuzhi* (1587 edition), j.28.6a, 985. Other sources state that it took place in the Northern Song. If indeed the magistrate in question was Dong Kai, then possibly there is a problem with the name of the reign period. Perhaps the event took place in the period following the Duanping, the Jiaxi 嘉熙 (1237–1240), rather than in Xining. However, there were only four years in the Jiaxi reign period, not ten. I have not been able to resolve this problem.

58. *Cao jiang xiaonü miaozhi*, j.9.1a–2b. A note indicates that the *Yuejun zhi* 越郡志 states that the death took place in the following year, 1094. Several poems dedicated to her are collected in the same chapter.

59. *Cao jiang xiaonü miaozhi*, j.1.4a. The 1899 *Guangxu Shangyu xianzhi jiaoxu* 光緒上虞縣志校續 (vol. 42, j.41.23b), quotes the *Bozhai bian* 泊宅編 of Fang Shao 方勺 (b. 1066): "In Shangyu County of Yuezhou, by the tomb of Filial Woman Cao on the bank of the river are two trees, one flourishing and the other withered. The twigs and branches of the flourishing one wrap around those of the withered one. From the outside, it has the appearance of embracing the father's corpse." This passage does not appear in the fragments reconstituted by Tao Zongyi

陶宗儀 (fl. 1360–1368) in his *Shuofu* 說郛, as far as I can judge. As Fang does not mention the temple, perhaps it had not been constructed when he visited the site. However, the appearance of the two trees were obviously seen as symbolic of Cao E's wrapping her arms round her father's corpse.

60. For Cai Bian's biography, see Tuotuo 脫脫 (1313–1355), *Song shi* 宋史 (Beijing: Zhonghua, 1977), ce 39, 13728–13730.

61. Beijing tushuguan jinshizu 北京圖書館金石組, ed., *Beijing tushuguan cang Zhongguo lidai shike tuoben huibian* 北京圖書館藏中國歷代石刻拓本匯編 (Zhengzhou: Zhongzhou guji, 1989), ce 4, "Bei Song" 北宋, 86. The rubbing is 158 cm long and 100 cm wide. See also *Shike shiliao xinbian disan ji* 石刻史料新編第三輯 (Taibei: Xinwenfeng, 1986), "Shaoxing fuzhi" 紹興府志, "Jinshi zhi" 金石志, vol. 9, j.76.25b, 43.

62. See Ari Daniel Levine, "Che-tsung's Reign and the Age of Faction," in *The Cambridge History of China: Volume 5 Part One: The Sung Dynasty and Its Precursors, 907–1279*, ed. Denis Twitchett and Paul Jacov Smith (Cambridge: Cambridge University Press, 2009), esp. 529–533.

63. *Cao jiang xiaonü miaozhi*, j.1.4b; 3.1b.

64. *Cao jiang xiaonü miaozhi*, j.4.1b.

65. *Cao jiang xiaonü miaozhi*, j.4.4b.

66. For the list of placards in the Cao E temple with the words and the names of the calligraphers, see *Cao jiang xiaonü miaozhi*, j.4.1b–14a. For an analysis of the deployment by the Kangxi Emperor of donations of his calligraphy to make his visage visible to his subjects, despite his actual absence, see Jonathan Hay, "The Kangxi Emperor's Brush-Traces: Calligraphy, Writing, and the Art of Imperial Authority," in *Body and Face in Chinese Visual Culture*, ed. Wu Hung and Katherine R. Tsiang (Cambridge: Harvard University Asia Center, 2005), 311–334. For placards more generally, see Luo Guanlin 羅冠林, "Bian'e wenhua yu chuantong minju huanjing" 匾額文化與傳統民居環境, MA thesis, Hunan University, 2008.

67. Placards require a separate study, as little has been done in Western scholarship on them in general and even less in religious buildings in particular.

68. Valerie Hansen, *Changing Gods in Medieval China, 1127–1276* (Princeton: Princeton University Press, 1990), 84.

69. Ari Daniel Levine, "The Reigns of Hui-tsung (1100–1126) and Ch'in-tsung (1126–1127) and the Fall of the Northern Sung," in *The Cambridge History of China: Volume 5, Part 1*, 581–582; Wu Fengpei 吳豐培, *Song Yuan zizhi tongjian (shang)* 宋元資治通鑒(上) (Beijing: Zhonghua quanguo tushuguan wenxian suowei fuzhi zhongxin, 1996), j.51.7b, 509. For a general discussion of Cai Jing and factionalism, see John Chaffee, "Huizong, Cai Jing, and the Politics of Reform," in *Emperor Huizong and Late Northern Song China: The Politics of Culture and the Culture of Politics*, ed. Patricia Buckley Ebrey and Maggie Bickford (Cambridge: Harvard University Asia Center, 2006), 31–77.

70. *Cao jiang xiaonü miaozhi*, j.1.4b, 87–446; 3.3ab, 87–452.
71. *Song Yuan zizhi tongjian (shang)*, j.53.6b, 521.
72. Levine, "The Reigns of Hui-tsung and Ch'in-tsung," 583. For a study of Huizong's Genyue Garden, see James M. Hargett, "Huizong's Magic Marchmount: The Genyue Pleasure Park of Kaifeng," *Monumenta Serica* 38 (1988–89): 1–48.
73. Hansen, *Changing Gods*, 79–104.
74. Hansen, *Changing Gods*, 79.
75. *Cao jiang xiaonü miaozhi*, j.1.5b.
76. *Cao jiang xiaonü miaozhi*, j.4.1b. Zheng Qingzhi lived ca. 1168, thus it is possible that the first placard described earlier was inscribed by him; perhaps the second one here was copied using the same calligraphy. For Zheng Qingzhi's dates, see: Chang Bide 昌彼得, ed., *Song ren zhuanji ziliao suoyin (dianzi ban)* 宋人傳記資料索引（電子版）*Index to Biographical Materials of Sung Figures* (digital edition) (Taibei: Dingwen, 1974), 20461.
77. Hansen, *Changing Gods*, 91. The local magistrate was to report the miracle to the fiscal intendant; the latter then sent another official from a neighboring county to check the claim in person, and then sent another official to double-check the veracity of the claim. Only after these two checks were completed did the fiscal intendant bring the matter to the attention of the emperor and, if all was in order, the title was formally granted.
78. *Cao jiang xiaonü miaozhi*, j.3.4ab. The father's grant of a title is recorded on 3.5ab.
79. *Cao E jiangzhi*, j.5.1b.
80. Photographic reprint of the copy held in the National Library, see: *Shaoxing congshu*, vol. 1, j.3.16b (423).
81. *Cao jiang xiaonü miaozhi*, j.1.5b.
82. *Cao jiang xiaonü miaozhi*, j.6.1ab. A great amount of folklore gathered around Liu Ji's name and texts attributed to his brush were subsequently published.
83. *Cao jiang xiaonü miaozhi*, j.6.2a.
84. The *Cao E jiangzhi*, j.5.3a, quotes the first line slightly differently: "E died for filial piety" (娥以孝而死).
85. See, for example, *Cao jiang xiaonü miaozhi*, j.1.6b–7b.
86. *Cao jiang xiaonü miaozhi*, j.1.6a.
87. *Cao jiang xiaonü miaozhi*, j.1.6b. *Juan* 10 of the *Cao jiang xiaonü miaozhi* is devoted to Madam Zhu's memory.
88. Xiaotian 小田, "Lun minzhong guannian de richang cunxu: Jiyu jindai 'Cao E wenhua' de kuozhan fenxi" 論民眾觀念的日常存續——基於近代"曹娥文化"的擴展分析, *Lishi yanjiu* 歷史研究 2013.4: 63–79.

3

An Examination of Commentaries to *Analects* 7.14, "Confucius Listened to the Shao Performance in Qi"

WANG YUNFEI

TRANSLATED BY CHRISTOPHER J. FOSTER

The "Shu'er" 述而 chapter of the *Lunyu* 論語 (Analects) includes a passage (7.14) that reads: "The master (Confucius) listened to Shao 韶 music in Qi 齊, and for three months lost his appetite for meat. He said: 'I did not expect that the performance of music reached such extremes'" (子在齊聞韶, 三月不知肉味, 曰: "不圖為樂之至於斯也").[1] One interpretation of this passage, perhaps the most familiar to readers today, holds that after Confucius heard this performance of Shao music, he extolled its beauty, and for three months found even meat to be flavorless in comparison. This is what I will call the "praising Shao" theory. Less well known is a second interpretation of this passage, the "distressed by Shao" theory, which argues that Confucius was so troubled by the fact that Shao was performed in Qi, he lost his appetite for meat for three months. By surveying the commentarial tradition to the *Lunyu*, the present chapter offers a new look at the "Confucius listened to the Shao performance in Qi" passage and the history behind its exegesis.

Han Commentaries to *Lunyu* 7.14

Both the *Shiji* 史記 and *Han shu* 漢書 record the event described in *Lunyu* 7.14. The *Shiji*, "Kongzi shijia" 孔子世家 chapter, states:[2]

> Confucius went to Qi and became a retainer of Gao Zhaozi, in the hopes that he might thereby meet with Duke Jing. He discussed music with the Grand Preceptor of Qi, and listened to the Shao piece. He studied it, and for three months forgot his taste for meat. The people of Qi commended him (for this).
>
> 孔子適齊, 為高昭子家臣, 欲以通乎景公. 與齊太師語樂, 聞韶音, 學之, 三月不知肉味, 齊人稱之.

The *Shiji* account augments the *Lunyu* by claiming that Confucius *xue zhi* 學之 ("studied it"), suggesting that Confucius studied the Shao piece and forgot his taste for meat for three months. This version exerted a strong influence on later thinkers, and Zhu Xi 朱熹, in particular, came to develop this theory further. In the *Han shu*, "Li yue zhi" 禮樂志 treatise on ritual and music, we find another anecdote about how "Confucius listened to Shao (written 招) music in Qi." It reads:[3]

> During the Spring and Autumn period, Gongzi Wan of Chen fled to Qi. The Chen (people) were the descendants of Shun, and the Shao music survived through them. Thus when Confucius went to Qi and heard the Shao performed, for three months he forgot his taste for meat. He said: "I did not expect that the performance of music reached such extremes." This was Confucius regarding it as very beautiful.
>
> 至春秋時, 陳公子完奔齊. 陳, 舜之後, 招樂存焉. 故孔子適齊聞招, 三月不知肉味, 曰: "不圖為樂之至於斯!" 美之甚也.

Note the final comment—"this was Confucius regarding it as very beautiful"—which unambiguously interprets Confucius's exclamation as one of praise.

Zheng Xuan's 鄭玄 (127–200 CE) commentary to the *Lunyu* was preserved among the cache of medieval manuscripts discovered at Dunhuang (P.2510) and is our earliest witness to the *Lunyu* commentarial tradition. It largely accords with the account given in the *Han shu*:[4]

Shao is the name for Shun's music. During the twenty-second year of Duke Zhuang of Lu's reign, Gongzi Wan of Chen fled to Qi with (knowledge of the) Shao (tradition). This is how Qi came to have Shao music. For three months (Confucius) lost his appetite for meat, pondering over it deeply. (He exclaimed:) "I never expected that the beauty of the Shao music composed by Shun reached such extremes."

韶, 舜樂名. 魯莊公二十二年, 陳公子完以奔齊, 故齊有焉. 三月不知肉味, 思之染 (深) 也. 昔時不圖舜作韶樂之美, 乃至於此也.

There are, however, various ways to interpret Zheng Xuan's commentary. Zheng's explanation is clear about how Shao is the name for Shun's music, that it came to Qi when Gongzi Wan of Chen fled there (in 672 BCE), and that when Confucius heard it, he lost his appetite for three months. The last line, however, includes subtle variations in interpretation, concerning what Confucius "pondered" and what he meant by "extremes." Was it that Confucius pondered over how Shao arrived in Qi, and was shocked that Shao's music could be found in this state? Or did he contemplate the Shao piece itself, marveling at its exquisite beauty? Might it be that while Confucius considered how Shao arrived in Qi, his expression of surprise is still at the beauty of the piece (and not its presence in Qi)?

The first issue we encounter upon an initial reading of Zheng Xuan's commentary is whether the line "for three months he lost his appetite for meat, pondering over it deeply" is read together with the sentence beforehand (the fact that knowledge of Shao was transferred to Qi), or with the statement following afterward (about its performance being extreme). If it connects to the prior sentences, then we get the first reading to Zheng Xuan's commentary (that pondered over how Shao arrived in Qi). If it connects to the sentences that follow afterward, then we have the second reading to Zheng Xuan's commentary (contemplating the beauty of the Shao piece). The third reading of Zheng Xuan's commentary combines elements from both of these two previous interpretations (Confucius is disconcerted by the arrival of Shao in Qi, yet marvels at the beauty of the music), implying both distress and praise in a self-contradictory fashion. The ambiguity of Zheng Xuan's commentary thus allows for either a "praising Shao" or a "distressed by Shao" reading.

If Zheng Xuan subscribed to the "praising Shao" theory, he could have removed the sentences detailing how Shao came to Qi with Gongzi Wan of

Chen entirely, without impacting the rhetorical force of the anecdote. Why retain this information? The reason Zheng Xuan specifically mentions how the Qi court came to possess knowledge of Shao music must have been to clear up contemporary confusion about the issue. The performance of Shao in Qi is an important stage in the development of the Shao musical tradition and there are different theories about how it actually came about. One theory is that Gongzi Wan of Chen brought it with him; another is that it was transmitted from Lu 魯; and, a third, is that it was always performed in Qi. While some textual support for each theory exists, comparatively speaking, the evidence is greatest for the theory that Gongzi Wan was responsible. His commentary makes clear that this is the account supported by Zheng Xuan as well.

If we, like Zheng Xuan, assume that Gongzi Wan of Chen brought Shao to Qi, then the question becomes whether such a transfer transgressed ritual propriety. This was a much-debated issue. Confucius, who cared deeply about ritual propriety, once reprimanded the Ji 季 clan's use of eight rows of dancers in their court performances by saying that "if this can be tolerated, what could one possibly not bear?" (是可忍也, 孰不可忍也) (*Lunyu* 3.1). As such, it is entirely possible that Confucius thought that Gongzi Wan bringing Shao music from Chen to Qi was a transgression of ritual propriety, and therefore hearing a performance of Shao in Qi would be so distressing that he would lose his appetite. Later commentators to the *Lunyu* each had their own opinion on how to interpret Confucius's feelings, complicated by the fact that contradictory statements even appeared within the *Lunyu* itself.

If we look just at the main text of the transmitted *Lunyu* 7.14 itself, however, there are no obvious contradictions. That is to say, this appears to be a debate manufactured by the commentarial tradition, split between the "praising Shao" and "distressed by Shao" theories. We need to keep in mind that, in its early textual history, there were multiple different editions of the *Lunyu*, including a Lu version (*Lu Lun* 魯論) and a Qi version (*Qi Lun* 齊論). Scholars in each state would have studied their own recensions. During the Western Han, the scholar official Zhang Yu 張禹 (d. 5 BCE) compiled the various versions and edited them into his own edition, called *Zhang Hou Lun* 張侯論 (Marquis Zhang's Analects). Then, based off this new edition, Zheng Xuan created yet another edition, in which he specifically referenced the *Qi Lun* and an "ancient-script" version (*Gu Lun* 古論). It is likely that he included heterogenous and contradictory content. It is also possible that his attempts to solve philological issues led to the selection of certain materials over others and, therefore, the loss of content. We find, for example, contradictory statements by Confucius both denouncing and praising the famous Qi minister Guan Zhong 管仲 (c. 720–645 BCE). The Qing scholar Tang Yan 唐晏 (1857–1920 CE) notes in his *Liang Han Sanguo xuean* 兩漢三國學案:[5]

> Alas! [Zhang] Yu, that wicked man, excelled at pandering to his peers. Serving as minister, he not only misled the Han royal house, but also muddled the teachings of Confucius when transmitting the classics. Thus the *Lunyu* at once denigrates and applauds Guan Zhong, while Zai Wo is only disparaged without a single word of praise. I suspect that such sentiments derive from the Qi version of the *Lunyu*, and that Yu included them within (his new edition). This is because Guan Zhong was revered by the people of Qi, yet Zai Wo was detested by them. Of the various Confucian classics, both the *Yi* (Changes) and *Chunqiu* (Spring and Autumn Annals) were disarranged by the men of Qi. [It appears that] the *Lunyu* encountered a similar sad fate. What misfortunes Confucius's teachings have endured!

> 嗟乎! 禹一邪人, 媚世之尤. 其為相也, 既誤漢室; 及傳經也, 又淆孔門. 故 "論語" 于管仲也, 忽毀忽譽; 於宰我也, 毀之無一嘉辭. 疑此皆出於 "齊論," 而禹合之者也. 蓋管仲齊人所尊, 宰我齊人所讎故也. 夫孔門諸經, "易" 與 "春秋" 皆為齊人所亂, 而 "論語" 又遭此阨, 何孔門之不幸也夫.

The "Distressed by Shao" Theory in Six Dynasty Period Commentaries to *Lunyu* 7.14

The "distressed by Shao" theory was the mainstream position in commentaries to the *Lunyu* 7.14 composed during the Wei, Jin, and Southern and Northern dynasties eras.[6] The importance of these medieval commentaries to *Lunyu* 7.14 is that, at this time, many ancient works not available today were still extant, some of which no doubt advocated a "distressed by Shao" position. The *Sui shu* 隨書 bibliographic treatise "Jingji zhi" 經籍志 claims:[7]

> Scholars in Qi transmitted a version (of the *Lunyu*) in twenty-two volumes. In the late Han period, Zheng Xuan took the *Zhang Hou Lun* as his base edition and referred to both the *Qi Lun*

and (ancient-script) *Gu Lun* when composing his commentary. During the Wei, Minister of Works Chen Qun, Chamberlain for Ceremonials Wang Su, and Erudite Zhou Shenglie all produced explanatory readings (for the *Lunyu*). Minister to the Ministry of Personnel He Yan also issued collected annotations (to the text). Later many other literati wrote commentaries, but the *Qi Lun* was thereupon lost.

齊人傳者二十二篇, 漢末鄭玄以 "張侯論" 為本, 參考 "齊論" "古論" 而為之注. 魏司空陳群, 太常王肅, 博士周生烈皆為義說. 吏部尚書何晏又為集解. 是後, 諸儒多為之注, "齊論" 遂亡.

It is thus evident that when scholars like Wang Su 王肅 (195–256 CE) and Zhou Shenglie 周生烈 (fl. 220 CE) were composing their commentaries to the *Lunyu* during the Wei, the *Qi Lun* was still extant.

The *Lunyu jijie* 論語集解 compiled by He Yan 何晏 (190–249 CE) is the earliest and most complete edition of the *Lunyu* bearing commentaries that has been transmitted to the present day. There are numerous differences between this work and Zheng Xuan's (newly discovered, but fragmentary) commentary to the *Lunyu*. One difference is that Zheng Xuan usually combines his thoughts into a single comprehensive commentarial note, whereas the *Lunyu jijie* instead splits that material into multiple separate statements interspersed after key sentences from the base text. The *Lunyu jijie* divides comments on *Lunyu* 7.14 in two parts, while Zheng Xuan treats the passage as a whole:[8]

> Zhou Shenglie states: "Confucius was in Qi, and listened to the overwhelming beauty of Shao music being performed. For this reason he forgot his taste for meat."
>
> 周生烈曰: "孔子在齊, 聞習韶樂之盛美, 故忽於肉味也."
>
> Wang Su states: "The word *wei* ('to do, perform') means *zuo* ('to compose, act'). He did not expect that playing Shao music reached this (place). 'This' refers to the state of Qi."
>
> 王肅曰: "為, 作也. 不圖作韶樂至於此. 此, 齊也."

Although Wang Su's commentary is appended to the final line of *Lunyu* 7.14, and clarifies the language used there, because Wang discusses the arrival of

Shao in Qi, it corresponds more closely to the first half of Zheng Xuan's commentary, on the first lines of *Lunyu* 7.14. Similarly, Zhou Shenglie's note about the overwhelming beauty of Shao relates to the second half of Zheng Xuan's commentary, even if these also were inspired by different lines in the base text.

In Huang Kan's 皇侃 (488–545 CE) *Lunyu yishu* 論語義疏, an expansion of the *Lunyu jijie*, a number of other commentators are quoted after Wang Su and Zhou Shenglie, including Guo Xiang 郭象 (d. 312 CE), Fan Ning 範甯 (339–401 CE), Jiang Xi 江熙 (4th c.), and Huang Kan himself:[9]

> Thus, Guo Xiang states: "He was aggrieved that, though the instruments (of the Shao music) existed, the Way (espoused therein) had been abandoned; that the sounds (of Shao) may be had (today), yet they were untimely (for this era)."

> 故郭象曰: "傷器存而道廢, 得有聲而無時."

> Fan Ning states: "Shao amounts to the perfection of music by the Great Yu (aka Shun). Qi was (a state of the) feudal lord. How could (Qi) possess this (music)? It is said that the Chen people were the descendants of Shun. The (Shao) music existed in Chen, but Jingzhong (aka Gongzi Wan) of Chen stole it away to Qi. Thus (Qi) misappropriated it."

> 範寧曰: "夫'韶'乃大虞盡善之樂, 齊, 諸侯也, 何得有之乎? 曰: 陳, 舜之後也. 樂在陳, 陳敬仲竊以奔齊, 故得僭之也."

> Jiang Xi states: "That (Mr.) He (Bian's valuable) *bi*-jade was thought akin to mere rubble, this is why Master Bian grew depressed; that the Shao music of Yu (aka Shun) was played alongside (the licentious tunes of) Zheng and Wei, this is why Confucius grieved for so long, losing his appetite the whole time. How far-reaching was the depth of his feeling?!"

> 江熙曰: "和璧與瓦礫齊貫, 卞子所以悁悵: 虞韶與鄭衛比響, 仲尼所以永歎, 彌時忘味, 何遠情之深也?"

> Huang Kan: Confucius arrived in Qi and heard the Lord of Qi perform the magisterial music of Shao, yet this aggrieved his heart, thus for a period of time his mouth lost all its appetite.

That period of time was for three months. Why was this so? Qi was ruled by a Lord who lacked the Way, yet he pompously performed the music of the sage kings. Though the instruments (to properly perform Shao) were present, the man was perverse. This is why he was so deeply aggrieved.

皇侃: 孔子至齊，聞齊君奏於韶樂之盛，而心為痛傷，故口忘完味，至於一時乃止也。三月，一時也。何以然也？齊是無道之君，而濫奏聖王之樂，器存人乖，所以可傷慨也。

Of these four men, Guo Xiang was an advocate of the "esoteric arts" (*xuanxue* 玄學, Neo-Daoism) active during the height of this philosophical movement in the Eastern Jin. Fan Ning, who lived shortly after Guo Xiang, was a classicist that opposed the esoteric arts and severely criticized He Yan and Wang Bi 王弼 (226–249 CE) for their interest, calling them even more abhorrent than Jie 桀 and Zhou 紂 (the cruel last rulers of the Xia and Shang, respectively). Jiang Xi, another Eastern Jin scholar, represents efforts to gather commentaries on the *Lunyu*. He was one of three scholars who collected previous *Lunyu* commentaries during the early medieval period, the other two being He Yan (Three Kingdoms, Wei) and Huang Kan (Southern dynasties, Liang). Guo Xiang, Fan Ning, Jiang Xi, and Huang Kan all adopted the "distressed by Shao" reading of *Lunyu* 7.14, but with slightly different rationales: for Guo Xiang, it was that Shao belonged to a bygone era, and its superficial performance had no effect in their present day; for Fan Ning, it was the misappropriation of sagely music by an unworthy Qi ruler; for Jiang Xi, it was the insult of playing Shao alongside the licentious tunes of Zheng and Wei; and Huang Kan offers a subtle combination of these factors.

With the sole exception of Zhou Shenglie, all other commentators to *Lunyu* 7.14 during the Wei, Jin, Southern and Northern dynasties eras advocated a "distressed by Shao" position. This is not because the "praising Shao" theory was unknown; to the contrary, these commentators weighed the merits of both the "distressed by Shao" and "praising Shao" theories. Sun Chuo 孫綽 (320–377 CE, Eastern Jin) was another scholar from this period in Chinese history who commented upon the *Lunyu*. Although his commentary to *Lunyu* 7.14 is no longer extant, in his *Orchid Pavilion Poems* (*Lanting shi* 蘭亭詩), composed in the ninth year of the Yonghe reign era (353 CE), he writes: "Seasonal delicacies—how are they not sweet? But one forgets flavor when listening to Shao" (時珍豈不甜，忘味在聞韶).[10] These lines are clearly an allusion to *Lunyu* 7.14 and suggest Sun Chuo ascribed to the "praising Shao" position. The poetry composed during the Orchid Pavilion gathering of 353 CE was extemporaneous and impromptu in nature; the "praising Shao" reading of *Lunyu* 7.14 therefore must have been well known and accepted by many at that time. Ruan Ji 阮籍 (210–263 CE) writes in his discourse on music, the *Yuelun* 樂論: "Thus when Confucius listened to Shao music in Qi, for three months he forgot his taste for meat. This shows how perfected music frees people of their desires, stilling their hearts and settling their *qi*, to the point that even meat is not regarded flavorful (by comparison)" (故孔子在齊聞韶, 三月不知肉好, 言至樂使人無欲, 心平氣定, 不以肉味滋味也).[11] Here Ruan Ji also adopts the "praising Shao" theory. It appears that, during the Wei, Jin, and Southern and Northern dynasties eras, the "praising Shao" theory was preserved primarily outside the *Lunyu* commentarial tradition.

Lu Deming's Commentary to *Lunyu* 7.14 in the Tang Dynasty

Lu Deming 陸德明 (556–527 CE) presents a reading for *Lunyu* 7.14 in his *Jingdian shiwen* 經典釋文 pertinent to our discussion. He records that one interpretation for Confucius's comment that he "did not expect that the performance of music reached such extremes" takes the verb *wei* 為 ("to do, perform") as *gui* 媯 instead, making it a proper name, Gui, in this context. Although Lu rejects this reading himself, it does reveal that the "distressed by Shao" theory remained influential in the early Tang. Lu notes:[12]

> (In regard to the phrase) "listened to Shao": [Shao] has a *fanqie* spelling of an initial *dzr-* (from MC *dzriX* 士) and final *-jew* (from MC *tsyew* 昭). The commentaries are in agreement.
>
> 聞韶: 士昭反, 注同.
>
> (In regard to the phrase) "perform music": Both characters are (read) as written. Wang Yun glosses *wei* as "to compose, act." Another edition writes it as *gui* 媯, pronounced with the *fanqie* spelling of an initial *k-* (from MC *kjo* 居) and final *-jwe* (from MC *ngjwe* 危). This is incorrect.
>
> 為樂: 並如字, 王雲: "為, 作也." 本或作 "媯," 音居危反, 非.

Lu Deming thus claims that in one edition, the word *wei* 為 ("to do, perform") in the *Lunyu* 7.14 line was written as *gui* 媯, changing the meaning of the line to: "I did not expect the music of Gui to reach here (in Qi)." Gui was the name of a river where Shun lived. According to the *Shiji* 史記 chapter "Wudi benji" 五帝本紀, "Shun lived by the banks of the Gui" (舜居媯汭). This alternative reading would then suggest that Confucius was surprised that the music of Gui reached Qi, in other words, that the Shao composed by Shun was played in Qi, and that this was the reason for losing his appetite. This is the argument central to the "distressed by Shao" position.

An Analysis of Song Dynasty Commentaries to *Lunyu* 7.14

Xing Bing's 邢昺 (932–1010 CE) *Lunyu zhushu* 論語注疏, composed in the Northern Song, is based off of Huang Kan's *Lunyu yishu* 論語義疏, with various abridgements and supplements.[13] For *Lunyu* 7.14, he removed the commentaries by Guo Xiang, Fan Ning, Jiang Xi, and Huang Kan, and only retained those of Zhou Shenglie and Wang Su. Owing to its early compilation, the *Lunyu zhushu* does not yet engage with one of the key debates that arises during the Song, namely how Confucius could "refrain from knowing the taste of meat" (不知肉味) for a full three months.

Cheng Yi 程頤 (1033–1107 CE) was the first to question if it would be improper for a sage to refrain from eating meat for three months. He proposed that the phrase *san yue* 三月 ("three months") was a mistake for *yin* 音 ("sound, tune"). This gives a new reading for *Lunyu* 7.14: "The master (Confucius) listened to the Shao tune in Qi and lost his appetite for meat. He said: 'I did not expect that the performance of music reached such extremes'" (子在齊聞韶音, 不知肉味, 曰: "不圖為樂之至於斯也"). It is entirely possible that *san yue* 三月 was a mistaken transcription for what was originally *yin* 音. The character *yin* 音 is graphically very similar to *san* 三 placed over *yue* 月, which is how these characters would appear in the vertical orientation of Chinese writing. This visual proximity could lead to the scribal error of writing *yin* as *san yue*, especially when handling manuscripts written in cursive forms. Cheng Yi had many disciples and was succeeded by Xie Liangzuo 謝良佐, Yang Shi 楊時, and Yin Tun 尹焞, all of whom echoed Cheng's theory that *san yue* was a mistake for *yin*. In the early Southern Song, Zhang Shi 張栻 (1133–1180 CE) also adopted Cheng's reading.

Zhu Xi 朱熹 (1130–1200 CE), on the other hand, followed the *Shiji* chapter "Kongzi shijia" 孔子世家, which emends the text by adding *xue zhi* 學之 ("studied it") before *san yue* 三月 ("three months"). He therefore claimed that "three months" refers to the period of time that Confucius spent studying the Shao musical piece. This renders *Lunyu* 7.14 as follows: "The master listened to Shao music in Qi, and studied it for three months, forgetting his taste for meat. He said: 'I did not expect that the performance of music reached such extremes'" (子在齊聞韶, 學之三月, 不知肉味, 曰: " 不圖為樂之至於斯也"). In his commentary, Zhu Xi explains that the reason Confucius forgot his taste for meat was "because he was singularly concentrated on this task (of studying Shao) and did not think of anything else (蓋心一於是而不及乎他也)." As further support, Zhu's commentary quotes Fan Zuyu 范祖禹 (1041–1098 CE):[14]

> Master Fan states: Shao is the most beautiful and most perfect, no (other piece) of music could improve upon it. Thus (Confucius) studied it for three months, forgetting his taste for meat, and touted such beauty, the epitome of sincerity and depth of feeling.
>
> 範氏曰: 韶盡美又盡善, 樂之無以加此也, 故學之三月, 不知肉味, 而歎美之如此, 誠之至, 感之深也.

Zhu Xi's commentary was highly influential. It was adopted both by Zhen Dexiu 真德修 (1178–1235 CE), known also as Master Xishan 西山先生, in his *Lunyu jibian* 論語集編 (in *Sishu jibian* 四書集編), as well as by Zhao Shunsun 趙順孫 (1215–1276 CE) in his *Lunyu zuanshu* 論語纂疏 (in *Sishu zuanshu* 四書纂疏), both composed at the end of the Southern Song. Zhu Xi had many disciples as well, and moreover his *Sishu jizhu* 四書集注 was eventually incorporated into the civil service examination. For these reasons, Zhu Xi's interpretation of *Lunyu* 7.14 quickly became the dominant position on the text.

A survey of commentaries on *Lunyu* 7.14 preserved in the *Siku quanshu* 四庫全書 reveals that Cheng Yi's interpretation of *san yue* ("three months") as a mistake for *yin* ("tune") and Zhu Xi's insertion of *xue zhi* 學之 ("studied it") before "three months" became the two mainstream readings for this passage. Yet during the Song there were some who criticized these positions. For example, in the early Northern Song, Chen Xiangdao 陳祥道 (1042–1093 CE) had earlier argued against the theory that Confucius "studied Shao" (*xue zhi* 學之) for three months, later espoused by Zhu Xi. Chen Xiangdao was a student of Wang Anshi 王安石 (1021–1086 CE), while Cheng Yi was a student of Zhou Dunyi 周敦頤 (1017–1073 CE). Chen Xiangdao and Cheng Yi were contemporaries but educated in divergent interpretations of the *Lunyu*. The "School of Luo (Region)" (*luoxue* 洛學) of Cheng Yi and Cheng Hao 程顥 (1032–1085 CE) was immensely influential, particularly after it was further synthesized by Zhu Xi and incorporated into his "School of Principle" (*lixue* 理學). On the other hand, Chen Xiangdao was a learned scholar in the three classics on ritual (*San li* 三禮), who refined his own teacher's reading of the *Lunyu*. Although Chen believed that Confucius was moved by the beauty of Shao, adopting the "praising Shao" position, he opposed the theory that Confucius "studied it" for three months.

Despite the prominence of Cheng Yi's and Zhu Xi's readings, the "distressed by Shao" theory did not disappear entirely. For instance, Zheng Ruxie 鄭汝諧 (fl. 12th c.), a contemporary of Zhu Xi, espoused:[15]

> The Chen (people) were the descendants of Shun, and as his descendants, could perform their ancestral music, therefore Shun's music survived in Chen. After Chen Jingzhong fled to Qi, his offspring ultimately usurped the rule, this is the reason why the Shao piece was performed there. To play music celebrating just abdication, in a state where the ruler's authority was usurped improperly, is this not deplorable! This is why (Confucius) lost his appetite for meat for all of three months. (With his comment that) "he did not expect that the performance of music reached such extremes," the word "such" refers to this, namely Master Chen's transgressions.

> 陳, 舜之後也, 為之後者, 得用先代之樂, 故舜之樂在陳, 自陳敬仲奔齊, 其子孫卒篡齊而有之, 是以韶樂作於齊. 夫以揖遜之樂而作於僭竊之國, 豈不大可痛惜乎! 是以三月之久不知肉味也. 不圖為樂之至於斯, "斯," 此也, 指陳氏之僭言之也.

Zheng Ruxie's courtesy name was Shunju 舜舉, and his honorary name was Donggu Jushi 東谷居士. He composed a number of works, including *Donggu Yi yizhuan* 東谷易翼傳, *Lunyu yiyuan* 論語意原, and *Donggu ji* 東穀集. Zheng was from the Yi-Luo 伊洛 region, but did not belong to the

Luo school of thought of the two Cheng brothers, and disagreed with Zhu Xi.

The Southern Song scholar Cai Jie 蔡節 (late 12th c.?) also espoused the "distressed by Shao" position, and although he acknowledges the debate over the propriety of Confucius refraining from meat for three months, he ultimately leaves this question open:[16]

> (Cai) Jie comments: Shao is the music of Shun. "Three months" expresses how long (he felt this way). The descendants of Shun were the Chen (people). After Chen Jingzhong fled to Qi, his offspring gradually monopolized rule of Qi, so that by the time of the reign of Duke Jing, the Chen clan had taken over in full. When Confucius listened to the Shao piece in Qi, for three months he lost his appetite for meat, because of how deeply distraught he felt, and he said: "I did not expect that the performance of music reached such extremes." "Such" (in this line) refers to Qi. Shao was originally a piece of music about just abdication, yet now it had come (to be performed in) the state of Qi. He bemoans the present and is nostalgic for the past. This is why (Confucius) lamented so! Some say that a sage must always temper his emotional responses, but when (Confucius) listened to the Shao piece in Qi, he was so distraught that he lost his appetite for three months—he perhaps should not have refrained (from eating meat) for so long. Nevertheless, an argument has yet to be raised to change this idea, so I will put (the issue) aside for the time being.

> 節釋曰: 韶, 舜樂也. 三月, 言其久也. 舜之後為陳, 自陳敬仲奔齊, 其後久專齊政, 至景公時, 陳氏代齊之形已成矣. 夫子在齊聞韶, 三月不知肉味, 蓋憂感之深也, 曰: "不圖為樂之至於斯," "斯"者, 指齊而言也, 韶本揖遜之樂, 今乃至於齊之國, 其殆傷今思古, 故發為此歎與. 或謂: 聖人之喜怒哀樂未有不中節者, 今在齊聞韶而憂感之深乃至於三月忘味, 恐不應固滯如此, 然未有一說可以易此說, 姑闕之.

Biographical information about Cai Jie is unfortunately quite spare, and all we know is that his representative work is the *Lunyu jishuo* 論語集說, preserved in the *Siku quanshu* 四庫全書 collection. When Cai Jie was active,

Zhu Xi's interpretation of the *Lunyu* was popular throughout the realm and Cai Jie's agreed with many of Zhu Xi's interpretations. But this was not always the case, and *Lunyu* 7.14 is one example. Cai Jie bravely went against the authority accorded Zhu Xi's reading and dared to promote the "distressed by Shao" position.

Jin Lüxiang 金履祥 (1232–1303 CE), a scholar active during the transition between the Song and Yuan, presents the most exhaustive discussion of *Lunyu* 7.14 thus far. Jin was a polymath who studied astronomy, geography, rituals, music, military strategy, yin and yang cosmology, and calendrics, among other fields, and his commentary to *Lunyu* 7.14 reflects this breadth of expertise. In his commentary, he notes that certain "literati in the north" (*beishi* 北士) claim that Confucius lost his appetite for three months out of distress after listening to the Shao performance in Qi, based on the *Han shu* claim that Chen Jingzhong fled with it to Qi. Jin disagreed with them, however, believing that Confucius certainly would not have let his indignation grow to the point of losing his taste for meat for three whole months. Instead, he praised Zhu Xi's reading, and accused supporters of the "distressed by Shao" position of failing to appreciate Zhu Xi's genius, while chasing after novel ideas.

In summary, by the Song dynasty, one of the major debates surrounding *Lunyu* 7.14 became whether Confucius would have refrained from eating meat for three months. What is certain is that, in the Song dynasty as before, a rivalry existed between the competing "distressed by Shao" and "praising Shao" theories. Yet during this period, "praising Shao" interpretations became the mainstream position, while "distressed by Shao" interpretations were marginalized; this stands in stark contrast to the Wei, Jin, and Southern and Northern dynasties, when the "praising Shao" theory was the weaker of the two. One reason why the "distressed by Shao" theory was marginalized during the Song is because of the dominance of the Cheng Yi and Zhu Xi schools; another crucial reason, however, is because the main advocates for the "distressed by Shao" position from the Wei, Jin, and Southern and Northern dynasties periods were preserved in Huang's *Lunyu yishu*, but it was lost during the Southern Song. This resulted in the loss of the strongest arguments raised in defense of the "distressed by Shao" theory.

Features of Yuan Dynasty *Lunyu* 7.14 Commentaries

Debates held by Yuan dynasty scholars concerning *Lunyu* 7.14 mainly concentrate on three areas:

1. Critiquing Cheng Yi's theory that *san yue* 三月 ("three months") was a miswriting of *yin* 音 ("tune"), and Zhu Xi's insertion of the words *xue zhi* 學之 ("studied it") before "three months." The works of Chen Tianxiang 陳天祥 (1230–1316 CE), Shi Boxuan 史伯璿 (fl. 14th c.), and Ni Shiyi 倪士毅 (1303–1348 CE) offer representative examples of this trend.

2. The question of how Qi could possess (knowledge of) Shao. There were two main views on this matter, that either Chen Wan 陳完 (aka Gongzi Wan of Chen, Chen Jingzhong) brought Shao with him when he fled to Qi, or that it occurred when Grand Preceptor Zhi 太師摯 of Lu 魯 went to Qi. Yuan Junweng 袁俊翁, Xiao Yi 蕭鎰, and Ni Shiyi all engage with this debate.

3. On how Confucius communed with the mind of Shun. Hu Bingwen 胡炳文 (1250–1333 CE) and Ni Shiyi both adopt this approach.

The Yuan scholars began to push back against the dominance of the Cheng and Zhu interpretations. Chen Tianxiang, for instance, believed that Cheng Yi's proposition to read "three months" as "tune" was too tenuous, preferring Wang Hunan's 王渾南 suggestion that *yue* 月 ("month") was instead a scribal error for *ri* 日 ("day"). Shi Boxuan lived in seclusion and never held office, but he studied Zhu Xi's philosophy in depth, and after thirty odd years of careful research, authored the *Sishu guanqie* 四書管窺, cementing his status as one of the Yuan dynasty's most eminent Confucian thinkers. Shi disagreed with both Cheng Yi's and Zhu Xi's textual emendations and argued that Confucius forgot his taste for meat because "he was deeply moved by the marvels of past and present" (感慨妙絕古今). Ni Shiyi was a representative figure in the Xin'an School of Principle 新安裡學 during the mid- to late Yuan, and a fifth-generation disciple of Zhu Xi. The *Sishu jishi* 四書輯釋 compiled by Ni Shiyi and annotated by Wang Yuanshan 王元善 made a point of defending Zhu's interpretations against detractors. This text incorporates the Song commentaries of Jin Lüxiang, Cheng Yi, Zhu Xi, and Wu Cheng 吳程. Furthermore, they argue that *san yue* ("three months") should be read together with the line preceding it, so that it becomes: "(Confucius) listened to Shao for three months" (聞韶三月). Yet the *Sishu jishi* also contends that the ancient-script version of the *Lunyu* discovered during the Han dynasty in the walls of Confucius's home originally wrote *yin* (as opposed to *san yue*), thus also supporting

Cheng Yi's position. Ni Shiyi, however, was not convinced by this theory and felt that the modern-script version of the text (with *san yue*) was more reliable. Whereas Song scholars defended Cheng Yi and Zhu Xi's teachings by repeating their interpretations, Yuan scholars, with all due reverence, attempted to correct and refine them.

Yuan scholars also debated the question of how Qi came to possess knowledge of Shao music. Yuan Junweng, in *Sishu yijie* 四書疑節, holds that, since the Chen people were Shun's descendants, listening to a performance of Shao in Chen would be most appropriate. He also argued that its performance in Lu was also appropriate, as the people in Lu performed musical pieces representative of all "six ages" (*liu dai* 六代) of China's antiquity (i.e., encompassing the Yellow Emperor, Yao, Shun, the Xia, Shang, and Zhou). The performance of Shao in Qi, however, was suspect to Yuan. After examining the various theories, Yuan argues evidence that Grand Preceptor Zhi of Lu brought Shao to Qi is only found in the Lu version of the *Lunyu* and is thus weak. The theory that Gongzi Wan of Chen fled to Qi, on the other hand, not only appears in the more reputable *Zuo zhuan* 左傳 and also the *Han shu* "Liyue zhi" treatise, but also is commented upon in *Mengzi* 孟子 (Mencius) and the *Shiji*. Xiao Yi, however, disagreed with this conclusion in his *Sishu daiwen* 四書代問, preferring the Grand Preceptor Zhi of Lu story. Ni Shiyi also weighed in on this debate in his *Sishu jishi* and promoted the Lu connection as well. Moreover, Ni believes that the reason Confucius lost his appetite for three months is because he lamented how Shao, which was once under Lu's stewardship, was now performed by Qi. Ni's interpretation, which adopted a "distressed by Shao" position, is unique among Yuan commentaries to *Lunyu* 7.14, as almost all other commentators argue that Confucius was so stunned by the beauty of the Shao performance that he forgot his taste for meat.

Yuan scholars also emphasized that hearing Shao made Confucius and Shun of a single mind (*xin wei yi* 心為一). Hu Bingwen, in his *Sishu tong* 四書通, stressed the intimacy of their communion, an idea further developed by Ming commentators. Hu's work was grounded in decades of study into Zhu Xi's philosophy. Despite the *Sishu tong*'s commitment to that school of thought, it preserves many varied textual sources and gives meticulous exegetical notes, making it an invaluable reference. Ni Shiyi, in his *Sishu jishi*, also claims that Confucius became one with Shun's mind when he listened to the Shao piece; it was as if Confucius had met with Shun in person.

Features of Ming Dynasty *Lunyu* 7.14 Commentaries

The only extant Ming commentary to *Lunyu* 7.14 is that of Hao Jing 郝敬 (1558–1639 CE), found in the *Lunyu xiangjie* 論語詳解. Hao Jing advocates a "distressed by Shao" position:[17]

> Confucius returned to Lu and rectified its music (*Lunyu* 9.15) in the eleventh year of Duke Ai, and at that time Preceptor Zhi was still in Lu. Thus (Confucius) said: "From when Preceptor Zhi begins (to play) up through to the final verse of 'Guanju,' how overwhelming it is (when the music) fills your ears!" (*Lunyu* 8.15). The historical records are mistaken that Zhi went to Qi after Confucius had rectified the music (of Lu). Lu already possessed (knowledge of) Shao music, so when Confucius was in Qi, this was not the first instance in which he listened to (its performance). But in this particular instance, because the Chen clan had usurped authority in Qi, and Confucius foresaw how they would depose of the ruling family there in the near future. With the ancestral state of Chen destroyed, members of its clan scattered about, residing in other domains, and behaving improperly, the sage (Confucius) lamented over how the majestic virtue (of a once great clan now) lacked any true heir, and sighed about how the rise and fall (of great clans and their states) followed no constant law. How could a state that is on the verge of being lost come to have this music, which (expresses) an age of flourishing? The principles of governance and the way of music are clearly out of accord (with one another)! Thus, surprised by this, (Confucius) exclaimed like so. (Other) commentators claim that "he did not expect that the beauty of the music reached such extremes," (but if so) then this (suggests he) thought poorly of Shun! Sagely words are of a depth difficult to fathom, one must savor them with great care.
>
> 夫子反魯正樂, 在哀公十一年, 時師摯尚在魯, 故曰: 師摯之始, 關雎之亂, 洋洋乎盈耳哉. 摯適齊, 在夫子正樂後, 史誤也. 魯自有韶, 夫子非至齊始聞, 特以是時陳氏擅齊, 夫子知其將有篡弒之禍, 而陳宗國破滅, 子孫流寓他邦, 為人亂賊, 聖人傷盛德之無後, 而歎興廢之靡常也. 國家將亡, 安得此盛世之音. 於政治之理, 聲

音之道，殊不相似，故詫之云爾，解者謂不意樂之美至於斯，則視
舜反為劣矣，聖言深永，宜詳味之.

In Hao Jing's opinion, Lu already knew and performed Shao, and therefore the Qi performance was not the first time Confucius had heard it. Instead, it was a matter of sagely foresight: while listening to the music of righteous government, he foresaw that the ruling family of Qi would soon be deposed. The irony caused Confucius to lose his appetite for three months.

Ming scholars also emphasized how Confucius communed with the mind of Shun. Hu Guang 胡廣 (1370–1418 CE) and a team of scholars worked on the *Lunyu* by imperial order, explaining not only Zhu Xi's commentary to *Lunyu* 7.14, but also those of Master Fu of Qingyuan 慶源輔氏, Master Feng of Houzhai 厚齋馮氏, Master Chen of Xin'an 新安陳氏, and Su Shi 蘇軾 (1037–1101 CE).[18] Master Fu of Qingyuan emphasized how Confucius learned about the virtue of Shun through his study of the sounds and rhythms of Shao. Master Chen of Xin'an focused on how Confucius did not just listen to the Shao performance with his ears alone, but rather felt it engraved upon his heart, causing him to exclaim over the beauty of Shun's sagely virtue and orderly reign. Su Shi claimed that through Confucius's mastery of the performance—its notes and movement—he could grasp the deeper intention of the music, allowing him to comprehend sages such as Shun and King Wen. Hu Guang thus concluded that Shun's music was of such perfection and beauty that it left an indelible mark upon Confucius's heart and mind.

Another Ming scholar, Lü Nan 呂柟 (1479–1542 CE), held that, when Confucius studied Shao, by learning the musical instruments and ritual movements, his inner nature joined with the Way of Heaven. Upon listening to the Shao music, Confucius, who lived in a chaotic and violent age, sensed the dignity of just abdication and the virtue of righteous civility, and because of this sighed deeply.[19] Sun Ying'ao 孫應鰲 (1527–1586 CE) argued that although the music of the ancients had been abandoned, their principles were not yet hidden. Through music, one may discover the subtleties of human nature and cosmic principles. Sun thus felt that Confucius was able to commune with the original intention of Shun.[20] Jiao Hong's 焦竑 (1540–1620 CE) likewise believed that, by listening to Shao, Confucius felt invited into Heaven's design. Desiring to follow the examples of past worthies, Confucius took great pleasure in the fact that Shun's music persisted in its antiquity.[21] Lu Shanji 鹿善繼 (1575–1636 CE) is another scholar who argued that, through music, Confucius understood

Shun's original goodness, an experience that marks Confucius as the foremost "appraiser" (of moral character).²² Ge Yinliang 葛寅亮 (1570–1646 CE), in his *Sishu Hunan jiang* 四書湖南講, also adopted this perspective, claiming that Confucius and Shun, although separated by many hundreds of years, could share emotions through music.²³ Shen Shouzheng 沈守正 (1572–1623 CE) followed the commentaries of Su Shi and a certain X Yi 口義 commentary, along with various colloquial interpretations, which claimed that "when the master (Confucius) listened to Shao, it was like a sage meeting another sage, and then knowing what weighed on the other's mind. No one less that a great worthy would be capable of this" (夫子聞韶, 如聖人見聖人, 便曉得他心事, 若大賢以下, 便不能如此).²⁴ Sun Zhaoxing 孫肇興 (fl. 1662 CE), in *Sishu yueshuo* 四書約說, moreover, wrote: "When the master (Confucius) listened to Shao, this was none other than the spirits of two sages melding together" (子聞韶, 直是兩聖精神融結了).²⁵

A Minor Revival of the "Distressed by Shao" Theory in Qing Dynasty *Lunyu* 7.14 Commentaries

In the Qing dynasty, special emphasis was given to textual exegesis in commentaries on *Lunyu* 7.14, including an evaluation of earlier commentaries, especially those of the Song and before. Because Huang Kan's *Lunyu yishu* was restored to China from Japan during Emperor Qianlong's 乾隆 reign (1733–1796 CE), scholars like Ling Shu 淩曙 (1775–1829 CE) were able to access once more the medieval commentaries of Wang Su, Huang Kan, Guo Xiang, and Jiang Xi, inspiring a minor revival in the popularity of the "distressed by Shao" theory.²⁶ By this point, however, the debate between the "distressed by Shao" and "praising Shao" positions had lost its intensity, and few cared which theory was correct.

Qing scholars attached particular importance to Han period sources for *Lunyu* 7.14. Pan Weicheng 潘維城 (fl. 19th c.), for instance, in *Lunyu guzhu jijian* 論語古注集箋 (published in 1880), cites Han passages related to *Lunyu* 7.14 found in the *Shiji* "Kongzi shijia," *Han shu* "Liyue zhi," and *Shuoyuan* 說苑 "Xiuwen pian" 修文篇, though of course these materials already were quoted often in previous scholarship.²⁷ Jiang Yong 江永 (1681–1762 CE), in his *Sishu guren dianlin* 四書古人典林, turns to commentaries to the *Yili* 儀禮, which happen to correspond with the content in the *Shuoyuan*. Jiang Yong's *Sishu guren dianlin* also records the *Shiji* story about Chen Wan fleeing to Qi.²⁸ Wu Changzong 吳昌宗 (c. 1500–1582 CE) included even more Han sources; besides the usual *Han shu*, *Shiji*, and *Shuoyuan* even, he cited from the *Shuowen* 說文, *Yueji* 樂記, and commentaries on the *Liji* chapter "Quli" 曲禮.[29]

Although special emphasis was placed on Han period sources, Qing scholars also paid close attention to early medieval commentaries to *Lunyu* 7.14 as well. Wu Qian 吳騫 (1733–1813 CE), for example, annotated Huang Kan's *Lunyu yishu* commentary in his *Huang shi Lunyu yishu canding* 皇氏論語義疏參訂.[30] Pan Weicheng's *Lunyu guzhu jijian* cites Wang Su, Zhou Shenglie, and Lu Deming's *Jingdian shiwen* commentaries to *Lunyu* 7.14.[31] Huan Maoyong's 宦懋庸 *Lunyu ji* 論語稽 cites Zhou Shenglie, Wang Su, Fan Ning, and Yuan Jie's 元玠 commentaries to *Lunyu* 7.14.[32] Zhai Hao's 翟灝 (1736–1788 CE) *Sishu kaoyi* 四書考異 cites Lu Deming's *Jingdian shiwen*, the *Shuoyuan*, and *Wenxuan* 文選.[33] Finally, as mentioned before, Ling Shu 淩曙 cites relevant content from the *Han shu* and *Shiji*, as well as the commentaries to *Lunyu* 7.14 by Wang Su, Huang Kan, Guo Xiang, and Jiang Xi, in his work. Thus, Qing scholars not only prioritized Han readings of *Lunyu* 7.14, they also respected early medieval commentaries.

In doing so, there was renewed interest in the "distressed by Shao" position to *Lunyu* 7.14. Wu Qian supported Huang Kan's interpretation that Confucius was shocked to find the Shao piece performed in Qi, as opposed to being struck by its beauty.[34] In *Sishu kaoyi*, Zhai Hao also argues that Wang Su read *wei* 為 ("to do, perform") as *gui* 媯 (a proper name), when Confucius exclaims over the extremity of *wei yue* / *gui yue* ("performance of music / music of Gui"). The music of the Gui clan should be in Chen, and therefore Confucius was surprised that it came to Qi.[35] That the performance of Shao in Qi was unexpected (and inappropriate) is a pivotal point in "distressed by Shao" interpretations.

One of the central questions to Song commentaries on *Lunyu* 7.14 was revived during the Qing as well: how could Confucius refrain from meat for "three months"? Mao Qiling 毛奇齡 (1623–1716 CE) challenged Cheng Yi's idea that *san yue* ("three months") was a miswriting of *yin* ("tune"). Zhai Hao documented various takes on this issue, including those in the *Chengzi yishu* 程子遺書, *Zhuzi huowen* 朱子或問, *Shiyijing wendui* 十一經問對, *Shiji bianhuo* 史記辨惑, and *Sishu bianyi* 四書辨疑.[36] Although Mao Qiling believed that the *Shiji* addition of *xue zhi* erroneously "altered a classic," Dai Dachang 戴大昌 (fl. 1796–1821 CE) disagreed, feeling that the addition was merited, as it "clarified the classic." In his *Sishu wenda* 四書問答, Dai further critiques the position that "three months" modifies the following sentence, on Confucius losing his appetite.[37]

Of the Qing commentaries to *Lunyu* 7.14, Liu Baonan's 劉寶楠 (1791–1855 CE) *Lunyu zhengyi* 論語正義 is perhaps the best known today. In *Lunyu zhengyi*, Liu cites Zhou Shenglie and Wang Su's commentaries, approving of the former and disagreeing with the latter. He, moreover, explains:[38]

> Yet this (expression of surprise by Confucius) follows after the line about how he "forgot his taste for meat." Because he admired Shao music, he listened and practiced it for a long time, to the point of forgetting his taste for meat. If *wei yue* ("to perform music") is *gui yue* ("the music of Gui"), and "to such extremes" refers to how Chen will supplant Qi, then this would mean he felt aggrieved. This does not make sense in light of the previous lines, so I suspect that this is incorrect.
>
> 然此句承"不知肉味"之下, 正以讚美韶樂, 所以聞習之久, 至不知肉味也. 若以"為樂"作"媯樂,""至於斯"為陳將代齊, 則別是感痛之義, 與上文不貫, 似非是也.

Liu thus offers here a clear critique of Wang Su's position, reminding us that, despite the renewed interest in "distressed by Shao" interpretations of *Lunyu* 7.14, limitations remained.[39]

Conclusions

This historical progression to *Lunyu* 7.14 commentaries reveals that both the "praising Shao" and "distressed by Shao" theories were always present in academic discourse. Han period texts allow for both "praising Shao" and "distressed by Shao" interpretations to this passage. In the early medieval period, the "distressed by Shao" reading became more mainstream. Thereafter, it gradually declined in popularity. Other debates then gained prominence, shifting attention away from the question of why Confucius lost his appetite. Consideration was given, for example, to the propriety of refraining from eating for so long (Song), to how Confucius communed with Shun through music (Yuan and Ming), or to other aspects of textual exegesis (Qing). In light of this survey of *Lunyu* 7.14 commentaries, another speculative argument may be raised. Following the death of Confucius, debates did indeed arise over whether he "praised Shao" or was "distressed by Shao" in Qi. It was only when Zhang Yu and Zheng Xuan unified the various prior *Lunyu* commentaries into a single edition during the Han, however, that the "distressed by Shao" reading was repressed initially, leading to the impression that it did not exist prior to the early medieval period.

Notes

1. Liu Baonan 劉寶楠 (1791–1855), *Lunyu zhengyi* 論語正義 (Beijing: Zhonghua, 2009), 264.

2. *Shiji* 史記 (Beijing: Zhonghua, 2007), 1910.

3. *Han shu* 漢書 (Beijing: Zhonghua, 1975), 1039.

4. Wang Su 王素, *Tang xieben Lunyu Zheng shi zhu ji qi yanjiu* 唐寫本論語鄭氏注及其研究 (Beijing: Wenwu, 1991), 77.

5. Tang Yan 唐晏 (1857–1920), *Liang Han Sanguo xuean* 兩漢三國學案 (Beijing: Zhonghua, 2008), 495.

6. Portions of this section appeared in the author's paper, "*Lunyu* 'Zi zai Qi wen Shao' yanjiu" 論語子在齊聞韶研究, presented at the Capital Region Forum on Aesthetics—and the First Early Career Aesthetics Forum Academic Workshop 京師美學論壇—暨第一屆青年美學論壇學術研討會, held in Beijing, August 2016.

7. Tang Yan, *Liang Han Sanguo xuean*, 520.

8. Huang Kan 皇侃 (Southern dynasties, Liang scholar, 488–545), *Lunyu yishu* 論語義疏, Rucang jinghua bian 儒藏精華編, vol. 104 (Beijing: Beijing daxue, 2007), 114.

9. Huang Kan, *Lunyu yishu*, 113–114.

10. Zhang Pu 張溥 (Ming scholar), *Han Wei Liuchao baisanjia ji* 漢魏六朝百三家集, in *Chizaotang Sikuquanshu huiyao* 攤藻堂薈要, Collection Section 集部 (Taipei: Taiwan shijie, 1985), under Zhang Pu, 27. Translation after Wendy Schwartz, "Revisiting the Scene of the Party: A Study of the Lanting Collection," *Journal of the American Oriental Society* 132, no. 2 (2012): 294.

11. Chen Bojun 陳伯君, *Ruan Ji ji jiaozhu* 阮籍集校注 (Beijing: Zhonghua, 1987), 95.

12. Lu Deming 陸德明 (Tang, 556–527), *Jingdian shiwen* 經典釋文 (Shanghai: Shanghai guji, 2016), 1363.

13. The following analysis draws from: Wang Yunfei 王雲飛, "*Lunyu* 'Zi zai Qi wen Shao' Songdai zhushi yanjiu" 論語子在齊聞韶宋代注釋研究, *Guanzi xuekan* 管子學刊 3 (2018): 71–76.

14. Zhu Xi 朱熹 (1130–1200), *Sishu zhangju jizhu* 四書章句集注, in *Wenyuange siku quanshu* 文淵閣四庫全書, vol. 197 (Taipei: Taiwan shangwu, 1983), 39.

15. Zheng Ruxie 鄭汝諧 (fl. 12th c.), *Lunyu yiyuan* 論語意原, in *Wenyuange siku quanshu*, vol. 199, 135.

16. Cai Jie 蔡節 (Song scholar), *Lunyu jishuo* 論語集說, in *Wenyuange siku quanshu*, vol. 200, 604.

17. Hao Jing 郝敬 (1558–1639), *Lunyu xiangjie* 論語詳解, in *Xuxiu siku quanshu* 續修四庫全書, vol. 153 (Shanghai: Shanghai guji, 2002), 187.

18. Hu Guang 胡廣 (1370–1418), *Sishu daquan* 四書大全*Lunyu jizhu daquan* 論語集注大全, in *Wenyuange siku quanshu*, vol. 205, 257. As for Master Feng of Houzhai, his commentary instead argues that the performance of Shao in Qi was surprisingly superior to that of Lu.

19. Lü Nan 呂柟 (1479–1542), *Sishu yinwen* 四書因問, in *Wenyuange siku quanshu*, vol. 206, 831.

20. Sun Ying'ao 孫應鼇 (1527–1586), *Sishu jinyu* 四書近語, in *Xuxiu siku quanshu*, vol. 160, 602. Sun Ying'ao also reflected upon the controversy over how Shao came to be performed in Qi. He believed that it was brought there initially by Grand Preceptor Zhi of Lu; Confucius's exclamation of surprise was over this fact.

21. Jiao Hong's 焦竑 (1540–1620), *Jiaoshi sishu jianglu* 焦氏四書講錄, in *Xuxiu siku quanshu*, vol. 162, 103. Jiao Hong subscribed to the theory that Gongzi Wan of Chen (aka Chen Jingzhong) brought Shao with him when he fled to Qi. Furthermore, Jiao did not accept Zhu Xi's addition of *xue zhi* ("studied it") before *san yue* ("three months").

22. Lu Shanji 鹿善繼 (1575–1636), *Sishu shuoyue* 四書說約, in *Xuxiu siku quanshu*, vol. 162, 572.

23. Ge Yinliang 葛寅亮 (1570–1646), *Sishu Hunan jiang* 四書湖南講, in *Xuxiu siku quanshu*, vol. 163, 199. Ge also supported the theory that Gongzi Wan of Chen brought Shao to Qi.

24. Shen Shouzheng 沈守正 (Ming scholar), *Chongding sishu shuocong* 重訂四書說從, in *Xuxiu siku quanshu*, vol. 163, 597.

25. Sun Zhaoxing 孫肇興 (Ming scholar), *Sishu yueshuo* 四書約說, in *Xuxiu siku quanshu*, vol. 164, 58.

26. Ling Shu 淩曙 (1775–1829), *Sishu diangu* 四書典故, in *Xuxiu siku quanshu*, vol. 169, 605.

27. Pan Weicheng 潘維城 (fl. 19th c.), *Lunyu guzhu jijian* 論語古注集箋, in *Xuxiu siku quanshu*, vol. 154, 69.

28. Jiang Yong 江永 (1681–1762), *Sishu guren dianlin* 四書古人典林, in *Xuxiu siku quanshu*, vol. 166, 320.

29. Wu Changzong 吳昌宗 (c. 1500–1582), *Sishu jingzhu jizheng* 四書經注集證, in *Xuxiu siku quanshu*, vol. 168, 145.

30. Wu Qian 吳騫 (1733–1813), *Huang shi Lunyu yishu canding* 皇氏論語義疏參訂, in *Xuxiu siku quanshu*, vol. 153, 670. For *Lunyu* 7.14, Wu discusses the placement of the two characters *Qi jun* 齊君 (Lord of Qi) (in Huang Kan's commentary); how the character *hu* 忽 ("forgot") from the line "forgot his appetite" (忽於肉味) (in Zhou Shenglie's commentary) is written as *wang* 忘 instead in the Ashikaga 足利 edition of the text; and how *ci* 此 ("this") from the line " 'This' refers

to the state of Qi" (此, 此齊也) (in Wang Su's commentary) is replaced with the word *si* 斯 ("this") in another edition. As for the subcommentaries to *Lunyu* 7.14, Wu Qian considers, for example, the difference between saying Confucius *zhi* 至 ("arrived at") or *zai* 在 ("was located in") Qi. He also examines relevant passages from the *Shuoyuan*, *Shiji* "Shijia," and Dan Qian's 丹鈆 *Xulu* 續錄.

31. Pan Weicheng, *Lunyu guzhu jijian*, in *Xuxiu siku quanshu*, vol. 154, 69.

32. Huan Maoyong 宦懋庸 (Qing scholar), *Lunyu ji* 論語稽, in *Xuxiu siku quanshu*, vol. 157, 309.

33. Zhai Hao 翟灝 (1736–1788), *Sishu kaoyi* 四書考異, in *Xuxiu siku quanshu*, vol. 167, 213.

34. Wu Qian, *Huang shi Lunyu yishu canding*, in *Xuxiu siku quanshu*, vol. 153, 670.

35. Zhai Hao, *Sishu kaoyi*, in *Xuxiu siku quanshu*, vol. 167, 213. Pan Weicheng also notes Zhai Hao's discussion of Wang Su's reading.

36. *Chengzi yishu* records Cheng Yi's argument that *san yue* is a miswriting of *yin*; *Zhuxi huowen* records Zhu Xi's critique of Cheng Yi's theory; *Shiyijing wendui* supports Cheng Yi's theory; *Shiji bianhuo* critiques the addition of *xue zhi* ("studied it [i.e., *Shao*]") before *san yue* in the *Shiji*; and *Sishu bianyi* argues against both the theories that *san yue* is miswritten *yin*, and that *yue* 月 is miswritten *ri* 日 ("day"). Zhai Hao, *Sishu kaoyi*, in *Xuxiu siku quanshu*, vol. 167, 213.

37. Dai Dachang 戴大昌 (fl. 1796–1821), *Sishu wenda* 四書問答, in *Xuxiu siku quanshu*, vol. 169, 320.

38. Liu Baonan, *Lunyu zhengyi*, 264.

39. Liu cites a "Zhou commentary" 周注 and "Wang commentary" 王注 in his discussion of *Lunyu* 7.14. The latter he clearly identifies as Wang Su's, but when it comes to the "Zhou commentary," Liu is less certain: "In the notes to the *Xiaofu* in the *Wenxuan*, this commentary is said to be by a 'Zhou Sheng,' perhaps at that time it was possible to differentiate between 'Zhou' and 'Zhou Sheng'" ("文選·嘯賦注" 引此注為 '周生,' 或當時周與周生能識別也"). Liu Baonan, *Lunyu zhengyi*, 264. Evidently, Liu did not know that this referred to Zhou Shenglie, or that there was a difference between Zhou Shenglie and Master Zhou, a Han commentator to the *Lunyu*.

4

The Xia-Shang-Zhou Chronology Project and Archaeological Research on the Xia Dynasty

Li Boqian

Translated by Constance A. Cook

Xia as a Critical Period of Ancient Chinese History

The Xia dynasty is mentioned in such classics as the *Guoyu* 國語, the *Yi Zhou shu* 逸周書, the *Guben zhushu jinian* 古本竹書紀年, the *Shiben* 世本, and in the most detail in *Shiji* 史記 "Xia Benji" 夏本紀 of Han scholar Sima Qian 司馬遷.

The Xia-Shang-Zhou Chronology Project was the most important initiative of the National Ninth Five-Year Plan for Science and Technology. It was supported by the Party, humanities and science scholars, and many notable international scholars abroad, such as Sarah Allan of Dartmouth College, who contributed helpful advice. Along with Li Xueqin 李學勤 (1933–2019), we all worked together and convened international discussions at Peking University, such as the International Conference on Recently Discovered Chinese Manuscripts 新出筒帛國際學術討論會. This chapter was composed and offered in Sarah's honor. It was later delivered as a lecture in Bengbu City Museum 蚌埠市博物馆 (August 2019), with a Chinese transcription published as: "Kaogu yanjiu zhong de Xia chao xunzong" 考古研究中的夏朝尋踪, *Guangmin ribao* 光民日報, December 28, 2019, 10.

During the twentieth century, there arose in Sinological circles an era of doubting the traditional accounts of ancient history; without material proof, for example, how do we know that a Xia dynasty actually existed? So many doubts have been expressed over the years that scholars are still caught in a stasis of half-doubt and half-belief. In 1924, when the debate was reaching a fevered pitch, Li Xuanbo 李玄伯 (1895–1974) wrote the article "The Only Method for Solving the Questions about Ancient History" (古史問題的惟一解決方法), in which he stated that "the only method for solving doubts about ancient history is archaeology. If we want to solve these questions, we must energetically move forward with excavations" (要想解決古史，唯一的方法就是考古學. 我們若想解決這些問題，還要努力向發掘方面走).[1] From that point on, everyone has recognized the value of pursuing archaeology. In 1926, Li Ji 李濟 (1896–1979) investigated and excavated sites in Xiyincun 西陰村, Xiaxian 夏縣, Shanxi, searching for traces of the Xia people.[2] No traces of the Xia were discovered, but instead painted pottery of the Yangshao 仰韶 culture was found.

In 1943, Xu Xusheng 徐旭生 (1988–1976) published the book *Zhongguo gushi de zhuanshuo shidai* 中國古史的傳說時代 (The Mythological Age of Ancient Chinese History) and then in 1959 at the age of seventy, proceeded to survey the Xiaxu 夏墟 (Wastes of Xia) site in western Henan and begin tests at the site of Erlitou 二里頭 in Yanshi 偃師.[3] His surveys and trial excavations can be seen as continuing the work of Li Ji. Xu claimed that Erlitou must be the site of the ancient capital Xibo 西亳, setting off a wave of archaeological searches for evidence of the Xia culture. All sorts of clues were discovered in the region by the Archaeology Research Institute 考古研究所 in the Science Academy 科學院 (later called the Social Science Academy 社會科學院), the students of archaeology in the History Department at Peking University, as well as archaeologists, sent individually or in teams, by the Shanxi Provincial Culture Relics and Archaeology Department.

In 1977, the Henan Provincial Cultural Relics and Archaeology Institute officially announced at a meeting the excavation of the Wangchenggang 王城崗 site, in Gaocheng town 告成鎮, Dengfeng 登封, Henan.[4] Archaeological team leaders and representatives from the excavations of the sites of Wangchenggang, Erlitou, Dongxiafeng 東下馮, and elsewhere reported on their efforts to uncover Xia cultural archaeology. The archaeologist Zou Heng 鄒衡 (1927–2005) gave a long speech and a heated debate ensued, resulting in the following four different scenarios:

1. Erlitou Stages 1–2 are Xia culture and stages 3–4 are Shang culture

2. Erlitou Stages 1–4 and Henan Longshan 龍山 culture are Xia culture

3. Erlitou Stages 1–4 are Xia and Henan late Longshan culture is not Xia culture

4. Erlitou Stages 1–3 are Xia, Stage 4 is Shang

The director of the Archaeology Institute for the Chinese Academy of Science at the time, Xia Nai 夏鼐 (1910–1985), summarized the problem of Xia culture in a speech:[5]

> First, we have to assume that the Xia dynasty existed in history and not deny its existence as the doubters do. Second, Xia culture had its own special features that reflect a specific Xia kingdom and people. As for considering Yangshao a Xia culture, even if it can be proved to be ancestral to Xia culture, it could only be considered as a Pre-Xia culture and not as Xia culture per se. Other peoples who existed at the same time as the Xia dynasty were not members of Xia culture, such as those in Inner Mongolia, Xinjiang, and other border regions. If there were Shang peoples and Zhou peoples during the Xia dynasty, they would not be the same as Xia people. You cannot label Pre-Shang culture or Pre-Zhou culture Xia culture.

He felt that the four possibilities mentioned here all had problems and that only Zou Heng's theory of Zhengzhou 鄭州 being the Shang capital of Bo 亳都 was worth further consideration.[6] This conference was a critical follow-up to Xu Xusheng's 1959 surveys of Xiaxu in western Henan and represented the first discussion dealing with the nature of Xia culture. In the twenty years hence, even though there had been some new discoveries and ideas, discussion remained focused on the four possibilities. There had been no change. However, the 1996 scientific and technical project, the Xia-Shang-Zhou Chronology Project 夏商周斷代工程 of the National Ninth Five-Year Plan, allowed for in-depth research on Xia culture, as well as presenting certain challenges.

The Xia-Shang-Zhou Chronology Project

The Xia-Shang-Zhou Chronology Project (hereafter, the Project) was a systematic attempt to engage experts in such fields as history, archaeology, astronomy, and dating technology. Its overall goal was to determine the chronology of the Xia, Shang, and Zhou eras on a scientific basis. But since the detail varied for each era, the chronologies for the early and late Shang and for the Western Zhou eras are more precise and concrete. For the Xia, it was a matter of "providing a basic chronological framework" (提出基本的年代框架). Compared with the Shang and Western Zhou, the requirements for dating the Xia were not high. The challenge was to confirm which archaeological remains actually belonged to the Xia culture, much less to date the sites. Project specialists set up a Xia Dynasty Dating Research taskforce headed by Zou Heng focused on the following four topics: (1) Early Xia culture, (2) Erlitou culture, (3) the Xia-Shang cultural boundary, and (4) astronomical events such as the Zhong Kang 仲康 eclipse and chronology recorded in the *Shangshu* "Yin zheng" 胤征 and in the *Da Dai liji* 大戴禮記 "Xia xiaozheng" 夏小正. Later, some of these evolved into other topics, such as evaluating the chronology and cultural layers for Donglongshan 東龍山 culture in Shangzhou 商州, researching the historicity of "Yu's punishment of the Three Miao" (禹伐三苗), and evaluating the layers in the site of Xinzhai 新砦. Specialists also engaged in scientific approaches to Xia dynasty chronology, turning to the use of carbon 14 (C14) and other technologies, bone sample preparation, AMS (accelerator mass spectrometry), and other tests. The following sites received official approval for excavation and support by the Cultural Relics Bureau: Dengfeng Wangchenggang, Yuxian Xinzhai, Yuxian Wadian 禹縣瓦店, Xinmi Xinzhai 新密新砦, Gongyi Shaochai 鞏義梢柴, Yanshi Erlitou, Shangzhao Donglongshan, among others. Except for Shaochai, the other sites have all been excavated with the requisite carbon samples examined. The preliminary report *Xia Shang Zhou duandai gongcheng 1996–2000 nian jieduan chengguo baogao* 夏商周斷代工程 1996–2000 年階段成果報告 was published in the year 2000 with the conclusion of the Project.[7] The section called "Xia Dynasty Chronological Research" (夏代年代學研究) used records on Xia history and archaeological data to identify Xia culture layers from those of Longshan at Erlitou.

Transmitted documentation of Xia history includes a reference to the *Zhuzhu jinian* 竹書紀年 preserved in the *Taiping yulan* 太平禦覽, *juan* 82: "From the time of Yu 禹 to Jie 桀 is 17 generations, during which sometimes there was a king and sometimes not; this was 471 years" (自禹至桀十七世，有王與無王，用歲四百七十一年).[8] Another theory is that the duration was 431 years, since "the 471 years includes Yi 羿 and Zhuo 浞, when Xia lacked rulers, and 431 years would not count those years when Xia was ruler-less."[9] Besides the length of the era, texts also record a lot of different capitals for the Xia. The collected commentary to *Shiji*, "Zhou benji" 周本紀, includes a quote from Xu Huang's 徐廣 (353–425) *Shiji yinyi* 史記音義: "Xia (meaning Yu, the first Xia ruler) resided in Henan, first in Yangcheng and later in Yangzhai" (夏居河南, 初在陽城, 後居陽翟).[10] The modern text *Zhushu jinian* records how Emperor Qi 帝啟 "enthroned in Xiayi on a *guihai* day and held a huge banquet for the local lords at Zuntai (referring to Yangzhai)" (癸亥帝即位於夏邑, 大饗諸侯於鈞台).[11] Zhang Shoujie 張守節 (8th c.) in the "Xia benji" of his *Shiji zhengyi* 正義 quotes the *Jizhong guwen* 汲塚古文 (Ancient Texts Recovered at Ji Mound): "Tai Kang resided at Zhenxun, and Yi and Jie had also lived there" (太康居斟尋, 羿亦居之, 桀又居之).[12] Wang Yinglin 王應麟 (1223–1296) of the Song dynasty in his *Tongjian dili tongshi* 通鑒地理通釋 on "Xia du" 夏都 quotes the *Shiben* 世本: "Xiang 相 crossed over to Diqiu 帝丘, which became Wei 衛 during the Zhou" (相徙帝丘, 於周為衛).[13] The first *juan* of the modern text *Zhushu jinian* records: "Shao Kang 少康 returned to Xiayi 夏邑 (referring to Yangzhai) from Lun 綸" (少康自綸歸於夏邑) and that "in his eighteenth reign year, he moved to Yuan 原" (十八年遷於原).[14] The *Taiping yulan* quotes the *Jinian* 紀年 to say the Emperor Ning 帝寧 (meaning Zhu 杼) "moved from (Yuan) to Laoqiu 老邱" (自[原]遷於老邱). And in *juan* 82 it cites the *Jinian* saying that "Emperor Jin 帝廑, also known as Yin Jia 胤甲 came to the throne and resided in Xihe 西河" (帝廑, 一名胤甲即位, 居西河).[15]

Despite the multitude of Xia capitals mentioned in texts, only two sites have any archaeological verification: Yangcheng, in Gaocheng, Dengfeng, and Zhenxun, near the Luo 洛 River. The site of Erlitou at Yanshi excavated by Xu Xusheng in 1959 lies next to the Luo River and is believed by some scholars to be the capital Zhenxun 斟鄩 as within the nine-square-kilometer area of the site appear evidence of palaces, large tombs, bronze foundries, fine jade workshops, bronze and pottery vessels.[16]

Erlitou culture has four distinct layers dated according to different numbered sets of data points:

Period 1: two points suggest the time span of 1800–1640 BCE
Period 2: nine for 1740–1590 BCE
Period 3: three for 1610–1555 BCE
Period 4: four for 1561–1521 BCE

Erlitou culture basically falls within the 359 years between dates 1880 and 1521 BCE, not enough to cover the 471 years suggested by texts, even if we exclude the stage without rulers. The C14 data provides a midpoint year of 1760 BCE for Period 1, which is far from the traditional year of 2071 BCE for the beginning of Xia. So, it seems that Erlitou culture must not represent the earliest stage of Xia culture. An Jinhuai 安金槐 (1921–2001) divided the layers of the late Longshan cultural remains at the Wangchenggang site in Henan into five periods. These have since collapsed into three stages by Fang Yanming 方燕明, who was responsible for the topic of Early Period Xia Culture Research 早期夏文化研究 for the Project.[17] The three stages subsume the data points for the original five periods as follows:

> Stage 1: originally Period 1 with two points for the date range 2190–2105 BCE
> Stage 2: originally Periods 2 and 3, with two points for Period 2 dates 2132–2064 BCE and two for Period 3 dates 2090–2030 BCE
> Stage 3: originally Periods 4 and 5, with three points for Period 4 dates 2050–1985 BCE and two points for Period 5 dates 2030–1965 BCE

The Project notes in its "Evaluation of the Basic Chronological Framework for the Xia Dynasty" (夏代基本年代框架的估定) section that scholars essentially hold two views on the upper limit of Xia culture: it is either Erlitou Period 1 or a stage of Henan Late Longshan culture. The Xinzhai Period 2 sites are recognized as a link between Henan Late Longshan and Erlitou Period 1. So, using 1600 BCE as the first year of the Shang and going back 471 years, then the Xia must have begun in 2071 BCE, placing it around the Henan Late Longshan Period 2 (2132–2030 BCE) (in Stage 2). In sum, the Project has made great strides from the perspective of the archaeology of Xia culture. We can understand the following points:

1. Erlitou culture represents middle and late Xia dynasty, and Henan Late Longshan culture must then belong to early Xia;
2. the existence of Xinzhai cultural sites with the one at Xinmi City 新密市 acting as a diagnostic for dating them between Henan Late Longshan and Erlitou Period 1 cultures. Based on secondary excavations in 1999, Xinzhai Period 2 culture fills the gap, with Xinzhai Period 1 dating to Longshan and Period 2 reaching to Erlitou Period 1;
3. from the large area, structures, and artifacts found at the Erlitou site, we know it must be Zhenxun. Henan sites

Wangchenggang in Dengfeng and Wadian in Yuzhou, dated to the Late Longshan, also reveal architectural structures, tombs, and fine jade and pottery work consistent with an Early Xia cultural identification.

Post-Project Accomplishments

The Project, one of the nine Five State Initiatives, ended productively in the year 2000. Since then some of the discoveries have continued to be subjects of archaeological analysis, producing even more information. For example:

1. The discovery of a large ancient city at the Wangchenggang site in Dengfeng, originally dated by An Jinhuai to Wangchenggang Period 3. The excavations that took place from 1976 to 1977 first revealed the site. The northern city wall in the site's northeastern section had destroyed the northern wall and moat of an older smaller city. Its western wall had been destroyed by the Ying River 潁河 and its eastern wall by the Wudu River 五渡河. A large pounded-earth platform was discovered in the northern section inside the walled city.[18]

2. The Xinzhai site in Xinmi revealed both Late Henan Longshan culture and Xinzhai Period 2 remains. There had once been a moat around the city wall. Analysis showed that the city was dated to a later stage than the late Longshan remains in Wangchenggang city. Structural foundations and smaller sized burials have also been found in Xinzhai city site.[19]

3. The Erlitou site reveals an inner palace compound, with encircling handicraft workshops and many palace foundations, as well as mid- to high-level elite tombs out of which were excavated stunning, turquoise-inlaid bronze chest plates.[20]

4. There is evidence of large-scale palace construction during Erlitou Period 4, a period of transition from Xia to Shang cultures.[21]

5. The Yuhuicun 禹會村 Longshan cultural site, jointly excavated by the Shandong team of the Archaeology Institute of the Academy of Social Sciences and the Bengbu City Museum

蚌埠市博物館, revealed a circular site including sacrificial platforms, pits, and ditches with a kind of work shed–like structure inside of it. Researchers feel that it might be the site described in texts such as Tushan 塗山, where Yu convened with the local lords.²²

6. Archaeological excavation revealed that the Shijiahe 石家河 cultural site includes many elements from Henan Late Longshan culture. Researchers feel that this may be evidence for Yu punishing the Sanmiao 三苗.²³

7. Updated C14 testing techniques have greatly improved the quality and quantity of results:

- Late Henan Longshan (An Jinhuai's Period 3) is 2090–2030 BCE;
- Xinzhai Stage 1 is 1870–1785 BCE, Stage 2 is 1790–1920 BCE;
- Erlitou Period 1 begins around 1735 BCE, Period 4 is 1565–1530 BCE, from Period 2 to Period 4 is 1680–1530 BCE.

These dates greatly advance our understanding of important issues concerning Xia culture and have been described in publications such as *Xia-Shang-Zhou Chronology Project Report (1996–2000)* 夏商周斷代工程報告 (1996–2000 年), *Xinmi Xinzhai 1999–2000 Field Archaeology Excavation Report 2000* 年田野考古發掘報告,²⁴ *Erlitou* 二里頭,²⁵ among others. As I explained in the *Xinmi Xinzai* field report, generally speaking Wangchenggang city represents Late Henan Longshan culture; and the Xinzhai Period (also called Xinmi culture) up through Erlitou culture represents the three major stages of Xia cultural history, from the beginning up through the end, roughly from the twenty-first through sixteenth centuries BCE. Besides the chronology of Xia cultural progression, there is stronger evidence to identify Wangchenggang city at Dengfeng as Yu's capital of Yangcheng, and Erlitou of Yanshi was Zhenxun where Taikang, Yi, and Jie resided. One can make the objective argument, based on the triangulation of transmitted history, archeology, and chronological data, that the Xia era of Chinese history existed and that Xia history can be believed, as will be affirmed in the new publication by Beijing University professor Sun Qingwei 孫慶偉, *Buried*

Traces of Yu: The Archaeological Reconstruction of a Trustworthy Xia History
鼏宅禹跡——夏代信史的考古學重建.²⁶

Conclusion

I have personally participated in and witnessed the progress of the Project from the beginning and can testify that, despite all the problems and conflicts, everyone firmly agreed that the target was reasonable and that the idea of "combining the best of humanities with natural sciences to jointly tackle the issues" was a pragmatic approach. We agreed on the possibility of reconciling data drawn from such diverse sources as transmitted literature, paleographical texts, astronomical calculations, and archaeological periodization of sites and burial ground materials, along with data points produced by C14 and AMS (accelerator mass spectrometry) techniques. Nevertheless, it is natural, with the numbers of people involved from many different academic backgrounds, that there would be different perspectives and opinions. There were lively debates held in fifty-two formal seminars and numerous informal meetings, from April 1996 to April 2000. While there was largely a consensus, minority opinions were preserved and not suppressed.

The Project concerned academic research on the chronology of Xia, Shang, and Zhou dynasties. Academic research has its own rules for determining goals and plans but drawing larger boundaries and setting up frameworks required directors. While there was largely a consensus, there were some details that could have been considered more thoroughly. For example, we find only the use of old excavation data for Wangchenggang in the section on "Research on Early Xia Culture" in the *Report of Possible Arguments in the Xia-Shang-Zhou Chronology Project* 夏商周斷代工程可行性論證報告. Focus on the data from the smaller inner-city ash pits was looked at without prioritizing expanding the parameters of the examination to include the Late Longshan city discovered there toward the end of the Project. Further, despite the fact that some people noted evidence for a cultural shift at Erlitou in which "late Yi replaced Xia" (後夷代夏), there was no relevant excavation until after the Project, resulting in research on the Xinmi Xinzhai site. Also, because it took a lot of time to upgrade the C14 equipment and employ new techniques, a stable specimen batch was not confidently managed until the end of the project, with most of the evidence revealed in the follow-up. Fortunately, those in charge understood the situation and supported the continuation of the work. In fact, it is due to the efforts of tireless uncompensated work after the end of the Project that the most satisfactory results were achieved.

Notes

1. Li Xuanbo 李玄伯, "Gushi wenti de weiyi jiejue fangfa" 古史問題的唯一解決方法, *Xiandai pinglun* 1 (1924) 3: 3. See also Gu Jiegang 顧頡剛, ed., *Gushi bian* 古史辨, reprint, vol. 1 (Shanghai: Shanghai guji, 1981), 268.

2. Li Ji 李濟, "Xiyincun shiqian de yicun" 西陰村史前的遺存, in *Li Ji wenji* 李濟文集 (Shanghai: Shanghai renmin, 2006), 170.

3. Xu Xusheng 徐旭生, "1959 nian xia Yuxi diaocha 'Xiaxu' de chubu baogao 1959" 年夏豫西調查'夏墟'的初步報告, *Kaogu* 考古 1959.11: 592–600.

4. Yu Bo 余波, "Guojia wenwuju zai Dengfeng zhaokai Gaocheng yizhi fajue xianchang hui" 國家文物局在登封召開告成遺址發掘現場會, *Henan wenbo tongxun* 河南文博通訊1978.1: 22–24.

5. Xia Nai 夏鼐, "Tantan shentao Xia wenhua de jige wenti" 談談探討夏文化的幾個問題, *Zhongyuan wenwu* 中原文物 1978.1: 32–33.

6. Zou Heng 鄒衡, "Zhengzhou Shangcheng ji Tang du Zheng Bo shuo" 鄭州商城即湯都鄭亳說," *Wenwu* 1978.2: 69–71.

7. Xia Shang Zhou duandai gongcheng zhuanjiazu 夏商周斷代工程專家組, *Xia Shang Zhou duandai gongcheng 1996–2000 nian jieduan chengguo baogao: jianben* 夏商周斷代工程1996–2000年階段成果報告: 簡本 (Beijing: Shijie tushu, 2000).

8. Wang Guowei 王國維, *Guben zhushu jinian jijiao Jinben zhushu jinian shuzheng* 古本竹書紀年輯校今本竹書紀年疏證 (Shenyang: Liaoning jiaoyu, 1997), 7.

9. 岳南 Yue Nan, *Qiangu xuean: Xia Shang Zhou duandai gongcheng jiemi ji* 千古學案: 夏商周斷代工程解密記 (Haikou: Hainan chubanshe, 2007), 67.

10. Sima Qian 司馬遷, *Shiji* 史記 (Beijing: Zhonghua shuju, 2014), 4.167.

11. Wang, *Guben zhushu jinian jijiao Jinben zhushu jinian shuzheng*, 49.

12. *Shiji*, 2.107.

13. Wang Yinglin 王應麟, *Tongjian dili tongshi* 通鑑地理通釋, in Wang Yunwu 王雲五 ed., *Congshu jicheng chubian* 叢書集成初編, vols. 3027–3028 (Shanghai: Shangwu yinchuguan, 1936), vol. 3027, *juan* 4 "Lidai duyi kao" 歷代都邑攷, 44.

14. Wang, *Guben zhushu jinian jijiao Jinben zhushu jinian shuzheng*, 53.

15. Wang, *Guben zhushu jinian jijiao Jinben zhushu jinian shuzheng*, 4–5.

16. Xu Xusheng 徐旭生, "1959 nian xia Yuxi diaocha 'Xiaxu' de chubu baogao 1959" 年夏豫西調查 '夏墟' 的初步報告, *Kaogu* 考古 1959.11: 592–600.

17. Fang Yanming 方燕明, "Xia Shang Zhou duandai gongcheng zhong de zaoqi Xia wenhua yanjiu" 夏商周斷代工程中的早期夏文化研究, *Zhongyuan wenwu* 中原文物 2001.2: 41–43.

18. Beijing daxue kaogu boxueyuan 北京大學考古文博學院 and Henansheng wenwu kaogu yanjiuyuan 河南省文物考古研究院, eds., *Dengfeng Wangchenggang kaogu*

faxian yu yanjiu 登封王城崗考古發現與研究 (2002–2005), 2 vols. (Zhengzhou: Daxiang, 2007).

19. Beijing daxue zhendan gudai wenming yanjiu zhongxin 北京大學震旦古代文明研究中心 and Zhengzhoushi wenwu kaogu yanjiuyuan 鄭州市文物考古研究院, *Xinmi Xinzhai 1999–2000 nian tianye kaogu fajue baogao* 新密新砦: 1999–2000 年田野考古發掘報告 (Beijing: Wenwu, 2008).

20. Zhongguo shehui kexueyuan kaogu yanjiusuo 中國社會科學院考古研究所, *Erlitou 1999–2006* 二里头 1999–2006 (Beijing: Wenwu, 2014), chap. 6, sec. 3.

21. Zhao Haitao 趙海濤, "Erlitou yizhi Erlitou wenhua siqi wanduan yicun tanxi," 二里頭遺址二里頭文化四期晚段遺存探析, *Nanfang wenwu* 南方文物2016.4: 115–123.

22. Zhongguo shehui kexueyuan kaogu yanjiusuo 中國社會科學院考古研究所 and Anhuisheng Bengbushi bowuguan 安徽省蚌埠市博物館, *Bengbu Yuhuicun* 蚌埠禹會村 (Beijing: Kexue, 2013).

23. Yang Xingai 楊新改 and Han Jianye 韓建業, "Yu zheng Sanmiao tansuo 禹征三苗探索," *Zhongyuan wenwu* 中原文物 1995.2: 46–55; Fang Qin 方勤, "Sanmiao yu nantu: Changjiang zhongyou wenming jincheng de kaoguxue guancha" 三苗與南土——長江中游文明化進程的考古學觀察, in *Sanmiao yu nantu: Hubeisheng wenwu kaogu yanjiusuo "shierwu" qijian zhongyao kaogu shouhuo* 三苗與南土——湖北省文物考古研究所"十二五"期間重要考古收穫, ed. Jianghan kaogu bianjibu 江漢考古編輯部 (Wuhan: Hubeisheng wenwu kaogu yanjiusuo, 2016), 10–14.

24. Beijing daxue zhendan gudai wenming yanjiu zhongxin, et al., *Xinmi Xinzhai*.

25. Zhongguo shehui kexueyuan kaogu yanjiusuo, *Erlitou 1999–2006*.

26. Sun Qingwei 孫慶偉, *Mizhuo Yuji: Xiandai xinshi de kaoguxue chongjian* 鼏宅禹跡——夏代信史的考古學重建 (Beijing: Shenghuo-dushi-xinzhi sanlian, 2018).

5

Formation of the "Nine Provinces" according to the Tribute Payments Recorded in Oracle-Bone and Bronze Inscriptions

Shen Jianhua

Translated by Constance A. Cook

Introduction

The continuous emergence of artifacts from the ground over the past decades provides invaluable data for our understanding of the rise and nature of China's ancient polities, including their conceptualization of time and space. In particular, the surprising correspondence between parts of the oracle-bone and bronze inscriptions—as well as with Warring States manuscripts and the received tradition articulated in transmitted texts—undoubtedly enhances our appreciation for the history of ancient Chinese civilization and provides much fodder for further contemplation.

According to tradition, the "Nine Provinces" (*jiu zhou* 九州) represented the boundaries of the realm and its geographical divisions. In the "Yu gong" 禹貢 chapter of the *Shangshu* 尚書, it is said that Yu 禹 demarcated the Nine Provinces during the Xia, with these divisions persisting through the Three Dynasties (i.e., the Xia, Shang, and Zhou eras).[1] Previously it was believed that the "Yu gong" chapter was compiled relatively late, with the concept of Nine Provinces taking shape no earlier than the Warring States period. Following the discovery of new archaeological sources, however, this theory has been called into question. Li Ling 李零 claims:

> Archaeological evidence exists for "Traces of Yu" (*Yu ji* 禹蹟) and the "Nine Provinces." This concept was not invented only in the Warring States, but can be pushed back into the Spring and Autumn period. With the songs and histories of the Shang and Zhou peoples, its antiquity may be extended even further. [The concept of Nine Provinces] is manifestly a "Three Dynasties" geographical ideology, and one that demonstrates a measure of flexibility: despite the fact that the Xia, Shang, Zhou, or even the states of Qi and Qin, had very different agendas, they all claim to fall within the "Traces of Yu." This is a point that deserves our close attention.[2]

When did the concept of Nine Provinces first form? How did its shape and structure evolve over the course of a thousand years, allowing it to persist as a model for ancient Chinese geographical divisions? Previous scholarship on the rise of urbanization in ancient China has largely neglected to treat *zhou* 州 as an analytical category, a gap that this essay seeks to address. In Li Ling's opinion, cited earlier, the Nine Provinces model was established at least by the Spring and Autumn period, with received songs and histories hinting at an even greater antiquity. Compared to such orally transmitted historical data, the records concerning *zhou* found on Shang and Zhou period paleographic sources offer tangible evidence for their existence. The recently discovered Western Zhou bronze inscription, Bin Gong *xu* 豳公盨, and the Warring States Chu bamboo-slip manuscript from the Shanghai Museum collection, *Rong Cheng shi* 容成氏, speak to the formation of the Nine Provinces system seen in the "Yu gong" chapter. Although certain differences arise between records concerning *zhou* in the Shang and Zhou paleographic sources, and the "Nine Provinces" (*jiu zhou*) discussed in transmitted texts, both in terms of their geographical extent and conceptualization, these differences are of only minor importance. More significant, however, is the fact that the *zhou* names, the tribute system, the function of officials and their organizational structure, as mentioned in the unearthed texts, all basically accord with those of the Nine Provinces system, as described in the "Five Tributaries" (*wu fu* 五服) model from the "Yu gong" chapter. Oracle-bone inscriptions (OBI) and other bronze inscriptions provide further insights into the origin and development of the concept of Nine Provinces.

The Concept of *Zhou* in Oracle-Bone and Bronze Inscriptions

In antiquity, *zhou* were understood as lands divided by mountain ranges and bodies of water, separated into the Nine Provinces. The *Shuowen jiezi* 說文解字 states: "Land surrounded by water on which people may reside is called a *zhou*. Water swirls around its sides, [hence the graph is formed] from two *chuan* 川 ('rivers'). Long ago, when Yao was dealing with the floods, people lived on high mounds [of earth] surrounded by water, sometimes called the Nine Provinces" (水中可居曰州. 水周繞其旁, 從重川. 昔堯遭洪水, 民居水中高土, 或曰九州).[3] In time the term Nine Provinces eventually referred to both the geographical and political "divine state" (the motherland, *shenzhou dadi* 神州大地), which by extension was the place where the Sons of Heaven resided in the Shang and Zhou political systems. The oracle bones record Shang kings in the "Celestial City Shang" (*tian yi Shang* 天邑商), "Four Quadrates" (*si fang* 四方), "Four Lands" (*si tu* 四土), and "Central Land" (*zhong tu* 中土); the bronze inscriptions document the Zhou kings as "making those far away pliant and enabling those close by" (*rou yuan neng er* 柔遠能邇), or saying "I may reside here in the Central Kingdom" (*yu qi zhai zi zhong guo* 余其宅茲中國). This suggests that the Shang and Zhou kings believed their political realms occupied the center of the world. Thus the *Shijing* 詩經 "Da Ya" 大雅 ode, "Wen Wang you sheng" 文王有聲, has "through the efforts of Yu, the Four Quadrates came together" (維之禹績, 四方攸同).[4] Confucius likewise claims, in the *Lunyu* 論語 chapter "Tai Bo" 泰伯, that, in King Wen's time, "two parts out of three in the world submitted to and served the Yin" (三分天下有其二, 以服事殷).[5]

The term *jiu zhou* 九州 ("Nine Provinces") does not appear in OBI. Similar terms to the Nine Provinces are found, however, in Shang hymns preserved within the *Shijing*. For instance, in "Xuan niao" 玄鳥 there is the line: "To those lands was he assigned as their lord; Into his keeping came all realms (i.e., the Nine Holdings)" (方命厥後, 奄有九有).[6] The Mao 毛 commentary explains that "the Nine Holdings, are the Nine Provinces" (九有, 九州).[7] The ode "Chang fa" 長發 writes, "God appointed him to be a model to all the lands (i.e., Nine Encirclements)" (帝命式於九圍) and "all the regions (Nine Holdings) were subdued" (九有有截).[8] The Mao commentary explains that "the Nine Encirclements are the Nine Provinces" (九圍, 九州也).[9] "Chang fa" also has the lines: "The waters of the Flood spread wide. Yu ranged the lands of earth below" (洪水茫茫, 禹敷下土).[10] This reveals that the division of the realm into Nine Provinces, as established by the Xia (Yu), were inherited by the Shang. With the emergence of numerous domains led by minor lords who "submitted to and served the Yin" (as cited from the *Lunyu* earlier), the Shang people, according to the late Spring and Autumn period Qi bell inscription, Shu Yi *zhong* 叔尸（夷）鍾, "filled out the Nine Provinces, living in the lands of Yu" (咸有九州, 處禹之堵[土]), having received grants of land gifted to them by the Shang kings that were then bequeathed to later generations.[11] Even though the precise phrase *jiu zhou* does not appear in the extant corpus of OBI, the *Shijing* and Shu Yi *zhong* statements suggest that the Shang sociopolitical organization incorporated aspects of the Nine Provinces model.

Records of *zhou* in the OBI, however, do offer more direct evidence that this was indeed the case. Pre-Qin texts often interchanged *zhou* 洲 ("isle") and *zhou* 州 ("province"), as any land mass surrounded by water was called a *zhou*; the Nine Provinces, accordingly, were envisioned as delineated by mountain ranges and rivers. Recall the *Shouwen jiezi* definition given earlier. In antiquity, "encircled land" (*yuantu* 圜土) referred to a jail. The ode "Zheng yue" 正月 has a line that reads: "And the people, quite innocent, are sentenced to be slaves and servants" (民之無辜, 並其臣僕).[12] To this, the *Mao shi zhengyi* 毛詩正義 cites Zheng Xuan's 鄭玄 explanation: "In olden times, if a criminal was not subjected to a mutilating punishment, they labored in an encircled land (*yuantu*) and were treated like servants. . . . (The first character of) *yuantu* is pronounced like *yuan* 圓 (which also means 'circular'). The *yuantu* was a jail" (古者有罪, 不入于刑則役之圜土, 以為臣僕 . . . 圜土, 音圓. 圜土, 獄也).[13] Inscriptions on the oracle bones suggest that the Shang built jails on islands to keep slaves from escaping, a practice similar to the use of moats as a deterrence. Consider the following example:

(1) On the *jiaxu* day . . . testing what was lost from the isle prison will be gained.

甲戌 . . . 貞奉（失）, 自㴲圉, 得. (*Ying* 英藏 540)[14]

The common term for an escaped slave or prey, as divined about by the Shang kings, is *shi* 失 ("loss"), the opposite of *de* 得 ("gain").[15] The graph with two water 水 elements is similar in connation to *zhou*, while the graph after is understood to be an early version of *yu* 圉, as in "prison" (*lingyu* 囹圄).[16] This inscription concerns a Shang king capturing an escaped convict and sending him to a jail surrounded by water. Three inscriptions mentioning *zhou chen* 州臣 ("isle servitors") concern a Shang king's capture of escaping servants:[17]

(2) Testing: the isle servitor will be captured.
貞: 州臣得. (*Heji* 合集850)
(3) Testing: the isle servitor will be captured.
貞: 州臣得. (*Heji* 851)
(4) Crack-making on a *yichou* day, Bin tests (the proposition) that the isle servitors who escaped will be captured in X.
乙酉卜亐貞, 州臣有𠆢 (失) 自賣得. (*Heji* 849)

Guo Moruo 郭沫若 claimed that *chen* ("servitors") were slaves,[18] but Gao Ming's 高明 subsequent study detailed how the position of the *chen* was more complex, with these figures sometimes serving as royal aides and at other times treated as slaves. The term *chen* in the "Wan Zhang" 萬章 chapter of *Mengzi* 孟子 refers to commoners: "The people within the state are called 'markets-and-wells *chen*,' and outside it they are called 'grasses-and-thickets *chen*'" (在國曰市井之臣, 在野曰草莽之臣).[19] In the "Fei shi" 費誓 chapter of the *Shangshu*, *chen* refers to slaves: "The slaves run away" (臣妾逋逃).[20] The OBI of the Wu Ding period also record: "Do not perhaps arrest *chen*" (臣不其幸) (*Heji* 163), and "do not perhaps capture *chen*" (臣不其得) (*Heji* 641). This shows that the *chen*, like slaves, could be chased down by the Shang kings.

The *Mozi*, "Shang xian, xia" 尚賢下 chapter, states: "Long ago Fu Yue lived on an isle in the Northern Sea, on an 'encircled land.' Dressed in coarse cloth belted with string, he labored building the walls of Fuyan" (昔者傅說居北海之洲, 圜土之上, 衣褐帶索, 庸築於傅岩之城).[21] This story finds support in the Tsinghua manuscript *Fu Yue zhi ming* 傅說之命. On slips #6–7 of *Fu Yue zhi ming*, it claims that the hamlet of Fu Yue was an "encircled land," on an isle in the Northern Sea, according with the description in the *Mozi*:

The hamlet of Yue, on an isle of the North Sea, was an "encircled land." Yue came from here to serve the Yin; the king commanded that Yue be made a lord.

亓 (其) 隹 (惟) 敓 (說) 邑, 才(在) 北𩫖 (海) 之州, 是隹 (惟) 鼎 (圜) 土. 敓(說) [六] 逨 (來), 自從事於𣪊(殷), 王甬 (用) 命敓 (說) 為公 [七].[22]

The term *zhou chen* 州臣, seen on inscription #4, thus refers to the "slaves" of a *zhou*, which was land delineated by water (e.g., "isle"). Although people often are named after places in the oracle bones, it is important to understand that *zhou* here is not a personal name. It functions akin to *dian chen* 奠臣 ("suburb servitors," *Heji* 635 verso, 7239, *Ying* 英1806), referring to commoners or slaves of a certain locality. Could the *zhou* described on the aforementioned oracle bones refer to this isle in the North Sea? While we may never be able to answer this question definitively, it is noteworthy that both the transmitted literature and recently discovered bamboo-slip manuscripts share the same record of a jail (*yuantu*) constructed on an isle of the North Sea. The fact that the OBI are concerned with slaves running away from *zhou* is suggestive in light of anecdotes about King Wu Ding of Shang finding Fu Yue on such an isle.

On the OBI, "Islet X" (*zhi* X 沚戜) is the name of a general and royal aide. The king at one point granted him land with thirty hamlets: "(The king) called on X *chen* Islet, and pledged as a gift thirty hamlets" (乎戜臣沚, 㞢册三十邑.) (*Heji* 707). Titles such as *bo* 伯, *hou* 侯, *gong* 公, and *zi* 子 are often found before personal names, signifying clan and polity connections, as well as connoting social ranks linked to marriage status, family generation, lineage membership, inherited position, performance in war, or, generally, marking a tribe's gradual political sophistication.²³ It appears that *zhi* serves a similar function in the name "Islet X" (*zhi* X 沚戜). Geographical terms were imbued with sociopolitical meaning, a process witnessed for the term *zhou* as well. The *zhou* were territories conferred to subjects by the Shang king; the *zhou chen* then are the servitors of such territories ("isle provinces"). They are of the same nature as *dian chen* ("suburb servitors") in OBI:

> (5) Testing the proposal of dispensing (it) from You city.
> . . . gather suburb servitors.
> Commercial goods imported, one.
> 貞叀自㞢邑
> . . . 奴奠臣. (甲橋刻辭 inscription on the back of the bridge)
> 貯入一. (甲橋刻辭 inscription on the back of the bridge)
>   (*Heji* 635 verso)
> (6) Order X to seek suburb servitors.
> 令弓希奠臣. (*Heji* 7239 recto)
> (7) Crack-making on a . . . *xu* day, X tests the proposal that
>   I . . . seek suburb servitors in . . .
> □戌卜, □, 貞余□希奠臣于□. (*Ying* 1806)

Judging from the relationship between "city, hamlet" (*yi* 邑) and "suburb servitors" (*dian chen*) in inscription #5, *dian* ("suburbs") were located outside the city walls. Chen Mengjia 陳夢家 claimed that *dian* in bronze inscriptions should be read as *dian* 甸, an administrative unit mentioned in the *Guoyu* 國語, "Zhou yu, shang" 周語上: "In the system of the former kings, the interior of the polity (consisted of) *dian* suburban tributaries" (先王之制, 邦內甸服).[24] Since *zhou chen* ("isle-province servitors") and *dian chen* ("suburb servitors") both fall under the jurisdiction of court officials, it appears that *zhou*—let us call them simply "provinces" now—were interposed between the royal capital and the *dian* suburbs. Up until the Zhou era, however, there was a lack of the strict geographical divisions seen in later conceptualizations of the Nine Provinces.

Exactly how large an area did the *zhou* mentioned in the oracle bones and bronze inscriptions encompass? We can only offer an estimate, but if a *zhou* was equivalent to an *yi* ("city, hamlet"), it should have an area between that of a *bi* 鄙 ("border region") and *dian* ("suburb"), equivalent to Chen Mengjia's description of the *situ* 四土 ("Four Lands") and *sifang* 四方 ("Four Quadrates") found within the limits of the kingdom.[25] The *Liji* 禮記 "Wang zhi" 王制 explains:[26]

> Beyond one thousand *li* (from the center), set up regional lords (*fang bo*) in such a way that five polities together make up a *shu* 屬 division, each *shu* with a *zhang* 長 head; ten polities together make up a *lian* 連 aggregation, each with a *shuai* 率 leader; thirty polities together make up a *zu* 卒 company, each with a *zheng* 正 regulator; 210 polities together make up a *zhou* 州 province, each with a *bo* 伯 elder.

千里之外設方伯, 五國以為屬, 屬有長; 十國以為連, 連有率; 三十國以為卒, 卒有正; 二百一十國以為州, 州有伯.

The *zhou bo* 州伯 in this text refers to the ruler of a province. Even though it is a post–Spring and Autumn title, it clearly derived from the Shang concept of *zhou*.

In the bronze inscriptions, *zhou* is equivalent to an *yi* 邑:

(8) (Of) Guo Bi's fields and of the hamlets, the three of Ke, Zhui (?), and Jia, and the two of Zhou and Hu . . .

鼒比田, 其邑競, 㭨, 甲三邑, 州, 瀘二邑 . . . (Guo Bi xu 鼒比盨, Jicheng 9.4466)[27]

(9) Bo Maifu then took those of the Shu Han, Zhong, and Zhou, named Jia and Ke, and their twenty men . . .

伯買父迺以厥戍漢, 中, 州曰叚, 曰𢼸, 厥人禺廿夫 . . . (Zhong yan 中甗, Jicheng 3.949)

(10) X Xing Hou's tributaries, with gifts of three types of servants: the people of Zhou, the people of Zhong, and the people of Yong . . .

𦔻邢侯服, 賜臣三品: 州人, 重人, 庸人 . . . (Rong zuo Zhou Gong gui 㦰作周公簋, Jicheng 8.4241)

According to Guo Moruo, the phrase X *xing hou fu* 𦔻邢侯服 in #10 means "continue Jing Hou's *interior tributaries*" (謂繼井侯之內服) along with the gifts to Xing Hou (aka Jing Hou) of three types of peoples—namely the Zhou, Zhong, and Yong peoples—indicates "tribal communities along the banks of the Wei River" (殆渭水沿岸之部落民族).[28] Inscription #9 names the Southern Yi 南夷 polities along the Han River: Shu Han 戍漢, Zhong 中, and Zhou 州. It is thus clear that, in these ancient inscriptions, the term *zhou* was used to name communities topographically linked by water systems. But while the earliest understandings of *zhou* may have referred to geographical features, it appears that, from the Shang down to the Zhou era, the term "isle servitors" (*zhou chen*) comes to refer to "Zhou peoples" (*zhou ren* 州人), with *zhou* in each case classified as a domestic tribute provider. This demonstrates that, during the Shang and Zhou, the concept of *zhou* gradually became that of an administrative unit. It is thus possible that these two terms, the "isle servitors" and "Zhou peoples," were connected geographically, the same basis on which the Nine Provinces in the "Yu gong" chapter was established.

It is noteworthy that the concept of *zhou* continued to evolve during the Western Zhou period, so that by the late Western Zhou there was already a Zhou Hall 州宮[29] and a Zhou Tower 州𥧤(就).[30] At this time, *zhou* had the emblems of a city-state, a temple and a capital. They had proto-cities, which were granted to the lords for their support. The *Shangshu dazhuan* 尚書大傳 states: "In antiquity, when the lords first received their land grants, they required lands for support: lords of one hundred *li* used thirty *li* (for their support), lords of seventy *li* used twenty *li* (for their support), and lords of fifty *li* used fifteen *li* (for their support)" (古者諸侯始受封, 必有采地: 百里諸侯以三十裡, 七十裡諸侯以二十裡, 五十裡諸侯以十五裡).[31] During the

Shang and Zhou eras, polities granted to non-heir sons (*shu bang* 庶邦), as described in the Da Yu *ding* 大盂鼎, first followed from the fact that "the former kings gave the people (fields) to set up border lands" (先王授民授 疆土). Therefore, the "isle servitors" (*zhou chen*) of the oracle bones, and the Zhou peoples (*zhou ren*) of the bronze inscriptions, refer to the hamlets and commoners granted by the royal house to the lords for their support. This explains why *zhou* lands were the objects of exchange in the Guo Bi *su* (#8) and the Rong zuo Zhou Gong *gui* (#10) inscriptions.

In its orthography, the graph for *zhou* 州 originally depicted land surrounded by water. People in the past used bodies of water as a way to delineate territory. At first just a general term for a geographical feature, this later became the origin of the Nine Provinces. This was the root meaning of *zhou* in the oracle bones. A vast quantity of data from prehistoric archaeological sites shows how natural land formations were used to delineate boundaries, reflecting a perhaps even more ancient way that humanity thought about geography. On this point, Shao Wangping 邵望平 presents strong archaeological evidence:[32]

> Ancient cultural regions are shaped by nature. But while each has its own core area, their boundaries were not clearly defined. The regions in-between are lively areas of interaction and cultural hybridity. The Nine Provinces described in the "Yu gong" basically follow along these lines.
>
> 古代文化區系是自然形成的，雖各有中心區域，卻無明確劃定的地界. 區系之間存在著相當機動的仲介地帶或仲介文化類型. "禹貢"所述九州的情況亦大體如此.

Examining the Origin of the Nine Provinces Model in the Shang Tribute System and Its Administration

Mentions of *zhou* on the oracle-bone and bronze inscriptions offer tantalizing hints of the antiquity of the Nine Provinces model. An examination of the Shang tribute system provides further evidence. The beginning of the newly discovered Bin Gong *xu* inscriptions prominently states: "Heaven commanded Yu to order the earth, following the mountains and digging the rivers, so as to divide up the land and set up the government" (天令禹 敷土, 隨山浚川, 乃差地設征).[33] This accords with the legend given in the

"Yu gong" preface: "Yu separated the Nine Provinces, following the mountains and digging the rivers, making each land responsible for providing tribute" (禹別九州, 隨山浚川, 任土作貢), proving that this was a popular belief during the Western Zhou era.³⁴ The institution of assigning tribute responsibility upon each land can be traced back to the Shang as well. The *Shijing* describes the Shang as a "one thousand *li* polity" (邦畿千里), referring to the expanse of land controlled by the royal house.³⁵ This expresses a clear worldview of the Shang as a state, with the Shang king controlling the lands outside the royal domain, that is, controlling the "Four Regions of Land Grants" (四封方) or "Four Lands" (四土) from the "Heavenly City Shang" (天邑商) or the "Central Land" (中土). The primary reason was to exact tributes from the outlying regions granted to the lords. The Shang administered their territory through a system of "lords" (*hou* 侯), "suburbs" (*dian* 甸), "landowners" (*nan* 男), "polities" (*bang* 邦), "support lands (for providing food)" (*cai* 采), and "frontier garrisons" (*wei* 衛); it is clear, from this, that the system of five *fu* (tributaries) and land-grants (*feng* 封) in the Western Zhou was simply an extension of the Shang's political organization.

The OBI indicates that the Shang already established a system of inner and outer *fu* tributaries, with a division of labor that betrays a sophisticated sociopolitical order. That the Zhou, after overthrowing the Shang, still demanded "homage to the king" (*zhong wang* 終王) through "annual tribute" (*sui gong* 歲貢) shows that they continued the Shang tribute system, though the number of *fu* tributaries was changed from four to five. The oracle bones include terms such as *nei yu shi* 內禦史 ("inner imperial archivist") and *nei yi* 內邑 ("inner city"), which reflect a strict division between inner and outer administration.³⁶ The graph for "outer, outside," *wai* 外, was written in a shortened form that looks similar to the graph *bu* 卜 ("crack-making") on the oracle bones:

> (11) Crack-making on a *renwu* day, Ze tested the proposal that there would be trouble in the outside and that on the inside here, it would not be favorable to proceed.
> 壬午卜 㚔 貞卜 (外) 有 希 (祟), 在茲入 (內) 出 不若. (*Heji* 2592)
>
> (12) Crack-making on a *jiayin* day, testing the proposal that there will be misfortune outside, rain.
> 甲寅貞在卜 (外) 有禍, 雨. (*Tunnan* 550)³⁷
>
> (13) Crack-making on a *xinsi* day, testing the proposal that it will not rain outside.
> 辛巳卜貞卜 (外) 不雨. (*Heji* 13004)

The graph for "inner, inside," *nei* 內, was shortened to *ru* 入 ("enter"):

> (14) Crack-making on a *xinyou* day, on the inside, on a *wu* day, there will be misfortune. 辛酉卜在入 (內) 戊有禍.
> (*Tunnan*, appendix 12)
> (15) Crack-making on a *guiyou* day, Chu tested the proposal that in ten days (something) would (occur) on the inside. 癸酉卜出貞旬在入 (內). (*Kyoto* 3008)[38]

Inscription #11 tests the proposal of whether there would be misfortune "on the outside" and unfavorable events "on the inside." The terms "on the inside" (*zai nei*) and "on the outside" (*zai wai*) refer to inner cities and outer cities (both *yi*) respectively. The reason the Shang were concerned about whether misfortune will befall these regions, is likely because of the impact this may have on the inner and outer tributaries (*fu*).

Titles for a variety of officials attached to these tributaries were also established during the Shang. According to the *Guoyu*, "Zhou yu, shang":[39]

> In the system of the former kings, the interior of the polity (consisted of) *suburban tributaries*. The outer regions of the polity (consisted of) lordly tributaries, as well the compliant tributaries of lords and frontier garrisons, the constrained tributaries of the Yi and Man peoples, and the wild tributaries of the Rong and Di peoples.
>
> 先王之制, 邦內甸服, 邦外侯服, 侯衛賓服, 夷蠻要服, 戎狄荒服.

The Shang kings distributed titles according to both official rank and the post's relative distance to the court. Lords protected the royal house and garrisoned the frontier. Moreover, they were responsible for paying tribute to the royal house, by conducting "day sacrifices, lunar rites, seasonal offerings, annual tributes, and homage to the king" (日祭, 月祀, 時享, 歲貢, 終王). The aim of these ritual activities was to ensure that provisions existed in case of emergency. Thus King Xiang of Zhou 周襄王 says in the *Guoyu*, "Zhou yu, zhong" 中:[40]

> Long ago, when the former kings controlled the whole world, they prescribed that a thousand square *li* would be the suburban tributaries. This was in order to provide for the rites to God on High (Shangdi), the [Spirits of] Mountains and Rivers, and

the Hundred Spirits; to satisfy the needs of the aristocratic lords and commoners; and to prepare against deprivation, in the event that [lords] do not submit to the court or other unforeseen disasters.

昔我先王之有天下也，規方千里以為甸服，以供上帝山川百神之祀，以備百姓兆民之用，以待不庭不虞之患。

Against the backdrop of Shang religious beliefs, instituting the aforementioned tributary system would have held a far greater significance than simply creating subservient officials to the Shang. By distributing responsibilities for "day sacrifices, lunar rites, seasonal offerings, and annual tributes" to their subjects, the Shang kings inspired loyalty toward the royal house and increased political cohesion. Participating in these sacrifices commemorated the Shang ancestors—they were the most important affairs of the states—and thereby acted as a mechanism for both ensuring social order and also maintaining support for the monarchy.

The oracle bones frequently document the Shang kings accepting tribute. In some cases, the inscriptions specify that the animals or human victims were to be used for sacrifices; in other cases, the kings have sent people off to hunt or work in the fields. For example:

> (16) Crack-making on a *gengzi* day, testing the proposal that the shepherds bring in Qiang slaves for the *beng* (gate) sacrifice.
> 庚子卜貞：牧氏 (致) 羌，於祊用。(*Heji* 281)
> (17) Crack-making on a *renyin* day, testing the proposal that the Xing region people will bring Qiang slaves for sacrifice to ancestors, beginning with the first Jia and ending with last Yi.
> 壬寅卜貞：興方氏 (致) 羌，用自上甲至下乙。(*Heji* 270 recto)
> (18) Crack-making on a *dingmao* day, order that people be arrested and brought forward, and for hunting in X. The eleventh month.
> 丁卯卜，令執氏 (致) 人，田于㴼。十一月。(*Heji* 1022 乙)
> (19) Crack-making on a *wuzhen* day, the king requested people brought forward, and the hunting of wild animals, for favor from the X ancestral altar.
> 戊辰卜，王乞氏 (致) 人，獸若于酺示。(*Heji* 1023)

The human victims used in sacrifices were mostly prisoners of war taken from outside the polity or from invading Qiang peoples. According to Qiu Xigui 裘錫圭, the "shepherds" (*mu* 牧) in #16 were officials sent by the Shang king to various regions outside the capital to carry out animal husbandry. Qiu argues that in ancient texts, the leader of the lords to each of the Nine Provinces was titled "shepherd."[41] Although this was likely a late usage, it is clear that, already during the Shang, the idea prevailed that "those of the suburban tributaries conduct (day) sacrifices, those of lordly tributaries perform (lunar) rites" (甸服者祭, 侯服者祀).[42]

Oracle-bone records such as these have stimulated research into the history of pre-Qin tribute and taxation systems, with the work of Wang Guimin 王貴民 in the 1980s especially representative. Compiling relevant data and conducting a thorough analysis, Wang discussed the seven types of tribute seen during the Shang, their quantities, and regional origins, making key observations.[43] Outlining how tribute was sent from various regions to the Shang king, as reflected in the OBI, brings us a step closer to understanding the origins of the Nine Provinces concept. The following evidence helps us to better understand this process.

There was a strict division of clan labor involved in the Shang kings' receipt of tribute. It was a complicated procedure. Tribute was not received directly at the royal capital, but first stored elsewhere. Most tribute first arrived in a suburb, such as a *dian* 奠, and later was brought into the capital. Item amounts, places of origin, and the names of handlers to the tribute were all documented. Oracle-bone records of this nature were often incised onto the socket of the scapula or the bridge of the plastron and signified with the graph 氐. Yu Xingwu 于省吾 explains that this graph is *di* 氐, read as *di* 厎, meaning "to bring forward" (*zhi* 致).[44]

Records of tribute received into *dian* suburbs:

(20) Into the *dian* suburb came thirty.
奠來三十. (*Heji* 9613 verso)
(21) Into the *dian* suburb came [tribute]. Ning.
奠來.宁. (*Heji* 4464 verso)
(22) At the *dian* suburb altar, ten piles and one. Yong.
奠示十屯又一. 永. (*Heji* 6527 socket)

Records of tribute into *yi* hamlets and cities:

(23) On a *bingyin* day, at the city altar, ten piles. (Lady) Fu Xiao.

丙寅邑示十屯. 小帚. (*Heji* 1534 socket)

(24) Crack-making on a *xinchou* day, Gu tests the proposal of bringing forward (tribute) to the city.
辛丑卜古貞邑氏(致). (*Heji* 9057 recto)

(25) To the city, seven captured rhinos.
邑執兕七. (*Heji* 10437)

Distribution of tribute was only decided after such inventories were sorted. This would have relieved the logistical pressures of storing and transporting tribute in the royal domain. Furthermore, having the tribute dispersed in this manner could anticipate any urgent needs that might arise due to warfare. Thus the OBI reveal that the Shang kings divined which of these two locations to select, for the import of tribute, or also if it should be sent directly out to the "border region" (*bi* 冋, read *bi* 鄙). For example:

(26) Crack-making on a *guisi* day, Wei tested the proposal that it be brought by road to the army camp, reaching the city. A second report. . . . testing the proposal that it be brought by road to the army camp, reaching the city.
癸巳卜韋貞: 行氏 (致) 有師暨邑. 二告.
. . . 貞: 行弗其氏 (致) [有師] 暨邑. (*Heji* 8985 recto)

(27) -*Hai* day . . . the king tested the proposal that X does not bring it to Yong, reaching the *dian* suburbs. The fourth month.
亥 . . . 王貞𠬝 弗其氏 (致) 雍暨奠. 四月. (*Heji* 8988)

(28) X . . . brings forward . . . to the border region.
𢀛 . . . 氏 (致) . . . 冋 (鄙) . . . (*Heji* 8989)

(29) Crack-making on an *yimao* day, Bin tests the proposal, saying "bring it to the city." 乙卯卜賓貞曰氏 (致) 乃邑.
(*Heji* 8986 verso)

In inscription #26, the Shang king queries whether the tribute goods should be sent to the army and capital. In #27, the question is whether to send them to Yong city and the *dian* suburbs. Inscription #28 asks if person X should send the tribute goods to the border region. These records suggest that the Shang implemented a tribute system that employed reliable and capable auxiliary teams in these locations. With such a division of labor, it would be inconceivable that while "two parts out of three in the world submitted to and served the Yin," all the peoples among the "Four Quadrates" would really come to court to pay tribute.

A key element of the Shang kings' organizational strategy, as evident from the previous discussion, was the development of transportation routes. The *Shiji* 史記, "Xia benji" 夏本紀, claims that Yu "opened up the Nine Provinces by connecting the nine roads" (以開九州, 通九道).[45] Inscription #26 offers a clear example of this, as tribute is "brought by road" (*xing di* 行氏). Besides the seven types of regional goods delineated by Wang Guimin, it is important to note that tribute also included critical transportation equipment, such as horses, chariots, and boats:

(30) . . . boat imports.
. . . 舟入. (*Heji* 17012 verso)
(31) X brings forward horses from Xie. The twelfth month. Yun brings forward three chariots.
牂 氏(致)馬自薛. 十二月. 允氏 (致) 三丙 (輛). (*Heji* 8984)
(32) Ning arrives with horses and two chariots; on the *xinsi* day it rained; bring forward . . . Lin.
宁征馬二丙 (輛), 辛巳雨, 氏 (致) □□□ (鄰). (*Heji* 21777)

It is important to note that the Shang tribute items largely correspond to those mentioned in the "Yu gong" chapter of the *Shangshu*. Furthermore, the import of horses, chariots, and boats as tribute suggests that the Shang's influence already was far-reaching, extending to the grasslands in the north, and the lakes and rivers in the south. The Shang could not have controlled the "Four Quadrates" without an extensive road system, including relay stations and hostels.[46]

The Nine Provinces from the Perspective of the Western Zhou Tribute System of *Ting Fang* 庭方 ("Regional Peoples Paying Court")

An analysis of Western Zhou institutions reveals that the concept of Nine Provinces from the early Zhou developed directly out of Shang antecedents. *Guoyu*, "Zhou yu, shang," relates how King Mu of Zhou 周穆王 failed to heed Lord Mou Fu of Zhai's 祭公謀父 remonstration against attacking the Quanrong 犬戎 tribe, leading to "(the Quanrong) from these wild tributaries not arriving (at court with their tribute)" (自是荒服者不至).⁴⁷ On the bronze inscriptions, we find the phrase "the regional peoples that do not pay court" (*bu ting fang* 不廷方), in which the graph *ting* 廷 is a verbalized *ting* 庭 ("court"). The *Shijing* ode "Chang Wu" 常武 exclaims: "In the Four Quadrates all is at peace; The peoples of Xu come in homage" (四方既平，徐方來庭).⁴⁸ The Mao 毛 commentary believes this refers to "coming to the royal court" (來王庭也).⁴⁹ The Mao Gong *ding* 毛公鼎 reads:⁵⁰

> The Greatly Manifest Wen and Wu, whom Brilliant Heaven extended and sustained in agreement with their virtue, possessed our Zhou and shouldered the responsibility of receiving the Great Mandate. They led and took in those regional peoples who did not come to court, with all (now) paying tribute to the radiant glory of Wen and Wu.
>
> 丕顯文武，皇天引厭，厥德配我有周，膺受大命，率懷不廷方，亡不閈于文武耿光. (*Jicheng* 2841)

The problem of "regional peoples who do not come to court" (不廷方) is seen on the oracle bones as well, with the query: "Do the lords not bring forward (tribute)?" (侯弗致, *Heji* 8990). These statements make it clear that, during the Shang and Zhou, visits to the court with tribute were tests of loyalty toward the royal house and expressions of subservience, making them extremely important in the eyes of the Shang and Zhou kings. Recently, a startling discovery was made of twenty-seven Shan 單 lineage bronze vessels, buried as a horde in Yangjia Village 楊家村, Majia Township 馬家鎮, Mei County 眉縣, Shaanxi 陝西. A line from an inscription on the Lai *pan* 逨盤 reads:⁵¹

> The Di Region peoples did not give offerings, (yet) with this action, King Cheng settled the ten thousand states in the Four Territories. Oh! My Brilliant High Ancestor, New Chamber the Second, was able to make his heart both deep and luminous, weakening those far away and empowering those nearby; he joined King Kang as an aide, annexing and drawing in those who did not come to court.⁵²
>
> 方狄不享，用奠四國萬邦. 雩朕皇高祖新室仲，克幽明厥心，柔遠能邇，會紹康王，方懷不廷.

The *Shijing* "Yin wu" 殷武 ode has, moreover: "Long ago there was Tang the Victorious; Of these, Di and Qiang, none dared not to make offering to him; None dare not to acknowledge him their king, saying 'Shang forever!'" (昔有成湯, 自彼氐, 羌, 莫敢不來享, 莫敢不來王, 曰商是常 (尚)).[53] The Di 狄 peoples mentioned in the Lai *pan* must refer to the Qiang Di 羌狄, with the line perhaps having a similar meaning as what is found in the "Yin wu" ode, when it talks about how, "of these, Di and Qiang, none dared not to make offering to him."[54] The Lai *pan* phrase, of "annexing and drawing in those who did not come to court" (方懷不廷), likewise recalls the Mao Gong *ding* statement that "they led and took in those regional states that did not come to court" (率懷不廷方). In the Five Tributaries system, the "offerings" (*xiang* 享) made by Di peoples represent the annual tribute to the Zhou king, which as one of the "wild tributaries" surrounding the Zhou royal house it was required to present.

As the Bin Gong *xu* states: "To give rise to subservience, one must be steeped in virtue" (乍臣厥沬唯德), thereby "making pliable all under Heaven" (憂 (柔) 在天下).[55] Yet regardless of how well a ruler "cultivates his civilized virtue" (*xiu wende* 修文德), he might still encounter opposition from other peoples who refuse to pay court and offer tribute. Thus, as the following bronze inscriptions record, Zhou King Li 厲 carried out wars against the southeastern Huai 淮 peoples, because they refused to pay tribute. Xi Jia *pan* 兮甲盤:[56]

> The king commanded Jia: "Tax and regulate the stored [goods] of the Four Quadrates of Chengzhou, all the way to the Southern Huai Yi people. For a long time, the Huai Yi have been people who paid us in silk. They shall not dare not to send out their silk, their stored [goods], their proffered people, or their commercial goods. They shall not dare not to approach the military outposts and the markets [with these things]. If they dare not to employ this command, then we will forthwith punish them and launch a coercive campaign."
>
> 王令甲政 (征) 嗣 (司) 成週四方責 (積), 至於南淮夷. 淮夷舊我帛晦人, 毋敢不出其帛, 其責 (積). 其進人, 其貯, 毋敢不即次, 即市. 敢不用命則刑, 剪伐. (*Jicheng* 10174)

Shi Huan *gui* 師寰簋:

The king agreeing (to the decree) said: "Master Huan, So! The Huai Yi, who have been our servants who paid in silk for a long time, now dare to rally their masses to not provide stored goods for our eastern territories. Now I initially ordered you to lead the army . . . to attack the Huai Yi."

王若曰: 師寰, 㢦! 淮夷繇 (舊) 我帛晦 (賄) 臣, 今敢博厥眾叚, 弗速 (積) 我東國. 今余肇令女 (汝) 率師 . . . 征淮夷. (*Jicheng* 8 4314)

Ju Fu *xu* 駒父盨[57]

Nanzhong Bang Fu commanded Ju fu: "Attain [the cooperation of] the lords of the south. Lead Gao Fu to visit the Yi peoples of Huai River and to see what they collect, what they contribute. Be cautious with regard to the Yi peoples' customs. May nobody then even dare not to respect and fear the king's command."

南仲邦父命駒父即南者 (諸) 侯, 率高父見南淮夷, 厥獻厥服. 我乃至於淮, 小大邦亡(無) 敢不具逆王命 . . . (*Jicheng* 9·4464)

In the phrase *bo hui chen* 帛賄臣 ("servants who paid in silk"), *bo* 帛 refers to a tax, while *hui* 賄 is the presentation of goods (later seen as a kind of bribe). This implies that, by the end of the Shang and the beginning of the Zhou, a system of taxes was already in place, where the "Yu gong" preface notes "each land was responsible for providing tribute" (任土作貢). Phrases like "their contributions and their tributes" (厥獻厥服) and "the collected goods of the Four Quadrates of Chengzhou" (成週四方積) refer to the clothing and local products levied from the suburban tributaries. If they went against the Zhou king's command, and "dared to not issue their silk or their collected goods" (敢不出其帛, 其積), then they were punished and violently coerced to do so (則刑, 剪伐).

On the Zhou tribute system, consider as well the following accounts from our transmitted corpus of texts. The *Guoyu*, "Lu yu, xia 魯語下," for instance claims: "Long ago, when King Wu conquered the Shang, he opened roads to the Nine Yi and the Eight Man peoples, so that each region paid tribute and no one forgot their duties. Thereupon the Xiaozhen clan contributed thorn arrows and stone crossbows" (昔武王克商, 通道於九夷八蠻, 使各以方賄來貢, 使無忘職業, 於是肅慎氏貢楛矢, 石弩).[58] In *Zuo zhuan* 左傳, Lord Zhao 昭公 year 13, this system is described clearly: "Long ago, the Son of Heaven arranged the tributes, ranking them from light to heavy. The (higher) the rank of respect (to be paid), the heavier the weight of the tribute: this constituted the Zhou system, so that those bearing the heaviest tributes were the suburban tributaries" (昔天子班貢, 輕重以列. 列尊貢重, 周之制也, 卑而貢重者, 甸服也). The Huai Yi lands must have belonged to the suburban tributaries, thus they bore a heavy burden in regard to tribute. Resistance by the southern and eastern Huai Yi tribes to this onerous duty provoked nearly every Zhou king to take up arms during the Western Zhou. This not only reveals the economic benefits at stake but also clarifies the relationships between conqueror and subjects. Even more importantly, it demonstrates the multilateral approach to governing adopted by the Zhou royal house. It is an approach founded upon an envisioned sociopolitical geography that they shared with the Shang, regardless of the animosity felt between the Shang and Zhou peoples through generations of conflict. Thus, we know that the concept of the Nine Provinces had deep roots.

Comparison of Province Names in "Yu gong" to Place Names Mentioned in Oracle-Bone and Bronze Inscriptions

Yan Province 兗州

From the oracle-bone and bronze inscriptions, we do not only witness early conceptualizations of *zhou* 州 ("isles, isle provinces, provinces") but also the origins of a tribute system, which hint indirectly at the Nine Provinces model. In fact, even more direct correlations may be found between province names in these paleographic sources, and those given to the Nine Provinces, as listed in the "Yu gong" chapter of the *Shangshu* and on Warring States period bamboo-slip manuscripts.

The earliest unearthed bamboo-slip manuscript with parallels to the "Yu gong" chapter is the Warring States–period *Rong Cheng shi* 容成氏 manuscript held by the Shanghai Museum.[59] Part of this manuscript narrates Yu's division of the world into the Nine Provinces, naming the various provinces. While some of the names differ, many are the same as those in the "Yu gong." Place names from the even more ancient oracle-bone and bronze inscriptions, meanwhile, corroborate the "Twelve Provinces" (*shi you er zhou* 十有二州) mentioned in the *Shangshu*, "Shun dian 舜典," a division allegedly prior to that of the Nine Provinces.[60] Before the full articulation of the Nine Provinces model in "Yu gong," knowledge of Xia history was transmitted through various scribal records and oral traditions. This historical consciousness was passed on through the Shang and Zhou to appear in later sources. Yan Province 兗州 serves as an example.

In the *Rong Cheng shi*, the following lines appear:⁶¹

He banked up the Ming Du (that is, Mengzhu) Marsh and cut beds for the nine rivers; hence, Jia Province and Xu Province could begin to be inhabited.⁶²

吕 波(陂)明者 (都) 之澤, 決九河之淺 (阻), 於是虖 (乎) 夾州, 澮 (徐) 州訇 (始) 可尻 (處). (Slips #24–25)

Li Ling explains that, "although the 'Yu gong' does not include a Jia Province 夾州 per se, since it was located as next to Xu Province 徐州 (in this anecdote), it could correspond to the Yan Province 兗州 in the 'Yu Gong' and in other received sources."⁶³ Why would Yan Province be called Jia Province on Chu bamboo-slip manuscripts? One possibility is that this difference stems from a confusion between the written form of graphs used to spell the province's ancient name. The graph *jia* 夾 (of Jia Province) looks similar to the complex form of *yin* 寅 (寅), as it was written on late period OBI.⁶⁴ Previously, the orthography of *jia* 夾 was thought to derive from the element 含豸, when in fact it is an alteration of *yin* 寅 and should share in the latter's pronunciation. Just as the word *yan* 奐 (燕) from the OBI takes *yin* as its phonetic, so too should the word *jia* 奐 (夾).⁶⁵ The ancient pronunciation of *yan* 兗 according to the *fanqie* system was "*yu* initial in the *yuan* category of finals" 余母元部 [*r-ən] and *yin* 寅 was "*yu* initial in the *zhen* category of finals" 餘母真部 [*r-in]. The pronunciations of these two words were similar enough that they could be loaned for one another. Moreover, the orthography of *yin* 因 and *jia* 夾 on the oracle bones is also similar. In fact, for the bone inscription now read as "the wind of Southern Regions is called Yin" (南方曰因風), scholars at first read *yin* as *jia* 夾 instead; only later did Qiu Xigui insist on reading it as *yin*.⁶⁶ As this debate suggests, we cannot eliminate another possibility, namely that there was confusion between *yin* 因 and *yan* 兗 as well. Thus, in Chu manuscripts like *Rong Cheng shi*, Jia Province was most likely just a way of writing Yan Province.⁶⁷

One of the hunting grounds mentioned on oracle bones is also called Yan. The graph writing this name is 沇, whose orthography entails a 允 element, with water elements of 〣 or 八 placed above and to the side of it. Yu Xingwu argues that this graph eventually evolved such that the water element was on the left and the phonetic on the right. He notes that *yan* 沇 in transmitted texts and on Han steles is written also as 兗 or 兖, with the elements 公 and 兖 at times interchanged as well, due to phonetic similarity. Yu further notes that the names of provinces in the "Yu gong" written in late Zhou times can be corroborated by OBI and points out that Yan Province derived its name from the Yan River 沇水.[68] The Yan 沇 lands mentioned on the oracle bones were one of the Shang's primary hunting grounds, especially in the Lin Xin 廪辛 (possibly the twenty-third Shang king) inscriptions:

> (33) The king may set up Yan and Li. The king went to the east. A tiger emerged and he caught it.
> 王其埶沇迺麓, 王於東立 (涖), 虎出, 擒. (*Heji* 28799)
> (34) On the next *wu* day, the king shall hunt in Yan without misfortune. He will make a capture.
> 翌日戊王叀沇田, 亡災, 擒. (*Heji* 29243)
> (35) Shall shoot deer in Yan, no cause for regret.
> 叀沇鹿射, 弗悔. (*Heji* 28353)
> (36) The king shall hunt in Yan without misfortune.
> 王沇叀田亡災. (*Tunnan* 4451)
> (37) Shall it be the shepherd of Yan.
> 叀沇牧. (*Tunnan* 2191)

The *Zhou li*, "Zhi fang shi," 職方氏 claims: "East of the River is called Yan Province" (河東曰兗州).[69] Yan Province was east of Ji Province 冀州, situated in the eastern section of the Shang capital near Jining 濟寧, which is the western part of modern Shandong. The phrase "the king went to the east" (王於東涖) in #33 implies that the Shang king went hunting in Yan, arriving in the east. The "Yu gong" says: "The Ji (River) and Yellow River make up Yan Province" (濟河惟兗州). It later describes how Yu "followed the Yan River. Flowing eastward it becomes the Ji, which enters the Yellow River. It then spills into the Ying, and to the east emerges north of Taoqiu. Yet eastward still, it reaches He, then Wen to the northeast, until joining the ocean even further northeast" (導沇水, 東流為濟, 入於河, 溢為滎, 東出於陶邱北, 又東至於荷, 又東北於汶, 又北東入於海).[70] The oracle bones mention other places in the proximity of Yan, including Wu 牢 (*Heji* 29248), You 斿 (*Heji* 28799), Xin 阞 (*Tunnan* 2191), Mu 穆 (*Heji* 4451), and X 虞 (*Heji* 41563), among others, which we may suppose were hunting grounds near the royal capital. Since this placement for hunting grounds makes sense in terms of the historical geography of the Shang, and these descriptions all accord with our received sources, Yu Xingwu's analysis is unassailable.

Ju Province 莒州

In the *Rong Cheng shi*, a Ju Province 䣄 (莒) 州 is listed immediately after Qing Province 競 (青) 州. This latter name appears in the Nine Provinces model from "Yu Gong," but Ju Province is not mentioned there. It was, however, a part of the earlier Twelve Provinces from the "Shun dian." According to the *Erya* 爾雅, "Shi di" 釋地, "Qi is called Ju Province" (齊曰營州), to which Guo Pu 郭璞 comments: "(This is) from Dai east to the ocean" (自岱東至海).[71] The geographical region Guo describes for Ju Province is essentially the same as that for Qing Province in "Yu gong," and it seems as if the two were combined together in the Nine Provinces model.

Bronze inscriptions record a place named Ju, which was located near modern-day Ju County 莒縣 in Shandong 山東. In his annotations of the *Rong Cheng shi*, Li Ling explains:[72]

> The inscriptions on Spring and Autumn–period Ju polity bronze vessels refer to their own state as 䣄 [i.e., the same character found in the *Rong Cheng shi*]. Ju's capital was located along the Yi River. Since "Yu gong" does not record a Ju Province, I suspect that this refers to the lands around this Ju polity. Note: the two provinces *both* seem to be in the region of Qi and Ju.

> 䣄州春秋莒國銅器以'䣄'自稱其國名. 莒國之域在沂水一帶. "禹貢"無莒州, 疑簡文'莒州'即莒國一帶. 案: 二州似在古齊, 莒之地.

The *Rong Cheng shi* reads:[73]

> Yu cut a river bed to link the Huai and Yi, so that they could flow East to the sea; hence, Jing Province and Ju Province could begin to be inhabited.

> 垂(禹)迵 (通) 淮與忻 (沂), 東忒 (注) 之海, 於是 . . . 启 (乎) 競州, 䣄 (莒) 州始可處也. (Slip #25)

The word *ju* 莒, in the name Ju Province, was a loan for an ancient metal called *lü* 鋁 ("aluminum"), seen on OBI and bronze inscriptions in the phrase "yellow aluminum" (*huang ju* [*lü*] 黃鑘 [鋁]). Consider, for example:

> (38) Crack-making on a *dinghai* day, Da . . . may cast yellow aluminum. . . . making a *pan* vessel shall benefit . . .

Formation of the "Nine Provinces" | 111

丁亥卜大... 其鑄黃呂(鋁)... 乍凡利 **重** ... (*Heji* 29687)
(39) The king may cast yellow aluminum, (for the) suburb covenant; It shall be beneficial to pray today on the *yi* day.
王其鑄黃呂(鋁), 奠盟, **重**今日乙奉利. (*Ying* 2567)
(40) I select those auspicious metals and yellow aluminum.
余擇其吉金黃鏞(鋁). (Zeng Bo X *fu* 曾伯霥簠, *Jicheng* 9·4631)

From the preceding examples, it appears that the graph *lü* 鏞 (鋁) was pronounced the same as *ju* on bronze inscriptions. Both it and the graph 薦 found in *Rong Cheng shi* were ancient forms for the word *ju* 莒. In bronze inscriptions from the Western Zhou, Spring and Autumn, and Warring States periods, the polity of Ju was written variously with the graphs 薦, 鄩, and 薦. For example:

(41) Ping, the Zhongzi (second son) of Ju (polity) Shu (younger) [A proper name, with titles].
薦(莒)叔之仲子平. (Ju Shu zhi Zhongzi Ping *zhong* 薦叔之仲子平鐘 *Jicheng* 1·172)
(42) Xi, the Xiaozi (youngest son) of the Lord of Ju, your filial descendant Buju. 鄩(莒)侯小子斨(析), 乃孝孫不巨. (Ju Hou Xiaozi *gui* 鄩侯少子簋 *Jicheng* 8·4152)
(43) Going to Lord Ling's court, Geng led two hundred boats entering Ju following the Yellow River.
於靈公之壬 (廷), 庚率二百乘舟入鄩(莒) 從河. (Geng *hu* 庚壺 *Jicheng* 15·9733)

Since the 1950s, large amounts of late Dawenkou 大汶口 period pottery with incised signs have been unearthed in Shandong, especially along the Yi River 沂水, south of Ju County as far as Zhucheng County 諸城縣.[74] By at least the Xia era, this region had a relatively dense population, which speaks to the possible antiquity of the Ju polity. Sun Yabing 孫亞冰 and Lin Huan 林歡 have compiled over fifty entries for "the names of places, peoples, and clan signs" relative to this geographical area in the OBI.[75] These records show how the Shang were "carrying in" (*yi* 以), "extracting" (*qu* 取), "contributing" (*gong* 共), "importing" (*ru* 入), and "bringing in" (*lai* 來) goods, while naming a myriad different clans, frontier lords, suburban shepherds, and other dependencies, in addition to all the officials employed. This proves that a sophisticated tribute system was already in place here by the Shang.

Transmitted historical works note that King Wu of Zhou 周武王 gave Ju as a land grant to the descendants of Shao Hao 少昊, surnamed Ying 盈

(嬴).⁷⁶ On the Spring and Autumn–era Ju bronze vessels discovered around 1975, including the Ju Shu zhi Zhongzi Ping *zhong* (bell) inscription in #41, we find the line: "Glistening and harmonious, (the bells) resound in the Eastern Xia"(戠(喊)戠(喊)雍雍, 聞于夏東).⁷⁷ The inscription thus refers to its lands as being the "Eastern Xia."⁷⁸ This corresponds to our transmitted texts, which claim: "Even though Ju was a small polity, it was a bastion for the Eastern Yi peoples that was afflicted but not destroyed by Jing and Wu" (莒雖小國, 東夷之雄者也, 其為患不滅荊吳). This reflects how Ju developed into a strong eastern polity and explains why it was used as the name for an eastern province.

Bing Province 並州

The *Rong Cheng shi* bamboo-slip manuscript mentions a Luo Province 蓏州:

> Yu then cut beds to link the Lou and Yi Rivers so they could flow east to the sea; hence, Luo Province could begin to be inhabited.

> 禹乃通蔞與湯, 東弢 (注) 之海, 於是虖 (乎) 蓏州始可處也. (Slips #25–26)

Li Ling noted that the Luo Province is not found in the "Yu gong." He suspected it was in fact the Bing Province described in the *Zhou li*, "Xia guan, Zhi fangshi" 夏官, 職方氏: "Its rivers include the Huchi and Ouyi, its lakes include the Lai and Yi" (其川虖池, 嘔夷, 其浸淶, 易). He notes that the ancient graphs for *bing* 並 and *luo* 蓏 looked similar and could be confused.⁷⁹ In the OBI, the word *bing* is written with the graph 𢓃, representing two people standing side by side. Should this graph be doubled, it could be confused easily with the graph for *luo*.⁸⁰

Furthermore, if we consider the divisions of the Nine Provinces, then Bing Province should be located in the modern-day Shanxi-Hebei region. To elucidate the "Shun dian" line of "initiating twelve provinces, granting the territory of twelve mountains, dredging out rivers" (肇十有二州, 封十有二山, 浚川), Kong Yingda 孔穎達 in *Shangshu zhengyi* 尚書正義 writes: "The word *zhao* (肇) means 'to initiate.' After Yu controlled the waters, Shun split You Province and Bing Province from Ji Province. He (also) split Ju Province from Qing Province, first establishing the Twelve Provinces" (肇, 始也. 禹治水之後, 舜分冀州為幽州, 並州, 分青州為營州, 始置十二州).⁸¹ Bing Province is not mentioned in the "Yu gong" or the *Erya*, but it is found in the *Zhou li*, "Zhi fang shi," which records: "Northern Zheng is Bing Province. Its mountain district is called Heng Mountain" (正北曰並州, 其山

鎮曰恒山).⁸² Zheng was a Zhou settlement taken over from the Shang. The graph for *bing* on Shang paleographic sources can be written as 𠨍, which was the same as the graph 竝 (竝), only differing in representing the two bodies as oriented sideways or straight forward. The Bing people were in intimate contact with the Shang kings. Not only did they often participate in the king's activities, they were responsible for submitting tribute to the royal house as well. The word *bing* appears as a place name and a name for peoples, for instance:

> (44) Crack-making on a *jihai* day, testing the proposal that the king may go hunting in Bing without misfortune.
> 己亥卜貞: 王其田並, 亡災. (*Heji* 33570)
> (45) On a *shen* day, in Bing.
> 申, 在並. (*Heji* 8137 verso)
> (46) Bi announced. . . . in Bing.
> 㠯告 . . . 在並. (*Heji* 33174)
> (47) Crack-making, you tested the proposal that. . . . together in Bing . . .
> 卜在攸貞 . . . 比在並 . . . (*Heji* 37519)
> (48) Bing imported ten (items).
> 並入十. (*Heji* 9247, 9248, 17085)
> (49) Testing the proposal that Bing may not bring them in, and that we will have to extract them.
> 貞並弗其氐 (致), 有取. (*Heji* 9105 verso)

Inscriptions on Shang bronze vessels record that the Bing people intermarried with the Ji 已, Shan 單, X 亻, Mu 木, and Qian 开 peoples, suggesting that they were powerful at this time (see for example *Jicheng* 3326, 7142, 8180, and 8182).

Peng Bangjiong's 彭邦炯 detailed research into the Bing clan in Shang bronze inscriptions has already demonstrated that the Bing lands on oracle bones were connected to the Bing peoples mentioned on a Shang *ge*-halberd unearthed from Shilou 石樓 in Shanxi 山西.⁸³ He likewise ties them to the Bing Province mentioned in transmitted texts. He notes that a nickname given for Taiyuan is Bing and that, previously, it was thought that this was because (Taiyuan) was in the administrative jurisdiction of Bing Province. In fact, this name, Bing Province, likely connects to the activities of the Bing peoples here during the Shang.⁸⁴ The discovery of Bing weapons dating to the Shang period is no coincidence. Peng's argument that the origin of Bing Province is certainly connected to the Bing people is correct.

Conclusion

In the 2003 issue of *Jiu zhou* 九州, the famous *Shangshu* scholar Liu Qiyu 劉起釪 discussed the origin of the Nine Provinces and the date of "Yu gong," amassing archaeological evidence to make his case. He concludes that we can now agree that the concept of Nine Provinces originated during the Xia, and that the "Yu gong" was drafted by hands of Shang scribes. He adds that the hypothesis of a late date of origin, however, still pertains to the final edition of the "Yu gong," which was edited by early Zhou scribes.[85] The recently discovered Bin Gong *xu* inscription, and the *Rong Cheng shi* Chu bamboo-slip manuscript, both refer to the Nine Provinces. This confirms that "Yu gong" was composed at least by the early Zhou period. Even though the Shang oracle bones do not provide the same amount of details that we find in the "Yu gong"—a much longer narrative text—they do reveal traces of the terminology and model given in the "Yu gong," the tribute listings and province names being prime examples. Both the paleographic sources and the "Yu gong" chapter of the *Shangshu* embody a geopolitical ideology that saw the power of the king unifying all of the realm, and that ideology was shared throughout the Three Dynasties (Xia, Shang, and Zhou). Thus the "Yu gong" proclaims: "The Nine Provinces eventually were put under the same order, with the four areas along the rivers made habitable. The nine mountains were cleared for travel and the nine rivers cleaned up to their sources. The nine marshes were well banked, and the four seas joined together" (九州攸同，四隩既宅．九山刊旅，九川滌源．九澤既陂，四海會同).[86] Despite the historical vicissitudes of dynastic change, this ancient geopolitical ideology remained constant in its core assumptions. Regardless of how the precise boundaries to the Nine Provinces may have changed in their conceptualization, it is a framework from which the Chinese people have never departed. Thus the He *zun* 何尊 states: "I shall reside here in the Central Kingdom" (余其宅茲中國)![87]

Notes

1. Kong Anguo 孔安國 (Han), Kong Yingda 孔穎達 (Tang), *Shangshu zhengyi* 尚書正義 (Shanghai: Shanghai guji, 2007), 6.189–256 ("Yu gong" 禹貢).

2. Li Ling 李零, "Zhongguo gudai dili da shiye 中國古代地理大視野," in *Jiu zhou* 九州 [1st series], ed. Tang Xiaofeng 唐曉峰 and Li Ling 李零 (Beijing: Zhongguo huanjing kexue, 1997), 5–18.

3. Xu Shen 許慎 (Han), Duan Yucai 段玉裁 (Qing), *Shuowen jiezi zhu* 說文解字注 (Nanjing: Fenghuang 2007), 989–990 (chap. 11, xia 下, 川部).

4. Mao Heng 毛亨 (Han), Zheng Xuan 鄭玄 (Han), Kong Yingda 孔穎達 (Tang), *Mao shi zhengyi* 毛詩正義, *Shisanjing zhushu* 十三經注疏 (Beijing: Beijing daxue, 2000), 16.1235 ("Wen Wang you sheng" 文王有聲). By comparison, Arthur Waley has "in the course made for it by Yu, Meeting-place for all the peoples." Arthur Waley, *The Book of Songs: [The Ancient Chinese Classic of Poetry]*, ed. Joseph Roe Allen, 1st ed. (New York: Grove Press, 1996), 242, ode no. 244.

5. He Yan 何晏 (Wei), Xing Bing 邢昺 (Song), *Lunyu zhushu* 論語註疏, *Shisanjing zhushu* 十三經注疏 (Beijing: Beijing daxue, 2000), 8.119 ("Tai Bo" 泰伯).

6. Waley and Allen, *Book of Songs*, 320, ode no. 303. Correspondence to "Nine Holdings" added.

7. *Mao shi zhengyi*, *Shisanjing zhushu* (Beijing: Beijing daxue, 2000), 20.1700 ("Xuan niao" 玄鳥).

8. Waley and Allen, *Book of Songs*, 321–322, ode no. 304. Correspondence to "Nine Encirclements" and "Nine Holdings" added.

9. *Mao shi zhengyi*, *Shisanjing zhushu* (Beijing: Beijing daxue, 2000), 20.1712 ("Chang fa" 長發).

10. Waley and Allen, *Book of Songs*, 320, ode no. 304, adapted.

11. Zhongguo shehui kexue kaogu yanjiusuo 中國社會科學院考古研究所, ed., *Yin Zhou jinwen jicheng* 殷周金文集成, 18 vols. (Beijing: Zhonghua, 1987–1994), #272–285. Hereafter *Jicheng*, followed by the number of the inscription. See also: Constance A. Cook and Paul R. Goldin, eds., *A Source Book of Ancient Chinese Bronze Inscriptions* (Berkeley: The Society for the Study of Early China, 2016), 256–262, esp. 259, 261.

12. Waley and Allen, *Book of Songs*, 167, ode no. 192, adapted.

13. *Mao shi zhengyi*, *Shisanjing zhushu* (Beijing: Beijing daxue, 2000), 12.829 ("Zheng yue" 正月).

14. Li Xueqin 李學勤, Qi Wenxin 齊文心, and Ai Lan 艾蘭 (Sarah Allan), eds., *Yingguo suo cang jiagu ji* 英國所藏甲骨集, 2 vols. (Beijing: Zhonghua, 1985). Hereafter *Ying*, followed by the number of the inscription.

15. Zhao Pingan 趙平安, "Zhanguo wenzi de 'shi' yu jiaguwen 'zhi' wei yi zi shuo" 戰國文字的 "幸" 與甲骨文 "達" 為一字說, *Guwenzi yanjiu* 古文字研究 22 (2000): 275–277.

16. On the graphs 幸 and 執, see Yu Xingwu 于省吾, "Shi Yan 釋㚔," in *Jiagu wenzi shilin* 甲骨文字釋林 (Beijing: Zhonghua, 1979), 295.

17. Guo Moruo 郭沫若, ed., Hu Houxuan 胡厚宣, comp., *Jiaguwen heji* 甲骨文合集 13 vols. (Beijing: Zhonghua, 1978–1982). Hereafter *Heji*, followed by the number of the inscription.

18. Guo Moruo notes that slaves originally came from captives and thus are often represented as bound in the orthography of ancient characters. See "Shi chen zai" 釋臣宰, *Jiagu wenzi yanjiu* 甲骨文字研究 (Beijing: Renmin, 1952), 3.

19. Zhao Qi 趙岐 (Han), Sun Shuang 孫奭 (Song), *Mengzi zhushu* 孟子註疏, *Shisanjing zhushu* 十三經注疏 (Beijing: Beijing daxue, 2000), 10 下.338 ("Wan Zhang, xia" 萬章下).

20. *Shangshu zhengyi* (Shanghai: Shanghai guji, 2007), 20.810 ("Fei shi" 費誓). Gao Ming 高明, "Lun Shang Zhou shidai de chen he xiaoxhen" 論商周時代的臣和小臣, in *Jinxin ji—Zhang Zhenglang xiansheng bashi qingshou wenji* 盡心集——張政烺先生八十慶壽文集 (Zhongguo shehui kexue, 1996), 107.

21. Wu Yujiang 吳毓江, ed., *Mozi jiaozhu* 墨子校注 (Beijing: Zhonghua, 2006), 2.96 ("Shang xian, xia" 尚賢下).

22. Li Xueqin, "Shuo ming" Part 1 說命, 上, in Li Xueqin, ed., *Qinghua daxue Zhanguo zhujian* 清華大學藏戰國竹簡 vol. 3 (Shanghai: Zhongxi, 2011), 122.

23. Shen Jianhua 沈建華, "Shangdai cefeng zhidu chutan" 商代冊封制度初探, in Xianggang Zhongwen daxue zhongwenxi 香港中文大學中文系, ed., *Dierjie guoji guwenzixue yantaohui lunwenji* 第二屆國際中國古文字學研討會論文集 (Hong Kong: Chinese University of Hong Kong, 1993), 188.

24. *Guoyu* 國語 (Shanghai: Shanghai guji, 1978), 4 ("Zhou yu, shang" 周語上 1). Chen Mengjia 陳夢家, *Yinxu buci zongshu* 殷墟卜辭綜述, chap. 9 on *Zhenzhi chuyu* 政治區域 (Beijing: Kexue, 1956), 324–325.

25. Chen Mengjia, *Yinxu buci zongshu*, 319.

26. Zheng Xuan 鄭玄 (Han), Kong Yingda 孔穎達 (Tang), *Liji zhengyi* 禮記正義, *Shisanjing zhushu* 十三經注疏 (Beijing: Beijing daxue, 2000), 407 ("Wang zhi 王制," 11).

27. Zhongguo shehui kexue kaogu yanjiusuo 中國社會科學院考古研究所, ed., *Yin Zhou jinwen jicheng* 殷周金文集成, 18 vols. (Beijing: Zhonghua, 1987–1994). Hereafter *Jicheng*, followed by the number of the inscription.

28. Guo Moruo, *Liang Zhou jinwen ci daxi kaoshi* 兩周金文辭大系考釋 (Tokyo: Nihon bunkyūdō shoten 日本文求堂書店, 1935), 40.

29. The Shi Xun *gui* has the line "made this treasure for use in the Hall of Zhou" 用作州宮寶 *Jicheng* 4342. See Cook and Goldin, *Source Book*, 114.

30. The San Shi *pan* 散氏盤 has the line . . . 之有辭囊, 州𥎦 (就) . . . , *Jicheng* 10176. Cf. ibid., 169–170, where Robert Eno reads the graph as *jing* 京, "officers Tuo Ke, Zhoujing, and Shu Congli." Explaining the graph 𥎦, Wang Guowei 王國維 argues: "The graph 𥎦 is commonly seen in oracle-bone and bronze inscriptions, as in the Ke *ding* 克鼎, Shi Dui *dun* 師兌敦, etc. phrase of '虩𥎦乃命,' where it has an emphatic meaning. In the archaic script of Scribe Zhou, it was shortened to *jiu* 就" (案殷墟卜辭與古金文多見 "𥎦" 字, "克鼎," "師兌敦" 等均云: "虩𥎦乃命" 乃重之意, 籀文就字當從省). Wang Guowei 王國維, *Yishu* 遺書, 17 vols., Shizhoupian shuzheng 史籀篇疏証, 19.

31. *Shangshu dazhuan* 尚書大傳.

32. Shao Wangping 邵望平, "'Yu gong' jiu zhou de kaoguxue yanjiu" '禹貢' 九州的考古學研究, *Jiu zhou xuekan* 九州學刊 2 (September 1987): 1, 11.

33. Li Xueqin 李學勤, "Lun Bin Gong xu ji qi zhongyao yiyi" 論豳公盨及其重要意義, *Zhongguo lishi wenwu* 中國歷史文物2002.6: 4–12, 89.

34. *Shangshu zhengyi* (Shanghai: Shanghai guji, 2007), 6.189 ("Yu gong" 禹貢).

35. Waley and Allen, *Book of Songs*, 320, ode no. 303, renders the line as: "Even their inner domain was a thousand leagues."

36. Shen Jianhua, "Buci suojian Shangdai de fengjiang yu nagong" 卜辭所見商代的封疆與納貢, *Zhongguoshi yanjiu* 中國史研究 2004.4: 3–15. *Heji* 151 and 23706 for *nei yu shi*, *Heji* 4476 for *nei yi*.

37. Zhongguo shehui kexueyuan kaogu yanjiusuo 中國社會科學院考古研究所, ed., *Xiaotun nandi jiagu* 小屯南地甲骨 (Beijing: Zhonghua, 1980). Hereafter *Tunnan*, followed by the number of the inscription.

38. Kaizuka Sigeki 貝塚茂樹, comp., *Kyōto daigaku jinbun kagaku kenkyūjo kura kōkotsumoji* 京都大學人文科學研究所藏甲骨文字 (Kyoto: Kyōto daigaku kagaku kenkyūjo, 1960). Hereafter *Kyoto*, followed by the number of the inscription.

39. *Guoyu* (Shanghai: Shanghai guji, 1978), 4 ("Zhou yu, shang" 周語上 1).

40. *Guoyu* (Shanghai: Shanghai guji, 1978), 54 ("Zhou yu, zhong" 周語中 2).

41. Qiu Xigui 裘錫圭, "Jiagu buci zhong suojian de 'tian,' 'mu,' 'wei' deng shiguan de yanjiu" 甲骨蔔辭中所見的'田''牧''衛'等職官的研究, *Gudai wenshi yanjiu xintan* 古代文史研究新探 (Nanjing: Jiangsu guji, 1992), 354–355.

42. *Guoyu* (Shanghai: Shanghai guji, 1978), 4 ("Zhou yu, shang" 周語上 1). Following these lines, the "day sacrifices, lunar rites, seasonal offerings, annual tributes, and homage to the king" (日祭, 月祀, 時享, 歲貢, 終王) are listed, providing context for the terms of *ji* 祭 and *si* 祀.

43. Wang Guimin 王貴民, "Shilun gong, gu, shui de zaoqi lichen—xian Qin shiqi gong, fushui yuanliu kao" 試論貢, 賦, 稅的早期歷程—先秦時期貢, 賦稅源流考, *Zhongguo jingjishi yanjiu* 中國經濟史研究1988.1: 13–29.

44. See Yu Xingwu on "Shi shi" 釋氏, in *Shuangjian chi Yin qi pianzhi* 雙劍誃殷契駢枝 (n.p.: lithographic version Shi yinben 石印本, 1940), 59.

45. *Shiji* 史記 (Beijing: Zhonghua, 2014), 2.66.

46. Yu Xingwu, "Yindai de jiaotong he yichuan zhidu" 殷代的交通和驛傳制度, *Dongbei renming daxue renwen kexue xuebao* 東北人民大學人文科學學報2 (1955): 5; and *Jiagu wenzi shilin* 甲骨文字釋林 (Beijing: Zhonghua, 1979), 277–280; Song Zhenhao 宋鎮豪, "Shangdai de daolu he jiaotong" 商代的道路和交通, *Huaxia wenming* 華夏文明 1992.3: 199–208.

47. *Guoyu* (Shanghai: Shanghai guji, 1978), 8 ("Zhou yu, shang" 周語上 1).

48. Waley and Allen, *Book of Songs*, 283, ode no. 263, adapted.

49. *Mao shi zhengyi*, *Shisan jing zhushu* (Beijing: Beijing daxue, 2000), 18.1476 ("Chang wu" 常武).

50. Adapted from Cook and Goldin, *Source Book*, 206.

51. Shaanxi sheng, Baojishi wewuju, Zhonghua shijitan yishuguan 陝西省, 寶雞市文物局, 中華世紀壇藝術館, eds., *Shengshi jijin—Shaanxi Baoji meixian qingtongqi jiaozang* 盛世吉金—陝西寶雞眉縣青銅器窖藏 (Beijing: Beijing, 2003), 34–35.

52. Cook and Goldin, *Source Book*, 237.

53. Waley and Allen, *Book of Songs*, 322, ode no. 305.

54. Wang Hui 王輝, "Lai pan mingwen yisi" 逨盤銘文箋釋, *Kaogu yu wenwu* 考古與文物2003.3: 83.

55. Zhu Fenghan 朱鳳瀚 argues that "these (lines) discuss how the king and his ministers both are able to wash their faces with virtue (是說王與臣皆能以德洗面)." See his: "Bin Gong xu mingwen chushi" 豳公盨銘文初釋, *Zhongguo guojiabowuguan guan kan* 中國歷史文物 2002.6: 31. Cook and Goldin, *Source Book*, 199, offer yet another take, with different transcriptions and punctuation.

56. Adapted from Cook and Goldin, *Source Book*, 185–186.

57. Adapted from Cook and Goldin, *Source Book*, 196.

58. *Guoyu* (Shanghai: Shanghai guji, 1978), 215 ("Lu yu, xia" 魯語下 5).

59. Shen Jianhua, "Chu jian *Rong Cheng shi* zhouming yu buci jinwen diming" 楚簡容成氏州名與卜辭金文地名, in *Guwenzi yanjiu* 古文字研究, no. 25 (Beijing: Zhonghua, 2004), 328–333. Sarah Allan also offers an analysis of the *Rong Cheng shi* in: *Buried Ideas: Legends of Abdication and Ideal Government in Early Chinese Bamboo-Slip Manuscripts* (Albany: State University of New York Press, 2015), 181–262.

60. *Shangshu zhengyi* (Shanghai: Shanghai guji, 2007), 2.88 ("Shun dian" 舜典).

61. See Li Ling's transcription of *Rong Cheng shi* in Ma Chengyuan 馬承源, ed., *Shanghai bowuguan cang Chu jian* 上海博物館藏楚簡, vol. 2. (Shanghai: Shanghai guji, 2002), 269.

62. Allan, *Buried Ideas*, 240.

63. Ma Chengyuan, *Shanghai bowuguan cang Chu jian*, vol. 2, 269.

64. Sun Haibo 孫海波, *Jiagu wenbian* 甲骨文編 (Beijing: Zhonghua, 1965), juan 14.17, 560.

65. *Jiagu wenbian* 甲骨文編, appendix 附4700, 4715. On the Xinyang 信陽 Chu bamboo slips, the graph *jia* 夾 is read as "overlapping collar" (*jia* 袷), akin to the later *Jiyun* 集韻 dictionary's definition of "overlapping garments" (*ren* 衽). See He Linyi 何琳儀, *Zhanguo guwenzi zidian* 戰國古文字字典 (Beijing: Zhonghua, 1998), vol. 2, 1428.

66. Qiu Xigui, "Shi nanfang ming" 釋南方名, in *Guwenzi lunji* 古文字論集 (Beijing: Zhonghua, 1992), 50–52.

67. Gu Jiegang 顧頡剛 claimed that *yan* was close in sound to *yi*, making Yi the name for Yin, a frontier garrison, but in fact from the Chu manuscripts we now are aware that *yi* 衣 was not the phonetic for *yan* 兗. See Gu's "Zhou yu dao de yanbian" 州與嶽的演變, *Shixue nianbao* 史學年報 1933.5: 11–33.

68. See Yu Xingwu, "Shi Yan," *Jiagu wenzi shilin*, 135–138.

69. Zheng Xuan 鄭玄 (Han), Jia Gongyan 賈公彥 (Tang), *Zhou li zhushu* 周禮註疏, *Shisan jing zhushu* 十三經注疏 (Beijing: Beijing daxue, 2000), 33.1026 ("Zhi fang shi" 職方氏).

70. *Shang shu zhengyi* (Shanghai: Shanghai guji, 2007), 6.198, 235–236 ("Yu gong" 禹貢).

71. Guo Pu 郭璞 (Jin), Xing Bing 邢昺 (Song), *Erya zhushu* 爾雅註疏, *Shisan jing zhushu* 十三經注疏 (Beijing: Beijing daxue, 2000), 7.209 ("Shi di dijiu" 釋地第九).

72. See Li Ling's transcription of *Rong Cheng shi* in Ma Chengyuan 馬承源, ed., *Shanghai bowuguan cang Zhanguo Chuzhu shu* 上海博物館藏戰國楚竹書, ed. Ma Chengyuan 馬承源 (Shanghai: Shanghai guji, 2002), 269.

73. Allan, *Buried Ideas*, 240.

74. Su Zhaoqing 蘇兆慶, "Shandong Jusian Liyanghe taowen yanjiu shuyao" 山東莒縣陵陽河陶文研究述要, *Xian Qin shi yanjiu dongtai* 先秦史研究動態1994.1: 25.

75. Sun Yabing 孫亞冰 and Li Huan 林歡, *Shangdai dili yu fangguo* 商代地理與方國 (Zhongguo shehui kexue, 2006), 198–200.

76. See, for example, *Shiji* (Beijing: Zhonghua, 2014), 5.277.

77. Zhongguo xian Qin shixuehui 中國先秦史學會, ed., *Ju wenhua yanjiu wenji* 莒文化研究文集 (Jinan: Shandong renmin, 2002), 20.

78. Li Jiahao 李家浩, "Qiguo wenzi zhong de 'sui'" 齊國文字中的"遂," *Li Jiahao juan* 李家浩卷 (Hefei: Anhui jiaoyu, 2002), 49.

79. Ma Chengyuan 馬承源, ed., *Shanghai bowuguan cang Zhanguo Chuzhu shu* 上海博物館藏戰國楚竹書, ed. Ma Chengyuan 馬承源 (Shanghai: Shanghai guji, 2002), 269.

80. Yu Xingwu pointed out that the basic meaning of the graph for *bing* is connected to the added one or two horizontal lines in the lower part of the graph, which signify two people linked together; see his "Shi guwenzi zhong fuhuai yin shen zhishizi" 釋古文字中附劃因聲指事字, *Jiagu wenzi shilin*, 457.

81. *Shang shu zhengyi* (Shanghai: Shanghai guji, 2007), 2.88 ("Shun dian" 舜典).

82. *Zhou li zhushu*, *Shisan jing zhushu* (Beijing: Beijing daxue, 2000), 33.1029 ("Zhi fang shi").

83. Yang Shaoshun 楊紹舜, "Shansi Shilou xinzhenji dao de jijian Shangdai tongqi 山西石樓新徵集到的幾件商代青銅器," *Wenwu* 1976.2: 94, fig. 1.

84. Peng Bangjiong 彭邦炯, "Bing qi, Bing shi yu Bing Zhou 竝器, 竝氏與並州," *Kaogu yu wenwu* 考古與文物 1981.2: 50–52.

85. Liu Qiyu 劉起釪, "'Yu gong' xiecheng niandai yu jiu zhou laiyuan zhuwenti tanjiu" "禹貢"寫成年代與九州來源諸問題探研, *Jiu zhou* 九州 2003.3: 1–13.

86. *Shang shu zhengyi* (Shanghai: Shanghai guji, 2007), 6.238 ("Yu gong" 禹貢).

87. *Jicheng* 11.6014.

6

The Tsinghua University *Yue Gong qi shi* Manuscript and Township Administration in the State of Yue during the Spring and Autumn Period

Wang Jinfeng

Translated by Christopher J. Foster

Introduction

In April 2017, the seventh volume of *Tsinghua University's Warring States Bamboo-Slip Manuscript Collection* 清華大學藏戰國竹簡 was published, containing four manuscripts: *Zifan Ziyu* 子犯子餘, *Jin Wen Gong ru yu Jin* 晉文公入於晉, *Zhao Jianzi* 趙簡子, and *Yue Gong qi shi* 越公其事.[1] Among them, *Yue Gong qi shi* is the longest manuscript, both in terms of the number of bamboo slips on which it was written (75 altogether) and its overall character count. *Yue Gong qi shi* is neither a philosophical treatise, nor masters literature; rather it offers a historical narrative for the state of Yue 越 at the end of the Spring and Autumn period. Since the manuscript was compiled no later than the mid–Warring States period, not long after the events described, we may regard it as a remarkably reliable account. For this reason, the *Yue Gong qi shi* rivals the *Zuo zhuan* 左傳 and *Guoyu* 國語 in its historical value.

The *Yue Gong qi shi* helps to fill a gap in our understanding of pre-Qin political administration of "townships" (*xian* 縣). Prior to the discovery of this manuscript, our extant historical data—whether from the received corpus or paleographic sources—included information on "townships" in the cities of Feng 豐 and Zheng 鄭 during the Western Zhou period;[2] in the states of Chu 楚, Jin 晉, Qin 秦, Qi 齊, and Wu 吳 during the Spring and Autumn period;[3] and even for the state of Yan 燕 and the territory belonging to the Three Jin 三晉 domains during the Eastern Zhou.[4] Yet up until now the evidence for any townships in the state of Yue has been missing. The *Yue Gong qi shi* manuscript provides ample content on Yue townships during the Spring and Autumn period, allowing for research on early territorial administration in this region.

A number of scholars have conducted research into Spring and Autumn period townships. This includes general overviews,[5] investigations into townships for individual states,[6] comparisons between different states,[7] and comparisons against later Warring States–period systems of township administration.[8] These previous studies have laid a solid foundation for research on Spring and Autumn period townships, yet they lacked information on Yue. The following chapter fills this gap, through an analysis of the *Yue Gong qi shi*.

The Size and Location of "Townships" in the State of Yue

On the Tsinghua *Yue Gong qi shi* manuscript, the word *xian* or "township" appears in the phrase "outlying township" (*bianxian* 邊縣), written in the following manner:

鄥㠯 (Slip #35)
鄥鄳 (Slip #39)
鄥遷 (Slips #44 and 52)

The editors of the Tsinghua collection read the first character as *bian* 邊 ("outlying") and the second character as *xian* 縣 ("township").[9] This archaic form for *bian* is found in the Shanghai Museum corpus of Warring States manuscripts, modifying the nouns "city" (*cheng* 城) and "person" (*ren* 人). For example, the *Cao Mo zhi zhen* 曹沫之陳 writes: "How should we defend the outlying cities?" (守鄥城奚如); while the *Zheng Zijia sang* 鄭子家喪, manuscript A (*jia* 甲), states: "When Zijia (Guisheng) of Zheng passed away, the frontiersmen came to report it" (鄭子家亡鄥人來告).[10] The three graphic variations for the second word all share the phonetic component of *huan* 睘 [*[ɢ]ʷˁ<r>en].[11] An ancient seal imprint (*Guxi wenbian* 古璽文編, no. 1903), read *huan shi* 睘史 ("township scribe"), replaced the word *xian* 縣 with *huan*.[12] This is also the case for the name Township of Fang City 方城睘, as inscribed on the Fang Cheng *huan* 方城睘 bronze badge (*Jicheng* 10423). These artifacts serve as proof that *huan* was used as a loan for *xian* [*Cə.[g]ʷˁe[n]-s].[13] It is thus correct to read the three pairs of characters from the Tsinghua *Yue Gong qi shi* manuscript listed earlier as "outlying township" (*bianxian*).

The townships in Yue, much like the cities, were positioned in the "hinterlands" outside of the Yue capital. Consider the following passage from the Tsinghua manuscript:

> Once the (people of the) state of Yue acted in good faith, the king thereupon desired to issue promotions. The king urgently dispatched men to inspect where (populations) had either gathered or dispersed among the cities and the outlying townships, both small and large, distant and near. . . . Once the king was informed of these inspections, he ordered them to submit reports, which he examined and heard in person. . . . Once the king examined and heard (the reports), he then evaluated the quality of the goods from the hinterlands (presented along with the) reports. . . . Some (managers) were promoted, and others demoted. Praise and condemnation were had, rewards and punishments given. Those who were skilled were appointed, and the dishonest were denied.

越邦服信，王乃好陞 (升) 人.[14] 王乃迿 (趣)[15] 使人䚋 (察)睹 (省) 成 (城)市，邊還 (縣)小大遠伲 (邇)之𨛜 (勾)，莕 (落) . . .[16] 王既察知之，乃命上會，王必親聖 (聽)之 王既必聽之，乃品巠 (野)會 . . . . 由 (有) 臤 (牽) 由 (有) 毀.[17] 有䖵 肯，有賞罰. 善人則由 (迪)，晉 (譖) 民則怀 (否).[18] (Slips #44–47)

The term *shang hui* 上會 means "to forward (up) accounts" (*shang ji* 上計) and refers to the periodic submission of status reports by the officials in charge of the cities and townships to the Yue king. The word *pin* 品, in its first appearance in the passage, is used as a verb, meaning "to evaluate the quality of."[19] The graph 巠 is an abbreviation for a variation of the usual graph for "hinterlands" (*ye* 野).²⁰ The phrase *pin ye hui* 品野會 means "to evaluate the quality of the goods from the hinterland that were presented along with the reports." This passage narrates how the Yue king dispatched men to survey changes in the population of all the cities and outlying townships, those small and large, distant and near. Afterward, the Yue king ordered the officials in charge of those cities and outlying townships to submit their accounts, and he personally listened to their reports. Finally, the Yue king evaluated the quality of the goods that were presented from the cities and outlying townships. It is thus evident that, in this bamboo-slip manuscript, the term "hinterlands" (*ye*) refers to where the cities and outlying townships were located.

During the Western Zhou and Spring and Autumn periods, the Zhou royal domain and the states of the regional lords commonly were divided into two general administrative regions: the "capital, city-state" (*guo* 國) and the "hinterlands" (*ye*).²¹ The *Zhou li* 周禮, "Tianguan zhongzai" 天官冢宰 chapter, for instance, states: "When the king established the state, he divided up the regions and rectified his position, he embodied the state and ordered the hinterlands, he set up officials and conferred roles, to serve as the guiding principles for his people" (惟王建國, 辨方正位, 體國經野, 設官分職, 以為民極).²² The word *guo* refers to the capital and neighboring suburbs in all four directions, while *ye* was the vast region beyond them. Jiao Xun 焦循 (1763–1820 CE) has argued previously: "If referring to a single state, then (the area) within the suburbs is the *guo*, and (the lands) outside (of the suburbs) are then the *ye*" (就一國言之, 則郊以內為國, 外為野).²³ The division between the capital and hinterlands is also expressed at times with the pairing of the words *guo* and *bi* 鄙 ("outskirts"). In the *Guoyu*, "Qi yu" 齊語 chapter, Guan Zhong 管仲 urges the ruler to "arrange the capital (in tripartite) and order the outskirts (in quintuple)" (叁其國而伍其鄙). To this, Wei Zhao 偉昭 (201–273 CE) comments: "The *guo* is the area within the suburbs; the *bi* is the area beyond the suburbs" (國郊以內也, 鄙郊以外也).²⁴ In the *Zuo zhuan*, Duke Zhuang 莊公, year twenty-eight, *bi* is mentioned: "All of the (Jin) noble sons were in the outskirts, only the sons of the two Ji women remained in Jiang (the Jin capital)" (群公子皆鄙, 唯二姬之子在絳).²⁵ Duke Xian of Jin 晉獻公 sent the heir apparent, Shensheng 申生, to reside in Quwo 曲沃, and his other sons, Chong'er 重耳 and Yiwu 夷吾, to reside in Pucheng 蒲城 and Qu 屈. These locations were all outside the Jin capital of Jiang. These two passages demonstrate how, at that time, the lands located outside of the capital city were referred to as "outskirts" (*bi*), also known as "hinterlands" (*ye*). Furthermore, the relationship between a capital and its hinterlands was denoted by the pairing of "metropolis" (*du*

都) and "outskirts" (*bi*) as well. For example, in the *Guoyu*, "Chu yu" 楚語 section, there is the line: "That a state has a metropolis and outskirts, this is an ancient institution" (國有都鄙, 古之制也).²⁶ Here the term *du* refers to the capital city, while the areas outside of the capital are called *bi*, the same as with the term *ye*. It is thus apparent that, during the Spring and Autumn period, any lands beyond those of the capital were regarded as "hinterlands" (*ye*). This is why, in the passage cited earlier from the Tsinghua manuscript, the cities and outlying townships are called "hinterlands."

Yue Gong qi shi, moreover, offers clues regarding the size of the Yue townships and their distance from the Yue capital:

Outlying townships, small and large, distant and near.
邊縣小大遠迡 (遖). (Slip #35)

Cities and outlying townships, small and large, distant and near.
城市, 邊縣小大遠迡 (遖). (Slip #44)

The character 迡 is a loan for "near" (*er* 遖). This same loan appears in the Shanghai Museum Warring States manuscript *Cong zheng* 從政, in the line: "It is said that a gentleman's relations need not be (found) nearby" (聞之曰君子之相就也不必在近迡). This confirms the reading of "near."²⁷ According to the *Shuowen jiezi* 說文解字, "*er* means to be near" (遖近也); the *Yupian* 玉篇 repeats this same definition.²⁸ In the first example (slip #35), the phrase "small and large, distant and near" (小大遠遖) modifies the term "outlying townships" (*bianxian* 邊縣). This is an instance of a postpositive attribute, which commonly appears in paleographic sources. For example, the phrase "a dark robe with embroidered border" (玄衣㶊屯(純)) is often seen in Western Zhou bronze inscriptions, where "embroidered border" is a postpositive attribute (e.g., in the Geng Ji *ding* 庚季鼎 inscription, *Jicheng* 2781, or the Xun *gui* 詢簋, *Jicheng* 4321). In the Mi Bo Shiji *gui* 弭伯耤簋 (*Jicheng* 4257), we find "pennant with five suns" (旂五日) instead of the more standard "five suns pennant" (五日旂).²⁹ Slip #44 of *Yue Gong qi shi*, cited earlier, writes "cities and outlying townships" (城市邊縣), yet on slips #50–52, "outlying townships and cities" (邊縣城市) appears twice instead. Comparing these two expressions, it is clear that "cities" and "outlying townships" are two separate entities, yet the attributes "small and large, distant and near" modify both. Thus, according to this manuscript, Yue townships were classified as either small or large in size and located either distant or near to the Yue capital.

What were the precise locations for these townships in Yue? In order to answer this question, we first must examine the term "outlying" (*bian*). In *Erya* 爾雅, "Shigu, xia" 釋詁下, *bian* is defined as "frontier" (*chui* 垂).[30] The two words, *bian* and *chui*, define one another in the *Shuowen jiezi* as well, where it claims that "*chui* means 'the distant margins'" (垂遠邊也).[31] The *Guoyu*, "Wuyu" 吳語, records how "Goujian, in command of but a few elders, blames himself for this serious crime, and pays respect (to Wu) in the borderlands" (句踐用帥二三之老, 親委重罪, 頓顙於邊). To this, Wei Zhao explains: "*Bian* is the outlying borderlands" (邊邊境).[32] These examples reveal that *bian* carries a connotation of "outlying borderlands." This same usage is found on *Yue Gong qi shi*, in the line:

> I thereupon led my scant brethren and hastened to report to the outlying borderlands.

孤用率我一二子弟以奔告于邊. (Slips #19–20)

In *Yue Gong qi shi*, the "outlying townships" (*bianxian*) must have been established in these borderland regions of the state of Yue.

We find similar examples of the formula *bian* + X in other Warring States sources. The term *bianren* 邊人 ("frontiersmen") appears in the *Guoyu*, "Lu yu" 魯語 section: "The people of Jin murdered Lord Li. The frontiersmen reported it and Lord Cheng held court. The Lord asked: 'Who would go so far as to murder their ruler?' (At first) no one replied, (but then) Li Ge said: 'It was the ruler's fault'" (晉人殺厲公, 邊人以告, 成公在朝. 公曰: "臣殺其君, 誰之過也?" 大夫莫對, 裏革曰; "君之過也"). Wei Zhao explains that the "*bianren* were the officers of the border battlefields" (邊人, 疆場之司), that is, the government officials in charge of the battlefields along the frontier.[33] In the *Zuo zhuan*, Duke Zhao 昭公, year twenty-four, it records: "When the men of Wu pursued Chu, the men at the frontier made no defense, and as a result Wu extinguished Chao and Zhongli before turning back" (吳人踵楚, 而邊人不備, 遂滅巢及鍾離而還).[34] Here the *bianren* are the people along Chu's borders. The *Zheng Zijia sang* manuscripts in the Shanghai Museum collection, as previously cited, begin with the statement that *bianren* came to report when Zijia of Zheng passed away.[35] The *bianren*, in this instance, are the same as those mentioned in *Guoyu*, namely government officials in charge of the battlefields along the frontier.[36] Similarly, in *Yue Gong qi shi* the term *bianren* appears in two passages:

It is my fault, that when wicked frontiersmen stirred up resentments, (causing) conflict between Wu and Yue, I directed kin from my two settlements to amass, morning and night, as if leopards and tigers, to feast (upon the enemy) in the mountains and open fields. . . . I thereupon led my scant brethren and hastened to report to the outlying borderlands. (But) the frontiersmen were unprincipled, and some disregarded my words.

孤所得罪，無良邊人稱怨惡，交鬥吳越，使吾二邑之父兄子弟朝夕粲然爲豺狼，食于山林草莽. . . . 孤用率我一二子弟以奔告於邊。邊人爲不道，或抗禦寡人之辭。(Slips #16–20)

The elite warriors had donned (their armor), the boats and chariots were ready, but the Wu army had not yet taken up arms. King Goujian of Yue (therefore) ordered the frontiersmen to voice their anger, making trouble for his personal ends. Agitating (long-standing) resentments, the frontiersmen (of both sides) then attacked one another, causing the Wu army to mobilize.

王卒既服，舟乘既成，吳師未起。越王勾踐命邊人聚怨，變亂私成，挑起怨惡，邊人乃相攻也，吳師乃起。(Slips #61–63)

In the first passage, *bianren* refers to the frontiersmen in the borderlands of both Wu and Yue; in the second passage, it refers to those from Yue. From these passages, it is clear that the term denotes those officials and commoners who are in the borderlands.

Consider also the term *bianyi* 邊邑 ("frontier settlement"). There is a passage in the *Shiji* 史記, "Wu Zixu liezhuan" 伍子胥列傳 chapter, that reads:[37]

Long ago, Zhongli, a frontier settlement of King Ping of Chu, and Beiliangshi, a frontier settlement of Wu, both raised silkworms. Women from the two (settlements) fought each other over mulberry trees. It caused such anger that both states (Chu and Wu) mobilized armies and fought one another. Wu sent Gongzi Guang to attack Chu. He seized Zhongli and Juchao, before returning.

久之，楚平王以其邊邑鍾離與吳邊邑卑梁氏俱蠶，兩女子爭桑相攻，乃大怒，至於兩國舉兵相伐。吳使公子光伐楚，拔其鍾離、居巢而歸。

Zhongli 鐘離 and Beiliangshi 卑梁氏 were the "frontier settlements" (*bianyi*) of Chu and Wu, respectively, located along the borders of these two states. The term "outlying townships" (*bianxian*) in the Tsinghua manuscript is used in the same sense as "frontiersmen" (*bianren*) or these "frontier settlements" (*bianyi*), as described earlier. It denotes townships located along Yue's borders. Many of Chu's townships were built out of the small rival states that Chu had destroyed around its peripheries, with a number of them utilizing the old capitals of those states.[38] A comparable situation can be imagined for the state of Yue. From the *Yue Gong qi shi*, it appears that, during the Spring and Autumn period, the "outlying townships" of Yue were established along its borderland regions, in the "hinterlands" (*ye*) outside of the state's capital. They were distinguished by their size, being large or small, and by their location vis-à-vis the capital, being distant or near.

The Role of Townships in Yue Territorial Administration

In the Tsinghua *Yue Gong qi shi* manuscript, "outlying townships" are often paired together with "cities." To better understand what the "outlying townships" constitute, it is therefore necessary to conduct a preliminary analysis of the "cities" as well. In transmitted texts, the term "cities" (*chengshi* 城市) first appears in the *Han Feizi* 韓非子 chapter "Ai chen" 愛臣, in the following passage:[39]

> This is why, even though a great minister's salary is large, he is not allowed to register (and thereby assume authority over) a city; though his clique be multitudinous, he is not allowed to employ soldiers. Thus, a subject of the state does not hold their own court, standing armies do not have private engagements, and warehouses or military stores are not allowed to lend out items on their own whim. This is how a wise ruler prohibits deviance.
>
> 是故大臣之祿雖大, 不得藉威城市; 黨與雖眾, 不得臣士卒. 故人臣處國無私朝, 居軍無私交, 其府軍不得私貸於家. 此明君之所以禁其邪.

The "cities" described in this passage were areas of concentrated populations, with developed industry and commerce, and residents who predominantly did not labor in the field. These cities generally are the political, economic, and cultural centers of their surrounding regions. This also describes the "cities" mentioned in the *Yue Gong qi shi*. The cities of Yue during the Spring and Autumn period were places of highly concentrated mercantile activities. *Yue Gong qi shi* mentions trade (而 □ (價)賈), shopkeepers (*shijia* 市賈), and legal disputes (*zhengsong* 爭訟) between merchants (slip #38). As we saw earlier, they are described along with the outlying townships as "small and large, distant and near" (slip #44). Since the Yue cities were economic hubs, they must have been positioned at the heart of each respective region of the polity. The townships, on the other hand, were established in the borderland areas. The complementary, yet contrastive, nature of cities and townships perhaps accounts for why *Yue Gong qi shi* often discusses them together as a pair.

Both were critical to the territorial administration of Yue. On slips #44–47 of *Yue Gong qi shi*, as previously discussed, the king of Yue dispatched men to inspect the cities and outlying townships, to see which were properly administered, and thereby issue promotions or demotions. Shortly after this passage, the text reads:

> In this way he enticed the people, in this way he received guests, in this way he gathered (populations in) settlements. . . . Thereupon the peoples of the four regions—Eastern Yin, the Western Yi, the Gumie, and Juwu—all heard that there was plenty to eat in the lands of Yue, that government oversight was modest, and (the ruler) valued trustworthiness. They thus came in waves upon waves, so that the lands of Yue held a great many people.
>
> 是以勸民，是以收賓，是以鄹(句)邑．．．．東夷、西夷、古蔑、句吳四方之民乃皆聞越地之多食，政薄而好信，乃波往歸之，越地乃大多人. (Slips #44–49)

One reason why the Yue king emphasized the proper administration of his "cities" and "outlying townships," was to attract people from other states to come settle in Yue. After enacting a series of measures, these "cities" and "outlying townships" were effectively governed, and as a result masses of immigrants entered Yue from other regions. Populating the "cities" and "outlying townships" was of vital concern for the Yue government. Consider also this other passage from the *Yue Gong qi shi*:

> Once the state of Yue was accustomed to promoting (worthy) people, and its population grew, the king thereupon desired to raise an army. As for each of the five types of blades, the king had their edges sharpened daily, and placed them within reach; as for the forging of equipment out of metal and hide, the king inspected its progress daily, to learn the state of his arsenal. The king then personally dispatched messengers to inquire which of his various lords, cities, and outlying townships were well equipped, and which were lacking, giving to them (what they needed for defense). Those oversupplied and those unequipped, this is what he investigated, inquiring everywhere. When the entirety of Yue, down to its outlying townships and cities, all valued their military, then the state of Yue commanded a massive army.
>
> 越邦皆服升人，多人，王乃好兵。凡五兵之利，王日習之，居諸左右；凡金革之攻，王日論省其事，以聞五兵之利。王乃親使人請問羣大夫及邊縣，城市之多兵，無兵者，王則與。唯多兵，無兵者是察，問於左右。舉越邦至於邊縣，城市乃皆好兵甲，越邦乃大多兵。(Slips #50–52)

The proper regulation of cities and outlying townships by the Yue king, through his tours of inspection, thus also served as a way for him to increase his military might. *Yue Gong qi shi* also records:

> Once the state of Yue had bountiful agriculture, the king thereupon desired trustworthiness.
>
> He then reformed the oversight of markets. Whenever any measure was out of order, or any insignia incorrect, the swindles who cheated honest folks were penalized . . . and conducted trade there, (the guilty party) was punished upon examination. Whenever the shopkeepers had a legal dispute, and there was a deviation (from the truth) or a trick was played, if (a claim) was found to be factual, (the guilty party) was punished upon examination. Penalties were determined according to the transgression that occurred.
>
> Whenever some resident or official leader from the outlying townships reported to the royal court, saying: "Previously the levies were not such-and-such, now they are too overbearing,

(you) have not balanced them (appropriately)," for all such cases, the king made certain to examine and listen (to the reports) personally. If (a report) was found to be trustworthy, the directors of affairs and official leaders from the settlement (in question) then were dismissed.

None of the directors of affairs and official leaders of the cities and settlements dared to exaggerate about their governance and present (such boasts) to the king. Whenever a claim was made to the royal court, saying: "Prior they gave their word (on such and such), but now it is not like they said," for all such cases, the king made certain to listen (to the claims) personally. If (a claim) was found to be trustworthy, regardless of whether (the guilty party) was of noble or mean status, they were punished.

酭越邦服農多食, 王乃好信. [Sec. 1]
　　乃修市政. 凡羣度之不度, 羣採物之不對, 伴媮諒人則刑也. □□□而□ (價)賈焉, 則詰誅之. 凡市賈爭訟, 反背欺詒, 察之而孚, 則詰誅之. 因其過以爲之罰. [Sec. 2]
　　凡邊鄙(縣)之民及有管(官)師之人或告於王廷, 曰: "初日政勿若某, 今政砫(重), 弗果(和)."⁴⁰ 凡此類也, 王必親見而聽之, 察之而信, 其在邑司事及官師之人則發(廢)也. [Sec. 3]
　　凡城, 邑之司事及官師之人, 乃無敢增歷 (益)其政, 以爲獻於王. 凡有獄訟至於王廷, 曰: "昔日與呂 (己)言員(云), 今不若其言." 凡此類, 王必親聽之, 旨(稽)之而信, 乃母(毋)有貴賤, 刑也. [Sec. 4] (Slips #37–42)

This passage may be divided into four sections based on its content. The first section introduces how the Yue king "desired trustworthiness" (*haoxin* 好信) and pursued a series of measures to ensure that the whole state acted in good faith. The next three sections then elaborate upon those specific measures. Although the term *chengshi* 城市 is not explicitly mentioned, nevertheless the second section concerns policies enacted in cities; the third section discusses policies for the outlying townships; and the fourth section summarizes governance of both cities and outlying townships. To encourage the adoption of trustworthiness throughout the state, the Yue king pressed for the proper administration of cities and outlying townships. *Yue Gong qi shi* thus reveals to us how Yue was governed through management of these cities and outlying townships. Based on this, we can chart out the ideal configuration of Yue's territorial administration (fig. 6.1).

In summary, the "cities" (*chengshi*) mentioned in *Yue Gong qi shi* were

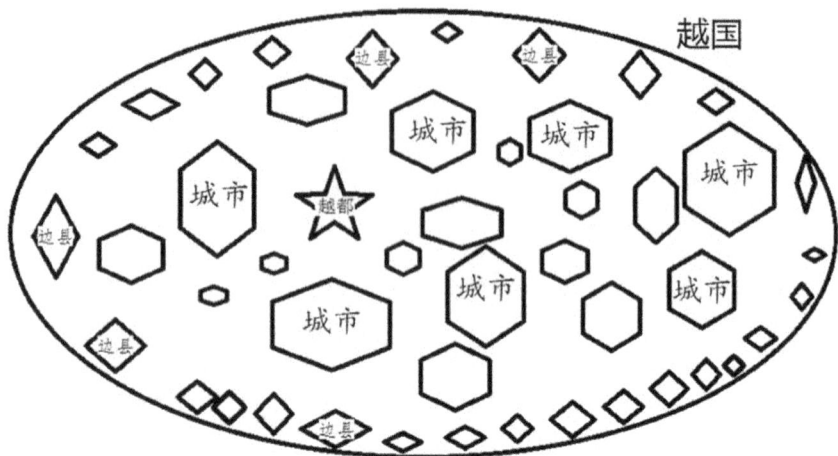

Figure 6.1. Idealized Diagram of Yue's Territorial Administration. *Key*: 越国 = Yue; 越都 = Capital of Yue; 城市 = City; 边县 = Outlying township. *Source*: Created by the author.

areas of concentrated populations, with developed industry and commerce, and residents who predominantly did not engage in agriculture. They served as the political, economic, and cultural centers for their surrounding regions. In their geographic distribution, cities and outlying townships formed a complementary pair, with the former located in the interior and latter along the state's borders. Furthermore, as *Yue Gong qi shi* has demonstrated, the administration of the entire state of Yue depended upon the establishment of these cities and outlying townships.

Administration within Yue Townships during the Spring and Autumn Period

Officials of varying status were assigned to govern townships in Yue. When the term "official leaders" (*guanshi zhi ren* 官師之人) first appears on the *Yue Gong qi shi* manuscript (slip #39), it refers to officials who issued reports on local affairs to the king. In its second appearance, the phrase instead refers to the people that these officials reported on. Although they are categorized together under this one phrase, in fact they constitute two different groups of people, with the latter potentially the superiors of, or colleagues to, the former. The *guanshi zhi ren* thus entailed many individuals. The "directors of affairs" (*sishi* 司事) must have been the highest ranking officials who handled the reported affairs. Note that further evidence for the roles of these officials is given on slips #40–42, though this time in the context of both cities and settlements.

Yue Gong qi shi also documents how officials of the cities and outlying townships periodically reported their accomplishments to the court, according to which the king then issued rewards or punishments:

> Once the king was informed of these inspections, he ordered them to submit reports, which he examined and heard in person. For those (cities and outlying townships where populations had) gathered, when the king met with the managers, he was joyful, yet he could not just smile with pleasure, but made certain to feast them and award gifts to them. For those (where populations had) dispersed, when the king met with the managers, he was aggrieved and displeased, and did not award them a feast.
>
> 王既察知之, 乃命上會, 王必親聖 (聽) 之. 其䢖 (勾) 者, 王見其執事人則台¹(怡) 愈 (豫)熹 (熹) 也, 不可□⁴¹芺 (笑) 芺 (笑)也, 則必飲食賜夋 (予) 之. 其苳 (落) 者, 王見其執事人, 則頋 (憂) 感 (慼) 不豫, 弗飨 (予) 飲食. (Slips #45–46)

Thus within the townships, there were governing officials who were the "managers" (*zhishi ren* 執事人). From these two passages, we may then categorize officials by the following titles and ranks (table 6.1).

The Yue king maintained close control over his townships, as reflected by the following points: First, the Yue king had the power to dispatch men to survey the townships, as the manuscript records (slip #44): "The king

Table 6.1.

Highest Order	Sishi 司事 Directors of Affairs	
Second Order	Guanshi zhi ren 官師之人 Official Leaders (liable to reporting)	Managers
Third Order	Guanshi zhi ren 官師之人 Official Leaders (who can issue reports)	

urgently dispatched men to inspect where (populations) had either gathered or dispersed among the cities and the outlying townships, both small and large, distant and near" (王乃趣使人察省城市, 邊縣小大遠邇之勾, 落). After this line, it states that "the king then participated" (王則與), revealing that the Yue king himself personally attended these tours.[42] Second, the officials in charge at the townships were required to "forward (up) accounts" (*shanghui* 上會) to the Yue king, which is to say, they reported to the Yue king on what they had accomplished while governing the townships. Third, based on these reports, the Yue king would then promote or demote officials in the townships, issuing rewards and punishments as warranted. For those officials who did a fine job, "(the king) made certain to feast them and award gifts to them" (必飲食賜予之), "promoted them" (*qian* 牽), and "assigned them to a post" (*di* 迪). For those who were less successful, "(the king) did not award them a feast" (弗餘飲食), "demoted" (*hui* 毀), and "denied posts" (*pi* 否). Fourth, it was the Yue king who held ultimate authority over the judicial cases in the townships. Both the residents of the townships and the official leaders who managed those territories could report to the royal court when "levies are overbearing" (*zheng zhong* 政重), or when the managers "exaggerate about their governance" (增益其政). Should an investigation find that this was truly the case, the Yue king could then dispose of the offenders.

It is thus apparent that, during the Spring and Autumn period, the state of Yue installed directors of affairs (*sishi* 司事) and official leaders (*guanshi zhi ren* 官師之人) in its townships. These officials were quite numerous and held varying ranks. They were the "managers" (*zhishi zhi ren* 執事之人) who governed the townships. As such, the Yue king maintained close control over his townships, for instance, by dispatching men to survey them. The officials in charge of those townships, moreover, reported their accomplishments (or lack thereof) to the king, by which he could promote or demote officials, rewarding and punishing them as warranted. The Yue king also held ultimate authority over the judicial cases in the townships.

Other Features of Yue Townships during the Spring and Autumn Period

The immigrants from other states who came to Yue did not only reside in cities but also settled in the townships. In *Yue Gong qi shi*, one of the primary reasons the Yue king sought to govern the outlying townships effectively was to entice people to move to Yue. Good governance would attract "the peoples of the four regions—Eastern Yin, the Western Yi, the Gumie, and Juwu" (東夷, 西夷, 古蔑, 句吳, 四方之民) (slips #48–49). This implies that foreign immigrants resided in the townships.

The townships of Yue were also referred to as "settlements" (*yi* 邑). A close reading of slips #39–40 of *Yue Gong qi shi*, cited earlier, reveals that the phrases "outlying townships" (*bianxian*) and "settlements" (*yi*) actually refer to the same entity. While residents or official leaders from *outlying townships* complain to the court about the injustices of overbearing levies, the directors of affairs and official leaders *from the settlement* (in question) are then punished for their poor governance. Furthermore, settlements are paired with cities later on slip #40 as well, in the phrase: "directors of affairs and official leaders of the cities and settlements" (城, 邑之司事及官師之人). This parallels how townships are paired with cities throughout the rest of the manuscript. For these reasons, we may conclude that Spring and Autumn–period townships in Yue were also called "settlements."

During this period, not all of the regional states established townships. Of those that did, there are a number of examples where the townships were also referred to as "settlements." For example, in *Zuo zhuan*, Duke Zhao, year five, it writes: "The territory from which Han exacts levies consists of seven settlements, all of them full-sized townships" (韓賦七邑, 皆成縣也).[43] This illustrates how settlements were equated with townships in Jin 晉. *Zuo zhuan*, Duke Cheng 成公, year seven, records:[44]

> When the troops returned after the campaign in which Chu had laid siege to Song, Zichong requested certain lands from Shen and Lü as reward. The king assented. Qu Wuchen, Lord of Shen, said, "This will not do. It is with these lands that Shen and Lü could become full-fledged settlements. From thence have come the levies and soldiers with which we defend ourselves against the north. If he takes those lands, there will be no more Shen and Lü."
>
> 楚圍宋之役, 師還, 子重請取於申, 呂以爲賞田, 王許之. 申公巫臣曰: "不可. 此申, 呂所以邑也, 是以爲賦, 以御北方. 若取之, 是無申, 呂也."

Shen 申 and Lü 呂 are actually Chu townships, and as such, these lines demonstrate that, in Chu also, townships and settlements were regarded as the same.

There are, moreover, a few states that never did establish townships, yet their settlements in fact functioned as townships. For instance, *Zuo zhuan*, Duke Xiang 襄公, year twenty-six, documents:[45]

> The Liege of Zheng rewarded his ministers for their achievement in entering the Chen capital. In the third month, on the *jiayin* day, the first day of the month, he offered Gongsun Shezhi ceremonial toasts and bestowed on him superior carriages and regalia appropriate to dignitaries of three commands, and these gifts were followed by eight settlements. He bestowed on Zichan second-tier carriages and regalia appropriate to dignitaries of two commands, and these gifts were followed by six settlements: "Going from above to below for each lower rank the number of gifts and honors is diminished by two. That is in accordance with ritual propriety. Your subject ranks fourth among the ministers. What is more, the achievement was Gongsun Shezhi's. I do not dare to be included in the ritual of rewards. I beg to decline the settlements." The lord insisted on giving them to him, so he accepted three settlements.
>
> 鄭伯賞入陳之功. 三月甲寅朔, 享子展, 賜之先路, 三命之服, 先八邑. 賜子產次路, 再命之服, 先六邑. 子產辭邑, 曰: "自上以下, 隆殺以兩, 禮也. 臣之位在四, 且子展之功也, 臣不敢及賞禮, 請辭邑." 公固予之, 乃受三邑.

Zuo zhuan, Duke Xiang, year twenty-seven:[46]

> The lord gave Gongsun Mianyu sixty settlements. He declined: "Only ministers are provided with a hundred settlements. I already have sixty. For the one below to have the emoluments of the one above creates disorder. I would not presume to hear of it. Moreover, it is precisely because Ning Xi had many settlements that he died. I fear that death will come to me soon if I accept." The lord insisted on giving them to him. He accepted half of them and was appointed junior tutor.
>
> 公與免餘邑六十, 辭曰: "唯卿備百邑, 臣六十矣. 下有上祿, 亂也, 臣弗敢聞.且寧子唯多邑, 故死. 臣懼死之速及也." 公固與之, 受其半. 以為少師.

Zuo zhuan, Duke Xiang, year twenty-seven:[47]

> Xiang Xu, minister of the left in Song, requested a reward: "I request to be granted settlements for having escaped death." The lord gave him sixty settlements.

> 宋左師 (向戌) 請賞, 曰: "請免死之邑." 公與之邑六十.

Compare these records to the *Yanzi chunqiu* 晏子春秋 (Outer Chapters, 7) dialogue between Duke Jing of Qi 齊景公 and Yan Ying 晏嬰, when the former claims: "In the past, our former ruler, Lord Huan, awarded Guan Zhong fox (furs) and grain, and those seventeen townships" (昔吾先君桓公, 予管仲狐與穀, 其縣十七);[48] and the line in *Shiji*, "Wu shijia" 吳世家: "In the third year of King Yuji, the prime minister of Qi, Jingfeng, committed a crime. He escaped from Qi to Wu, where he was granted the township of Zhufang" (王餘祭三年, 齊相慶封有罪, 自齊來奔吳, 吳予慶封朱方之縣);[49] or the bell inscription on the Spring and Autumn–period Shu Yi *bo* 叔夷鎛 that reads: "The Lord said: '. . . I award you the cities of Lai, Mi, Jiao, and three hundred of their townships'" (公曰: 夷 . . . 餘賜汝萊都朕鰲其縣三百).[50] It is evident that the settlements in the states of Zheng 鄭, Wei 衛, and Song 宋 could also be called "townships."

To recapitulate the preceding, some of the immigrants that moved to Yue from other states during the Spring and Autumn period resided in Yue's townships, which could also be called "settlements" (*yi*).

Conclusions

Transmitted texts and paleographic sources provide data for the township administration in various regional states during the Spring and Autumn period. Yet, only with the publication of the Tsinghua *Yue Gong qi shi* manuscript is there data provided for the state of Yue. We now know that townships in Yue during the Spring and Autumn period were established in the state's borderland region, thus they were called "outlying townships" (*bianxian*). They varied in size and distance from the capital. The "cities" (*chengshi*), by contrast, were centrally located in each region of Yue. They too were classified as either large or small, distant or near, and functioned as hubs for mercantile activities. Through "cities" and the "outlying townships," Yue was able to govern the entirety of its state.

The officials established in Yue townships during the Spring and Autumn period include directors of affairs (*sishi*) and official leaders (*guanshi zhi ren*). These officials were quite numerous and held varying ranks. They were the "managers" (*zhishi zhi ren*) of the townships. The Yue king maintained control over his townships through inspections, by requiring the managers to submit reports on their governance, by issuing promotions or demotions to township officials, and by serving as the ultimate judicial authority in township matters.

The region in which Yue established its townships during the Spring and Autumn period was known as the "hinterlands" (*ye*), and the townships in them could also be called "settlements" (*yi*). Immigrants who moved to Yue often settled in these areas.

Through an analysis of townships in the state of Yue during the Spring and Autumn period, we can now better understand the early history and nature of townships as a unit of territorial administration.

Notes

1. Qinghua daxue chutu wenxian yanjiu yu baohu zhongxin 清華大學出土文獻研究與保護中心, ed. (Li Xueqin 李學勤 as lead editor), *Qinghua daxue cang Zhanguo zhujian (qi)* 清華大學藏戰國竹簡(柒) (Shanghai: Zhongxi, 2017).

2. The inscription on the Mian *fu* 免簠 vessel (*Jicheng* 集成 4626, mid-Western Zhou) mentions a Zheng township 鄭縣, while the inscription on the First Year Shi X *gui* 元年師旋簋 vessel (*Jicheng* 4279, late Western Zhou) includes a Feng township 豐縣. These inscriptions both offer invaluable evidence for township-level administration during the Western Zhou period. Zhongguo shehui kexue kaogu yanjiusuo 中國社會科學院考古研究所, ed., *Yin Zhou jinwen jicheng* 殷周金文集成, 18 vols. (Beijing: Zhonghua, 1987–1994). Hereafter *Jicheng*, followed by the number of the inscription.

3. Gu Jiegang 顧頡剛 conducted a comprehensive survey and detailed examination of all data related to the administration of townships found among works in our received corpus, introducing materials pertaining to the states of Chu, Jin, Qin, Qi, and Wu during the Spring and Autumn period. See his "Chunqiu shidai de xian" 春秋時代的縣, published in *Yu gong* 禹貢, vol. 7, nos. 6–7, 1937, 169–193, and again in *Gu Jiegang gushi lunwenji* 顧頡剛古史論文集, vol. 5, from *Gu Jiegang quanji* 顧頡剛全集 (Beijing: Zhonghua, 2011), 231–274.

4. Li Jiahao 李家浩 in the late 1980s compiled all the evidence available on "townships" found among the Zhou paleographic sources extant at that time, bringing to light data for townships in the states of Qi, Yan, and the Three Jin

domains during the Eastern Zhou. See his: "Xian Qin wenzi zhong de 'xian'" 先秦文字中的縣, Wenshi 文史, 1987.28: 49–58; reprinted in Li Jiahao, Zhuming zhongnian yuyan xuejia zixuan ji—Li Jiahao juan 著名中年語言學家自選集, 李家浩卷 (Hefei: Anhui jiaoyu, 2002), 15–34.

5. See for example: Gu Yanwu 顧炎武 (Qing), "Rizhi lu Junxian" 日知錄郡縣, in Rizhi lu jishi 日知錄集釋 (Shanghai: Shanghai guji, 2006), 1238; Yao Nai 姚鼐 (Qing), "Junxian kao" 郡縣考, in Xibao Xuan shi wenji 惜抱軒詩文集 (Shanghai: Shanghai guji, 1992), 12; Zhao Yi 趙翼 (Qing), "Junxian" 郡縣, in Gaiyu congkao 陔餘叢考 (Shanghai: Shangwu, 1957), 293–295; Gu Jiegang 顧頡剛, "Chunqiu shidai de xian" 春秋時代的縣, Yu gong 禹貢, vol. 7, nos. 6–7 (1937): 169–193, reprinted in Gu Jiegang gushi lunwenji 顧頡剛古史論文集, vol. 5, of Gu Jiegang quanji 顧頡剛全集 (Beijing: Zhonghua, 2011), 231–274; Tatsuo Masubuchi 增淵龍夫, "Shuo Chunqiu shidai de xian" 說春秋時代的縣, in Riben xuezhe yanjiu Zhongguoshi lunzhu xuanze 日本學者研究中國史論著選擇, vol. 3, ed. Liu Wenjun 劉文俊, trans. Huang Jinshan 黃金山 and Kong Fanmin 孔繁敏 (Beijing: Zhonghua, 1993), 189–213; Li Jiahao 李家浩, "Xian Qin wenzi zhong de 'xian'" 先秦文字中的縣, Wenshi 文史 28 (1987): 49–58, see also Li Jiahao, Zhuming zhongnian yuyan xuejia zixuan ji—Li Jiahao, juan 28; Zhou Zhenhe 周振鶴, "Xian zhi qiyuan san jieduan shuo" 縣制起源三階段說, Zhongguo lishi dili luncong 中國歷史地理論叢 3 (1997): 28–38.

6. On Chu 楚 townships, see: Yang Kuan 楊寬, "Chunqiu shiqi Chu guo xian zhi de xingzhi wenti" 春秋時期楚國縣制的性質問題, Yang Kuan gushi lunwen xuanji 楊寬古史論文選集 (Shanghai: Shanghai renmin, 2003), 61–83; Xu Shaohua 徐少華, "Guanyu Chunqiu Chu xian de jige wenti" 關於春秋楚縣的幾個問題, Jiang Han luntan 江漢論壇1990.2: 69–77. For studies of Jin 晉 townships, see: Zhou Suping 周蘇平, "Chunqiu shiqi Jin guo de xian zhi" 春秋時期晉國的縣制, Shixue yuekan 史學月刊 1986.2: 12–18; Lü Wenyu 呂文鬱, "Chunqiu shidai Jin guo de xian zhi" 春秋時代晉國的縣制, Shanxi shida xuebao 山西師大學報1992.5: 73–76. For research on Wu 吳 townships, please refer to: Zhang Xiaofang 張曉芳, "Chunqiu Wu guo junxian zhi kaolun" 春秋吳國郡縣制考論, Bianjiang jingji yu wenhua 邊疆經濟與文化 2008.9: 78–79.

7. See for instance: Zheng Dianhua 鄭殿華, "Lun Chunqiu shiqi de Chu xian yu Jin xian" 論春秋時期的楚縣與晉縣, Qinghua daxue xuebao 清華大學學報 2002.4: 3–8. See also Lü Wenyu, "Chunqiu shidai Jin guo de xian zhi," which compares the townships in Jin with those in Qin 秦 and Chu.

8. The final section of Zhou Suping's "Chunqiu shiqi Jin guo de xian zhi" discusses the differences between Spring and Autumn and Warring States–period townships.

9. Qinghua daxue chutu wenxian yanjiu yu baohu zhongxin, ed., Qinghua daxue cang Zhanguo zhujian (qi), 10–11, 130, 133, 137, and 140. CF: Note that there is one additional instance of "outlying townships" (邊縣) on slip #51, in which the orthography of xian appears to miswrite what should be the component 睘. See Qinghua daxue cang Zhanguo zhujian (qi), 140.

10. See Bai Yulan 白於藍, *Zhanguo Qin Han jianbo gushu tongjiazi huizuan* 戰國秦漢簡帛古書通假字匯纂 (Fuzhou: Fujian renmin, 2012), 761–762.

11. CF: Old Chinese reconstructions are taken from William H. Baxter and Laurent Sagart, *Old Chinese: A New Reconstruction* (Oxford: Oxford University Press, 2014); see also their updated reconstructions at http://ocbaxtersagart.lsait.lsa.umich.edu/.

12. Gugong bowuyuan 故宮博物院 et al., eds., *Guxi wenbian* 古璽文編 (Beijing: Wenwu, 1981).

13. Li Jiahao, "Xian Qin wenzi zhong de 'xian,'" offers further examples where the archaic graphs for *huan* were used as loans for *xian*.

14. The Tsinghua editors read *sheng* 陞 as *zheng* 徵 ("to summon"), but the Old Chinese pronunciations for these two words are rather different. More likely, *sheng* 陞 is *sheng* 升, meaning "to raise up." In the *Chuci* 楚辭, "Yuanyou" 遠遊, among the "Jiu tan" 九歎 songs, there is the line, "wishing (to search) high and low, in great haste" (志升降以高馳), to which an ancient commentary notes that "*sheng* 升 is written *sheng* 陞 in another edition" (升一作陞). The phrase *shengren* 升人 in the Tsinghua manuscript means, literally, "to raise up people," which here should be interpreted as "to bring in masses of people."

15. The word "urgently, speedily" (*qu* 趣) is defined in the *Shuowen jiezi* 說文解字 as "urgent" (*ji* 疾). *Shuowen jiezi* (Beijing: Zhonghua, 2017), 118. Bao Biao's 鮑彪 (Song) commentary to the line "soon we will be urged to attack (the state of) Western Zhou" (即且趣我攻西周), from *Zhanguoce* 戰國策, "Dong Zhou ce" 東周策, likewise defines *qu* 趣 with *ji* 疾. See *Zhanguoce zhushi* 注釋 (Beijing: Zhonghua, 1990), 9.

16. The character 匓 is a loan for *jiu* 勼, which is defined as *ju* 聚 ("assemble, gather") in the *Shuowen jiezi* (under the *bao* 勹 radical), *Shiming* 釋名 ("Shi gongshi" 釋宮室) and *Yu pian* (*bao* 勹 radical). See *Guxun huizuan* 古訓匯纂 (Beijing: Shangwu, 2003), 1928. The character *ge* 菳 is a loan for *luo* 落, which means "scatter, disperse." See Bai Yulan, *Zhanguo Qin Han jianbo gushu tongjiazi huizuan*, 467, for this loan. In *Yi Zhou shu* 逸周書, "Fengbao" 酆保, there is a discussion of the "five dispersals" 五落, on which Zhu Youzeng 朱右曾 in *Yi Zhou shu jixun jiaoshi* 逸周書集訓校釋 comments that "*luo* 落 means to disperse" (落散也). See *Yi Zhou shu huijiao jizhu* (Shanghai: Shanghai guji, 2007), 119. Yan Shigu 顏師古 (581–645 CE) gives the same gloss in his commentary to the line "(their) retainers gradually left" (賓客益落), from the *Han shu* 漢書, "Zheng Dangshi zhuan" 鄭當時傳 (Beijing: Zhonghua, 1962), 50.2325. This line appears in *Shiji*, "Ji Zheng liezhuan" 汲鄭列傳, as well, to which Sima Zhen 司馬貞, in *Shiji suoyin* 史記索隱, explains: "*Luo* 落 is like 'to scatter,' it refers to dispersing" (落猶零落謂散也) (Beijing: Zhonghua, 1959), 120.3113.

17. *Qian* 臤 is a loan for "to pull, to lead along" (*qian* 牽). See Bai Yulan, *Zhanguo Qin Han jianbo gushu tongjiazi huizuan*, 860–861, for additional examples.

The *Shuowen jiezi* (under the *niu* 牛 radical), glosses *qian* 牽 as "to draw forward" (*yin qian* 引前), which is repeated in the *Yupian* (likewise under the *niu* radical) (Beijing: Zhonghua, 2017), 93, and *Guxun huizuan*, 1405. In the *Yue Gong qi shi*, it means to promote certain personnel to higher offices. The term *hui* 毀 means "to remove or cast aside." This is, for example, how it is used in *Liang shu* 梁書, "Rulin zhuan" 儒林傳 (sec. Sima Yun 司馬筠), in the line: "(Veneration) through the fifth generation of kin was thereupon removed" (五世親盡乃毀) (Beijing: Zhonghua, 2020), 749. The word *hui* 毀 on slip #40 of *Yue Gong qi shi* is used in the same way, meaning "to demote or remove from office." Thus when it writes (rendered more literally as) "some were brought forward, and others cast aside" (有牽有毀), this refers to the fact that promotions and demotions were made.

18. *You* 由 here is a loan for *di* 迪, meaning "to appoint to a post." *Shangshu*, "Mushi" 牧誓, records: "[The Shang king] casts off his paternal and maternal relatives, not appointing them" (昏棄厥遺王父母弟不迪). See *Shangshu zhengyi* 尚書正義 (Shanghai: Shanghai guji, 2007), 424. Wang Yinzhi 王引之, in his *Jingzhuan shici* 經傳釋詞, vol. 6 (Changsha: Yuelu, 1982), 11, notes that in the *Shiji*, "Zhou Benji" 周本紀, the phrase "not employ" (*bu yong* 不用) is used instead of *bu di* 不迪. See *Guxun huizuan*, 1477. The *Shijing* 詩經, ode "Sangrou" 桑柔, in the "Daya" 大雅, writes: "These good men are neither sought nor appointed" (維此良人弗求弗迪); the Mao Commentary 毛傳 explains that "*di* is to advance" (迪進也). Zheng Xuan 鄭玄 further explains: "There are good people in the state, yet the king does not seek them out, nor employ them" (國有善人王不求索不進用之). See *Mao Shi zhengyi* 毛詩正義 (Beijing: Beijing daxue, 1999), 1187. The term *zen* 譖 means "to be untrustworthy." In the *Shijing* ode "Zhanyang" 瞻卬, in the "Da ya," there are the lines: "Using (the words of) others, (their gossip) is harming and unsettling; (merely) untrustworthy at first, it ends in unrest" (鞫人忮忒譖始竟背); to which Zheng Xuan explains that "*zen* means to be untrustworthy" (譖不信也). *Mao Shi zhengyi*, 755. The character *pi* 否 is a loan for "to block, denounce" (*pi* 否). The phrase *zenming ze pi* 譖民則否 means: "Those who are untrustworthy are then denounced."

19. Qinghua daxue chutu wenxian yanjiu yu baohu zhongxin, ed., *Qinghua daxue cang Zhanguo zhujian (qi)*, 138.

20. Zhao Ping'an 趙平安, "Tantan Zhanguo wenzi zhong yongwei 'ye' de 'ye' zi" 談談戰國文字中用為野的冶字, paper presented at Wenming de hexie yu gongtong fanrong—Huxin, hezuo, gongxiang 文明的和諧與共同繁榮—互信合作共享, Beijing, 2016.

21. Hu Xinsheng 胡新生, "Xi Zhou Chunqiu shiqi de guoye zhi yu buluo guojia xingtai" 西周春秋時期的國野制與部落國家形態, *Wenshizhe* 文史哲 2 (1985): 57–65.

22. *Zhou li zhengyi* 周禮正義 (Beijing: Zhonghua, 2015), 775.

23. *Zhou li zhengyi*, subcommentary to the *Dianshi* 甸師 section, 118.

24. *Guoyu jijie* 國語集解 (Beijing: Zhonghua, 2002), 219.

25. *Chunqiu Zuo zhuan gu* 春秋左傳詁 (Beijing: Zhonghua, 1987), 257. Translation is adapted from Stephen Durrant, Wai-yee Li, and David Schaberg, trans., *Zuo Tradition*; *Zuozhuan* 左傳 (Seattle: University of Washington Press, 2016), vol. 1, 212–213. Note however that they translate *bi* as "lowly rank."

26. *Guoyu jijie*, 499.

27. Ma Chengyuan 馬承源, ed., *Shanghai bowuguan cang Zhanguo Chu zhushu (er)* 上海博物館藏戰國楚竹書(二) (Shanghai: Shanghai guji, 2002), *Cong zheng*, *jia* (slip #13), 71, 226.

28. *Shuowen jiezi*, 142; for *Yu pian*, see *Guzun huizuan*, 2316.

29. Pan Yukun 潘玉坤, *Xi Zhou jinwen yuxu yanjiu* 西周金文語序研究 (Shanghai: Huadong shifan daxue, 2005), 205–211.

30. *Erya* (Beijing: Zhonghua, 2016), 9.

31. *Shuowen jiezi*, 1138.

32. *Guoyu jijie*, 538.

33. *Guoyu jijie*, 172.

34. Translation by Durrant, Li, and Schaberg, *Zuo Tradition*, vol. 3, 1630–1631.

35. See n. 10 in this chapter.

36. Chen Wei 陳偉, *Xinchu Chu jian yanjiu* 新出楚簡研究 (Wuhan: Wuhan daxue, 2010), 306.

37. A similar passage is found in *Shiji*, "Wu Taibo shijia" 吳太伯世家: "Previously, women from Chu's frontier settlement, who resided in Beiliangshi, fought with women from Wu's frontier settlement over mulberry trees. The families of the two women were incensed and destroyed one another. When the leaders of the two states' frontier settlements heard about this, they too were incensed and attacked one another, resulting in Wu's frontier settlement being destroyed. The king of Wu was angry and consequently attacked Chu, seizing two cities before leaving" (初, 楚邊邑卑梁氏之處女與吳邊邑之女爭桑, 二女家怒相滅, 兩國邊邑長聞之, 怒而相攻, 滅吳之邊邑. 吳王怒, 故遂伐楚, 取兩都而去). See *Shiji*, 31.1462. Both passages provide similar information on "outlying settlements."

38. Yang Kuan, "Chunqiu shiqi Chu guo xian zhi de xingzhi wenti," 61–83.

39. *Han Feizi jijie* 韩非子集解 (Beijing: Zhonghua, 1998), 25.

40. According to the *Guangya* 廣雅, "Shigu, san" 釋詁三 section, the word *mou* 某 ("such-and-such") refers to "an unspecified name" (*mou ming ye* 某名也). Wang Niansun 王念孫 (1744–1832) clarifies in *Guangya shuzheng* 廣雅疏證: "Whenever *mou* 某 is mentioned, this is how the text replaces a proper name (with an unspecified one)" (凡言某者皆所以代名). See *Guxun huizuan*, 2100. In this line from the *Yue Gong qi shi*, *mou* stands for whatever the current state of the township in question may be. The word *guo* 果 is used here as a loan for *he* 和 ("harmonious"). On the Mawangdui 馬王堆 silk manuscript *Yi zhi yi* 易之義, this same loan occurs in the line: "This is why Lu (Tread Upon) is used to harmonize actions, and the Qian (Humility) is used to order rituals" (是故履以果行也, 謙以制禮也). See: Hunan

sheng bowuguan 湖南省博物館 and Fudan daxue chutu wenxian yu guwenzi yanjiu zhongxin 復旦大學出土文獻與古文字研究中心, eds., *Changsha Mawangdui Hanmu jianbo jicheng* 長沙馬王堆漢墓簡帛集成 (Beijing: Zhonghua shuju, 2014), *Zhong yi* (i.e., *Yi zhi yi*), line 46, lower register: vol. 1, 37; vol. 3, 107, 108, n. 15. The *Shangshu*, "Gao Yao mo" 皋陶謨 chapter, writes "respectful of one another, oh how harmonious they will be!" (同寅協恭, 和衷哉), to which the pseudo-Kong commentary 孔傳 (ca. 3rd–4th c.) comments: "By regulating the regional lords with the five rites, it makes them equally honored and respectful together, harmonious and kind" (以五禮正諸侯, 使同敬合恭而和善). See *Shangshu zhengyi*, 151. Likewise, *Mengzi* 孟子, "Gongsun Chou, xia" 公孫丑下, states: "(Fortunate) timing granted by Heaven does not compare to favorable terrain, yet favorable terrain does not compare to harmony among men" (天時不如地利, 地利不如人和). See *Mengzi zhengyi* (Beijing: Zhonghua, 1987), 251. These are two examples where the word *he* 和 is used in a similar way, to mean "harmonious."

41. I suspect that the character before "*xiaoxiao* 笑笑," left without transcription, was originally a word that meant "only." If this is the case, then the line reads that "he could not just smile with pleasure" (不可笑笑也) but also had to give out actual rewards.

42. The word *yu* 與 ("participate"), is written as ▨ on the manuscript, for which the Tsinghua editors give 賊 as the transcription. The left component is *jian* 見, while the right component is written ▨, which the editors believe to be *bi* 必 (Qinghua daxue chutu wenxian yanjiu yu baohu zhongxin, ed., *Qinghua daxue cang Zhanguo zhujian* (*qi*), 137, 138 n. 3). The character *bi* 必 itself is seen elsewhere in the *Yue Gong qi shi*, however, where it is written as ▨ (slip #42) and ▨ (slip #61). The three lines at the bottom of these graphs are slanted strokes that run parallel to one another, without intersecting. The bottom of the right component to 賊, however, includes two lines that cross, ▨, which differs from how *bi* is written in these other instances. This suggests that the right component is not *bi*. Instead, I believe that its orthography matches that of *yue* 戉 instead, giving a transcription of 䦱. Compare, for instance, against the examples listed in Tang Yuhui 湯余惠, *Zhanguo wenzibian* 戰國文字編 (Fuzhou: Fujian renmin, 2001), 823.

In *Yue Gong qi shi*, this graph is used to write the word *yu* 與 ("to participate, be with"). *Yue* 戉 is the phonetic, and its OC pronunciation is similar enough to *yu* 與 to allow for a loan. See Tang Zuofan 唐作藩, *Shangguyin shouce* 上古音手冊 (Nanjing: Jiangsu renmin, 1982), 162. Yu Yue 俞樾, in his *Qunjing pingyi* 群經平議 (from *Qing Guangxu Chunzaitang quanshu* 清光緒春在堂全書, "Shangshu, san" 尚書三 (27–32), comments that, in the "Jiugao" 酒誥 chapter of the *Shangshu*, the word *yue*, which shares the same phonetic as the graph on our manuscript, is the same as *yu*. In *Yue Gong qi shi*, *yu* means "to participate in." It is used in this way, for instance, in *Lunyu* 論語, "Bayi" 八佾: "If I am not present (*yu*) at the sacrifice, it is as if I did not sacrifice at all" (吾不與祭如不祭) (see *Lunyu jishi* [Beijing: Zhonghua, 1990], 175); *Liji* 禮記, "Wangzhi" 王制: "At fifty they do not attend violent campaigns, at sixty they do not participate in dressing for war, and at seventy they do not participate in hosting guests" (五十不從力政, 六十不與服戎, 七十不與賓客之事) (see *Liji jijie* [Beijing: Zhonghua, 1989], 384); *Han shu*, *Wang Mang zhuan* 王莽傳 (pt. 1): "Kong Guang was made Grand Preceptor, participating in the governance of the Four Supports" (以光為太師, 與四輔之政). See *Han shu*, 99a.4047.

    43. Adapted from Durrant, Li, and Schaberg, *Zuo Tradition*, vol. 3, 1394–1395.
    44. Durrant, Li, and Schaberg, *Zuo Tradition*, vol. 2, 764–765.
    45. Durrant, Li, and Schaberg, *Zuo Tradition*, vol. 2, 1166–1167.
    46. Durrant, Li, and Schaberg, *Zuo Tradition*, vol. 2, 1192–1193.
    47. Durrant, Li, and Schaberg, *Zuo Tradition*, vol. 2, 1202–1203.
    48. *Yanzi chunqiu jiazhu* (Beijing: Zhonghua, 2014), 363.
    49. *Shiji*, 31.1452.
    50. *Jicheng* 285. Cf. Constance A. Cook and Paul R. Goldin, eds., *A Source Book of Ancient Chinese Bronze Inscriptions*, Early China Special Monograph Series no. 8 (Berkeley: Society for the Study of Early China, 2020), 258–264.

7

Marriage and Social Networks in Zhou China
Reflections on the Rules Governing Female Names in Bronze Inscriptions

LI FENG

The Problem and Its Significance

Rules that underlay the various names of women in the bronze inscriptions and the received texts of the Zhou dynasty have long been disputed among the scholars. The rules functioned essentially to regulate marriage relations among the states or lineages and were critical stabilizers of the foundation of Zhou social order. The present chapter examines the reasons behind the establishment of these rules from a social-historical perspective. In continuation, the chapter also reviews some of the recent debates about the formation and significance of these rules and discusses methodological issues in modern historical studies based on paleographical materials.

"A Splendid Woman": The *Book of Poetry* ("Airs of Wey" section):

A splendid woman and upstanding;
Brocade she wore, over an unlined coat,
Daughter of the Ruler of Qi,

Wife of the Ruler of Wey,
Sister of the Crown Prince of Qi,
Called sister-in-law by the Ruler of Xing,
Calling the Ruler of Tan her brother-in-law.
Hands white as rush-down,
Skin like lard,
Neck long and white as the tree-grub,
Teeth like melon seeds,
Lovely head, beautiful brows.
Oh, the sweet smile dimpling,
The lovely eyes so black and white.
This splendid lady takes her ease;
She rests where the fields begin.
Her four steeds prance,
The red trappings flutter.
Screened by fans of pheasant-feather
she is led to Court.
Oh, you Great Officers, retire early,
Do not fatigue our lord.
Where the water of the river, deep and wide,
Flows northward in strong course,
In the fish-net's swish and swirl
Sturgeon, snout-fish leap and lash.
Reeds and sedges tower high.
All her Jiang ladies are tall-coiffed;
All her knights, doughty men.

碩人其頎, 衣錦褧衣. 齊侯之子, 衛侯之妻. 東宮之妹, 邢侯之姨, 譚公維私.
手如柔荑, 膚如凝脂, 領如蝤蠐, 齒如瓠犀, 螓首蛾眉, 巧笑倩兮, 美目盼兮.
碩人敖敖, 說於農郊. 四牡有驕, 朱幩鑣鑣. 翟茀以朝. 大夫夙退, 無使君勞.
河水洋洋, 北流活活. 施罛濊濊, 鱣鮪發發. 葭菼揭揭, 庶姜孽孽, 庶士有朅.

It is probably hard to find another work in pre-Qin Chinese literature that achieved such a high level of exaltation about a woman's beauty.[1] The poem, especially the line "巧笑倩兮, 美目盼兮" (Oh, the sweet smile dimpling; the lovely eyes so black and white), with its adorable sense of liveliness and even temptation, has captured the hearts of generations of scholars and their like, distantly echoed in the most famous line of all time, "回眸一笑百媚生" (If she but turned her head and smiled, there were cast a hundred spells), from Bai Juyi's 白居易 "Song of Everlasting Sorrow" ("Chang hen ge" 長恨歌) extolling the beauty of the Tang emperor's famous concubine. It is the rich vocabulary in the archaic language of Zhou that adds another layer of deeply felt beauty.

The beauty of the poem's protagonist, however, cannot be fully understood and appreciated until we put her in the social context described by the lines referring to the hardworking ministers and the many Jiang 姜 women and minor gentlemen who attended her on her day of marriage. Indeed, everyone would be perplexed by the complex network of social relations ascribed to her in the first stanza of the poem. As it goes, she was the wife of Duke Zhuang of Wey 衛 in northern Henan, daughter of the ruler of the state of Qi 齊 in Shandong, sister to the crown prince of Qi, sister-in-law of the ruler of the state of Xing 邢, and younger sister to the wife of the ruler of Tan 譚. In this network formed through marriage, the fine lady stood in unique status with respect to each of the four regional states of Zhou: Qi, Wey, Xing, and Tan.

It is traditionally known that the states of Wey and Xing were descended from the Zhou royal Ji 姬 clan, as Wey was founded by a brother of King Wu and Xing by a son of the Duke of Zhou. Qi, on the other hand, was from the Jiang 姜 clan, a longtime ally and marriage partner of the Zhou.[2] Here, the ruler of Qi married his younger daughter to the ruler of Wey and had previously married his elder daughter into the state of Xing, whose ruler could then call the lady "sister-in-law." Another well-known marriage partner of Qi was its southern neighbor, the state of Lu 魯, to which Qi sent multiple brides over generations, including the ill-reputed Wen Jiang 文姜.[3] The state of Tan, on the other hand, is known as a state of the Si 姒 clan with which Qi was also related by marriage,[4] in addition to the aforementioned Ji states. This marriage network, centered on the state of Qi, was typical of Zhou society that had clans (*xing* 姓) and lineages (*shi* 氏) as its essential formational structures and closely observed the taboo that prohibited marriage between lineages of the same clan kin groups.[5] In fact, the Western Zhou state was founded on the principle of delegation of authorities to the royal Ji members over regional settlements augmented by the institution of marriage between the Ji states and the non-Ji states, including Qi.[6]

The importance of marriage relationships and the social network thereby formed in Zhou politics is fully documented in the bronze inscriptions from both the Western and Eastern Zhou periods. In fact, marriage was one of the most popular topics, besides bureaucratic affairs and military conduct, that was recorded in the inscriptions. Unlike the perspective of the poems in the *Book of Poetry*, which often speak about marrying ladies from the third person, the poet's viewpoint, inscribed bronzes that refer to marriage or married ladies were often cast by individuals involved in that relationship or by their close relatives. They offer more genuine insights into the actual operation of marriage in Zhou society and the political and social web formed through it. Moreover, the information in the inscriptions is advantageous in that, when excavated from particular sites, identifies the particular local states or lineages, often indicating their clan origins and their marriage partners.[7] Therefore, inscribed bronzes offer an important basis for the reconstruction of regional social networks as typified in the poem "A Splendid Woman."

However, correctly understanding this information in the bronze inscriptions involves a number of methodological challenges. Similar to the poem "A Splendid Woman" in which the name of the protagonist is not announced, in the bronze inscriptions, not only is this often true, but the same lady can also be called by different terms, most often using the lineage name (*shi* 氏) and/or clan name (or surname, *xing* 姓) combined in different ways, depending on the circumstances under which the bronzes were cast and on their specific purposes. Moreover, due often to the abstract nature of the language of the relevant inscriptions, it is not always clear who was casting vessels for whom, or, therefore, who was marrying into whose lineage or state. But, on the fundamental level, when faced with a corpus of hundreds of inscriptions, only a systematic approach can bring order to the various sources that span across China over a period of nearly eight hundred years. Such an analysis should aim not only to explain particular names of women who have relationships to specific lineages or states but also to systematically explain the raison d'être behind these inscriptions. Only such an analysis can make the hundreds of bronze inscriptions cast for/by elite women valuable sources for the social history of early China.

The Rules and Their Rationale

In 2015, I began to develop a theory that I think can logically explain the reasons behind the various names of women in bronze inscriptions and, by extension, also in the received texts from the Zhou period. I called it Rules of Name Differentiation.⁸

A straightforward description of Rule I may be charted as in figure 7.1. Let us suppose that the Ji 姬 clan had three consanguineous lineages (A, C, and D), whereas the Jiang 姜 clan also had three lineages (B, E, and F) that engaged in marriage relationships with the lineages of the Ji clan. The marriage relationship was constructed not in a parallel fashion, in which each lineage identified one specific lineage in the opposing party as its exclusive marriage partner; instead, it had considerable freedom to choose one from the three or more consanguineous lineages—each time determined by political circumstances—as long as the prohibition of marriage between members of the same clan was observed. This was indeed the case in Zhou society.

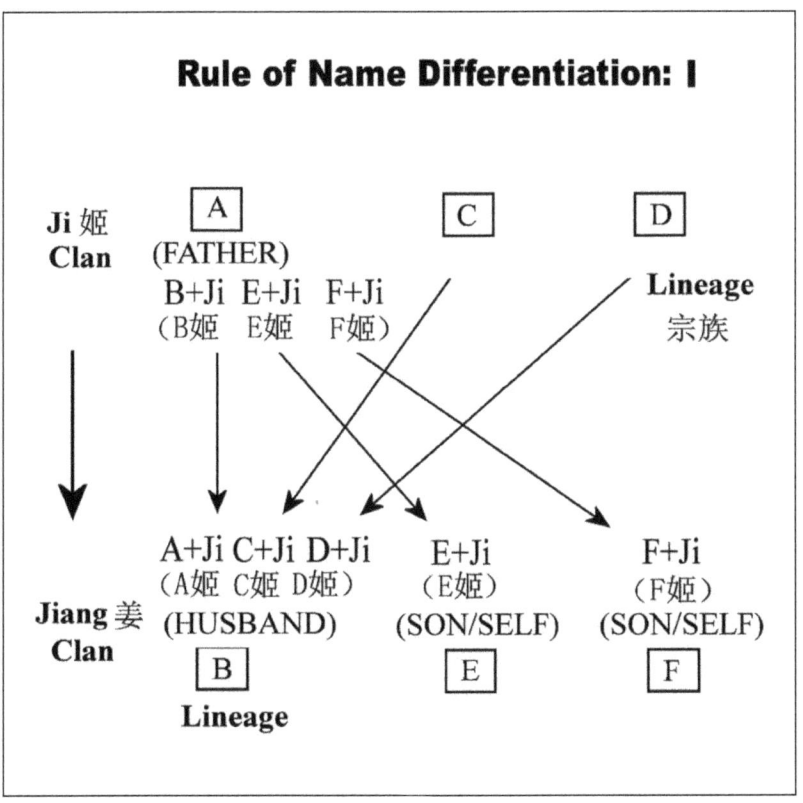

Figure 7.1. Rule I. *Source*: Created by the author.

Taking Lineage A of the Ji clan as the starting point and assuming that its patriarch had sent three daughters into marriage into three different lineages (B, E, and F) of the Jiang clan (of course, this does not exclude the possibility of marrying his daughter to lineages belonging to a third clan), the father would have to name his daughter "B Ji," "E Ji," and "F Ji"; that is, by his (and their) clan name (or surname), combined with the lineage names of their respective husbands (husband's lineage name + her clan name). Otherwise, if he were to use his (their) lineage name to call them, he might have had multiple daughters who had to share the same name "A Ji," which is to be avoided. In other words, her husband's lineage name was an important component in the designation of a married woman on cast bronzes, and hence the name called by her parents, usually her father. Examples of such usage are numerous in bronze inscriptions, typically cast on dowry vessels that would accompany the marrying lady into her new home. For instance, a set of four *gui* tureens (JC: 3775–3776, NA: 0055–0056),[9] cast by the ruler of Deng 鄧, was found in the cemetery of the state of Ying 應 in Pingdingshan 平頂山, Henan, and was inscribed: "鄧公作應嫚𦬱此媵簋，其永寶用" (Duke of Deng makes for Ying Man, Bi, [this] dowry *gui* vessel; may [she] eternally treasure and use it!). We know that Man 嫚 is the clan name of Deng, not that of the state of Ying, which was Ji; therefore, on the dowry bronze cast by her father, the lady is designated "Ying Man" 應嫚. To give an example from the Eastern Zhou period, the Lu Bo Yufu *li* 魯伯愈父鬲 (JC: 0692) is inscribed: "魯伯愈父作邾姬仁媵羞鬲" (Bo Yufu of Lu makes for Zhu Ji, Ren, [this] dowry food-serving *li* tripod). Here, the character *ji* 姬 in the lady's name "Zhu Ji" 邾姬 is the clan name of the state of Lu, and Zhu 邾 identifies her husband's state; in fact, the bronze was found in Tengxian 滕縣 in Shandong, near the capital site of the state of Zhu 邾, currently under excavation by Shandong University. The same is true in the Chenhou *gui* 陳侯簋 (JC: 3815), a bronze cast by the ruler of the state of Chen in Henan who married his daughter to the Zhou king, hence referring to his daughter as "Wang Wei" 王媯 on her dowry vessel; *wang* 王 here identifying the Zhou king as her husband (functions the same as a lineage name), and Wei 媯 identifying her clan origin. Unusually, these bronzes were found in areas close to the husband's state and were clearly marked as *yingqi* 媵器, or "dowry vessels." A new example is the Pengzhong *ding* 倗仲鼎 (JC: 2462), which says: "Pengzhong makes for Bi Kui 畢媿 (this) dowry *ding* vessel; may (she) for ten thousand years eternally use it!" The bronze was cast by an elite member of the state of Peng of the Kui clan in Shanxi who married his daughter into the famous Bi lineage in the royal domain of Shaanxi. Although the vessel comes with no provenance, it forms an interesting pair with the Pengbo *ding* 倗伯鼎, to be discussed later.

However, when a husband casts a bronze for his wife, whether for her personal use or for her use in worship, he would change the preceding rule. Let us suppose that if a husband in Lineage B (of the Jiang clan) casts a vessel for his wife from Lineage A (of the Ji clan), he ought to call her "A Ji"—"A" identifying her father's lineage and Ji identifying her father's (and her) clan origin—(father's lineage name + her clan name). This gives rise to a problem, depending on who is calling her, where "A Ji" and "B Ji" actually refer to the same lady who was married from Lineage A into Lineage B. The opposition between these two names for the same person confused many scholars, particularly when they tried to use the relevant inscriptions to determine the clan identity of the local states or lineages. Nevertheless, the reason for this switch of position is also clear, and it operates on the same rule of name differentiation. If a husband calls his wife by his own lineage name and her (or her father's) clan name, then, if he were to receive wives who were also from Linages C and D, he would completely fail to differentiate them. On the contrary, by using their fathers' lineage names, he can effectively differentiate them as "A Ji," "C Ji," and "D Ji." Demonstrating this rule in the inscriptions can be straightforward. The Sanbo *gui* 散伯簋 (JC: 3777) was cast by the lineage head of San 散 for his wife from the state of Ze 夨, which descended from the Ji clan, calling her "Ze Ji" 夨姬;[10] the Earl of Yu (Yubo 𩵋伯) cast two *ding* cauldrons (JC: 2676–2677) for his wife from the Jing 井 lineage of the Ji clan in Shaanxi, calling her "Jing Ji" 井姬; the Han Huangfu *ding* 函皇父鼎 (JC: 2548) was cast by the eminent Han Huangfu for his wife from the Zhou 琱 lineage, calling her "Zhou Yun" 琱妘, "Yun" 妘 being the clan identity of the Zhou lineage.[11] Usually, these vessels were found in or close to the areas where the husband's lineage or state was located. Recently, a very good proof of this rule came from the archaeological excavation of the cemetery of the state of Peng 倗 at Hengshui 橫水 in Jiangxian 絳縣, Shanxi. The two tombs discovered there were separated by four meters only from north to south. Three bronzes, cast for Pengbo's 倗伯 own use, were excavated from tomb no. 2, which was identified as the burial place of the ruler of Peng. Tomb no. 1, by the features of its buried goods, was identified by most scholars as belonging to the spouse of the ruler; from which four vessels, including one *ding* and one *gui*, all cast by Pengbo for his wife (one such bronze was also found in tomb no. 2), were excavated from this tomb. The inscription was: "Pengbo makes for Bi Ji 畢姬 (this) treasured travel *ding* (or *gui*) vessel."[12] Apparently, Pengbo's wife was from the famous

Bi 畢 lineage of the Ji clan, which was descended from the prominent Duke of Shao; therefore, she was called "Bi Ji" 畢姬 by her husband. In contrast, the Pengzhong *ding* 倗仲鼎 (JC: 2462) was a dowry vessel for a lady who married from the state of Peng into the Bi lineage; therefore, she is referred to as "Bi Kui" 畢媿 by her father.

Here arises a problem: If a husband took two or more wives from a single lineage of a different clan, how could he then differentiate them? He would insert a seniority designation between her father's lineage name and clan name, such as in the case of "Jing Meng Ji" 井孟姬 in the Zhong Shengfu *li* 仲生父鬲 (JC: 0729) or "Mao Zhong Ji" 毛仲姬 in the Shanfu Lübo *ding* 膳夫旅伯 (JC: 2619), and so forth. In Zhou inscriptions, women's seniority was designated by four terms: *meng* 孟, *zhong* 仲, *shu* 叔, and *ji* 季; just as men were differentiated by four terms: *bo* 伯, *zhong* 仲, *shu* 叔, and *ji* 季. Jing Meng Ji 井孟姬 was the oldest daughter of the Jing lineage, and Mao Zhong Ji 毛仲姬 was the second daughter of the Mao lineage, both traditionally known to have belonged to the Ji 姬 clan. Therefore, their husbands cast bronze for them and called them "Jing Meng Ji" 井孟姬 and "Mao Zhong Ji" 毛仲姬, respectively, complying with format of father's lineage name + her clan name.

What about a son casting a sacrificial vessel for his mother or a married lady casting a bronze for her own use? We have typical cases that suggest that a son would call his mother by her clan name, which is prefixed by his own lineage name (son's lineage name + her clan name). For instance, when a woman was married from Lineage A of the Ji clan into Lineage E of the Jiang clan, her son born of the marriage would have to call her "E Ji," in contrast to what her husband would call her, "A Ji." The reason for this lies in the fact that her husband needed to differentiate her (A Ji) from possibly his other wives (C Ji or D Ji) from the same Ji clan, but her son had only one biological mother and therefore there is no need to differentiate. The typical case is the Yuan *pan* 褱盤 (JC: 10172), dating to the late Western Zhou period. According to the inscription, this *pan* was cast for his father "Zhengbo" 鄭伯 and his mother "Zheng Ji" 鄭姬. Since male elites were by rule referred to after their lineage names, in his case, it is clear that the caster Yuan refers to his mother by the same lineage name as his father's, "Zheng" 鄭, and his mother was from the Ji 姬 clan. In the case of a married woman who cast a bronze with an inscription that referred to herself, she usually used her husband's lineage name and her own clan name. For instance, the San Ji *ding* 散姬鼎 (JC: 2029) is inscribed: "散姬作尊鼎" (San Ji makes [this] sacrificial *ding*). We know that San Ji 散姬 was from the state of Ze 夨, whose clan name was Ji 姬.[13] Another bronze, the Xu Ji *li*

許姬鬲 (JC: 0575), is inscribed: "Xu Ji makes (for) Xu Hu 虎 (this) travel *li* vessel." The state of Xu was of the Jiang clan; apparently the bronze was cast by a lady from the Ji clan who married into the state of Xu, so she called herself "Xu Ji" 許姬. She made the bronze for a person named "Jiang Hu" 姜虎. In addition, Guo Jiang 虢姜 cast multiple vessels excavated in the cemetery of the state of Guo 虢 in Sanmenxia 三門峽, for instance, Guo Jiang *ding* 虢姜鼎 (NB: 1100), inscribed: "Guo Jiang makes (this) travel *ding* vessel; may (she) eternally use it!" Guo was a state of the Ji clan, and Guo Jiang was apparently a lady of the Jiang clan who married into Guo; therefore, she called herself "Guo Jiang" 虢姜 on bronzes she made, using husband's lineage name + her clan name. The famous Jin Jiang *ding* 晉姜鼎 (JC: 2826) cast by Jin Jiang 晉姜 was another typical case and its long inscription best speaks of the relationship between Jin Jiang 晉姜 and her husband's state, Jin 晉. However, there seemed to be some flexibility in the way women called themselves as there are a small number of inscriptions in which they also refer to themselves by the lineage names of their fathers. For instance, the Lü Jiang *gui* 呂姜簋 (JC: 3348) is inscribed: "Lü Jiang makes (this) *gui* vessel." The state of Lü 呂 was of the Jiang clan, probably the state in which Lü Jiang was born. This might be a vessel cast by an unmarried woman for herself or by a married woman who, for political reasons, needed to emphasize her origin in the state of Lü.

In sum, the varying ways in which women were referred to in bronze inscriptions cast for/by them are the result of the operation of three principles that governed marriage relationships in Zhou society: 1) the cross-marriage between the Zhou elite lineages; 2) the exogamic rule that prohibited marriage between the consanguineous lineages of the same clan; 3) the practice of polygamous marriage where a husband by convention takes more than one wife. This is very different from the situation of monogamy commonly practiced in the ancient states of the Mediterranean world (although there are also exceptions to this rule).[14] It created very complex social relationships. Therefore, for each Zhou male elite, there was a class of lineages from which he could take wives, which excluded consanguineous ones. There is, thus, the need for the Zhou elites to use different designations for wives from different lineages or for daughters who were married into different lineages. Because of the prominent position of lineages in Zhou society, such lineage designations always constituted an essential part of a woman's name, prefixing or replacing her given name, which in the majority of the cases is omitted. However, the impact of the aforementioned principles goes beyond women's names to the names, and hence the social standing, of young elite males born of such marriages.

For a very long time, scholars were perplexed by certain names like "Zhousheng" 琱生, "Guosheng" 虢生, "Fansheng" 番生, and so on, all including *sheng* 生 as their ending character. It has been famously proposed by Zhang Yachu 張亞初 that in such names the character *sheng* 生 should be read as *sheng* 甥, "nephew," implying that the character prefixing it designates his mother's father's lineage, of which he is a nephew. In other words, Zhousheng 琱生 was a son born to a woman married out of the Zhou 琱.[15] Now this reading is widely accepted among scholars for such names that total more than thirty, but there is a complete lack of explanation of the reason behind these unconventional names. What is even more puzzling is the fact that individuals such as Zhousheng 琱生 and Fansheng 番生 enjoyed very high political standing in the central bureaucracy of the Western Zhou state,[16] and yet they continued to be referred to by their mothers' fathers' lineage names, as against the normal practice that elite males of Zhou be referred to by their own (thus their fathers') lineage names. Now, I think this can be explained by the Rule of Name Differentiation: II, as in figure 7.2.

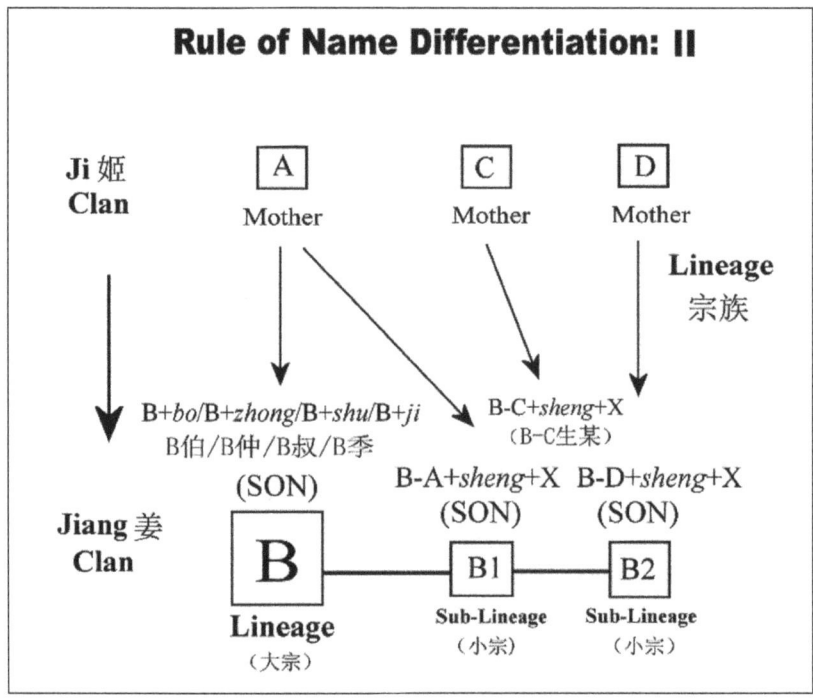

Figure 7.2. Rule II. *Source*: Created by the author.

Again, we may assume that the Ji 姬 clan had three lineages, A, C, and D, that were engaged in marriage relationships with lineages belonging to the Jiang 姜 clan. However, in this case we focus on one lineage of the Jiang clan, which is Lineage B, by the rule of lineage segmentation, that is over time there developed a distinction between the main branch of the lineage and sublineages established by the offspring of the trunk lineage. Because of the practice of primogeniture, sons born of a lineage in any generation would have been differentiated by four terms, *bo* 伯, *zhong* 仲, *shu* 叔, *ji* 季, with *bo*, the eldest son standing as the normative heir of the lineage. As a rule, the Zhou males were called by these seniority terms, prefixed by the lineage name of their fathers, as in names like Maobo 毛伯, Guozhong 虢仲, Jingshu 井叔, Sanji 散季. In theory, this is probably true of all lineages, main or derivative; but in practice, since sons of the main lineage were already referred to by the conventional seniority terms prefixed by the lineage name, this would make it infeasible and confusing for sons of the sublineages to also use the same set of names. In order to avoid this confusion, it was required that the sons of a sublineage adopt the lineage names of their mothers' fathers, using it alone or together with the name of the main lineage, followed by the character *sheng* 甥. Thus, when a lady of Lineage A of the Ji clan was married into the main branch of Lineage B, the sons born of the marriage would be referred to as "B-*bo*," "B-*zhong*," "B-*shu*," and "B-*ji*"; but, if she was married into a sublineage of Lineage B, B1, or B2 for instance, the son born of the marriage would have to be referred to as "B-A-*sheng*," followed by his seniority name or personal name if necessary. If his mother was from Lineage C or Lineage D, he would have to be referred to as "B-C-*sheng*" or "B-D-*sheng*." Or he could simply be called "A-*sheng*," "C-*sheng*," or "D-*sheng*."

Thus, Zhousheng 琱生 was a person who was born to a lady from the Zhou 琱 lineage. Since he cast vessels for his ancestor the Duke of Shao 召, there can be no doubt that he belonged to the prominent Shao lineage and thus could also have been referred to as "Shao Zhousheng" 召琱生, although this latter name does not appear in the inscriptions. A lady from the Zhou 琱 lineage had also married into the prominent Han 函 family, as is evident from the Han Huangfu *gui* 函皇父簋 (JC: 4141). The duplication of two lineage names is exemplified by names such as "Zhou Jisheng" 周𩁢生, or the textually known "San Yisheng" 散宜生. The latter, "San Yisheng," was known as a minister to King Wen and a member of the San lineage, born to a lady from the lineage of Yi 宜. The former, "Zhou Jisheng," appears on the Zhou Jisheng *gui* 周𩁢生簋 (JC: 3915) and was a member of the

Zhou 周/琱 lineage, born to a lady from the Ji 鸏 lineage; the vessel was being cast by him for a lady marrying out of the Ji 鸏 lineage.[17] Examples of personal names included in such terms are "Chensheng Que" 陳生雀 in the Chensheng Que *gui* 陳生雀簋 (JC: 2468) and "Junsheng Hufu" 麇生曶父 in the Shi Hai *gui* 師害簋 (JC: 4117), the latter name being Junsheng's courtesy name. Only when we understand the rule of lineage segmentation, and the principle that governed the exogamic marriage network of Zhou, can we fully understand the varying ways in which these unconventional elite names were constructed.

In short, lineages were essential building blocks of early Chinese society. The correct management and presentation of lineage relations were critical measures to the formation and operation of Zhou society. As women provided the essential means for the reproduction of society, strict rules determining the ways in which they were called and remembered by their lineage membership and clan origin worked to demarcate the correct marriage groups for the future. On the other hand, as the prominent transmitters of power and property, elite males were required to correctly identify their lineage positions as an important path to achieve social order. Even when they were able to rise to the top of the Zhou bureaucratic government, they continued to be referred to by the names adopted when they were young, names based on their status in the lineage and the lineage's standing in Zhou society.

Challenges by Wu Zhenfeng

In June 2016, Wu Zhenfeng 吳鎮烽, a senior scholar of bronze inscriptions in Shaanxi, published an article in which he refuted the views I suggested in my essay published in the *Wenhuibao*. In all, Wu's view is that the rules proposed in my essay are but specific "forms" (*fangshi* 方式) of women's names, not rules, which, if they were, everyone should obey. According to Wu, there are various other "forms" that women called themselves or were called by their family member and, in the majority of cases, women's names did not include lineage names. In conclusion, Wu stressed that the situation was rather ad hoc, and there were simply no rules that might have governed it.[18]

With regard to the way in which women were called by their fathers on dowry vessels, for instance, Wu Zhenfeng listed nine such "forms."[19] However, a look at the list quickly reveals that these can be best understood as variations of the essential structure, husband's lineage name + her clan name, particularly with respect to forms 1–4, to which seniority order and/or personal given name were added perhaps to further distinguish the lady from her siblings. This is completely legitimate and the use of more complex forms like these certainly would not undermine the importance of the normative structure, much less overturn it. As for forms 5–9, they constitute various abbreviations of the more complex forms by simply calling a woman by her clan name, or personal name, or seniority, or by combining any two or three of these elements. Ultimately, however, they constitute no counterevidence to the normative rule according to which women were referred to by their fathers or mothers on their dowry vessels. In Zhou elite society, depending on the social and economic power of the family and the personal relations the parents have to their daughters and their husbands, parents certainly had the freedom to use such simpler forms of names in bronzes cast for their daughters' marriage; but, while the normative rule remained, they would not violate it.

It was further argued by Wu Zhenfeng that, among the 230 dowry vessels cast by Zhou parents for their daughters, only 93 mention the lineage name of the husband as part of the name of the wife, thus complying with the normative structure I suggested; in contrast, 112 cases do not, so the structure husband's lineage name + her clan name cannot be considered a rule. However, when we look at the 112 cases, they include five "forms": 6) +2; 7) +4; 8) +19; 9) +53; 10) +34, the largest numbers being that of the simple use of seniority and/or personal names (9–10). In other words, Wu was effectively comparing the 93 cases that mention the husband's lineage name with the total number of inscriptions that do not mention "lineage name" at all (not only those that do not mention the husband's lineage name). This is a logically wrong comparison, as the subject of comparison and the object to which it is being compared are not on the same level of the classification system. The legitimate comparison should be that between cases that mention the husband's lineage name and cases that do not mention the husband's lineage name, *all within the realm of inscriptions that mention "lineage names."* However, in contrast to 93 (40%) of the total 230 cases of dowry vessels with inscriptions in which parents call their daughters by "husband's lineage name + her clan name," there is not a single case of a dowry bronze inscription that mentions a "lineage name" that is not her husband's. In other words, *dowry vessels that mention lineage names must mention husband's lineage name, and this is certainly the rule*. Moreover, the number 93 is much higher than that of actual cases in any other comparable categories (i.e., #5–10). The aforementioned situation certainly constitutes a very strong base that "husband's lineage name + her clan name" was the normative structure of women's names on dowry vessels. More importantly, rules are based on principles that govern the operation of the whole system; in this case, the preceding rule can be fully explained by the principles that governed marriage in Zhou society.

Wu Zhenfeng also made similar arguments in his effort to invalidate other rules about women's names that I suggested, but his arguments can be refuted on the same grounds as those demonstrated.[20] Of all the inscriptions Wu has gathered, there are only three cases in which a woman commissioning a bronze gives her father's lineage name, thus presenting possible counterevidence to the normative structure of "husband's lineage name + her clan name": Qi Jiang *ding* 齊姜鼎 (JC: 2148), Lu Ji *li* 魯姬鬲 (JC: 0593), and Zhai Ji *jue* 祭姬爵 (*Mingtu* 銘圖08426). But three is a very small number and the three are restricted to the situation in which women, themselves, were the casters of the bronzes. Moreover, two of them, the Qi Jiang *ding* and Zhai Ji *jue* were both found in the Zhou capital Feng 豐 in Shaanxi, evidently commissioned by elite women who were married into the Zhou royal domain from two regional states in the east. They suggest a certain flexibility in the ways women referred to themselves under special circumstances, when, for instance, their purpose was to commemorate their origins in the eastern states.

In my October 2017 response to Wu Zhenfeng, I further discussed the complex relationship that emerged from the gift of dowry vessels to the daughters of another state and the rules that governed the names of women that appear in pairs in such a context.[21] Our current evidence for this is mainly from the regional states in the Yangzi region centering on the hegemonic state of Chu 楚; correctly interpreting these names is key to understanding the regional geopolitics of southern China during the Spring and Autumn period. There are three inscriptions that testify to the situation in which two women's names appear on the same vessel:

1. **Zenghou *fu* 曾侯簠 (JC: 4598):**

    叔姬霝乍（作）黃邦, 曾侯作叔姬, 邛嬭媵器將彝.

    Shu Ji Ling makes way to the state of Huang, and the Ruler of Zeng makes (for) **Shu Ji** and **Qiong Mi** (this) dowry vessel as her sacrificial vessel.

2. **Xuzi Zhuang *fu* 鄦子妝簠 (JC: 4616):**

    唯正月初吉丁亥, 鄦子妝擇其吉金, 用鑄其簠, 用媵孟姜, 秦嬴.

It was the first month, first auspiciousness, on *dinghai* day, the Ruler of Xu, Zhuang, chose auspicious metal, with which he casts the *fu* vessel, using it as a dowry vessel for **Meng Jiang** and **Qin Ying**.

3. **Shangruo Gong** *fu* 上鄀公簠 (NA: 0401):

唯正月初吉丁亥，上鄀公擇其吉金，鑄叔嫚，番改媵簠.

It was the first month, first auspiciousness, on *dinghai* day, the Duke of Shangruo chose auspicious metal, casting a dowry *fu* vessel for **Shu Mi** and **Fan Ji**.

It is first to be recognized that the first woman on the first two vessels shares the same clan name as the state rulers who cast the bronzes; for instance, Zeng's 曾 clan name was Ji 姬 and Xu's 鄁 was Jiang 姜. Therefore, it is evident that the bronzes were cast as dowry vessels primarily for the first woman in each pair, who were daughters of their casters. But the inscriptions suggest no clear connection between the second woman and the caster of any of these bronzes. How can we explain this?

The most reasonable explanation is: Two women, from two different lineages/states, were married into the same lineage/state at the same time; therefore, the vessel was cast as a dowry vessel for both. The caster, usually the father of one of the women, called the lady from this one state (usually his daughter, state A) by a name in accordance with the normative "husband's lineage name + her clan name" structure (or by using a seniority name instead of lineage name). But, since he entered into a relationship with the second woman (from C) only through his daughter's husband's family (state B), he adopted the position of the husband's lineage in calling the second woman by the normative structure of "father's lineage name + her clan name." Specifically, the first bronze was cast by the Ruler of Zeng 曾 (A) for his daughter Shu Ji 叔姬 who married into the state of Huang 黃 (B), into which the state of Qiong 邛 (of Mi 嫚 clan name, C) also sent a lady in marriage, so the vessel was cast for both Shu Ji 叔姬 and Qiong Mi 邛嫚. In the second inscription, the Ruler of Xu 鄁 (A) cast a vessel for both his daughter Meng Jiang 孟姜 and Qin Ying 秦嬴 (from state C), who married into an unknown state (B). In the third inscription, however, there is a high possibility that Shu Mi 叔嫚 was a daughter of the King of Chu 楚 (A) and Shangruo 上鄀 was its dependent state (state D). In this case, the Duke of Shangruo was actually casting a dowry bronze for the

160 | Li Feng

daughter of his master the King of Chu. Since the small state Fan 番 (C) was sending a daughter to accompany the Chu princess in her marriage to an unnamed state (B), the Duke of Shangruo cast the vessel for both women, but called the latter, Qin Ying, according to the position of the state of the husband of the Chu princess (B). The important point here is the following: when a bronze was cast as a dowry vessel for two women, the first woman, as the primary bride, is named from the standpoint of her father and in accordance with the normative "husband's lineage name + her clan name" structure. The second woman, however, is named from the standpoint of their husband and in accordance with the normative "father's lineage name + her clan name" structure (fig 7.3).

Understanding this rule opens new ways for us to correctly interpret some of the previously difficult-to-understand inscriptions. For instance, the Quanbo *ding* 夐伯鼎 is inscribed: "唯正八月既生霸丙申, 夐伯作楚叔妊,

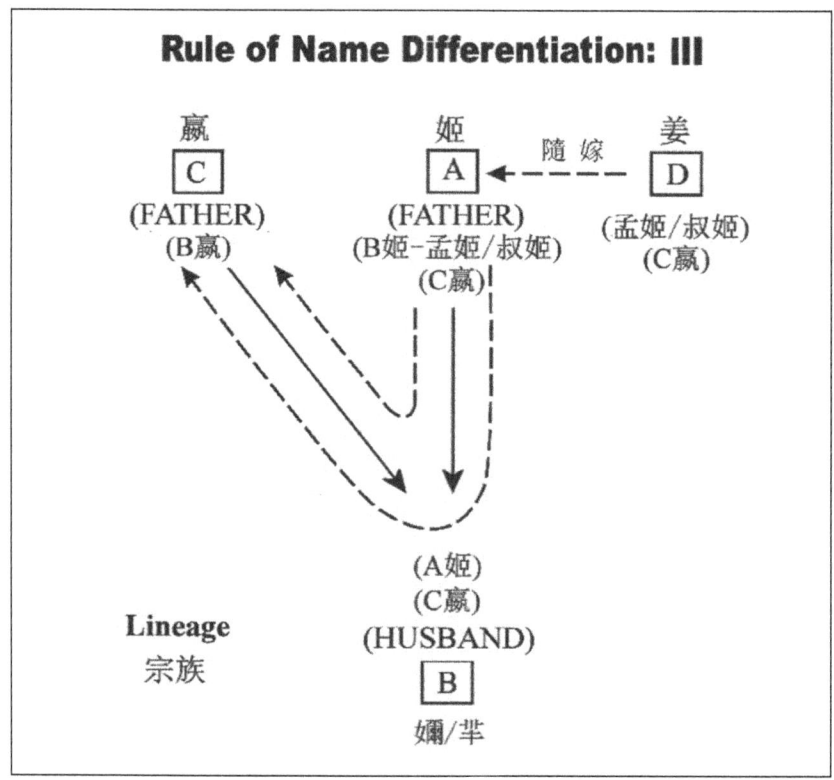

Figure 7.3. Rule III. *Source*: Created by the author.

樂姬媵盂鼎" (it was the formal eighth month, after dying brightness, on *bingshen* day, Quanbo casts [for] Shu Ren of Chu and Le Ji [this] dowry deep-belly *ding*).²² It is confusing that the lady from Chu was referred to by the clan name Ren 妊, instead of Mi 嬭, which is the traditionally known clan name of Chu. So, it is no wonder that some scholars thought that the two ladies named in the inscription were married into two different states.²³ It is now clear, however, according to the rules discussed earlier, that the Quanbo 曩伯 (in the position of state D) was casting a dowry vessel for a lady from an unnamed state (A)—possibly the state of Xue 薛 in Shandong, whose clan name was Ren 妊—who married into the state of Chu (B); but it is also clear that the vessel was cast as a dowry for the second lady, Le Ji 樂姬, who, at the same time, married into Chu from the state of Le 樂 (C) and adopted the normative structure of the name from the position of her husband (father's lineage name + her clan name). Only a systematic understanding of the complex relationships of marriage and the rules that governed the various names of women in such relationships can fully reveal the social and political meaning of such inscriptions.

Further Reflections

Soon after my response was published, Wu Zhenfeng published his second paper to defend his early criticism of my views.²⁴ Wu opened his paper with a strong argument against the concept of "rule" in my essays, but in doing so he made another logical mistake. Targeting the structure of "husband's lineage name + her clan name" as the normative structure of names used by parents for their daughters, Wu argued that, if this structure represented a "rule," then neither of the two constituent parts should be missing; if missing, then the aforementioned structure is not a "rule." This, Wu argued, should be the case in all inscriptions cast by parents for their daughters. In order to support his position, he gives as an analogy the Chinese Communist Party's (CCP) organizational rule, the so-called "Democratic Centralism" (*minzhu jizhong zhi* 民主集中制), and argues that both concepts are indispensable for the doctrine to be considered a "rule" in the CCP; he further states that this is similar to the formulation of "Water = H_2 + O" in which neither "H_2" nor "O" can be missing.

If Wu had intended to use a political argument to counter my "rule," then I would not have been able to respond because of my total lack of interest in discussing political issues in what is purely an academic context. But, I feel compelled to point out that the two examples he gave are self-evident propositions in logic and that any denial of them is, in itself, contradictory. What Wu is saying, therefore, is that this is the same way that people from East Asia form their names: family name (surname) first, followed by personal name (Name = Surname + Given Name). While this is certainly correct, it proves nothing about my proposed "rules." Whether the format "Surname + Given Name" can be regarded as a "rule" cannot be determined by the format itself but must be determined by its extensive or rare use in East Asia, or even in the world. Therefore, the two cases of analogy suggested by Wu Zhenfeng are meaningless in the current debate and simply cannot support Wu's position. Furthermore, in making his argument, Wu was apparently confused about the two propositions: the "composition of rule" and the "application of rule." It is simply wrong in logic that Wu used the answer to this conceptual truth to answer the question about the validity of rule based on its practical application. As a senior scholar, Wu knows well whether the rule of the so-called "Democracy + Centralism" was always strictly obeyed, or whether any of the two constituent parts were ever ignored or purposely undermined, despite the fact that, as a rule, these two combined constituent parts are clearly written in the party's doctrine. So, Wu's argument is not only oversimplistic, it is simply misplaced. Ultimately, whether the structure of "husband's lineage name + her clan name" constituted a rule in Zhou society depends on the number of instances of actual cases of inscribed bronzes to which the rule was applied. Using figures provided by Wu, I have already pointed out that 93 inscriptions cast on dowry vessels include "husband's lineage name" as part of the designation of their daughters' names, while not a single inscription on a dowry vessel that mentions lineage name does not mention "husband's lineage name" of the woman. In other words, when a woman was referred to by her lineage identity by her parents, she must be called by her husband's lineage identity. This certainly was the rule, although simplified forms of names that refer to her only by her personal name and/or seniority order were also valid practices in Zhou society.

  A larger part of Wu's paper was taken up by discussions of examples in which Wu thinks invalidate the rules I suggest were practiced in Zhou society. The nature of the language of some of these examples, the Guozhong *li* 虢仲鬲 (JC: 0708), for instance, has ambiguities that are open to different interpretations,[25] to which Wu added only more reasoning but not evidence. Another inscription, the Huangzi *li* 黃子鬲 (JC: 0624), for instance, was taken out of its archaeological context in which twelve vessels from the same tomb clearly show that the name "Huang Meng Ji" 黃孟姬 was the abbreviation of "Huang furen Meng Ji" 黃夫人孟姬. None of these are qualified counterevidence to the normative structure, "father's lineage name + her clan name," used by husbands casting vessels for their wives. Since I have already pointed out problems with these inscriptions, there is no need to discuss them again. But two examples, stressed by Wu at length, show important methodological differences between Wu and myself in the analysis of bronze inscriptions that need to be discussed here.

The first is the Yuan *pan* 寰盤 (JC: 10172), a *pan* basin that was cast in the twenty-eighth year of King Xuan of Zhou (r. 827–782 BCE). The *pan* was cast by Yuan for his father Zhengbo 鄭伯 and his mother Zheng Ji 鄭姬, the latter being clearly referred to in accordance with the normative structure "son's lineage name + her clan name." In other words, Zheng Ji was a lady who was married into the Zheng lineage from an unknown lineage of the Ji clan 姬, so that Zheng was not a member of the Ji clan. In his first paper, Wu accepted this reading and clearly stated that Zheng 鄭 in Zheng Ji's 鄭姬 name refers to her husband's (son's) lineage, and, according to the well-known marriage taboo of the Zhou, this Zheng lineage must have been a non-Ji 姬 lineage.[26] However, in his second paper and in order to criticize me, Wu abruptly changed his position and strongly defended the traditional textual view that Zheng 鄭 was founded by King Xuan's brother You 友 (i.e., Duke Huan of Zheng 鄭桓公), therefore, Zheng was of the Ji clan; on the other hand, Wu denied the existence of a non-Ji lineage by the name of "Zheng" 鄭.[27] Wu concluded that the Yuan *pan* was an example demonstrating that a son casting a vessel for his mother did not use her father's (his maternal grandfather's) lineage name but used, instead, his (son's) lineage name and his mother's clan name. Wu's conclusion, however, is not only consistent with the normative structure (son's lineage name + her own clan name) that I suggested for sons casting vessels for their mothers, which he criticized, but further created a contradiction by having a woman of the Ji clan marry into a lineage, Zheng 鄭, that belonged to the Ji clan (in Wu's view). It is unfortunate that Wu missed my special analysis of the problem of Zheng, already published in 2007.[28] In that study, I have shown that, since the Zheng of the Ji clan (that of Duke Huan of Zheng) was established in 806 BCE, but the Yuan *pan* was cast in 800 BCE, six years after the founding of Zheng (Ji clan), by which time Yuan's father and mother were already dead (but the tradition is strong on the death of Duke Huan of Zheng in 771 BCE), it is clear that the Zheng in the Yuan *pan* was not the Zheng of the Ji clan. The existence of this non-Ji Zheng

鄭 (evidently of the Jiang 姜 clan instead) long before and even after the founding of the Zheng of the Ji clan is not only indicated by inscriptions such as that on the Yihou Ze *gui* 宜侯夨簋 (JC: 4320) and the Zheng Jiangbo *ding* 鄭姜伯鼎 (JC: 2467), cast by the head of the Zheng lineage of the Jiang clan, but this "Jiangbo" 姜伯 was previously misread as "Yibo" 義伯 by Wu Zhenfeng,[29] but it is also corroborated by inscriptions cast by Zheng's neighbors, for instance, the Zewang *guigai* 夨王簋蓋 (JC: 3871) that was cast by the King of Ze 夨 for his wife Zheng Jiang 鄭姜, a lady from the Zheng lineage whose own clan name was Jiang. If Wu had read my paper published in 2007, he might not have intended to switch his position, being misguided by the restriction of textual tradition on Zheng.

The second case involves the identity of the state of Wu 吳 and begins with the inscription of the Bo Junfu *ding* 伯䂇父鼎 (JC: 2649), which says: "伯䂇父作朕皇考犀伯,吳姬寶鼎" (Bo Junfu makes [for] my august deceased father Xibo 犀伯 and Wu Ji [this] treasured *ding* vessel). However, this is both a historical problem and a historiographical problem, and a full analysis of it is beyond the scope of the present chapter. Wu thinks that this is Bo Junfu making a vessel for his father Xibo and his mother Wu Ji 吳姬, who was a lady of the Ji surname from the state of Wu 吳. If this were true, it would contradict the normative structure—"son's lineage name + her clan name"—that is used on vessels cast by a son for his mother. In his second paper, Wu strongly defends the textual (basically Han) account of Wu (吳姬) as a member of the Ji clan, located in the Yangzi Delta, based on Wu's alleged ancestral line going back to the Zhou royal brothers, Taibo 太伯 and Zhong Yong 仲雍. Wu argues that there can be no other Wu than this Wu of the Ji clan in the Zhou dynasty. I have earlier pointed out that Wu's connection to the Zhou royal house and the alleged clan name Ji 姬 of Wu was most likely fabricated by later historians. This view, with which I concur, is based on our current information from the archaeological finds in the area of the Yangzi Delta and the consideration of the geopolitical position of the region in the contemporary Western Zhou time period.[30] In fact, inscriptions such as, for instance, that on the Caihou Shen *pan* 蔡侯申盤 (JC: 10171) are good evidence of this point: the ruler of Cai cast a dowry vessel—in accordance with the marriage taboo—for his daughter Da Meng Ji 大孟姬, who was married to the King of Wu 吳, which certainly indicates that Wu was not of the Ji clan; similarly, the Zi *yi* 自匜 (JC: 10186) was a dowry vessel cast for Wu Ji 吳姬, who married into the state of Wu.

As discussed earlier, on all dowry vessels, the lineage name represents the lineage into which the woman was married. On the other hand, inscriptional evidence clearly shows that there was another state, Wu 吳, probably a member of the Ji clan, originating in the royal domain of Shaanxi. This was the lineage of Wubo 吳伯, mentioned in the Ban *gui* 班簋 (JC: 4341), and probably also of Wu Hui 吳朹, mentioned in the Jing *gui* 靜簋 (JC: 4273). Both men were officials at the Zhou royal court in Shaanxi, and the Zhou king once also visited the settlement of Wu 吳, mentioned in the Shi You *gui* 師酉簋 (JC: 4288). Without acknowledgment of the existence of two Wu states in the Zhou periods, Wu Zhenfeng was in no position to argue that the Wu Ji 吳姬 in the Bo Junfu *ding* was married from the Wu state, not a woman who married into the Wu state. It is ultimately wrong to cling to textual records to deny information in the bronze inscriptions; instead, modern historians should first clarify the information on the contemporaneous bronze inscriptions before comparing that information to the received textual tradition, especially when the same tradition dates no earlier than the Han dynasty. This is the essential attitude a modern historian must have.

Conclusion

When Wu Zhenfeng says, "The Zhou dynasty never promulgated rules for elite names. The 'rules that governed female names' suggested by Professor Li are, in fact, merely a form of women's names. This is the fundamental difference between me and Professor Li,"[31] I agree with him about the difference in our approaches; there certainly is a conceptual distinction to be made between "rule" and "form." However, I think that the most fundamental difference between our views in the current debate lies not in our conclusions, but in our different understanding of the purpose of historical studies and the nature of history as a discipline. Wu's method is to try to identify as many variants of a phenomenon as possible, which he calls *fangshi* 方式 (forms), and correctly display them as the results of his research in an article. Accordingly, in his first paper, Wu gave nine "forms" of women's names that they are called by their parents (increased to eleven in his second paper); eight "forms" of women's names that they are called by their sons; six "forms" of women's names that they are called by their husbands; twenty "forms" of women's names that they are called by themselves; and, in addition, some small categories of a small number of "forms," such as women's names that they are called by their brothers or friends. Wu's comprehensive survey of sources and the clear display of them is of great value to our field, so long as we recognize where his approach leads.

Regrettably, however, the conclusion he draws from such a thorough survey is merely: "There was no rule that governed the names of women, as there was no rule for the names of men. The Zhou dynasty never promulgated rules for elite names."[32]

However, I think that modern historians should and can do much more than just surveying sources and correctly displaying them. They should no longer find satisfaction in *what really happened in history*, but should make the effort to understand *why the events happened the way they did*.[33] Comprehensive and accurate surveys of sources are the important first step of a research project, but the historian should move on to analyze the sources, not just for the purpose of displaying them as they are, but for the purpose of detecting regularities and pervasive patterns in history. More importantly, the historian should make an effort to understand the causes for these regularities and whether certain regularities were random gatherings of facts or were determined by certain rules. Rules are based on principles that link practices by individuals or groups with the social structures in which they live. Societies with different structures and different cultural practices certainly had different rules. The purpose of studying bronze inscriptions lies ultimately not in uncovering their conditions of existence, which is certainly important, but in achieving a logical and systematic understanding of the institutions and cultural traditions of Zhou society through the discovery of "rules."

Notes

1. Arthur Waley's translation with minor modification. See Waley, *The Book of Songs: The Ancient Chinese Classic of Poetry* (New York: Grove Press, 1996), 48–49.

2. For the marriage between the Ji clan and the Jiang clan, see Edwin Pulleyblank, "Ji and Jiang: The Role of Exogamic Clans in the Organization of the Zhou Polity," *Early China* 25 (2000): 1–27.

3. Wen Jiang's 文姜 story is told in the *Zuo zhuan*. She was the daughter of Duke Xi of Qi and married Duke Huan of Lu (711–694 BCE). But, on a home visit, she committed adultery with her half-brother, the reigning Duke Xiang of Qi. Duke Xiang of Qi eventually arranged the murder of Duke Huan of Lu, and this caused long-lasting turmoil in the state of Lu. See *Zuo zhuan* 左傳 (Beijing: Zhonghua, 2006), 152.

4. On the clan origin of Tan, see Chen Pan 陳槃, *Chunqiu dashi biao lieguo juexing ji cunmie biao zhuanyi* 春秋大事表列國爵姓及存滅表譔異 (Shanghai: Guji, 2009), 467–469.

5. On the distinction between clan and lineage, see Li Feng, *Early China: A Social and Cultural History* (Cambridge: Cambridge University Press, 2014), 140–141. Essentially, clans were kin groups bound together by a common ancestry, and clan names usually were related to the maternal origin of the clan's founding ancestor. Lineages were recent and contemporary social, political, and economic entities of the Zhou elites; they usually existed in relatively smaller units and were related to each other through clan ties.

6. On the importance of marriage relationships in Zhou society and the Western Zhou state, see Edward L. Shaughnessy, "Marriage, Divorce and Revolution: Reading between the Lines of the Book of Changes," *Journal of Asian Studies* 51 (1992) 3: 587–599; Li Feng, *Landscape and Power in Early China: The Crisis and Fall of the Western Zhou, 1045–771 BC* (Cambridge: Cambridge University Press, 2006), 292–293.

7. Regional states were localized polities of Zhou (and some non-Zhou) elites in eastern China that were installed with autonomous rights under the overall Zhou royal authority. Lineages were social entities that held landed property and population in the Zhou royal domain, and that later also gradually gained power within the eastern states. On the difference between regional state and lineage, see Li Feng, *Bureaucracy and the State in Early China: Governing the Western Zhou* (Cambridge: Cambridge University Press, 2008), 43–49.

8. I explained these rules first in December 2015 at a conference in Beijing, jointly hosted by the University of Chicago and Beijing University. The same contents were then presented in a seminar that I gave at East China University of Political Science and Law in Shanghai and, subsequently, published in: Li Feng 李峰, "Xi Zhou zongzu shehui xia de chengming qubie yuanze" 西周宗族社會下的稱名區別原則, in *Wenhuibao* 文匯報 (February 19, 2016), 14–15. In English, these rules were first published in: Li Feng, "The Western Zhou State," in *Routledge Handbook of Early Chinese History*, ed. Paul R. Goldin (London: Routledge, 2018), 101–102.

9. Serial numbers of inscribed bronzes, abbreviated as JC for *jicheng*, follows *Yin Zhou jinwen jicheng* 殷周金文集成, ed. Zhongguo shehui kexueyuan kaogu yanjiusuo (Beijing: Zhonghua, 1984–1994); adopted in the Academia Sinica database of bronze inscriptions: http://bronze.asdc.sinica.edu.tw/qry_bronze.php.

10. It has recently been clarified that Ze 矢 descended from the Ji 姬 clan; see Li Feng 李峰, "Xi Zhou jinwen zhong de Zheng di he Zheng guo dongqian" 西周金文中的鄭地和鄭國東遷, *Wenwu* 2006.9: 70–78.

11. The Zhou 珘 lineage (of the Yun 妘 clan) should not be confused with the royal Zhou 周 lineage (of the Ji 姬 clan) that founded the Western Zhou dynasty.

12. Shanxi sheng kaogu yanjiu suo 山西省考古研究所 et al., "Shanxi Jiangxian Hengshui Xi Zhou mu fajue jianbao" 山西絳縣橫水西周墓發掘簡報, *Wenwu* 2006.8: 4–18.

13. See Li Feng, "Xi Zhou jinwen zhong de Zheng di he Zheng guo dongqian," 70–78.

14. Richard Saller, "Household and Gender," in *The Cambridge Economic History of the Greco-Roman World*, ed. Walter Scheidel, Ian Morris, and Richard Saller (Cambridge: Cambridge University Press, 2007), 90.

15. Zhang Yachu 張亞初, "Liang Zhou jinwen suojian mou sheng kao" 兩周銘文所見某生考, *Kaogu yu wenwu* 考古與文物 1983.5: 83–89.

16. See Li Feng, *Bureaucracy and the State in Early China*, 66, 124.

17. Dong San 董珊, "Shilun Yinxu buci zhong de Zhou wei jinwen zhong de Yun xing zhi Zhou" 試論殷墟卜辭中的周為金文中的妘姓之猸, *Zhongguo guojia bowuguan guankan* 中國國家博物館館刊 2013.7: 48–63.

18. See Wu Zhenfeng 吳鎮烽, "Yetan Zhou dai nüxing chengming de fangshi" 也談周代女性稱名的方式, website of the Center for the Study of Excavated Manuscripts and Paleography, Fudan University, June 7, 2016, accessed September 3, 2017, http://www.gwz.fudan.edu.cn/Web/Show/2822. For my *Wenhuibao* article, see n. 8.

19. The list includes: 1) husband's lineage name + her clan name; 2) husband's lineage name + her clan name + her personal name; 3) husband's lineage name + her seniority order + her clan name; 4) husband's lineage name + her seniority order + her clan name + her personal name; 5) [missing]; 6) her clan name; 7) her personal or courtesy name; 8) her clan name + her personal name; 9) her seniority order + her clan name; 10) her seniority order + her clan name + her personal or courtesy name.

20. See Li Feng 李峰, "Zailun Zhou dai nüxing de chengming yuanze: Da Wu Zhenfeng xiansheng" 再論周代女性的稱名原則：答吳鎮烽先生質疑, published on the website of the Center for Bamboo and Silk Manuscript Studies, Wuhan University, October 6, 2017, http://www.bsm.org.cn/?guwenzi/7649.html.

21. Li Feng, "Zailun Zhou dai nüxing de chengming yuanze: Da Wu Zhenfeng xiansheng."

22. Wu Zhenfeng, *Shang Zhou qingtongqi mingwen ji tuxiang jicheng* 商周青銅器銘文暨圖像集成 (Shanghai: Guji, 2012), 128–131.

23. See Liu Li 劉麗, "Yi qi ying er nü xianxiang bushuo" 一器媵二女現象補說, *Guwenzi yanjiu* 古文字研究 31 (2016): 199–204.

24. See Wu Zhenfeng, "Zaitan suowei de 'Zhou dai nüxing chengming qubie yuanze': Da Li Feng jiaoshou" 再談所謂的"周代女性稱名區別原則"—答李峰教授, published on the website of the Center for the Study of Bamboo and Silk Manuscripts, October 21, 2017, accessed December 5, 2018, http://www.bsm.org.cn/show_article.php?id=2930.

25. Liu Shegang 劉社剛, "Guozhong xu jiqi xiangguan wenti kao" 虢仲盨及其相關問題攷, *Wenbo* 文博, 2011.6: 26–27. (攷 = 考.)

26. See Wu Zhenfeng, "Yetan Zhou dai nüxing chengming de fangshi," 4.

27. See Wu Zhenfeng, "Zaitan suowei de Zhou dai nüxing chengming qubie yuanze," section 2.

28. See Li Feng 李峰, "Xi Zhou jinwen zhong de Zheng di he Zheng guo dongqian," 70–78.

29. See Wu Zhenfeng, *Jinwen renming huibian* 金文人名彙編 (Beijing: Zhonghua, 1987), 301. In this book, under "Zheng Yibo" 鄭義伯, is listed the Zheng Yibo *ding* 鄭義伯鼎, which is indeed the Zheng Jiangbo *ding* 鄭姜伯鼎.

30. See Li Feng, *Landscape and Power in Early China*, 324–325, and *Bureaucracy and the State in Early China*, 239–240.

31. See Wu Zhenfeng, "Zaitan suowei de Zhou dai nüxing chengming qubie yuanze," introduction.

32. See Wu Zhenfeng, "Zaitan suowei de Zhou dai nüxing chengming qubie yuanze," introduction.

33. The reader is advised to read the preface to the Chinese edition of my book on bureaucracy: Li Feng 李峰, *Xi Zhou de zhengti: Zhongguo zaoqi de guanliao zhengdu he guojia* 西周的政體: 中國早期的官僚制度和國家 (Beijing: Sanlian, 2010), i–ix.

8

The Faces of Cao Gui

Fact and Meaning in Warring States and Early Han Historiography

ANDREW MEYER

Extending Lévi-Strauss's Model from Prehistoric to Historical Narratives

In her seminal study of early Chinese dynastic legends, *The Heir and the Sage*, Sarah Allan demonstrated that accounts of early dynastic transitions (such as the putative abdication of Yao to his successor Shun) served as vectors for an extensive and enduring debate, the effect of which was "to mediate an inherent social conflict . . . [between] the demands of virtue and heredity" during the Warring States 戰國 (481–221 BCE).[1] Allan noted that the dynastic legends of early China were produced within a discursive dynamic like that described by Claude Lévi-Strauss for the legends of South American peoples such as the Bororo. In Lévi-Strauss's analysis the composers of legend were analogous to bricoleurs—craftspeople who create artifacts out of sundry materials that they find handy. In the same way that bricoleurs

---

The author would like to thank the editors, the anonymous reviewers, and his colleagues in the Late Antique, Medieval, and Early Modern studies seminar at Brooklyn College, who offered feedback on this work.

are only limited by the materials available in their "treasure chests," the composers of legend were limited by the materials made available to them in the body of legend that they inherited from prior generations, which could then be reworked into new patterns on the basis of current needs.²

Implicit in Allan's study of early Chinese dynastic legends was the suggestion that these narratives were isomorphic to the stories studied by Lévi-Strauss because all were rooted in "prehistoric" mythology (i.e., an oral discourse that preceded the existence of written records). In this chapter, however, I would like to extend this type of analysis to discourses surrounding events and figures set in historical times, arguing that we can see a similar dynamic at work. I will focus here on one such figure, the Spring and Autumn–era 春秋 (771–481 BCE) knight Cao Gui 曹劌 (fl. ca. 670 BCE),³ by way of investigating this phenomenon and exploring its implications for the study of early China.

Cao Gui was most prominently immortalized during the Former Han 前漢 (206 BCE–8 CE) by Sima Qian 司馬遷 (145–ca. 86 BCE) as the first of the "Assassins" 刺客 whose biographies are arrayed in the *Records of the Historian* (*Shiji* 史記).⁴ But he had a long and varied career in the literature of the Warring States and early empire. Anecdotes about him are recorded in the *Zuo zhuan* 左傳,⁵ the *Guoyu* 國語, the *Guanzi* 管子, the extant fragments of the *Shenzi* 慎子, the *Lüshi chunqiu* 呂氏春秋, the *Huainanzi* 淮南子, and the *Xinxu* 新序. He is mentioned as an exemplar of martial prowess in the *Zhanguoce* 戰國策 and the *Sunzi bingfa* 孫子兵法.⁶ An extended text recording dialogues between Cao Gui and his ruler, Duke Zhuang of Lu 魯莊公 (r. 693–662 BCE), was discovered among the bamboo manuscripts housed at the Shanghai Museum.⁷ We thus have a rich array of testimony regarding the treatment of Cao Gui within the historiography of Warring States and Former Han literati.

Cao Gui as an Exemplar of Dignity and Efficacy

The sheer frequency with which Cao Gui appears in the textual record suggests how provocative and intriguing a figure he was for early literati. Why this was so becomes immediately apparent when we turn to the particular instances of his literary persona. It is difficult to determine with any certainty which story is the locus classicus of Cao Gui lore, but a convenient point of departure for investigation is a famous anecdote recorded in the *Zuo zhuan*:⁸

In the tenth year [of Duke Zhuang], the army of Qi attacked us. The Duke was about to do battle when Cao Gui requested an audience.

His neighbors told him, "The highborn (lit., 'those who eat meat') are planning [for battle], why should you get involved?"

—[Cao] Gui replied: "The highborn are benighted, they cannot make long-range plans."

Thus, he entered for an audience and asked what cause they were fighting for.

The Duke said, "When I have food and clothing to make myself secure, I do not dare hoard it, I share it with others."

—[Cao] replied, "That is a small grace, it is not universal. The people will not follow you."

The Duke said, "I do not dare embellish my sacrificial offerings of animals, jade, and silk. They are always faithful."

—[Cao] replied, "This is small faithfulness that does not inspire confidence. The spirits will not grant you luck [on this account]."

The Duke said, "For cases great or small, even if I cannot investigate them [personally], I always decide them according to the facts."

—[Cao] replied, "This is the kind [of conduct that inspires] loyalty, for this you may do battle one time. If you go into battle I ask to come along."

The Duke mounted a chariot with [Cao Gui], and they battled at Changshao.

The Duke was about to sound the drums [to advance], but [Cao] Gui said, "Not yet."

The men of Qi attacked three times, [then Cao] Gui said, "Now we may [attack]."

The Qi army was routed.

The Duke was about to pursue, [but Cao] Gui said, "Not yet."

Dismounting, he looked at their wheel tracks. Climbing up onto the crossbar of the chariot, he observed them. "Now we may [pursue]," he said.

Thus they pursued the Qi army. When they had triumphed, the Duke asked his reasons.

—[Cao Gui] replied: "Battle depends on the *qi* of courage. The first roll of the drums arouses the *qi*. On the second roll it diminishes. By the third roll it is exhausted. The enemy was depleted, and we were full, thus we defeated them. A great state is difficult to fathom. I feared they had set an ambush, [but] I saw that their tracks were chaotic and their flags disordered, so we pursued them.

十年, 春, 齊師伐我, 公將戰, 曹劌請見. 其鄉人曰: 肉食者謀之, 又何間焉. 劌曰: 肉食者鄙, 未能遠謀, 乃入見, 問何以戰. 公曰: 衣食所安, 弗敢專也, 必以分人. 對曰: 小惠未遍, 民弗從也. 公曰: 犧牲玉帛, 弗敢加也, 必以信. 對曰: 小信未孚, 神弗福也. 公曰: 小大之獄, 雖不能察, 必以情. 對曰: 忠之屬也, 可以一戰. 戰則請從, 公與之乘, 戰于長勺, 公將鼓之, 劌曰: 未可. 齊人三鼓, 劌曰: 可矣. 齊師敗績, 公將馳之, 劌曰: 未可. 下視其轍, 登軾而望之, 曰: 可矣. 遂逐齊師, 既克, 公問其故. 對曰: 夫戰, 勇氣也. 一鼓作氣, 再而衰, 三而竭, 彼竭我盈, 故克之, 夫大國難測也, 懼有伏焉, 吾視其轍亂, 望其旗靡, 故逐之.

This passage is remarkable for the sheer density of logical and polemical assertions compacted into its rhetorical formulations. As in the dynastic legends examined in *The Heir and the Sage*, the tension between virtue and heredity is a central focus. Cao Gui is a lowly knight, not ensconced within the circle of high-born aristocrats and ducal kin entitled to a share of meat from the ancestral temple. It is nevertheless he who possesses the key to preserving the state that is putatively the patrimony of "those who eat meat." Cao Gui is thus an exemplar who embodies the basic dignity and political efficacy of the very literati who composed and circulated his story.

Complexity or Contradiction in the Cao Gui Persona

Beyond engaging the question of merit and lineage, Cao Gui sits at the confluence of other lines of tension: between "civil" and martial prowess (*wen* 文 and *wu* 武);[9] between virtue and force (*de* 德 and *li* 力).[10] Though Cao secures victory on the battlefield, he does not do so through a feat of personal courage or skill-at-arms, but through knowledge and intellectual acumen. He reads the enemy in the same way that a literatus would read a text; he thus stands testimony to the manner in which literati are essential to all functions of the state, even its military operations. Indeed, Cao demonstrates that the literatus contributes more to the military enterprise than the "heroic" warrior, establishing the supremacy of *wen* over *wu*.

Cao's interrogation of the Duke before the battle asserts the authority of literati to stand in moral judgment of the state's hereditary leaders, and to the primacy of moral concerns in the conduct of power. Cao must first assess whether the Duke possessed the minimum threshold of moral potency that would empower him to take up arms, only then was it possible to secure victory. This demonstrates not merely the supremacy of *de* over *li*, but that the latter effectively does not exist in the absence of the former.

The urgency of these aggregated concerns would in itself go a long way to explaining why the figure of Cao Gui would be so alluring to the composers and compilers of many texts. But if we pick at the different strands in the tapestry of Cao Gui's legend, we find that his persona is extremely complex. In the *Guanzi*, we find this account that diverges sharply in its depiction of Cao from that found in the *Zuo zhuan*:[11]

> For four years [the state of Qi] trained soldiers, until it had one hundred thousand mailed warriors and five thousand chariots. [Duke Huan of Qi (r. 685–643 BCE)] spoke to Guan Zhong (ca. 730–645 BCE), saying, "My knights have been trained, my soldiers are many, I want to subjugate Lu."
>
> —Guan Zhong sighed deeply, saying, "The state of Qi is endangered! You do not exert your virtue (*de*) but exert your military. The states in the world that can field one hundred thousand mailed warriors are not few. If we [thus] want to send our small military to subjugate a great military (i.e., the combined militaries of the many states), we will lose the masses in our own state. If the lords of the land prepare against us and our own people turn on us, can we fail to be endangered?"
>
> The Duke did not listen, he indeed invaded Lu. Lu did not dare to give battle. They set the pass [between the two states] fifty *li* from the capital [of Lu].
>
> Lu asked to be treated as a "vassal within the passes," to follow Qi, if Qi would not invade Lu again. Duke Huan agreed.
>
> The men of Lu asked for a covenant, saying, "Lu is a small state, we never wear swords. If now you wear swords it will be said among the vassal lords that this was an armed meeting. It is best for you to stop, please put aside your swords."

—Duke Huan said, "Agreed."

Thus he ordered his entourage to be without weapons.

—Guan Zhong said, "This may not be. The lords of the land were afraid of you. If you had withdrawn at that point, it would have been all right. Now that you have genuinely weakened the ruler of Lu, the lords of the land further consider you greedy. If after that there is some incident [during the covenant ceremony], the small states will become more recalcitrant, the great states will become more wary. None of this will profit the state of Qi."

The Duke did not listen.

—Guan Zhong again remonstrated, saying, "If you are determined not to leave Lu, why will you not use weapons? As a man, Cao Gui is stubborn and envious, he cannot be restrained by an agreement."

Duke Huan did not listen, and finally met [with Lu]. Duke Zhuang [of Lu] concealed a sword, Cao Gui also brought a hidden sword up onto the altar.

—Duke Zhuang pulled his sword from his bosom and said, "If the border of Lu is to be only fifty *li* from the capital, all I can do is die!"

With his left hand he grabbed Duke Huan, with his right hand he held his sword against himself, saying, "Since it is to be death, I will die in front of you!"

Guan Zhong moved toward his lord, but Cao Gui drew his sword and stood between the two steps [of the altar], saying, "The two rulers are changing the map, no one will come forward."

—Guan Zhong said, "My lord cedes territory, let the Wen River be the boundary."

Duke Huan agreed, they set the Wen River as the boundary and withdrew.

When Duke Huan returned he reformed his government and did not cultivate his military.

四年, 修兵, 同甲十萬, 車五千乘. 謂管仲曰" :吾士既練, 吾兵既多, 寡人欲服魯." 管仲喟然嘆曰: "齊國危矣, 君不競於德而競於兵, 天下之國, 帶甲十萬者不鮮矣, 吾欲發小兵以服大兵, 內失吾眾, 諸侯設備, 吾人設軸, 國欲無危, 得已乎?" 公不聽, 果伐魯,魯不敢戰，去國五十裡而為之關。魯請比於關內，以從於齊，齊亦毋復侵魯，桓公許諾。魯人請盟曰："魯，小國也，固不帶劍，今而帶劍，是交兵聞於諸侯，君不如已，請去兵。桓公曰："諾。"乃令從者毋以兵。管仲 曰："不可. 諸侯加忌於君，君如是以退可，君果弱魯君，諸侯又加貪於君，後有事，小國彌堅，大國設備，非齊國之利也。"桓公不聽，管仲又諫曰："君必不去魯，胡不用兵，曹劌之為人也，堅強以忌，不可以約取也。胡不用兵，曹劌之為人也，堅強以忌，不可以約取也。桓公不聽，果與之遇，莊公自懷劍，曹劌亦懷劍踐壇，莊公抽劍其懷曰："魯之境去國五十裡，亦無不死而已。"左揕桓公，右自承，曰："均之死也，戮死於君前。"管仲走君，曹劌抽劍當兩階之間曰："二君將改圖，無有進者。"管仲曰："君與地，以汶為竟。"桓公許諾，以汶為竟而歸. 桓公歸而修於政，不修於兵革。

Perhaps the most remarkable observation that emerges from the juxtaposition of these respective passages is the degree of logical and rhetorical overlap that they exhibit. On key points both texts agree. Guan Zhong's relationship to Duke Huan in the *Guanzi* affirms the same supremacy of merit over birth as that implied by the dialogue between Duke Zhuang of Lu and Cao Gui recorded in the *Zuo zhuan*. Though not as lowly in status as Cao Gui, Guan Zhong is his Duke's inferior by birth but his clear superior in judgment and ability: the narrative shows that Duke Huan should have been guided by Guan Zhong from the outset.

Moreover, the supremacy of civil over martial prowess and virtue over military force are likewise points of consensus between the *Guanzi* and the *Zuo zhuan*. Guan Zhong reads his ruler's opponents like a text, and if his advice had been heeded it would have garnered the same kind of tactical success secured by Cao Gui in the *Zuo zhuan*. The *Guanzi* anecdote begins with Guan Zhong predicting that Duke Huan's choice to rely on military might over virtue will lead to danger and concludes with the Duke being converted to the correct path after Guan Zhong's prediction proves true.

Given this foundation of consensus, the divergence between the two texts in their depiction of Cao Gui might appear somewhat puzzling. Where the *Zuo zhuan* presents Cao as an unambiguous paragon of virtue, the *Guanzi* paints him a villain: "stubborn and envious" and wholly without honor. Not only is he brutish and devious, but in abetting his ruler's profanation of the covenant ceremony, the Cao Gui of the *Guanzi* demonstrates utter contempt for the sanctity and austerity of ritual in general. This likewise diametrically contradicts Cao Gui's portrayal in the *Zuo zhuan*, where (in a different anecdote than the one cited earlier[12]) he admonishes his ruler to cleave to ritual so as to set a good example for present and future generations. In terms of plot and characterization the two passages presented are thus effective inversions of one another. All of the exemplary qualities borne by Cao Gui in the *Zuo zhuan* are shifted onto Guan Zhong in the *Guanzi*; while in the *Guanzi* Cao Gui becomes reduced to a moral status even worse than that occupied by the faceless Qi invaders in the *Zuo zhuan*.

Why is this? One factor might be simple geopolitics. If (as is possible, and as I have argued elsewhere is likely[13]) the anecdote taken from the *Guanzi* was first produced in Qi and that taken from the *Zuo zhuan* was first produced in Lu, a clear motive for the apparent inversion would be state propaganda: the Qi text promotes a hero of its home state and impugns the agents of its opponents; the Lu text vice versa.

Even if this is true, however, the divergence between the two passages cannot be reduced to a case of simple transposition. More is at stake than the dignity or reputation of particular states or dynasties. This can be seen in the comparison between the behavior of the protagonist in either anecdote. Both Guan Zhong and the Cao Gui of the *Zuo zhuan* provide their respective rulers with congruent forms of service, but the *Zuo zhuan* narrative makes clear that Cao Gui's support of Duke Zhuang is conditional in a way that (in the *Guanzi*) Guan Zhong's service of Duke Huan is not (it is, in fact, literally unconditional).

In the *Zuo zhuan* anecdote, Duke Zhuang avails himself of Cao Gui's talents only after submitting to the knight's interrogation and providing a satisfactory justification on his third attempt. Even then, Duke Zhuang earns Cao Gui's service for one battle, with no guarantee of further loyalty. By contrast, Guan Zhong relentlessly serves Duke Huan of Qi and continues to offer new advice, despite the fact that, over the course of the anecdote, the Duke repeatedly ignores and contravenes Guan Zhong's counsel. More than this (and in further stark disparity from the case of Cao Gui in the *Zuo zhuan*), Guan Zhong persistently modulates his advice to account for the obstinate foolishness of his ruler: Duke Huan should (in the *Guanzi*'s enumeration of Guan Zhong's assessments) rely on virtue over military might; barring that, he should stop when he has frightened the lords of the land; barring that, he should refrain from acquiring a reputation for greed; barring that, he should at least have the good sense to go into the covenant meeting with Lu armed (and thus avoid being tricked in a way that will cause others to see him as not only threatening and greedy, but vulnerable).

The Cao Gui Persona: Clash of Interpretive Constructs

These contrasts suggest that the figure of Cao Gui sat at a contested boundary between Qi and Lu, and that the conflict demarcated by this frontier was both deeper and more abstract than a mere rivalry between competing states. The "Qi position" staked out in the *Guanzi* is articulated in a phrase used by Guan Zhong: "the profit of the *state* (of Qi)" (*guo zhi li* 國之利). "The profit of the state" is the one concern imbuing Guan Zhong's counsel with consistency and integrity, and it provides the fundamental rationale for Guan's behavior overall: it would be best for the state if it had a ruler that listened to his wise advisor, but barring that it would be better for the ruler's wise advisor to continue to serve him than for the state to lack a ruler altogether.

The "Lu position" implicit in the *Zuo zhuan* does not treat the state as an equivalently ultimate concern. Cao Gui's support of both ruler and state is contingent upon Duke Zhuang's fulfillment of moral ideals that transcend and give meaning to the state of Lu itself. If state power is not being used in service of those moral imperatives, the existence of the state as a polity is no longer worthy of concern. In the terms of the texts in which they are inscribed, the Qi position could be summarized as "the Way exists to support the state," while the Lu position was that "the state exists to fulfill the Way."

The labels "Lu position" and "Qi position" are obviously interpretive constructs, but they are not wholly alien impositions upon the sources themselves. The acknowledgment of such an opposition is broadcast in many formulations found in Warring States texts. For example, *Analects* 6.24 declares, "With one change, Qi can become Lu; with one change, Lu can achieve the Way" (齊一變, 至於魯; 魯一變, 至於道).[14] Not only does this passage evince a general awareness of a Qi-Lu conceptual divide, but it stands as a concrete instance of the "Lu position" in particular: Qi must obviously become more like Lu, but even the state of Lu itself must aspire to more perfectly embody the moral Way to be ultimately worthy of loyalty.

Much evidence suggests that advocacy of these opposed positions served as focal points (among others) of group identity for distinct communities of literati operating in Qi and Lu, respectively. As the divergence in their perspectives suggests, these groups were organized differently, or at least represented themselves as such in the surviving literature they produced. The Lu partisans composed material such as that found in the *Analects* and *Mencius*, which celebrate the Master-disciple fellowship, its cultivation of intimately personal relationships between literati in the realm outside of government service, and its commitment to the propagation of moral teaching. Qi partisans, by contrast, produced writings such as those found in the *Guanzi* and *Yanzi chunqiu* that valorize state service as the highest object and ideal to which a literatus might aspire, subordinating each knight's individual qualities, talents, and personal relationships to the needs of the state itself.[15]

Though the conceptual Qi-Lu rivalry was most likely (at least for a time) socially institutionalized within the political geography of the Warring States, this does not compel us to read every observable articulation of the "Qi position" or the "Lu position" as the product of a particular group at a particular time or place. Both positions were amenable to abstraction and literary transmission: "Qi" and "Lu" could serve as signifiers analogous to the use of "Athens and Jerusalem" in the polemical literature of early Christianity.[16] Thus as literary tropes these positions could circulate beyond the ambit of the groups that first formulated them even while those groups remained coherent and active, and could (and did) persist into the early empire, long after any concrete social rivalry between geographically and organizationally distinct groups had collapsed.

The portability of these formulations is amply evinced by the archaeologically discovered text *Cao Mie zhi zhen* 曹蔑之陳 (The Battle Formations of Cao Mie), archived among the bamboo manuscripts at the Shanghai Museum. Though the exact provenance of these manuscripts is unknown, lexical and other evidence suggest that they were originally interred in the state of Chu in the late fourth century BCE.[17] Though the text was thus removed from any immediate geographic affinity with any "Qi-Lu" rivalry, the conflicts mediated by passages such as those excerpted earlier remain:[18]

> Duke Zhuang of Lu was about to make a great bell. When the mold was complete, Cao Mie went in for an audience, saying, "Of old when the Zhou house chartered Lu as a state, it was seven hundred [*li*] from east to west, five hundred from north to south. There were no mountains or marshes, no territory in which there was no people. Now your state gets smaller while your bells get bigger. My lord think on it. Of old when Yao feasted Shun they ate from earthen plates and drank from earthen bowls, yet they controlled the world. Is not this being poor in adornment yet rich in virtue?

魯莊公將為大鐘, 型既成矣. 曹蔑入見, 曰: 昔周室之邦魯, 東西七百, 南北五百, 匪山匪澤, 亡有不民. 今邦彌小而鐘愈大. 君其圖之. 昔堯之饗舜也, 飯於土簋, 歠於土鉶, 而撫有天下. 此不貧於美而富於德歟?

What is most remarkable about this passage (and by extension, the entire manuscript of the *Cao Mie zhi zhen*) is that it deploys its eponymous protagonist, a celebrated hero of the state of Lu, as a logical and rhetorical proponent of the "Qi position." This is broadcast in several ways. In logical terms, the basic assumption that the inverse relationship between the size of the bells and that of the territory of Lu is a negative indicator precludes there being a more transcendentally moral justification for state policy (i.e., the resolution of the story rests on the assumption that ritual and music must necessarily exist for the good and support of the territorial state, not vice versa).

In rhetorical terms, the text deploys several tropes that telegraph its affinity with the "Qi position" over that of Lu. The preceding anecdote mirrors one contained in the *Yanzi chunqiu* 晏子春秋, in which the eponymous protagonist likewise admonishes his ruler for plans to cast a bell.[19] In thus problematizing the occasion of the production of a musical instrument, both the *Cao Mie zhi zhen* and *Yanzi chunqiu* evoke a heated controversy within the discourse of Warring States literati: the conflict between the latter-day disciples of Mozi and those of Confucius over the validity of music.[20] Texts aligned with Confucius acknowledge the merit of government frugality[21] but virtually never assent to the idea that music is a legitimate realm in which to seek "cost savings," precisely because the followers of Mozi condemned music as wrong on the charge that it is wasteful of resources.[22] By allowing that frugality may apply even to the domain of music, *Cao Mie zhi zhen* (like the *Yanzi chunqiu*) broadcasts that it is not bound by the same rhetorical obligations and allegiances as Lu partisans. The evocation of the Confucius-Mozi controversy is made very explicit in *Cao Mie zhi zhen* by use of language that mirrors phrasing found in the *Mozi*: "In antiquity when Yao ruled the world . . . he ate from earthen plates and drank from earthen bowls" (古者堯治天下 . . . 飯於土塯, 啜於土形).[23]

Though it provisionally aligns itself with the followers of Mozi in this opening passage, *Cao Mie zhi zhen* distinguishes itself from the position of the *Mozi* in later passages, where Cao Gui is depicted as assenting to "assault" (*gong* 攻) as a legitimate exercise of state power:[24] the *Mozi* bans "assault" in the same terms and for the same reasons as it does music.²⁵ At the same time, Cao Gui's discussion of the means of assault distinguishes him from Confucius as the latter was depicted in the *Analects*. In *Analects* 15.1, when the ruler of Wei asks Confucius about battle formations (*zhen* 陳) the Master becomes so offended that he leaves the state.²⁶ By contrast, Cao Gui is so blithe about answering such questions from the ruler of Lu that the whole series of dialogues were entitled *The Battle Formations of Cao Mie* (*Cao Mie zhi zhen*).²⁷

This move to distinguish Cao Gui's position from that of *both* Confucius and Mozi is very typical of "Qi-partisan" texts: a means of signaling that the producers of the text are not bound by the commitments of the latter-day disciples of either figure. Though this suggests that *Cao Mie zhi zhen* was perhaps produced in the same context as the material anthologized in texts such as the *Guanzi* and *Yanzi chunqiu*, this was not necessarily the case. Even if *Cao Mie zhi zhen* was produced in Qi, that fact would not (and obviously did not, given its appearance among texts buried in Chu) have limited its usefulness to literati operating within Qi itself.

Though the texts produced by latter-day disciples of Confucius and Mozi depict those figures as vehemently disagreeing with one another on many counts, they likewise present both Masters as advocating the determinative supremacy of a moral Way that transcends the state and necessarily imbues it with legitimacy. Confucius would define "the Way" differently than Mozi, but both would assent to the proposition that "the state exists to fulfill the Way." Any articulation of the Qi position would thus be useful to someone who desired to promote the concept that "the Way exists to support the state."

This is exemplified by the appearance of the opening passage of *Cao Mie zhi chen* among the extant fragments of the text attributed to Shen Dao. Shen is recorded as having accepted the patronage of the Qi state at Jixia, but little in his eponymous text marks him as a "Qi partisan." The anecdote about Cao Gui is chiefly useful within the purview of the *Shenzi* in support of its advocacy of the state as an ultimate concern and focus of loyalty.²⁸

If we follow the evolution of Cao Gui as a figure into imperial times, the picture becomes even more complex. In the *Huainanzi* we find this anecdote:²⁹

> In days of old, Caozi commanded an army on behalf of Lu. Three times in battle he was not victorious and lost thousands of *li* in territory. If Caozi had persisted in his plans and had

not reversed course, had [planted his] feet without budging, he [might have] had his throat cut at Chenzhong or ended his days as the captive commander of a defeated army. But Caozi was not embarrassed by his defeat and did not die in shame and without merit. [Instead], during the interstate meeting at Ke, he took a sword three feet long and pointed it at the midriff of Duke Huan [of Qi]. Thus the effects of three defeats in battle were reversed in the course of a morning. His courage was heralded throughout the world, and his accomplishments were established in the state of Lu.

昔者, 曹子為魯將兵, 三戰不勝, 亡地千里. 使曹子計不顧後, 足不旋踵, 刎頸于陳中, 則終身為破軍擒將矣. 然而曹子不羞其敗, 恥死而無功. 柯之盟, 搚三尺之刃, 造桓公之胸, 三戰所亡, 一朝而反之, 勇聞於天下, 功立于魯國.

This account of Cao Gui is remarkable for combining elements from many other *mutually divergent* accounts. Its overall structure corresponds most closely to the account in the *Guanzi*, but the included detail that "three times in battle [Cao] was not victorious" suggestively echoes the *Zuo zhuan*'s narrative, in which Cao orders the assault only after "the men of Qi attacked three times." Moreover, the conclusion of the meeting at Ke in this account diverges from that of the *Guanzi*: in the earlier text Cao threatens suicide, in the *Huainanzi* he achieves his goal by threating the life of Duke Huan. This different version of events is echoed in Sima Qian's later account found in the *Shiji*, where it is instrumental in the overarching narrative of the "Assassin Retainers" chapter as a whole.

Most surprisingly, both this *Huainanzi* account and the *Shiji* biography that parallels it invert the normative frame of the structurally similar narrative that appears in the *Guanzi*. Where Cao is a brute and a villain in the *Guanzi*, in the *Huainanzi* and *Shiji* he has become a hero whose "courage was heralded throughout the world, and . . . accomplishments were established in the state of Lu." Taken all together, the various accounts of Cao Gui suggest a kind of "agglutinative" process, in which alterations of the narrative do not entail rejection or repudiation of prior elements, but the retention of old components in a new formulation that evolves in the manner of a snowball going downhill.[30]

The plasticity of Cao Gui's literary persona and his movement back and forth across polemical frontiers demonstrates that the type of "legend transformations" studied by Sarah Allan in *The Heir and the Sage* were not confined to the orally transmitted lore of high antiquity or limited to a narrow range of concerns (such as a particular focus upon the conflict between heredity and virtue) but were foundational to the general practice of historiography among early Chinese literati. As a figure of the seventh century BCE, Cao Gui belonged to an era that produced ample written records that would have been available to literati of the Warring States. The prominent place his story occupies in texts such as the *Zuo zhuan* and *Shiji* demonstrates that, to the extent that a historical methodology can be reconstructed for the Warring States and Former Han, the treatment of Cao Gui exemplifies it.

What, then, can we learn about early Chinese historiography from an examination of the different faces of Cao Gui? Here Sarah Allan's work provides guidance in her use of Lévi-Strauss's analogy of the bricoleur. This analogy might be fruitfully combined with the oft-used heuristic concepts of "fact" and "meaning" as component dimensions of historical inquiry.[31] These categories are amenable for the examination of early Chinese discourse because the sources contain signifiers and formulations that are nearly equivalent. "Facts"—discrete events, figures, locations—are designated by terms such as *shi* 事 or *gu* 故 in early Chinese writings. "Meaning" is denoted by terms like *yi* 義 or *li* 理.[32]

Fact-Meaning Bricolage

European and American historiography of the late nineteenth and early twentieth centuries generally treated these factors as separate and qualitatively dissimilar. "Facts" were tied to evidence that they should form a ground for consensus among competent historians. The generation of "meaning" required the intervention of the historian as interpreter, thus it was possible for different historians to derive divergent meanings from the same set of facts.

In the bricoleur-like operation of the early Chinese historian, however, "facts" and "meanings" were never as mutually independent as nineteenth- and twentieth-century convention once held to be the norm. The composers of the different anecdotes regarding Cao Gui were obviously borrowing "facts" from one another and reshaping them within discrete parameters, with an eye toward making the facts serve new or different meanings. This is not to suggest that early Chinese historians were wholly unconcerned with the "truth value" of discrete facts. Such an attitude would be self-subverting. If the persona of Cao Gui were completely fluid it would become unrecognizable in the migration from one text to another, and the potential to derive any larger "meaning" from his story would be nullified. But the general principle at work was that the "truth" of Cao Gui's story lies as much in its meaning as in the particular facts that comprise it. The value of the historian's output was derived from the *bricolage entier*, the integral synthesis of fact and meaning, rather than being validated only by the rigor or adequacy of its distinct components.

Any informed observer will no doubt note that the kind of interplay I have described between fact and meaning is not unique to early China. One can see the manipulation of "fact" in service of meaning and appeals to alter or abandon particular meanings on the basis of (oftentimes dubious) "facts" in virtually all societies at all times. But there is good evidence that early Chinese historians were constructing the past in this bricoleur fashion quasi-systematically, in accordance with the deliberate and self-conscious conventions of a loosely bound but broadly inclusive discourse. We do not have coherent treatises outlining historiographical method, but we do have frequent statements that reflect on the methods and goals of history. For example, among the anecdotes recorded concerning Cao Gui, we find this one in the *Zuo zhuan*:[33]

> In his twenty-third year [of rule], in summer, the Duke went to Qi to view the [ceremonies] at the Altar of the Soil. This was not in accordance with ritual. Cao Gui admonished him, saying, "This is impermissible. Ritual is that by which the people are made correct. Thus meetings are for the purpose of articulating the order of superior and inferior and regulating the use of resources. Court audiences are for correcting the dutifulness of the aristocratic ranks and manifesting the order of senior and junior. Punitive expeditions are for the sanctioning of wrongdoing. The lords of the land have their [obligatory] visit to the royal court, the king has his inspections and hunts, for the purpose of broadly training [his vassals]. Other than these the ruler does not undertake. The actions of the ruler must be recorded. If it is recorded and cannot serve as a model, how will later generations look upon it?

> 二十三年, 夏, 公如齊觀社, 非禮也, 曹劌諫曰, 不可, 夫禮, 所以整民也, 故會以訓上下之則, 制財用之節, 朝以正班爵之義, 帥長

幼之序，征伐以討其不然，諸侯有王，王有巡守，以大習之，非是
君不舉矣，君舉必書，書而不法，後嗣何觀.

The clear traces of the Qi-Lu partisan conflict are visible here. It is unclear whether Cao is objecting to the trip in question because it is excluded as a rule from the proper forms of travel for the ruler, or whether there is some particular deviation planned by the rulers of Qi that make this occasion anathema. In either case, however, the parameters of the Qi-Lu conceptual divide are manifest: the Qi rulers are instigating an occasion that glorifies the dignity and the power of their own state; Cao is objecting that this instance is invalidated by a moral Way that transcends parochial loyalties.

Beyond providing a snapshot of a moment in the Qi-Lu discourse, however, the anecdote provides a comment on how its composers (and by extension, the larger historiographical community in which they were operating) constructed the larger task they were undertaking. In adducing the reasons that Duke Zhuang should relent, Cao Gui reveals underlying assumptions about the processes underpinning the production of history itself. The Duke must take care about the nature of his actions as future historical *facts*, because of the damage that he will do in the realm of historical *meaning*.

A somewhat divergent but complementary anecdote can be found in the *Mencius*. In that text, we read:[34]

> King Xuan of Qi (r. 319–301 BCE) asked: "Tang overthrowing Jie, King Wu marching on Zhou (last ruler of Shang), did these things occur?"
>
> —Mencius answered, "It is in the records."
>
> "Is it permissible for a vassal to murder his ruler?" [the king] asked.
>
> —[Mencius] answered: "One who violates humanness is called a felon, one who violates rightness is called a tyrant. Those who are tyrants and felons are called 'single commoners.' I have heard of punishing the single commoner Zhou; I have never heard of murdering [Zhou the] ruler."

齊宣王問曰: "湯放桀，武王伐紂，有諸?" 孟子對曰: "於傳有之."
曰: "臣弒其君可乎?" 曰: "賊仁者謂之賊，賊義者謂之殘，殘賊之
人謂之一夫. 聞誅一夫紂矣，未聞弒君也."

Here the King of Qi and Mencius agree about the basic facts of the past (Tang overthrew Jie, King Wu killed Zhou), but the king demonstrates his ignorance of history because he does not understand the meaning of the common facts to which both he and Mencius assent. The *Zuo zhuan* and the *Mencius* thus emphasize different dimensions of the historical "bricolage." The *Mencius* expresses historiographic confidence: any facts from the past may be assimilated into an efficacious history as long as their meaning is interpreted correctly. Meaning thus implicitly controls the historiographic process.

This confidence is contradicted by the story taken from the *Zuo zhuan*. According to Cao Gui's admonition, the facts of Duke Zhuang's actions will necessarily narrow the range of meanings that can be derived from the present moment by future historians. This formulation thus implies that facts, not meanings, control the historical process. This induces a sense of historiographic pessimism. Because the ancestral rulers of a state are by definition models for their descendants to emulate, and since the ruler's actions must be recorded faithfully, Cao Gui's warning suggests that the Duke's actions might create a paradox making the task of future historians of Lu impossible: since fact and meaning will not be reconcilable, history itself will be unachievable.

Distinctions between Classical Chinese and Greco-Roman Models of Historiography

Though the passages express different degrees of emphasis and historiographical confidence, in the triangulation revealing their shared assumptions we can discern a common orientation toward history as bricolage. Both passages assume that history is only arrived at through correctly amalgamating fact and meaning. Neither passage allows that either of these dimensions can stand autonomously, or that the validity of the historical enterprise as a whole is dependent upon rigor or accuracy in either or both domains independently.

This is not to imply that early Chinese literati were uniquely exotic in their orientation to the past or to the relationship between fact and meaning. Many texts acknowledge the possibility of simply getting the facts wrong, or make the argument that particular meanings collapse in the face of countervailing facts.[35] But in their representation of the social enterprise of historiography early Chinese literati implicitly articulated a set of conventions that can be distinguished from the historiographical cultures of other societies in the ancient world. For example, in book 1 of Herodotus's *Histories*, we read: "The Persians . . . find in the sack of Troy the origin of their hostility toward the Hellenes. But the Phoenicians disagree with the Persians. . . . I myself have no intention of affirming that these events occurred thus or otherwise."[36]

Such pronouncements of neutrality regarding conflicting facts are very common in Greco-Roman historiography[37] but are virtually absent from that of early China. This does not stem from a failure of mutual intellectual comprehension, but from divergent conventions regarding the proper methods and outcomes of historiography. Since early Chinese literati proceeded from the assumption that the historian's intrinsic role resided in necessarily recording *both* the facts *and* meaning of the past, a decision like that made by Herodotus (to refrain from choosing between two conflicting sets of facts) implicitly constituted an abrogation of the historian's task. Because the meaning embodied in any particular passage was necessarily unitary, embedding it within two conflicting sets of facts would be gratuitously confusing. The historian's role as understood by early Chinese literati thus compelled a choice that Herodotus was not obligated to make in the construction of his history.

The contrast between these disparate constructions of the historian's role can be further illustrated by juxtaposing the preceding quote from Herodotus with the following famous anecdote from the *Zuo zhuan*, recording part of the aftermath of a palace coup launched by the minister Cui Zhu (d. 546 BCE) against his ruler, Duke Zhuang of Qi 齊莊公 (r. 553–548 BCE):[38]

> The Grand Scribe [of Qi] recorded: "Cui Zhu murdered his ruler." Cuizi killed him. His younger brother succeeded [to the post] and wrote [the same], and the two [brothers] were then dead. Their younger brother wrote the same, and finally he was spared. The Scribe of the South, on hearing that the Grand Scribes had all been killed, grabbed his bamboo slats and headed [to court], only on hearing that the record had been made [correctly] did he return home.
>
> 大史書曰:"崔杼弒其君."崔子殺之. 其弟嗣書, 而死者二人. 其弟又書, 乃舍之. 南史氏聞大史盡死, 執簡以往, 聞既書矣, 乃還.

Although this anecdote was likely an idealized depiction of the historian's work that was rarely (if ever) realized in practice, for the anecdote to be rhetorically meaningful, a typical Chinese literatus would need to be able to understand what was at stake. The Grand Scribe's offense here was not in recording the mere fact of the ruler's death, or even that it happened at the hands of his minister Cui Zhu, but in his insistence on the formula "murdered his ruler" (*sha qi jun* 弑其君). This is the same phrase that was the subject of King Xuan's question to Mencius in the anecdote cited earlier.[39] By using this recognized formula, the scribe was moving to fix the meaning of Cui Zhu's act, marking it as different in kind from justified uprisings like those of the ancient sages Tang and King Wu. The anecdote illustrates that the achievement of this proper synthesis of fact and meaning was deemed of ultimate importance, meriting the sacrifice of the historian's very life if necessary.

This latter phenomenon distinguishes the conventions of historiography in early China from those in the ancient Mediterranean world exemplified (and, in part, established) by Herodotus. Though, if we translated the preceding passage into ancient Greek and presented it to Herodotus, he would most likely have understood its rhetorical message and appreciated the courage and integrity of its protagonists, and he would not have seen anything in the conduct of history it depicted that was structurally analogous to the enterprise embodied by his own text. There is no circumstance imaginable in Herodotus's *Histories* (or indeed in virtually all of Greco-Roman historical letters) in which the writing of a single line by a historian was a goal worth sacrificing one's life to achieve. The case of the Grand Scribe of Qi is as alien to the historiographical world constructed in the *Histories* as Herodotus's noncommittal preservation of conflicting sets of facts is to that of the *Zuo zhuan*. Thus, though the divergent historiographical conventions of early China and the early Greco-Roman world produced very distinct intellectual milieus, the roots of that gap are sociohistorical rather than epistemological.

Why this was so can be seen through observation of the case of Cao Gui. The sources show that his image was persistently being appropriated by partisans on opposing sides of a conceptual divide. We might thus expect that at some point a statement like Herodotus's regarding the Persians and Phoenicians would appear in the record, to the effect that the facts about Cao Gui were too complicated and mutually contradictory to be sorted out. At the very least we might expect some accusations of bias or infidelity, charges that one or another of the portraits of Cao Gui was based in lies. Rather, what we perceive over time is an amalgamation of Cao Gui's historical persona. All of the conflicting stories about Cao Gui continued to shape his image as the historiography of his deeds accumulated and evolved into the Former Han.

This process was facilitated by the "bricolage historiography" that the Cao Gui accounts themselves exemplify. Since the final aim of historiography was to produce an alloyed expression of both fact and meaning, the discarding or discrimination of inconvenient facts was less useful than their appropriation, transfiguration, and reinterpretation. But the preference for this mode of historiography itself was driven by the sociopolitical circumstances of the literati that produced our sources, as indicated by the debates that they used Cao Gui to mediate.

Early Chinese literati were locked in dispute over the relationship between virtue and heredity, virtue and the state, and virtue and power precisely because they all operated in a complex and conflicted relationship with the social and political leaders of their own time. Literati lacked wealth, status, and coercive force, and were subject to the arbitrary power of the hereditary aristocracy and the state apparatuses the aristocracy controlled. Control over the past (through the mediation of the written word) was one of the few sources of power that literati could unequivocally claim as their own.

This is one of the main rhetorical messages of the story of the Grand Scribe of Qi: "We knights must support one another in the control of the past or leave ourselves vulnerable to the arbitrary whims of highborn aristocrats like Cui Zhu." Falling into dispute over contested facts (or allowing that such disputes were ultimately unresolvable) would diminish the value and coherence of that control. The bricolage historiography exemplified by the discourse surrounding Cao Gui allowed literati to debate alternative understandings of the past and its logical significance without yielding the shared authority that they enjoyed as the past's chroniclers and interpreters.

Reconciling Tensions in Recent Scholarship

An appreciation of this dimension of early Chinese historiography helps reconcile tensions expressed in recent scholarship on the sources. David Schaberg, in his study *A Patterned Past*, noted that the anecdote was a form uniquely adapted to the purposes of early Chinese historiographers, enabling them to make "the world and its history a laboratory for their own notions of ritual."[40] Wai-yee Li, in her *The Readability of the Past in Early Chinese Historiography*, likewise acknowledges the functionality of the anecdote in generating a readable "meaning" out of the facts of the past. But she notes that when we step back from the individual anecdote to take in broader fields of expression (chapters and sections of the *Zuo zhuan*, the text of the *Zuo zhuan* as a whole, the larger hermeneutical literature on the *Chunqiu* of which the *Zuo zhuan* is a part), the picture becomes murkier. The particular interpretations instantiated in disparate anecdotes are mutually conflicted and difficult to reconcile, leading Li to characterize the historiographic enterprise as a whole as marked by an irreducible "anxiety of interpretation."[41]

What Li labels the anxiety of interpretation might, in fact, be an emergent property of the bricolage historiography as it was practiced during the Warring States and early empire. The past was engaged by literati at a variety of contested boundaries (often, as we saw in the case of Cao Gui, several at once), and was useful to mediating those conflicts. At the same time, literati needed their collective control of the past to bolster the dignity and authority of their position within the larger political economy of the early Chinese social world. They thus gravitated toward a historiography that privileged the synthesis of fact and meaning in representations of the past. This facilitated sophisticated debate as literati deployed various logical and rhetorical techniques to make the past serve desired ends, and denied utility to simplistic or reductive claims of falsehood, bias, or incoherence that would undermine the readability of the past altogether and deprive literati of the political capital to be garnered from its control. As the case of Cao Gui evinces (and as many sources generally corroborate[42]), however, this intrinsically interpretive historiography forced literati to treat the past as a shared bequest. The need to deal with opposing texts on the basis of both fact and meaning (rather than fall back on outright denial of conflicting facts) meant that the boundaries between different historiographic traditions would necessarily remain porous, and any historical account that covered sufficient ground would (by virtue of incorporating source materials of varying and dispersed provenance) exhibit some degree of inconsistency and internal dissonance. The anxiety of interpretation occasioned by such complexity was no doubt real, but as the evolution of Cao Gui's historical persona over time shows, that anxiety was counterbalanced by a corresponding potential and fertile versatility.

Notes

1. Sarah Allan, *The Heir and the Sage: Dynastic Legends in Early China* (San Francisco: Chinese Materials Center, 1981), 142–143.

2. Claude Lévi-Strauss, *The Savage Mind* (La Pensée Sauvage) (Chicago: University of Chicago Press, 1966), 17.

3. Cao Gui is identified in different texts variously by the given name Gui 劌, Hui 翙, Mo 沬, or Mie 蔑. There is little doubt that the variant names refer to the same figure—for almost any instance of Cao Gui lore there exist permutations for two or more of the variants. The proliferations of names may have resulted from phonetic borrowing (see Ernest Caldwell, "Promoting Action in Warring States Political Philosophy: A First Look at the Chu Manuscript *Cao Mie's Battle Arrays*," *Early China* 37 [2014]: 261, n. 6). I have adopted the name given to Cao Gui in the sources that figure most prominently in my analysis, as a matter of convenience.

4. Sima Qian 司馬遷, "Cike liezhuan" 刺客列傳, *Shiji* 史記, in Zhang Youluan 張友鸞, ed., vol. 86 (Beijing: Zhonghua, 1959), 2515–2516.

5. D. C. Lau 劉殿爵 and Chen Fong Ching 陳方正, eds., *Chunqiu Zuo zhuan zhuzi suoyin* 春秋左傳逐字索引, ICS: Ancient Chinese Text Concordance Series (Hong Kong: Commercial Press, 1995), B3.10.1/46/17–21, B.23.1/57/17–20. Unless otherwise noted, all references to transmitted primary sources in this chapter will be to ICS Concordance Series editions (D.C. Lau and Chen Fong Ching, eds.). Citations will be in the form: chapter/page/line(s). If the ICS edition is broken into *juan* 卷 rather than *pian* 篇, the *pian* number will be provided in parentheses: *juan* (*pian*)/page/line. In subsequent references the publication year will be given for the first citation of each text.

6. D. C. Lau 劉殿爵 et al., eds., *Guoyu zhuzi suoyin* 國語逐字索引, ICS Ancient Chinese Text Concordance Series [= ICS: ACTCS] (Hong Kong: Commercial Press, 1999), 2.1/25/3–20; idem., *Guanzi zhuzi suoyin* 管子逐字索引, ICS: ACTCS (Hong Kong: Commercial Press, 2001), 7.1/54/30–55/10; idem., *Shenzi zhuzi suoyin* 慎子逐字索引, ICS: ACTCS (Hong Kong: Commercial Press, 2000), 8/6/13; idem., *Lüshi chunqiu zhuzi suoyin* 呂氏春秋索引, ICS: ACTCS (Hong Kong: Commercial Press, 1994), 19.7/126/28–127/11; idem., *Huainanzi zhuzi suoyin* 淮南子逐字索引, ICS: ACTCS (Hong Kong: Commercial Press, 1992), 13/126/28–127/2; idem., *Xinxu zhuzi suoyin* 新序逐字索引, ICS: ACTCS (Hong Kong: Commercial Press, 1992), 4.7/18/28–19/6; idem., *Zhanguo ce zhuzi suoyin* 戰國策逐字索引, ICS: ACTCS (Hong Kong: Commercial Press, 1992), 129/62/24, 145/76/5–7, 440/215/26; idem., "Sunzi bingfa suoyin" 孫子兵法索引, in *Bingshu si zhong (Sunzi, Weiliaozi [Yuliaozi], Wuzi, Simafa) zhuzi suoyin* 兵書四種 (孫子, 尉繚子, 吳子, 司馬法) 逐字索引 ICS: ACTCS (Hong Kong: Commercial Press, 1992), 11/12/3.

7. Ma Chengyuan 馬承源, ed., *Shanghai bowuguan cang Zhanguo Chu zhushu* (4) 上海博物館藏戰國楚竹書 (四) (Shanghai: Shanghai guji, 2004), 89–156, 239–285. For an extensive discussion of the manuscript, see Caldwell, "Promoting Action," 259–290. A very useful study and transcription of the manuscript can be found in Li Xusheng 李旭升, ed., "*Shanghai bowuguan cang Zhanguo Chu zhushu (4)" du ben* "上海博物館藏戰國楚竹書(四)" 讀本 (Taibei: Wanjuanlou, 2007), 137–268.

8. *Zuo zhuan* B3.10.1/46/17–21. All translations are my own.

9. For the conceptual pairing of *wen* and *wu*, see: Robin McNeal, *Conquer and Govern: Early Chinese Military Texts in the Yi Zhou shu* (Honolulu: University of Hawai'i Press, 2012), 13–39.

10. For the opposing linkage of *de* and *li*, see: Mark Edward Lewis, *Sanctioned Violence in Early China* (Albany: State University of New York Press, 1990), 128–129, 203, 224, 274 n. 50.

11. *Guanzi* 7.1/55/1–10.

12. *Zuo zhuan* B.23.1/57/17–20.

13. Andrew Meyer, "'The Altars of the Soil and Grain Are Closer than Kin': The Qi Model of Intellectual Participation and the Jixia Patronage Community," *Early China* 33 (2011): 42–53.

14. D. C Lau, *Lunyu zhuzi suoyin* 論語逐字索引, ICS: ACTCS (Hong Kong: Commercial Press, 2006), 6.24/14/3.

15. I laid out the arguments for this analysis in greater detail in Meyer, "The Altars of the Soil and Grain Are Closer than Kin," 53–66.

16. A formulation initiated by the Carthaginian scholar and Christian apologist Tertullian (ca. 160–220 CE), who "affected to despise the Classical tradition, coining the rhetorical question which sums up the preoccupation of second-century Catholic theologians, 'What has Athens to do with Jerusalem?'" (Diarmaid MacCulloch, *Christianity: The First Three Thousand Years* [New York: Viking Penguin, 2010], 144).

17. Ma Chengyuan 馬承源, ed., *Shanghai bowuguan cang Zhanguo Chu zhushu (1)* 上海博物館藏戰國楚竹書（一） (Shanghai: Shanghai guji, 2001), 1–2.

18. Ma Chengyuan, *Shanghai bowuguan*, vol. 4, 91–94, 243–245; Li Xusheng, "*Shanghai bowuguan (4) du ben*," 142, 158.

19. D. C. Lau, *Yanzi chunqiu zhuzi suoyin* 晏子春秋逐字索引, ICS: ACTCS (Hong Kong: Commercial Press, 1993), 2.11/15/1–5. As I have argued elsewhere (Meyer, "The Altars of the Soil and Grain," 59–66) the *Yanzi chunqiu*, like the *Guanzi*, most likely originated as the product of Qi state patronage.

20. One of the anonymous reviewers called my attention to a passage in the *Guoyu* 國語 that deals with similar themes. In that anecdote one of the ducal officers at the Zhou court admonishes the king against the casting of a costly bell but argues on the basis of *both* fiscal prudence and musical aesthetics. The passage thus charts a course *between* "Confucian" and "Mohist" positions in ways similar to what can be perceived in the *Yanzi chunqiu* and the *Cao Mie zhi zhen*. See: D. C. Lau, *Guoyu zhuzi suoyin* 國語逐字索引, ICS: ACTCS (Hong Kong: Commercial Press, 1999), 1.30/21/12–22/25. Given the mixed composition of the *Guo yu* it is difficult to infer when and where this anecdote might have been produced, but it well evinces the ways in which structurally similar arguments could be transposed to different settings according to the perceived needs of the historian.

21. For example: *Lunyu* 9.3/20/10–11.

22. D. C. Lau, *Mozi zhuzi suoyin* 墨子逐字索引 (Hong Kong: Commercial Press, 2001), 9.3 (35)/58/11–60/13.

23. *Mozi* 6.2 (21)/37/14.
24. Ma Chengyuan, *Shanghai bowuguan*, 4, 280.
25. *Mozi* 5.1 (17)/30/14–5.3(19)/35/28.
26. *Lunyu* 15.1/41/28–29.
27. The manuscript was remarkable (though not unique) for having a formal title inscribed on the reverse side of the second bamboo slip on which it was recorded (Ma Chengyuan, *Shanghai bowuguan*, 4:93, 245). The mention of "battle formations" is particularly evocative of *Analects* 15.1.
28. Paul M. Thompson, *The Shen Tzu Fragments [Shenzi yiwen* 慎子] (Oxford: Oxford University Press, 1979), 3–12; Eirik Lang Harris, *The Shenzi Fragments A Philosophical Analysis and Translation* (New York: Columbia University Press, 2016), 9–104.
29. *Huainanzi* 13/126/28–127/2. *The Huainanzi: A Guide to the Theory and Practice of Government in Early Han China*, trans. John Major, Sarah Queen, Andrew Meyer, and Harold Roth (New York: Columbia University Press, 2010), 511.
30. The transmutation of Cao Gui in the *Huainanzi* and *Shiji* demonstrates that his lore could be useful even in a discourse in which the controversy between "Qi" and "Lu" positions was no longer salient. Liu An and his guest scholars were chiefly interested in Cao Gui as a figure who preserved the autonomy of the fief of Lu against encroachment by Qi (in the same way that they and their text defended the autonomy of Huainan against encroachment by the imperial court). This might explain their motive for reversing the role of Cao Gui within the framework depicted in the *Guanzi*.
31. For a discussion of the interplay of "fact" and "meaning" in modern historiography, see Hayden V. White, *The Content of the Form: Narrative Discourse and Historical Representation* (Baltimore: Johns Hopkins University Press, 1987), 40–44.
32. An exemplary instance of these usages can be found in the "Grand Historian's Afterword" by Sima Qian 司馬遷 (2nd–1st c. BCE) in *Shiji* 史記 130, "Taishigong zixu" 太史公自序, in *Shiji xuanjiang* 史記選講, ed. Zheng Quanzhong 鄭權中 (Beijing: Zhongguo qingnian, 1959), 3296–3298.
33. *Zuo zhuan* B.23.1/57/17–20.
34. D. C. Lau, *Mengzi zhuzi suoyin* 孟子 逐字 索引, ICS: ACTCS (Hong Kong: Commercial Press, 1995), 2.8/11/9–16.
35. See, for example, the discussion of *Han Feizi* in David Schaberg, "Chinese History and Philosophy," in *The Oxford History of Historical Writing*, ed. Andrew Feldherr and Grant Hardy, vol. 1, *Beginnings to AD 600* (Oxford: Oxford University Press, 2011), 404–409.
36. Herodotus, *The Landmark Herodotus: The Histories*, ed. Robert B. Strassler; trans. Andrea L. Purvis; introduction by Rosalind Thomas (New York: Pantheon Books, 2007), 5–6.
37. John Marincola, *On Writing History: From Herodotus to Herodian* (London: Penguin Classics, 2017), xxxvii–xl.

38. *Zuo zhuan* B9.25.2/283/25–26.

39. In this echoing we see traces of the Qi-Lu debate. Depicting Qi leaders as sensitive to the charge of "murdering their rulers" was an allusion to the fact that the Tian clan had risen to become rulers of Qi through just such a stratagem.

40. David Schaberg, *A Patterned Past: Form and Thought in Early Chinese Historiography* (Cambridge, MA: Harvard University Asia Center, 2001).

41. Wai-yee Li, *The Readability of the Past in Early Chinese Historiography* (Cambridge, MA: Harvard University Asia Center, 2007), chapter 5, 321–410.

42. For example, the *Zuo zhuan*'s preservation of calendrical systems from different states, indicating that it brings together material of varying geopolitical provenance (Li, *The Readability of the Past*, 24).

9

Historical Narratives in Early Chinese Classics
The Case of the "Great King Leaving Bin" in Transmitted Texts and the Bamboo Slips of the *Zhou xun*

Cui Xiaojiao

Introduction

The construction of thought, its development, and transmission in Western philosophy often relies on specific notions or theories. As Alfred North Whitehead once noted, the entire history of philosophy in the West can be regarded as footnotes to Plato. From a certain point of view, Whitehead's comment speaks about the specific way in which Western philosophy is constructed: "ideas," "being," and other key notions connect the development of Western philosophy from its very beginning and serve as the ideological background or theoretical cornerstone of the construction of philosophy by philosophers in different periods. In a world where ideas or

---

This work is supported by the Fundamental Research Funds for the Central Universities (00900-310422114). A Chinese version of this chapter has been published as: Cui Xiaojiao 崔曉姣, "Zaoqi jingdian zhong de lishi xushi: Yi chuanshi wenxian ji Beida zhushu *Zhou xun* zhong de 'Da wang qu Bin' weili" "早期經典中的歷史敘事: 以傳世文獻及北大竹書《周馴》中的 '大王去邠' 為例," *Beijing daxue zhexuemen* 北京大學哲學門 18 (2017) 2: 69–82.

concepts hold a dominant position, the role of history or certain historical events naturally may be considered relatively marginal in the construction of philosophical ideology.

In contrast, the situation is very different in the construction and development of ancient Chinese philosophy—constructing ideology in ancient China had always placed importance on history; ideologies were often implied or "woven"[1] into the narrative or into the continuous reconstruction of historical events. A classic example is rendering Kongzi 孔子 (Confucius) as the compiler of the *Chunqiu* 春秋 (Spring and Autumn Annals). Through the composition of historical events, Kongzi conveys specific political notions and ideals for later generations. "On the surface, it is 'transmitting and not creating,' but actually this 'creating' is incorporated into the 'transmission.'"[2] In the world of thought in ancient China, historical narratives cannot be separated from the production of classics and the construction of thought. On the one hand, philosophers express and transmit their philosophical ideologies through historical narratives.[3] In ancient Chinese classics, the ways in which historical narratives develop are often not mere records of the historical event, or, in other words, are not conducted for the purpose of recording historical facts and preserving actual data. Instead, historical narratives are inseparable from the ideological inclinations and argumentative theories conveyed in different texts or promoted by different thinkers. On the other hand, the construction of ideologies and the composition of classics constantly alter the concrete manifestation of historical events. Thinkers and commentators often rewrite or reconstruct historical events according to their specific ideological interests. In other words, each historical event has a fixed outline or even a certain "deep structure"[4] that serves as a basis for thinkers. However, while the deep structure serves as their base, the details they described alter, and some thinkers even go as far as changing the protagonist or the time the event occurred in order to present the ideas they aspire to transmit.

In this chapter I examine the case of the "Great King Leaving Bin"[5] as a typical example. To date, the earliest known record of this event is found in the *Shijing* 詩經 ode "Mian" 緜. The record in the *Shijing* serves as the prototype of this story as found in later literature. Subsequently, the *Mengzi*, the *Zhuangzi*, the *Huainanzi*, the *Lüshi chunqiu*, the *Shiji*, the *Shuoyuan*, and other documents record related historical narratives. Among those materials, the descriptions found in the *Shiji* and the *Shuoyuan* are based on the *Mengzi*, while the accounts in the *Huainanzi* and the *Lüshi chunqiu* are more similar to those found in the *Zhuangzi*. The recently published manuscript *Zhou xun* 周馴,⁶ in the Peking University collection of Western Han bamboo slips, also describes a similar historical narrative of the "Great King Leaving Bin." However, the protagonist of this event is switched from "King Tai of Zhou" 周大(太)王 to "King Zhao of Chu" 楚昭王, and the contextual event is changed from (1) the Di 狄 tribes attacking Bin and causing the king to move his residence to the foot of Mount Qi 岐, as described in the *Shijing*, to (2) King Helü 闔閭 of Wu 吳 (d. 496 BCE) attacking the state of Chu and King Zhao fleeing to Sui 隋.⁷

Generally speaking, the story as recorded in the *Shijing* is described in a rather simple manner, the main purpose in creating this narrative being to praise King Tai of Zhou for moving the people from Bin to Qi and opening up new territories. The *Mengzi*, *Zhuangzi*, and *Zhou xun* versions concentrated on the conflict between King Tai and the Di tribes in order to promote issues in political philosophy. In addition, while on the surface the descriptions in the *Mengzi* and the *Zhuangzi* seem to be very similar, a closer examination reveals a clear distinction between them. Although in the *Zhou xun* the protagonist of the story is replaced, there are many phrases similar to the narrative recorded in the *Zhuangzi*.

I maintain that the event as recorded in the *Shijing* can serve as the prototype with the *Mengzi*, *Zhuangzi*, and *Zhou xun* versions serving as three variants. Historical narratives in early Chinese classics often conceal deeper structures. Without changing the deep structure of a historical event, a writer could adapt or reconstruct details to fit a prevailing philosophical purpose. Thus, we find different variants of the same event, revealing a certain fluidity to historical narratives in early Chinese classics.

Part 1: The *Shijing*—The Prototype Story of the "Great King Leaving Bin"

As previously described, the earliest written evidence we have today of the story of King Tai of Zhou moving his residence from Bin to the foot of Mount Qi is found in the *Shijing* ode "Mian" 緜, from the *Daya* 大雅 section:⁸

> In long trains ever increasing grow the gourds.
> When [our] people first sprang,
> From the country about the Ju and the Qi,
> Ancient Duke Danfu,
> Made for them kiln-like huts and caves,

Ere they had yet any houses.
Ancient Duke Danfu,
Came in the morning, galloping his horses,
Along the banks of the western rivers,
To the foot of [Mount] Qi;
And there, he and the lady Jiang,
Came, and together looked out for a site on which to settle.
The plain of Zhou looked beautiful and rich,
With its violets and sow thistles [sweet] as dumplings.
There he began with consulting [his followers];
There he signed the tortoise shell, [and divined].
The responses were—there to stay, and then;
And they proceeded there to build their houses.
He encouraged the people and settled them;
Here on the left, there on the right.
He divided the ground into larger tracts and smaller portions;
He dug the ditches; he defined the acres;
From the west to the east,
There was nothing which he did not take in hand.
He called his superintendent of works;
He called his minister of instruction;
And charged them with the building of the houses.
With the line they made everything straight;
They bound the frame-boards tight, so that they should rise regularly.
Up rose the ancestral temple in its solemn grandeur.
Crowds brought the earth in baskets;
They threw it with shouts into the frames;
They beat it with responsive blows;
They pared the walls repeatedly, and they sounded strong.
Five thousand cubits of them arose together,
So that the roll of the great drum did not overpower [the noise of the builders].
They set up the gate of the enceinte;
And the gate of the enceinte stood high.
They set up the court gate;
And the court gate stood grand.
They reared the great altar [to the spirits of the land],
From which all great movements should proceed.

Thus though he could not prevent the rage [of his foes],
He did not let fall his own fame.
The oaks and the Yu were [gradually] thinned,
And roads for traveling were opened.
The hordes of the Hun disappeared,
Startled and panting.
[The chiefs of] Yu and Rui were brought to an agreement,
By King Wen's stimulating their natural virtue.
Then, I may say, some came to him, previously not knowing him;
And some, drawn the last by the first;
And some, drawn by his rapid success;
And some, by his defense [of the weak] from insult.

緜緜瓜瓞.
民之初生, 自土沮漆.
古公亶父, 陶復陶穴, 未有家室.
公亶父, 來朝走馬.
率西水滸, 至於岐下.
爰及姜女, 聿來胥宇.
周原膴膴, 堇荼如飴.
爰始爰謀, 爰契我龜.
曰止曰時, 築室於茲.
迺慰迺止, 迺左迺右, 迺疆迺理, 迺宣迺畝, 自西徂東, 周爰執事.
乃召司空, 乃召司徒, 俾立室家.
其繩則直, 縮版以載, 作廟翼翼.
捄之陾陾, 度之薨薨, 築之登登, 削屢馮馮, 百堵皆興, 鼛鼓弗勝.
迺立皋門, 皋門有伉.
迺立應門, 應門將將.
迺立冢土, 戎醜攸行.
肆不殄厥慍, 亦不隕厥問.
柞棫拔矣, 行道兌矣.
混夷駾矣, 維其喙矣.
虞芮質厥成, 文王蹶厥生.
予曰有疏附, 予曰有先後, 予曰有奔奏, 予曰有禦侮.

The description here focuses on how Ancient Duke Danfu, fleeing from the danger posed by the Di tribes, spurred his horses on eastward to the foot of Mount Qi where he found fertile soil. After divining with a tortoise shell, he settled there. He prepared the land for his people "and so he established new territories, divided up the land, taught them to plant and cultivate the land."⁹ Once the people were content, Ancient Duke Danfu then assigned the Superintendent of Works and the Minister of Instruction duties.¹⁰ After that, the people constructed the walls of the shrine and gradually opened up the land for cultivation, causing everyone to be happy. Finally, King Wen inherited the ways of Ancient Duke Danfu: "King Tai established the role of the king; King Wen extended it further, making kingship much greater."¹¹

Unlike the accounts in later texts, the ode does not offer a detailed description as to how the Di tribes posed a threat nor the exact process of how Ancient Duke Danfu moved his residence. We see in later texts—such as the *Mengzi* and the *Zhuangzi*—the focus of the narrative of the "Great King Leaving Bin" shifts from the details of settling into the new place to a description of the departure; that is, the situation of the repeated invasions and attacks from the Di tribes, and even of King Tai's failed efforts to appease the tribes with offerings of money, silks, hounds and horses, pearls and jade. Since King Tai could not bear the suffering and loss of his people, he decided to leave Bin and change his residence. The people eventually followed him to Mount Qi.¹²

In general, the narrative structure of the *Zhou xun* is similar, but it has a different protagonist. It tells how King Zhao of Chu suffered attacks from King Helü of Wu and so decided to leave *Ying* 郢 (the ancient capital of Chu) in favor of *Sui* 隋, and finally, the people followed. Clearly, the versions told in the *Mengzi*, *Zhuangzi*, and *Zhou xun* were based on the *Shijing* but with added details and enriched contents, making the historical event of the "Great King Leaving Bin" livelier and more concrete. While adding to the plot, those texts simultaneously changed the focus of the narrative. This was not done merely for the sake of telling a better story but obviously for purposes of ideological persuasion. The ideological intention of the original version in "Mian" is described in the Han-era Mao commentary: " 'Mian' describes the rise of King Wen, as begun by King Tai." Kong Yingda 孔穎達 (574–648 CE) expands this, saying:

> The poet who wrote "Mian" was talking about the rise of King Wen, which is based on the achievements of King Tai. The achievements of King Tai serve as the foundation for King Wen who succeeded and gained power. Now we see that the rise of King Wen originated in the achievements of his predecessors, thus the story of King Tai is idealized.

作 "緜" 詩者，言文王之興，本之於太王也. 太王作王業之本，
文王得因之以興. 今見文王之興，本其上世之事，所以美太王也.

Thus, according to the commentaries, the purpose of giving an account of the story of the "Great King Leaving Bin" was mainly to trace and praise the origin of "the rise of King Wen"—the "kingly conduct" of King Tai is ultimately a song in the praise of King Wen's virtuous deeds. It seems that, for the commentators, the narrative of King Tai opening up a new frontier was really to explain the success of King Wen: "Respect for him was widespread, the people flourished and the military was strong."[13] The tale transforms King Tai's failure over the barbarians into King Wen's overawing them and pacifying the states of Yu and Rui.

To summarize, the core content of the ode records and praises what happened after Ancient Duke Danfu left Bin and relocated to the foot of Mount Qi, leading to the successful rise of King Wen; it does not comment on the role of the Di tribes. Yet, interestingly, the missing contents become the core of the historical narrative as presented in the *Mengzi*, the *Zhuangzi*, the *Zhou xun*, and other later texts. Through altering the focus of the narrative and describing in detail the political conflict, these texts, rather than merely leading the readers to appreciate the virtues of the early leaders, invite them to ponder issues such as the legitimacy of political power, the ultimate goals of political endeavors, and other fundamental issues in political philosophy. Furthermore, as the descriptions in the *Mengzi*, *Zhuangzi*, and the *Zhou xun* are not entirely the same, they can be seen as three different ideologies promoting varying humanistic values. They also reflect key characteristics of historical narratives in early Chinese classics.

Part 2: Two Variants—The *Mengzi* and the *Zhuangzi*

As previously mentioned, in the *Mengzi*, *Zhuangzi*, *Zhou xun*, and other documents expanded upon *Shijing* account, the *Zhou xun* took the changes one step further by changing the identity of the protagonist. Here, I first examine the narratives as told in the *Mengzi* and the *Zhuangzi*. The *Mengzi* records:[14]

> Duke Wen of Teng said: "Teng is a small state. If it tries with all its might to please the large states, it will only bleed itself white in the end. What is the best thing for me to do?

In antiquity, answered Mencius, when King Tai was in Bin, the Di tribes invaded the place. He tried to buy them off with skins and silks; he tried to buy them off with horses and hounds; he tried to buy them off with pearls and jade; but all to no avail.

Then he assembled the elders and announced to them, 'What the Di tribes want is our land. I have heard that a man in authority never turns what is meant for the benefit of men into a source of harm to them. It will not be difficult for you, my friends, to find another lord. I am leaving.'

And he left Bin, crossed the Liang Mountains, and built a city at the foot of Mount Qi and settled there.

The men of Bin said: 'This is a benevolent man. We must not lose him.'

They flocked after him as if to market. Others expressed the view, 'This is the land of our forebears. It is not a matter for us to decide. Let us defend it to the death.' You will have to choose between these two courses."

滕文公問曰："滕，小國也，竭力以事大國，則不得免焉．如之何則可？"

孟子對曰："昔者大王居邠，狄人侵之，事之以皮幣，不得免焉；事之以犬馬，不得免焉；事之以珠玉，不得免焉．乃囑其耆老而告之曰：'狄人之所欲者，吾土地也．吾聞之也，君子不以其所以養人者害人．二三子何患乎無君，我將去之．'去邠，逾梁山，邑於岐山之下居焉．邠人曰：'仁人也，不可失也．'從之者如歸市．或曰：'世守也，非身之所能為也，效死勿去．'君請擇於斯二者．"

The *Zhuangzi* says:[15]

When the Great King Danfu was living in Bin, the Di tribes attacked his territory. He offered them skins and silks, but they refused them; he offered them dogs and horses, but they refused them; he offered them pearls and jades, but they refused them. What the men of the Di tribes were after was his land. The Great King Danfu said: "To live among the older brothers and send the younger brothers to their death; to live among the fathers and send their sons to their death—this I cannot bear! My people, be diligent and remain where you are. What difference does it make whether you are subjects of mine or of the men of Di? I have heard it said, one must not injure that which he is nourishing for the sake of that by which he nourishes it." Then, using his riding whip as a cane, he departed, but his people, leading one another, followed him and, in time, founded a new state at the foot of Mount Qi. The Great King Danfu may be said to have known how to respect life. He who knows how to respect life, though he may be rich and honored, will not allow the means of nourishing life to injure his person. Though he may be poor and humble, will not allow concerns of profit to entangle his body. The men of the present age, if they occupy high office and are honored with titles, all think only of how serious a matter it would be to lose them. Eyes fixed on profit; they make light of the risk to their lives. Are they not deluded indeed?

大王亶父居邠，狄人攻之，事之以皮帛而不受，事之以犬馬而不受，事之以珠玉而不受，狄人之所求者，土地也. 大王亶父曰："與人之兄居而殺其弟，與人之父居而殺其子，吾不忍也. 子皆勉居矣. 為吾臣與為狄人臣，奚以異? 且吾聞之，不以所用養害所養." 因杖策而去之，民相連而從之，遂成國於岐山之下. 夫大王亶父可謂能尊生矣. 能尊生者，雖貴富不以養傷身，雖貧賤不以利累形. 今世之人居高官尊爵者，皆重失之. 見利輕亡其身，豈不惑哉!

Aside from the two preceding examples, the "Annals of Zhou" (Zhou Benji 周本紀) of the *Shiji*, the *Lüshi chunqiu*, the "Daoying xun" 道應訓 chapter in the *Huainanzi*, the *Shuoyuan*, and other texts give similar accounts. Notably, the narratives in the *Shiji* and the *Shuoyuan* are similar to the one told in the *Mengzi*, while those in the *Lüshi chunqiu* and the *Huainanzi* are closer to the account given in the *Zhuangzi*.

From the perspective of intellectual history, when one historical event appears in different texts and various forms, this is not a mere coincidence. On the one hand, this may have some connection to the mutual influence early texts had on one another and their common desire to transmit a shared cultural background. However, and to some extent even more importantly, repeated copying of an event implies its extremely important ideological significance and its role in presenting fundamental issues of political philosophy such as legitimacy and goals. This is the deep structure and what explains the variations.

The focus of the historical narrative and even the concrete plot of the "Great King Leaving Bin" has been switched to the conflict between King Tai and the Di tribes. Emphasis is on the failure of King Tai's bribes, his decision to flee, and the people's decision to follow. The belligerence of the Di tribes is contrasted to virtues such as "benevolence" (*ren* 仁) in the *Mengzi* or the ideal of "valuing life" (*gui sheng* 貴生) in the *Zhuangzi*. For these philosophers, King Tai effortlessly handled the crises and succeeded without resorting to war. Warring States controversies over "force" and "virtue" are at play.

In both the *Mengzi* and the *Zhuangzi*, the descriptions of the conflict between the Di tribes and King Tai basically lead to the same question: What is the ultimate guarantee or ultimate protection for the legitimate rise and employment of political power? Is it the necessary result of an external force as represented by the Di aggressions, or is it just an inherent political ideal or belief as represented by King Tai?

Regardless of the differences in the details of the descriptions in the *Mengzi* and the *Zhuangzi*, and regardless of the fundamental differences in the understanding of politics that the two represent, in both cases the underlying issues of humanistic motivations and values are concealed behind narration of the historical event. It is for these reasons that the narrations have been expanded.

R. G. Collingwood notes:

> The historian, investigating any event in the past, makes a distinction between what may be called the outside and inside of an event. By the outside of the event I mean everything belonging to it which can be described in terms of bodies and their movements: the passage of Caesar, accompanied by certain men, across a river called the Rubicon at one date, or the spilling of his blood on the floor of the senate-house at another. By the inside of the event I mean that in it which can only be described in terms of thought: Caesar's defiance of Republican law, or the clash of constitutional policy between himself and his assassins. The historian is never concerned with either of these to the exclusion of the other. He is investigating not mere events (where by a mere event I mean one which has only an outside and no inside) but actions, and an action is the unity of the outside and inside of an event. . . . His work may begin by discovering the outside of an event, but it can never end

there; he must always remember that the event was an action, and that his main task is to think himself into this action, to discern the thought of its agent.[16]

Collingwood showed that historical events not only include the figurative "body and their movements" that constitute their outside but also contain abstract ideologies and thoughts that constitute their "inside." It is the latter that enables historical events to be associated with the history of thought. Philosophers, by retelling a narrative, can leave an ideological mark on the actual historical process and produce a practical impact on the political world.

In the case of the "Great King Leaving Bin," the content of the historical events reflects the deep structure. In the earliest version, in the "Mian," it is King Tai's and the Duke of Zhou's virtuous conduct. In the *Mengzi* and the *Zhuangzi*, it concerns questions of political legitimacy and the ultimate goal of political acts. It is precisely because of the differences in the contents, the deep structures, that the details of the outer story changes.

The subtle differences in the *Mengzi* and the *Zhuangzi* versions are key to their different approaches to issues of conflict and competition in the political world, between force and some political or philosophical ideal, and whether the legitimacy of a regime requires an external force. However, in the *Mengzi*, the reason why the people followed the king and left Bin is because King Tai was benevolent and could protect the people:[17]

> Such as sensitive heart was possessed by the Former Kings and this manifested itself in compassionate government. With such a sensitive heart behind compassionate government, it was as easy to rule the empire as rolling it on your palm.
>
> 先王有不忍人之心, 斯有不忍人之政矣. 以不忍人之心, 行不忍人之政, 治天下可運之掌上.

According to the *Mengzi*, as long as the ruler possesses the seeds of goodness and promotes benevolent governance, the people's hearts will necessarily follow and easily result in ruling the empire. However, in the *Zhuangzi*, the reason why the masses approved and praise King Tai's rule was because he was able to "value life." That is, King Tai understood how to respect and cherish life; he esteemed the value of each individual's life. Zhuangzi was more focused on the discourse between individual life and political power than other philosophers of his time. He believed that power alone was an insufficient rationale for rule and that in fact the entire political world was nothing compared to the value of a human life. Ideal governance required respect for the individual's right to preserve and find his own unique nature. The slight differences in the outer form of the historical narrative we find in the *Mengzi* and the *Zhuangzi* reflect the great ideological distance and theoretical differences between the two thinkers.

Part 3: A Third Variant—The Peking University Bamboo Manuscript of the *Zhou xun*

Unlike the recollections in the *Mengzi* and the *Zhuangzi*, the Peking University bamboo slips of the *Zhou xun* preserve the main plot of the story but change the identity of the protagonist. It tells the story of how King Helü of Wu's attacks on Chu caused King Zhao to flee to Sui. Nevertheless, the text bears similarities to the *Zhuangzi*:[18]

> On the first day of the fourth month when the crown prince sought an audience with the king, Duke Zhaowen of Zhou 周昭文公 gave an imperial decree using the following historical incident. He said: "In the past Wu attacked Ying. King Zhao [of Chu] addressed his people in tears bidding farewell, he said: 'I cannot live with the elder brothers while their younger brothers are killed. Why would I desire to rule a country in which the sons are killed while I reside with their fathers? There is no difference between acting as ministers for me or for others . . . I am about to leave for a distant location . . .' In the middle of the night, the people searched for their lord but did not find him, they felt as if they lost their close relative. There was not one who did not sob. They carried the children and assisted the elders . . . to follow King Zhao's path. They spoke to King Zhao and said: 'Chu's population cannot compare to Wu, but in bravery the people of Wu cannot compare to the people of Chu. The people ask you to return and use braveness against the enemy.' King Zhao returned to King Wu's territory, causing King Helü of Wu to move his campsite thrice in one night. Therefore King Helü . . . returned Ying to King Zhao, just as it was to begin with. If King Zhao was to lose Ying, without bestowing virtue on his people, then his sacrifices would be to no avail, how could he have remained the ruler? This is what the

Odes call: 'the one who governs with virtue pacifies the country.' How can a ruler abandon virtue in his rule?"

維歲四月更旦之日, 恭大子朝, 周昭文公自身敕之, 用茲念也. 曰: "昔吳攻郢, 昭王垂泣以辭其民曰: '與人之兄處而殺其弟, 吾弗忍也. 與人之父居而殄其子, 吾何以國為? 為他人臣與為吾臣, 豈有以異? . . . 吾將去汝, 往適遠方.' . . . 夜半, 郢人求君弗得, 師若失親, 莫不瀾泣. 於是乃掛幼扶老 . . . 以從昭王. 謂昭王曰: '以眾則楚不如吳, 以勇則吳不如楚. 民請還, 為致勇之寇.' 乃反至於邗王之所, 令吳闔閭一夜未嘗不三徙臥. 闔閭 . . . 乃復歸郢, 若其始也. 昭王有失郢之行, 而無德於民, 其乏祀必矣, 豈又尚得為君? 此詩"所謂'懷德為寧'"者也. 人君其胡可以毋務懷德?"

The "Chu shijia" 楚世家 (House of Chu) chapter in the *Shiji*,[19] the "Yu cheng" chapter of the *Xinshu*,[20] and the "Taizu xun" chapter of the *Huainanzi*[21] all record the event of King Zhao leaving Ying. The historical record of the event in the *Shiji* is quite different from the *Zhou xun*, whereas the *Xinshu* and the *Huainanzi* accounts are somewhat similar. While describing a different event, the *Zhou xun* reveals a close literary connection to the description in the *Zhuangzi*. Table 9.1 shows this connection. Although the descriptions in both the *Zhuangzi* and the *Zhou xun* are short, the contents of the speeches given by both kings are almost identical and the storylines completely homogeneous.

Table 9.1.

Zhuangzi	*Zhou xun*
The Great King Danfu said: "To live among the older brothers and send the younger brothers to their death; to live among the fathers and send the sons to their death—this I cannot bear!"	King Zhao addressed his people in tears bidding farewell, he said: I cannot live with the elder brothers while their younger brothers are killed. Why would I desire to rule a country in which the sons are killed while I reside with their fathers?
What difference does it make whether you are subjects of mine or of the men of Di?	There is no difference between acting as ministers for me or for others.

While discussing the Warring States controversy over the hereditary right to rule versus abdication, Sarah Allan mentioned that "legendary material in ancient Chinese texts is always difficult to date because it is frequently copied from one text to another. The texts themselves are usually composite works compiled from various sources or by more than one hand rather than the product of a single author."[22] It is plausible that this is the situation in the *Zhou xun* and the *Zhuangzi*. The entire text of the *Zhou xun* manuscript takes the form of the Duke Zhaowen of Zhou reprimanding the crown prince, using historical stories that reflect a concern for governmental issues. These stories "begin from Yao and Shun and reach the times of Duke Xian of Qin 秦獻公 in the mid-Warring States period."[23] They are largely found in texts such as the *Huainanzi*, the *Lüshi chunqiu*, the *Shuoyuan* and other classics that are composed as anthologies.

Based on the *Zhou xun* as well as the characteristics and contents of the other texts, cross-textual copying or even textual mixtures among them is likely. Furthermore, according to the Peking University editors, the *Zhou xun* was compiled during the late Warring States period, which was close in time to the compilation of the miscellaneous chapters in the *Zhuangzi*, which would include "Giving Away a Throne." Since the two accounts came from the same historical period, it is safe to assume that there was mutual interaction between writers and intertextuality, perhaps even a common source of dissemination.

The Beijing University editors go so far as to categorize the *Zhou xun* as belonging to the school of "Huang-Lao Daoism."[24] Indeed, the bamboo slips of the *Zhou xun* do elucidate ideological concepts that are closely related to Huang-Lao Daoism,[25] such as the unity between body and state, the distinction between the roles of ruler and ministers, and the proper distribution of rewards and punishments. For example, the text gives us statements such as: "If one can rule his own body then the state is also governed," "the distance between heaven and earth is very far, whereas the distance between the ruler and ministers are even further than that of heaven and earth," "for those who act as the ruler, rewards and punishments cannot be inappropriate, if rewards and punishments are inappropriate then there is no way to command the people." Therefore, classifying the *Zhou xun*—just as some of the outer and miscellaneous chapters of the *Zhuangzi* are—as Huang-Lao Daoism is quite plausible and similarities between the two are to be expected.

As mentioned in parts 1 and 2 of this chapter, historical narratives in early Chinese classics often present some fluidity based on the deep structure of the narrative, thus forming different variations. This is manifested through changing the protagonist of the historical narrative in the *Zhou xun*. Similar to the account of the "Great King Leaving Bin" as described in the *Mengzi* and the *Zhuangzi*, the *Zhou xun* also presents a concern for the issues of political legitimacy and the ultimate goal of government. Duke Zhaowen of Zhou told the crown prince the historical narrative for this reason. The function of the historical narrative is to present this deep structure and to convey the narrator's point of view through this variant. Thus, the "Great King Leaving Bin" as recorded in texts such as the *Mengzi* and *Zhuangzi* can be regarded as belonging to the same textual group as the "Zhao King Fleeing to Sui" story recorded in the *Zhou xun*, the *Xinshu*, the *Huainanzi*, and other texts. In essence it is intended to show the conflicts between different political forces, thereby presenting and discussing major issues in political philosophy. As far as the specific documents of textual groups are concerned, the " 'history' in these texts could be transformed, at least within a certain range, and ancient Chinese writers used these transformations as a means of expressing political and social attitudes."[26]

Part 4: Conclusions

Through the case study of the prototype narrative of the "Great King Leaving Bin," presented in the ode "Mian" of the *Shijing* and three later variants presented in the *Mengzi*, *Zhuangzi*, and *Zhou xun*, we can arrive at some conclusions regarding the form and characteristics of historical narratives in early Chinese classics. Unlike recording historical facts, the details of historical narratives often contain a certain amount of flexibility, which can be adapted or altered by different narrators. The basis and purpose of doing so was to express the narrators' specific ideological position or value ideal. At this point, the narrator simultaneously presents a "nonhistorical view of history."[27] That is, using a specific historical incident as the blueprint for a "rhetorical method"[28] to express a specific philosophical position or ideological concern.

In context of this chapter, we saw how the *Mengzi*, *Zhuangzi*, and the *Zhou xun* expanded the storyline presented in the ode "Mian" of the *Shijing* and how they highlighted the conflict in the story to interrogate core issues in political philosophy. Meanwhile, the fact that the contents of the three texts are not entirely the same shows the different ideological interests and humanistic concerns of their authors. This represents the deep structure inherent to the construction of historical narratives.

Notes

1. See Wang Bo 王博, "Shuo 'Yu zuo yu bian'" 說 "喻作於編," *Zhongguo zhexue shi* 中國哲學史 2006.1: 5–23.

2. Wang Bo, *Zhongguo ruxue shi, Xian Qin juan* 中國儒學史, 先秦卷 (Beijing: Beijing daxue, 2011), 83.

3. To clarify, the "historical narrative" I discuss here differs from actual historical statements or historical texts. In general terms, the purpose of the latter is inclined more toward restoration, presentation, or explorations of historical facts, while the former serves more as some kind of "material" or "framework" that functions to carry or express the personal intentions or ideas of the author.

4. Sarah Allan discussed the deep and superficial structural layers of ancient legend narratives in terms of Lévi-Strauss's theory of mythological analysis in *The Heir and the Sage: Dynastic Legend in Early China*, revised and expanded edition, SUNY series in Chinese Philosophy and Culture (Albany: State University of New York Press, 2017).

5. The "Great King" described here is King Tai of Zhou 周太王, who was also known by the title Ancient Duke Danfu 古公亶父. This chapter makes use of the different names according to their appearance in different texts.

6. According to the speculations made by the editorial team, based on the diversity and complexity of the contents and literary style of the *Zhou xun*, the composition of the text "could not have been the work of one person, nor could it have been compiled in one time and place. It most likely was gradually collected from different sources." Among the historical figures the *Zhou xun* refers to, the earliest is Duke Xian of Qin 秦獻公 (424–362 BCE), while the actions of Duke Zhaowen of Zhou and the crown prince took place in the latter half of the fourth century BCE, "thus the text could not have been formed before the end of the fourth century BCE." From the historical events recorded in the *Zhou xun* and the characteristics of the language, vocabulary, and grammar, we can conclude that it was probably composed toward the end of the Warring States period. See Han Wei 韓巍, "Xi Han zhushu Zhou xun ruogan wenti de taotan" 西漢竹書《周馴》若干問題的探討, in *Beijing daxue cang Xi Han zhushu, di san ce* 北京大學藏西漢竹書第三冊 (Shanghai: Shanghai guji, 2015), 249–98, with the quotes on 254.

7. Interestingly, in addition to the *Zhou xun*, the "Yu cheng" 諭誠 chapter of the *Xinshu* 新書 and the "Taizuxun" 泰族訓 (Exalted Lineages) chapter of the *Huainanzi* also record the event of King Helü of Wu attacking Chu and King Zhou fleeing to Sui. The difference is that the details of the narrative in the *Zhou xun* and the language it uses are extremely close to the description of the event of the "Great King Leaving Bin" in the *Zhuangzi*.

8. Zheng Xuan 鄭玄, Kong Yingda 孔穎達, comm., *Maoshi zhengyi* 毛詩正義, *Shisanjing zhushu* 十三經注疏 (Beijing: Beijing daxue, 2000), 986. Translation is

after: James Legge, *The Chinese Classics: The She King; Or the Book of Poetry* (Taibei: SMC, 1991), 437–441.

9. Zheng Xuan, Kong Yingda, *Maoshi zhengyi*, 1147–1167.

10. Zheng Xuan, Kong Yingda, *Maoshi zhengyi*, 1156.

11. Zheng Xuan, Kong Yingda, *Maoshi zhengyi*, 1166.

12. As mentioned in the introduction to this chapter, although on the surface the narratives in the *Mengzi* and *Zhuangzi* seem to resemble one another, they actually differ in their political philosophies. This is further discussed later. For a more detailed reading, refer to Ding Sixin 丁四新, "Renmin yu zunsheng: 'Gu gong qianqi' de rudao jieshi" 仁民與尊生: "古公遷岐"的儒道解釋, *Jianghuai luntan* 江淮論壇2012.3: 101–108; and Cui Xiaojiao 崔曉姣, "Cong 'Dawang qu Bin' kan ru, dai zhengxhi zhexue zhi fentu" 從"大王去邠"看儒, 道政治哲學之分途 *Wuhan keji daxue xuebao* 武漢科技大學學報2016.3: 312–17.

13. Zheng Xuan, Kong Yingda, *Maoshi zhengyi*, 1165.

14. *Mengzi*, "Lianghui wang, xia" 梁惠王下, see D.C. Lau, *Mencius*, book 1 part B (London: Penguin Books, 1970), 71–72.

15. *Zhuangzi* 莊子 "Rang Wang" 讓王, see Burton Watson, *The Complete Works of Zhuangzi* (New York: Columbia University Press, 2013), 240–241.

16. R. G. Collingwood, *The Idea of History* (Oxford: Oxford University Press, 2005), 210.

17. *Mengzi*, "Gongsun Chou, shang" 公孫醜上, see D. C. Lau, *Mencius*, book 1 part B (London: Penguin Books, 1970), 82.

18. The character variants in the text are based on Han Wei, "Zhou Xun shiwen zhushi" 周馴釋文注釋, *Beijing daxue cang Xi Han zhushu, di san ce* 北京大學藏西漢竹書第三冊 (Shanghai: Shanghai guji, 2015), 123–145.

19. The *Shiji* "Chu shijia" records: "In the winter of the tenth year (506 BCE), Helü, the king of Wu, Wu Zixu 伍子胥, and Po Pi 伯嚭, together with Tang 唐 and Cai 蔡, all attacked Chu 楚. Chu was crushed. The troops of Wu then entered Ying and disgraced King Ping's tomb for the sake of Wu Zixu. When the troops of Wu came, Chu sent Zichang 子常 to meet them with troops. They drew up in formation on both sides of the Han 漢 River. Wu attacked and defeated Zichang, and Zichang escaped and fled to Zheng 鄭. When the troops of Chu fled, Wu, taking advantage of its victory, pursued them. After five battles they reached Ying. On the Ji-mao day, King Zhao went out of the capital and fled. On the Geng-chen day, the men of Wu entered Ying." Translation after: William H. Nienhauser Jr., *The Grand Scribe's Records*, vol. 1 (Bloomington: Indiana University Press, 2006), 413–414.

20. The "Yu Cheng" 諭誠 chapter of the *Xinshu* 新書 says: "King Zhao of Chu stood in his room and worried about the cold, saying: 'When I had breakfast, I drank two goblets of wine and wore my furs, yet I still felt cold. How can the people bear it?' On that day, he distributed furs from the storehouse to clothe those who were cold; he also distributed food from the granary to feed those who were

hungry. Two years later, King Helü attacked Ying, and King Zhao fled to Sui. The people, remembering his deeds, begged him to return and put the invaders to death. Helü moved his campsite ten times that night, but still could not occupy Chu and had his forces retreat. King Zhao returned, that is the virtue of his entire lineage." Jia Yi 賈誼 (Han), Yan Zhenyi 閻振益 and Zhong Xia 鍾夏 (commentators), *Xinshu jiaozhu* 新書校注 (Beijing: Zhonghua shuju, 2000), 279. Translation by author.

21. The "Taizu xun" (Exalted Lineage) chapter of the *Huainanzi* says: "King Helü of Wu attacked Chu and, after five battles, entered the capital Ying. He burned the grain in the tall granaries, destroyed the Nine Dragon array of bells, flogged King Ping's tomb, and occupied King Zhao's palace. King Zhao escaped to Sui. With fathers and elder brothers carrying the young and supporting the old, the one hundred surnames followed him. They roused one another to courage and directed it at the enemy; committing their lives, they raised their bare arms and fought with them. At this time, without a general to lead them, they still fell into formation, each man risking his life, and forced the Wu armies to retreat, regaining their Chu territory." Translation after: John S. Major et al., *The Huainanzi* (New York: Columbia University Press, 2010), 2246.

22. Allan, *The Heir and the Sage*, 16.

23. See Han Wei, "Zhou xun shuoming" 周馴說明, *Beijing daxue cang Xi Han zhushu, di san ce* 北京大學藏西漢竹書第三冊 (Shanghai: Shanghai guji, 2015), 121–122.

24. Han, "Zhou xun shuoming," 121–122.

25. Yuan Qing 袁青, "Lun Beida Han jian Zhou xun de Huanglao xue sixiang" 論北大漢簡"周馴"的黃老學思想, *Zhongguo zhexue shi* 中國哲學史 2017.3: 69–74.

26. Allan, *The Heir and the Sage*, preface, xiv.

27. For further details see Chen Shaoming's 陳少明 analysis of Zhuangzi's "historical view" in his "Lishi de yanyuhua: dui Zhuangzi lishi lunshu de yizhong jiedu" 歷史的寓言化——對莊子歷史論述的一種解讀, *Zhongguo zhexue shi* 中國哲學史 2013.2: 41–47. Aside from the *Zhuangzi*, historical narratives in many manuscripts also express this kind of "nonhistorical view of history" attitude to a certain extent.

28. Chen Shaoming, "Lishi de yanyuhua."

10

Rebuilding King Wen

Paratext as Intellectual Biography in the *Yi Zhou shu* Preface

PAUL NICHOLAS VOGT

Introduction

Over the millennium separating the end of the Shang dynasty from the common era, the figure known posthumously as King Wen of Zhou 周文王 (ca. 12th–11th c. BCE) assumed a role of unusual complexity in early Chinese intellectual production. Situated at the boundary between history and prehistory, King Wen represented a transition point between models of social and intellectual organization, providing a convenient vehicle for debate over a host of issues surrounding the relationship between religious and political knowledge, practitioners, and institutions.[1] Depictions of King Wen in the Warring States and Han intellectual milieus were thus many and varied; the scale of that variation, in fact, has become clearer over the last few decades, as Warring States manuscripts touching on the history of the Zhou royal house have come to light.[2]

As textual traditions concerning the early reaches of Chinese history coalesced during the Warring States and Han periods, different approaches to the memory of King Wen as a character construct emerged. The opening sequence of the collection commonly known as the *Yi Zhou shu* 逸周書 is perhaps the most inclusive of these, uniting several texts of substantive formal, argumentative, and philosophical diversity into a "King Wen cycle" covering the period from the last years of Shang through King Wen's death. The heavy lifting of this attributive process is performed, however, not by the chapters themselves, but by the combination of the collection's traditional nomenclature and, especially, the "preface" that typically accompanies transmitted editions. Reading the first portion of the *Yi Zhou shu* as the intellectual legacy of King Wen depends, in other words, on the paratextual power of its preface to frame its discrete textual units within a common historical vision.

With the term "paratextual," I refer to the literary theorist Gérard Genette's famous model of the paratext, referring to the materials that accompany the main "text" of a text—whether physically or in the public consciousness—and shape its reception.[3] These materials, taken together or separately, negotiate between the text and its audience, guiding the reader in interpreting the work to which they are attached without, in theory, interfering with the text itself. As Genette puts it, they create "a kind of canal lock between the ideal and relatively immutable identity of the text and the empirical (sociohistorical) reality of the text's public."[4] In a certain respect, applying Genette's model of the paratext to the *Yi Zhou shu* preface stretches its bounds, given that he intended it specifically for materials claimed, directly or indirectly, by a putative author figure.[5] However, the various formal and functional characteristics of paratexts that Genette enumerates nicely encompass the relationship of the *Yi Zhou shu* preface to the collection it accompanies, and, given that Genette himself includes prefaces written well after the author's death in his discussion, I feel justified in deploying the term.[6]

The following analysis explores the details of the *Yi Zhou shu* preface's paratextual framing. Approaching the preface as a work in its own right, the study considers how the preface contextualizes individual chapters within the life of King Wen and how its framings of those chapters relate to each other in style, content, and assumed historical background, giving brief, secondary consideration to how they relate to the chapters themselves. Based on the resulting vision of the preface's internal logic, the study then considers the implications of this paratextually constructed biography of King Wen as an example of the ascription of authority to diverse textual content, rediscovering the impact of this alternate lens through which generations of readers have encountered the character of King Wen not only as a moral paragon, but also as a pragmatically minded intellectual.

Basics of the *Yi Zhou shu*

The *Yi Zhou shu* is a collection of short texts from early China that theoretically relate to the activities of the royal house during the Western Zhou period (ca. 1045–771 BCE).⁷ Some of the texts in the collection claim that relationship explicitly, typically in the form of framing devices (*Yi Zhou shu*, "Bao dian" 寶典):⁸

> In his third regnal year, on the day Bingchen, first day of the second month, the king [i.e., King Wu] was at Hao. [He] summoned Dan, the Duke of Zhou, saying . . .
>
> 維王三祀, 二月丙辰朔, 王在鄗, 召周公旦曰 . . .

However, many of the work's chapters contain no such internal indicators, and the understanding that the *Yi Zhou shu* might preserve part of the intellectual heritage of the Western Zhou relies on its historical range of titles, the earliest comments on the origin of the text, and the claims made in the preface that has long accompanied it. The *Yi Zhou shu* as a product of the Western Zhou is thus first and foremost a paratextual construct.⁹

As the complex textual history of the *Yi Zhou shu* has been addressed elsewhere, I will not delve into the details.¹⁰ Here it will suffice to say that the collection contains some material from the Warring States period or earlier, as well as some of likely Han dynasty vintage, but seems first to have reached a form approximating that in which it is known today during the Western Han.¹¹ By the early Period of Disunion, when the main commentary to the text was composed, part of these "original" contents had already disappeared from some lines of transmission.¹² The discovery of the Jizhong tomb texts, which included materials relating to the Western Zhou kings, complicated the matter further; transmission lines of the *Yi Zhou shu* were afterward often confused with these Jizhong texts, and it remains possible that elements of the Jizhong materials may have been interpolated into the extant versions of the collection.¹³ Along the way, portions of the collection were once more lost, such that modern editions of the *Yi Zhou shu* lack eleven chapters that are listed in the preface.¹⁴ As an exercise in paratextual organization, then, we might expect the *Yi Zhou shu* to be both relatively consistent and representative of a certain spectrum of Han dynasty interests, but we should be prepared to encounter locations in which its contents conflict with these interpretive criteria in whole or in part.

Basics of the *Yi Zhou shu* Preface

The "preface"¹⁵ to the *Yi Zhou shu* comprises a series of brief statements corresponding to each of the fifty-nine extant texts making up the collection, as well as eleven further chapters that received editions lack (though some such statements fall within a lacuna in the received text of the preface; see later discussion). Each of the component line entries mentions an individual king of the Western Zhou period, describes the social or political circumstances of a time in that king's reign, and then specifies a chapter of the *Yi Zhou shu* as the product of that historical moment (see the following translation). The line entries assign the chapters to specific kings with varying degrees of explicitness, but if one reads the series in sequence, relying on context clues and accepting the general principle that a particular entry may be grouped with the one preceding it unless otherwise specified, the logic of their attributions becomes relatively clear.

As Edward Shaughnessy has pointed out, the preface in all likelihood took its current form sometime during the first century BCE, while the missing chapters were probably lost during the Song dynasty.[16] The circumstances of the preface's composition, however, and thus the intent behind it, remain subjects of debate. One line of argument suggests that it followed a model set by the preface of a hundred-chapter version of the *Shangshu*, though there is some question as to whether the model in question was the "pseudo–Kong Anguo preface," preserved in the *Wenxuan* and considered a post-Han work, or some other document that accompanied an original, lost version of a hundred-chapter *Shangshu* recension.[17] Niu Hong'en supports the opinion that Liu Xiang both compiled the *Yi Zhou shu* collection and wrote the preface.[18] Huang Peirong, in contrast, notes that a few of the preface's entries mischaracterize the contents of their chapters, concluding on this basis that the compiler(s) of the collection and author(s) of the preface must have been different people.[19] Lacunae in the text of the preface that overlap partly with chapters now missing from the collection itself complicate such efforts to divine the relationship between the two.

The *Yi Zhou shu* preface assigns the first twenty-five chapters of the collection to the time of King Wen, apart for two textual irregularities that are discussed later. Piecing the building blocks of the collection's chapters together, it constructs a life story of the sage sovereign King Wen like a house built with stones scavenged from a ruin. In some places, it does violence to those blocks in order to fit them into its framework, but the result, by and large, is an internally consistent, conceptually coherent intellectual biography of a figure of outsized importance to the Chinese political and philosophical tradition.

The pages that follow examine the details of that construct, tracing how the textual and paratextual motives blended in a preface that stands as a compelling work in its own right. The assignations for these chapters appear here in translation, in the same order in which they occur in the text.[20] Proposing a division of the portion dealing with this "King Wen cycle" into sections based on its own internal logic, this study searches for the reading experience that the arrangement conveyed, exploring how content and chronology shaped each other to produce the most detailed intellectual biography of King Wen known from early China.[21]

"Instructions and Models" Sequence (Shang-Zhou Transition Period)

1. 昔在文王, 商紂並立, 困於虐政, 將弘道以弼無道, 作 "度訓." Formerly, when King Wen reigned simultaneously with Zhou of Shang, beset by oppressive governance, [King Wen] used the expansive Way in order to help [those] without the Way; [thus] "Du xun" (Instructions on Degrees) was composed.[22]

2. 殷人作教, 民不知極, 將明道極以移其俗, 作 "命訓." When the men of Yin created teachings, the people did not understand [their] guiding principle. [King Wen] used the illumination of the Way's guiding principle to shift the customs [of the people]; [thus] "Ming xun" (Instructions on Commands) was composed.

3. 紂作淫亂, 民散無性習[23]常, 文王惠和化服之, 作 "常訓." Zhou [of Shang] gave rise to lewdness and chaos, and the people scattered and lacked character in conducting their normal activities.[24] King Wen, benevolent and harmonious, transformed them and led them to submit; [thus] "Chang xun" (Instructions on Norms) was composed.

4. 上失其道, 民散無紀, 西伯脩仁明恥示教, 作 "文酌." When those above lost their Way and the people scattered and lacked a connecting thread, the Elder of the West cultivated humaneness, illuminated shame, and demonstrated teachings; [thus] the "Wen zhuo" (Deliberation[25] of [King] Wen) was composed.

5. 上失其道, 民失其業, X X 凶年, 作 "糴匡." When those above lost their Way and the people lost their trades, X X lean years; thus "Di kuang" (Correction of Stores) was composed.

The first five preface entries adopt the idea that chaos dominated the realm in the late years of the Shang dynasty, taking the time when the inept and tyrannical King Zhou of Shang set policy as their backdrop. Though King Wen is traditionally understood to have operated within the Shang political system at this time—hence the *Shiji* account refers to him as "Lord of the West" (Xi Bo 西伯) during these years[26]—the *Yi Zhou shu* preface begins by stating that he and King Zhou of Shang *bing li* 並立, "were simultaneously established," depicting a parity of legitimacy, if not legal authority, even in the days before the proper separation of Zhou from Shang.

Generally, these first five entries of the preface characterize their chapters' content in terms of King Wen's efforts to fill the leadership vacuum left by the failures of King Zhou. The first entry, for "Du xun," sets this premise in general terms, describing King Wen's goal simply as to "assist [those] lacking the way" (*bi wu dao* 弼無道). The second and third entries add some specificity to this construct. The second entry postulates a breakdown in communications between the Shang leadership and the general populace, describing the "Ming xun" chapter as King Wen's attempt to bridge that gap. In the third entry, the preface holds that King Zhou's depredations have prevented the people from holding to their normal standards of behavior; the "Chang xun" chapter, it claims, captures King Wen's efforts to calm their concerns and restore social order. The exhortation in the fourth and fifth entries that "leaders lost their Way" is more generic than the attribution of these problems to Zhou himself. Again, however, the "Wen zhuo" entry construes King Wen's intervention as a moral failure of existing leadership, to be corrected through the explanation and modeling of morally correct behavior. Whereas the "Wen zhuo" entry seems to address the dissolution of the general social fabric binding the populace—literally, the *ji* 紀, "[connecting] thread"—the entry for "Di kuang" puts an economic spin on the topic, in accordance with the general thrust of the chapter.[27]

Throughout this sequence, King Wen conducts a second-order intervention, fixing problems that Zhou of Shang caused to arise in the populace rather than addressing them at the source. King Wen is generally said to rely on "instruction" (*xun* 訓, *jiao* 教) and "illumination" (*ming* 明) rather than direct implementation of policies, though the slightly anomalous "Di kuang," depending on one's interpretation of *kuang* 匡, may represent a counterexample.[28] Overall, the logic of the sequence of entries is both consistent and progressive—the first establishes a historical frame for interpreting the chapters, and the second through fifth deploy that frame to contextualize their chapters in greater detail.

"Martial Endeavors" Sequence

6. 文王立, 西距昆夷, 北備獫狁, 謀武以昭威懷, 作 "武稱." Once King Wen was established, [he] held off the Hunyi in the west and defended against the Xianyun in the north. By planning martial affairs, [he] illuminated [his ability to] awe [these groups] and bring [them] to submission;[29] [thus] "Wu cheng" (Martial Balance)[30] was composed.

7. 武以禁暴, 文以綏德, 大聖允兼, 作 "允文." With war [he] prevented violence, and with civility [he] pacified the virtuous.[31] [His] great sagacity was truly double; [thus] "Yun wen" (Truly Civil) was composed.[32]

8–10. 武有七德, 文王作 "大武," "大明武," "小明武" 三篇. War has seven virtues. King Wen composed the three chapters called "Da wu" (Great Martial), "Da ming wu" (Greater Illumination of the Martial), and "Xiao ming wu" (Lesser Illumination of the Martial).

Chapters 6–10 of the *Yi Zhou shu* concern themselves with military strategy construed at its broadest—that is, including both the tactics and strategy of war itself as well as the conduct of governance in conquered regions. The preface shows an awareness of this, describing all five of these chapters as products of King Wen's martial efforts.[33] Robin McNeal has convincingly argued for the conceptual coherence of this sequence, suggesting that these chapters may have been read and transmitted as a collective before their incorporation into the *Yi Zhou shu*.[34] Here I will offer only a few words on the preface's historical framing of this group of chapters as part of a broader intellectual biography of King Wen.

The statement that "King Wen was established" (Wen Wang *li* 文王立), at the beginning of the entry for "Wu cheng," suggests that a new section of the preface's biographical construct was meant to begin with chapter 6. However, the very first line of the preface uses the same term, *li*, to describe King Wen's status throughout the preceding chapters. The following sequence of the "Cheng" chapters (11–13; see following) represents a less-described period in the King Wen biography, judging from other sources. However, whether or not one accepts the traditional model that King Wen's reign technically "began" with the conferral of a "Mandate of Heaven" nine years before his death, it is difficult to claim that the residence of the Zhou at

Cheng represents a less independent period of "establishment" than whatever relationship between King Wen and Shang may have preceded it.[35]

The idea that the Zhou handled military relations with populations known as the Kunyi and the Xianyun, even in the era before the conquest of Shang, appears in various sources.[36] There is some ambiguity about the chronology of these relationships and the figures involved; for instance, the *Bamboo Annals* assigns the activities of Nanzhong against the Kunyi to the third year of Di Yi, the second-to-last king of the Shang period.[37] The *Hou Han shu*, however, specifically construes King Wen's interactions with these two groups as part of the Zhou relationship with Shang.[38] Of course, it is perfectly possible to understand the Kunyi and the Xianyun as posing ongoing problems for the hegemonic powers of the Central States, and in the case of the latter, there is good evidence for this viewpoint.[39] Still, viewed through this lens, it is difficult to understand the "establishment" of King Wen proposed in the chapter 6 line item as a claim of independence from Shang. The preface's line item for chapter 6 thus seems all the more to introduce a thematically rather than chronologically distinct section, dealing with King Wen's military activities as a separate category from his domestic pursuits. There is every reason, in other words, to read this second group of chapters, as defined by the preface, as a distinct section, potentially overlapping in time with the materials that came before and after it, and construed historically as the product of King Wen's efforts to incorporate belligerent external populations into the Shang—soon to be Zhou—realm.

Residence at Cheng

> 11. 穆王遭大荒, 謀救患分災,[40] X "大匡."
>
> When King Mu met with a great shortage, [he] made plans to rescue [the people] from misfortune and mitigate disaster, [composing] "Da kuang" (Great Restoration).

Chapters 11–13 of the *Yi Zhou shu* present a variety of interpretive difficulties centering around the proposition that King Wen briefly resided at a place called Cheng 程. Foremost among these is that the received version of the *Yi Zhou shu* preface seemingly assigns chapter 11 to King Mu, King Wen's fifth-generation descendant, rather than to King Wen himself. General consensus suggests that this is an error, in the sense that the intent of the chapter's "author" was to cast it as a product of the reign of King Wen.[41] The precise nature of that error is somewhat in question, however, and since its implications relate directly to the reading strategy adopted here, it bears further discussion.

The "Da kuang" chapter itself begins with the statement:

維周王宅程三年, 遭天之大荒.

> In the third year of his residence at Cheng, the Zhou king encountered a great shortage [sent by?] Heaven.[42]

In theory, the phrase *Zhou wang*, "the Zhou king," could, if taken out of context, refer to any of the many generations of Zhou rulers.[43] Why the compilers of the *Yi Zhou shu* preface would choose King Mu from among them is less than clear. To my knowledge, no other early Chinese source associates King Mu of Zhou with the location known as Cheng 程.[44] On the other hand, King Wen's residence at Cheng is attested in the *Bamboo Annals*, which notes also that he eventually relocated to Feng—the center of Zhou power for most of the Western Zhou period, located near modern Xi'an—due to "great famine" (*da ji* 大饑), very close to the "great shortage" 大荒 mentioned in the preface's line item for the "Da kuang" chapter.[45] In fact, the suggestion that King Wen dwelt in Cheng for a time seemingly appears in no other received texts of early date—an intriguing fact in light of the complicated relationship between the textual histories of the *Yi Zhou shu* and the *Bamboo Annals*.[46] Yet new corroboration provided by the "Cheng wu" text from the Tsinghua University slips suggests that the idea that King Wen had occupied Cheng was extant well before the composition of the *Yi Zhou shu* preface.[47] The assignation of a chapter with a framing device mentioning Cheng to the King Wen cycle, along with texts bearing titles that argued for such a connection, is thus quite easy to imagine. This model of King Wen's biography was, however, clearly not universally accepted in the Han dynasty, given that the *Shiji*'s "Basic Annals of Zhou" make no mention of Cheng in their treatment of King Wen.[48] It is thus equally conceivable that the preface might have originally assigned it to the King Wen cycle, only for that attribution to be changed later, whether intentionally or by accident; or that the compilers of the preface might have misunderstood the connection of King Wen to Cheng and therefore attributed the chapter to a different king.[49]

This quandary speaks to broader issues concerning the textual history of the preface and its relationship to the *Yi Zhou shu* collection, namely: Was the preface composed by the same person or persons who compiled the collection, and/or those who set the order of the chapters? The sparse information on the collection's early transmission means that we may never be able to answer these questions. As this brief study shows, however, the structure of the King Wen cycle as presented in the preface shows a sophisticated understanding of the relationship between chronological sequence and content type. Though there is no question that the preface occasionally mischaracterizes the content of the chapters, it does so, I would say, in the interest of maintaining the coherence of that structure. My preliminary inclination is thus to see the King Mu attribution of the "Da kuang" chapter as a later change, intentional or unintentional, rather than an original feature of the preface.

The question remains, however, just how the Cheng chapters, including "Da kuang," relate to the broader sequence of the King Wen cycle. While the preface proposes a bit of social context for "Da kuang," received editions lack any entries for chapters 12, "Cheng wu" (Awakening at Cheng), and 13, "Cheng dian" (Statutes of Cheng), due to a substantial lacuna. However, the *Maoshi zhengyi* cites a claim made in a work it calls "Zhou shu" that King Wen composed these two chapters while at Cheng—a natural assumption, given the titles—and it may well be, as Lu Wenchao 盧文弨 has suggested, that the claim originally formed part of the text now missing from the preface.[50] I thus tend to see a transition point between a section devoted to military affairs, ending with the combined assessment of chapters 8–10 seen earlier, and a separate one beginning with the chapter 11 assessment. This would suggest a reading in which the Cheng chapters constituted an independent section in their own right—perhaps an artifact of the perception that they related to a marginal tradition within the King Wen biography. Unfortunately, the lacuna that appears here encompasses the preface's entries for the following three chapters, "Qin yin," "Jiu zheng," and "Jiu kai." As such, it remains impossible to gauge precisely how the summaries of the Cheng chapters might have related to those immediately following them when the preface was first compiled. Without such corroboration, one can only note that the extant Cheng chapters, "Da kuang" and "Cheng dian," are quite different from each other in form, content, and language, connected only by their common historical framing.[51]

"Rule-Setting" Section

17. 文王唯庶邦之多難，論典以匡謬，作"劉法。"

> Considering[52] the many difficulties of the various states, King Wen discussed the use of statutes to correct errors; [thus] the "Liu fa" (Models for the Axe) was composed.[53]

18. 文王卿士諗發教禁戒，作"文開。"⁵⁴

King Wen's ministers counseled the promulgation of teachings to restrict and admonish; "Wen kai" (Opening of Culture/Opening of [King] Wen?) was composed.

The "next" eight chapters of the received *Yi Zhou shu*, from "Cheng wu" through "Ba fan," are missing from the line of transmission.⁵⁵ Meanwhile, the long lacuna in the preface overlaps but does not coincide perfectly with the missing chapters. Specifically, the entries for "Qin yin" and "Jiu zheng," or chapters 14 and 15 in the received edition, are entirely missing, and of the entry for "Jiu kai," only the simple phrase "composed 'Jiu kai'" (*zuo jiu kai* 作九開) remains.⁵⁶ It is unlikely, then, that the lacunae resulted from complementary editorial processes.

The sequence of chapters in the preface picks back up with "Liu fa," chapter 17 in the preface order. The preface's framing of this chapter still suggests a "crisis mode" in which King Wen filled a gap left by the poor leadership of Shang. In the early portion of the preface, however, King Wen's action in this regard was presented as modeling of and instruction in moral principles; here it is construed instead as a process of legal reform, wherein "statutes" (*dian* 典) are brought into alignment. The different language implies that King Wen has begun to usurp the capacity of an official ruler for the "various states" (i.e., the realm of Shang hegemony), a role conflict that was the subject of much angst in early treatments of King Wen, both within the *Yi Zhou shu* and elsewhere.⁵⁷

This contextualization of chapter 18 follows upon the previous entry enough that one might read them as a logical sequence: once King Wen went about establishing uniformity of policy across the "various states," his advisors consulted with him on these new policies and conducted a public awareness campaign, ensuring that King Wen's rules were known across the realm. The "rule-setting" block formed by these two entries may be seen as related to the sequence that follows, but differs from it in both scope (public, rather than directed to high-ranking individuals) and purpose (keeping the general peace rather than defending against the threat of Shang).

"Individual Instructions" Section (Preparation for Conquest of Shang)

19. 維美公命于文王，脩身觀天以謀商難，作"保開。"

When Duke Mei received a command from King Wen, he cultivated himself and observed Heaven in order to plan for difficulties [from] Shang; "Bao kai" (Opening of the Protector?) was composed.

20. 文王訓乎武王以繁害之戒，作"八[58] 繁。"

King Wen instructed King Wu with admonishments about the proliferation of harm; the "Ba fan" (Eight Proliferations) was composed.

21. 文王在酆，命周公謀商難，作"酆保。"

At Feng, King Wen ordered the Duke of Zhou to plan for difficulties [from] Shang; the "Feng bao" (Protection of Feng) was composed.

Whereas the former two entries framed their chapters as general policy, the preface construes the next few chapters as individual instructions to specific, powerful figures within the Zhou elite sphere. No "Duke Mei" (*Meigong* 美公), specified as the target of King Wen's commands in the chapter "Bao kai," is known from other received texts or bronze inscriptions, but it has been suggested that the phrase might represent any of several powerful figures working closely with the crown in the years surrounding the conquest, including Taigong Wang 太公望, Shaogong Shi 召公奭, or even the Duke of Zhou.[59] Though "Ba fan," the putative eighteenth chapter, is lost, the preface's description of it accords with various extant writings that employ an address from King Wen to King Wu as a framing device. Typically, these take the form of warnings, as in the "Wen jing" chapter appearing later in the King Wen cycle; and often, as in both "Wen jing" and "Wen zhuan," they include accounts of dream interpretation, a skill sometimes attributed to King Wen.[60]

Since the preface's description of chapter 21 begins with an expositional statement of the king's location, one might easily take it as an effort to begin a new section of the sequence addressing the events following King Wen's relocation of the Zhou to Feng.[61] I am inclined, however, to see the chapter's framing—as an order to the individual, famous figure of the Duke of Zhou—as a meaningful commonality connecting the entry to the two preceding it. Notably, chapters 19 and 21 are both construed as preparations against the threat posed by Shang; and while chapter 20 makes no mention of Shang, readers would undoubtedly know that its specified addressee, Fa/King Wu, would ultimately carry out its conquest. In fact, as Huang Peirong notes, the content of the "Feng bao" chapter has little to do with the Shang-Zhou conflict, offering instead a general statement on statecraft.⁶² Chapters 19–21, as contextualized by the preface, thus combined a common thematic thread (conflict with Shang) with a common formal context (individual addresses from the king to important allies). That the preface takes some trouble to fit "Feng bao" into this mold hints at its significance to the composer's vision of the *Yi Zhou shu* collection.

"Preparing a Legacy" Section

The closing portion of the preface's "King Wen cycle" defines a series of chapters as products of King Wen's efforts to prepare his posterity for his eventual passing.

> 22–23. 文啟謀乎後嗣以脩身敬戒，作"大開，""小開"二篇.
>
> > [King] Wen first counseled his posterity to cultivate themselves and respect admonitions; the two chapters "Da kai" (Great Opening) and "Xiao kai" (Lesser Opening) were composed.
>
> 24. 文王有疾，告武王以民之多變，作"文儆."
>
> > When King Wen was ill, he told King Wu about the many changes of the people; "Wen jing" ([King] Wen's Warning) was composed.
>
> 25. 文王告武王以序德之行，作"文傳."
>
> > King Wen told King Wu about conduct according to virtue; "Wen zhuan" (Bequeathal of [King] Wen) was composed.

Internally, the two chapters "Da kai" and "Xiao kai" bear little resemblance to each other, despite the fact that the preface treats them together; the much shorter "Da kai" consists mainly of a numerical list of admonitions, while "Xiao kai" is formatted as a speech, with customary utterances such as *wuhu* 嗚呼, and so forth. The introductory lines of both chapters, however, specify their intent as instructions for descendants, in good accordance with the preface's definition of their purpose; both chapters carry brief framing devices designating them as royal products, and both, in the received edition, close with variants of the same formula (found also at the closing of the Tsinghua text *Baoxun*).[63]

The preface construes both "Wen jing," chapter 24, and "Wen zhuan," chapter 25, as admonitions preparing King Wu for the eventuality of King Wen's death. Intriguingly, however, the text of the former makes no explicit reference to illness or infirmity, describing itself instead as the result of King Wen's interpretation of a dream.[64] Its reading as part of his end-of-life preparations stems entirely from the preface entry, in addition, perhaps, to assumptions stemming from the reader's general familiarity with many similarly framed texts.[65] The latter chapter, on the other hand, is quite explicit about its relationship to King Wen's last days.[66] Yet the preface's framing thereof makes no note of King Wen's impending death other than that implied by the title of the chapter itself ("Wen zhuan," or The Bequeathal of [King] Wen). The line statement for the following chapter ("Rou wu," chapter 26) serves that function instead.[67]

Conclusion: Toward an Intellectual Biography of King Wen in the *Yi Zhou shu* Preface

In this chapter, I have proposed a reading of the "King Wen cycle" of *Yi Zhou shu* chapters, as defined by the preface, that groups them into the following sequence:

1. "Instructions and models" sequence (chapters 1–5)
2. "Martial endeavors" sequence (chapters 6–10)
3. "Residence at Cheng" sequence (chapters 11–13)
4. "Rule-setting" section (chapters 17–18)
5. "Individual instructions" section (chapters 19–21)
6. "Preparing a legacy" section (chapters 22–25)
7. Chapters 14–16, partly or wholly absent from both preface and main text, are not addressed.

Most of these proposed sections coincide roughly with stages in the traditional chronology of King Wen's political life as presented in the *Shiji*,

"Zhou ben ji," and evoked partially in many other early texts, including the *Yi Zhou shu* preface itself. However, points of potential chronological overlap abound, particularly between the first and second sections, which situate themselves in the early stages of King Wen's exercise of authority; the fourth and fifth, which characterize King Wen's executive efforts in terms of the quantity and effect of their targets; and the fifth and sixth, both of which include texts of the "address to a successor" variety. The understanding of King Wen's life that emerges from the preface's construct, in other words, is informed by chronology but not determined by it. Chapters are gathered instead based on their communicative modes (instruction vs. command, mass vs. individual) and/or understood purposes (informing the conduct of war, securing the succession). The chronology of King Wen's life emerges as an explanatory feature, in that chapters of similar type are assumed to emerge from the same periods of King Wen's life circumstances; hence, for example, those chapters that are understood as instructions on behavioral models are assigned to the period before King Wen's assumption of independent power, while those construed as policy implementations are situated later in the sequence. The model of King Wen's life that emerges from the preface, however, is first and foremost an intellectual biography, with chronology as a second-order sorting criterion.

One effect of adopting biography as an organizational principle is to create a sequence where no obvious one exists. In the case of a figure of cultural memory such as King Wen, the ordering potential of biography is twofold, fusing the general and obvious sequence endemic to human life in general—birth, early life, prime, aging, death—with an overlay of the specific ordering of historical memory associated with the figure's social endeavors. Tension between these sequences can produce tragedy, as with dead Achilles's words to Odysseus in the underworld or adult Oedipus's return to Thebes, or triumph, as in the many tales of heroes giving their lives in pursuit of a signature accomplishment. King Wen's tale, however, is that of a founding hero, favored by the powers that be, who, like Moses, built a legacy for his people and brought them to the brink of independence from tyranny, only to die before he could see their project fully accomplished. The drama of the King Wen story thus comes not from a contrast between the general and individual narratives of King Wen's life, but from the arrested momentum of the two sequences working in parallel: The Zhou, as led by King Wen, must and will conquer the Shang, but King Wen himself, the architect of Zhou supremacy, will never see that happen. This contrast called for explanation, and the effort to do so produced some of early China's most incisive commentaries on violence, death, and the creation of a cultural legacy.

The openness of the historical traditions surrounding King Wen, however, meant that the range of visions of his core competencies, and thus of the legacy that would power the success of the Zhou, was quite broad. The Confucian-inflected biography proposed by the *Shiji* leaned hard into a vision of King Wen's moral exemplarity as an explanatory feature of the Shang conquest, a vision that had become influential enough to call into question the veracity of at least one *Yi Zhou shu* chapter, "Shi fu," that failed to live up to Mencius's moral expectations. Other sources, however, attributed King Wen's success to his supernatural perspicacity, or, as the *Yi Zhou shu* chapters on which McNeal has focused show, to his military prowess, broadly construed. The complex structure of the *Yi Zhou shu* preface offers one model for accommodating the ambiguities and contradictions endemic in these early sources. Like the Buddhist doctrine of expedient means, the preface's structural model embeds the different chapters in the social circumstances and political needs of different stages of King Wen's life story, construing all of them as legitimate responses to given circumstances while still, through the end-orientation of the King Wen tale, admitting the possibility of a hierarchy among them.

This study has endeavored to show one logic of reading that emerges from the *Yi Zhou shu* preface: to build an intellectual biography for King Wen that helps the reader contextualize the diversity of material available concerning him, and thus to permit the reader, against the backdrop of narrower and more idealized visions of King Wen, to regard most or all of that material as (differently) legitimate. Many aspects of the preface's compositional logic and its relationship to the collection, however, invite deeper inquiry. Some of these materials must have been associated with King Wen long before either the compilation of the *Yi Zhou shu* or the composition of the preface (though the references to King Wen in some chapters are peripheral enough to have been introduced as part of a late editorial process). Many, however, carry no obvious internal ties to King Wen; their connection to him comes entirely from their treatment in the preface and position in the collection. What was to be gained by framing these materials, which could stand and may well earlier have stood on their own, as part of King Wen's intellectual production? Did the preface compilers structure the preface so as to deploy the implied valuation inherent in the biographical sequence of King Wen, proposing a hierarchical relationship in which the later chapters best captured the "real" essence of King Wen's intellectual legacy? These and other questions will require a more thoroughly integrated reading of the preface entries accompanying the King Wen chapters, the formal logic of those chapters, and the political-philosophical ideas they contain. McNeal's work on chapters 6–10 has shown that such work can offer convincing explanations. The observations offered here will, I hope, support further such efforts for the rest of the King Wen cycle.

Notes

1. The Tsinghua manuscript *Baoxun* 保訓 captures this succinctly; see Li Xueqin 李學勤, ed., *Qinghua daxue cang Zhanguo zhujian* (1) 清華大學藏戰國竹簡 (一) (Shanghai: Zhongxi, 2010), 8–9, 55–62, 142–148; Rens Krijgsman, "Cultural Memory and Excavated Anecdotes in 'Documentary' Narrative: Mediating Generic Tensions in the *Baoxun* Manuscript," in *Between History and Philosophy: Anecdotes in Early China*, ed. Paul van Els and Sarah Queen (Albany: State University of New York Press, 2017), 301–330.

2. These include multiple texts published in the first volume of the Tsinghua manuscripts, including *Baoxun* (cited earlier), *Cheng wu* 程寤, *Zhou Wu Wang you ji Zhougong suo zi yi dai wang zhi zhi* 周武王有疾周公所自以代王之志, *Huangmen* 皇門, and *Zhaigong zhi guming* 祭公之顧命 (encompassing most of the volume); *Xinian* 繫年, published as Li Xueqin, ed., *Qinghua daxue cang Zhanguo zhujian* (2) 清華大學藏戰國竹簡 (二) (Shanghai: Zhongxi, 2011); as well as *Wu Wang jianzuo* 武王踐阼, found in Ma Chengyuan, ed., *Shanghai bowuguan cang Zhanguo Chu zhushu (qi)* 上海博物館藏戰國楚竹書 (七) (Shanghai: Shanghai guji, 2008), 13–30, 147–168 (recently treated, along with its counterpart from *Da Dai liji* 大戴禮記, in Zhou Boqun, "A Translation and Analysis of the Shanghai Museum Manuscript *Wu Wang Jian Zuo," *Monumenta Serica* 66 (2018) 2: 1–31.

3. On the paratext as a frame of inquiry, see Gérard Genette, *Paratexts: Thresholds of Interpretation*, trans. Jane E. Lewin (Cambridge: Cambridge University Press, 1997), 1–15, and on prefaces (and postfaces) as a form thereof, 161–293.

4. Genette, *Paratexts*, 407–408 (the quote is from page 408).

5. Genette, *Paratexts*, 9.

6. Genette, *Paratexts*, 268–270 (though Genette does suggest that the prefaces to ancient works may push the boundary between paratext and "metatext").

7. The dates given here follow Edward L. Shaughnessy, *Sources of Western Zhou History: Inscribed Bronze Vessels* (Berkeley: University of California Press, 1991), xix.

8. Huang Huaixin 黃懷信, Zhang Maorong 張懋鎔, and Tian Xudong 田旭東, *Yi Zhou shu huijiao jizhu (xiuding ben)* 逸周書彙校集注(修訂本), 2 vols. (Shanghai: Shanghai guji, 2007) *Yi Zhou shu*, 279, hereafter *Yi Zhou shu huijiao jizhu*. All excerpts from the *Yi Zhou shu* follow this work unless otherwise noted,

though I have made extensive use of the Chinese Text Project database (ctext.org) in preparing this chapter. A critical summary of the various *Yi Zhou shu* editions now available appears in Robin McNeal, *Conquer and Govern: Early Chinese Military Texts from the Yi Zhou shu* (Honolulu: University of Hawai'i Press, 2012), 189–190 n. 3.

9. See Genette, *Paratexts*, vii–x, 1–15, 210–212, 263–265. Famously, the "Yiwenzhi" 藝文志 section of the *Han shu* 漢書 mentions a work with seventy-one chapters under the name "Zhou Documents" (*Zhou shu* 周書), concerning which Yan Shigu 顏師古 notes that Liu Xiang 劉向 characterized it as materials related to the Zhou; while Xu Shen's 許慎 *Shuowen jiezi* 說文解字 cites an "I Chou shu" 逸周書 in several locations, including one quotation that appears in the current "Wang hui" 王會 chapter. On these points see Edward L. Shaughnessy, "I chou shu 逸周書," in *Early Chinese Texts: A Bibliographical Guide*, ed. Michael Loewe (Berkeley: Society for the Study of Early China, 1993), 231; Luo Jiaxiang 羅家湘, *Yi Zhou shu yanjiu* "逸周書" 研究 (Shanghai: Shanghai guji, 2006), 9, 85; Tang Yuanfa 唐元發, *Yi Zhou shu cihui yanjiu* "逸周書" 詞彙研究 (Hangzhou: Zhejiang daxue, 2015), 3; see also Ban Gu 班固, *Han shu* 漢書 (Beijing: Zhonghua, 1962), 1705–1706; Xu Shen 許慎 (Zang Kehe 臧克和 and Wang Ping 王平), eds., *Shuowen jiezi xinding* 說文解字新訂 (Beijing: Zhonghua, 2002), 9, 227, 373, 529, 665, 692, 847.

10. Treatments include Huang Peirong 黃沛榮, "Zhou shu yanjiu" "周書研究, PhD dissertation, National Taiwan University, 1976, 17–82; Shaughnessy, "I Chou shu," 229–233; Zhou Yuxiu 周玉秀, *"Yi Zhou shu" de yuyan tedian jiqi wenxianxue jiazhi* "逸周書" 的語言特點及其文獻學價值 (Beijing: Zhonghua, 2005), 8–84; Luo Jiaxiang, *Yi Zhou shu yanjiu*, 59–86; Shaughnessy, *Rewriting Early Chinese Texts* (Albany: State University of New York Press, 2006), 177–181, 183; McNeal, *Conquer and Govern*, 73–96; Tang Yuanfa, *Yi Zhou shu cihui yanjiu*, 1–10.

11. See, for example, Shaughnessy, "I Chou shu," 230–231; Huang Peirong, "Zhou shu yanjiu," 20; McNeal, "The Body as Metaphor for the Civil and Martial Components of Empire in *Yi Zhou shu*, Chapter 32: With an Excursion on the Composition and Structure of the *Yi Zhou shu*," *Journal of the American Oriental Society* 122, no. 1 (January–March 2002): 47–49. Some (e.g., Niu, 728) have suggested that the Han scholar Liu Xiang himself was responsible for editing the work; see Luo Jiaxiang, *Yi Zhou shu yanjiu*, 85–86; Niu Hong'en 牛鴻恩, *Yi Zhou shu xinyi* 逸周書信譯, 2 vols. (Taibei: Sanmin, 2015), 728. Luo Jiaxiang cites a "Zhou zhi" from early Spring and Autumn as the earliest core of the work (*Yi Zhou shu yanjiu*, 85–86), while Huang Peirong has suggested that a group of early chapters from the Warring States period formed an initial "main body" (*zhuti* 主體) for it; see Huang Peirong, "Zhou shu yanjiu," 82–94. McNeal, "The Body as Metaphor," 48, questions the latter assertion.

12. Luo Jiaxiang, *Yi Zhou shu yanjiu*, 9–10, 85–86; Shaughnessy, "I Chou shu," 231.

13. Luo Jiaxiang, *Yi Zhou shu yanjiu*, 10, 57–58, 85–86. Luo notes the puzzle of the "Qi fu" chapter, which strongly resembles the *qiance* ("tomb inventory") genre of writings and therefore offers some oblique evidence that remnants of a

manuscript edition might have survived in the received text. However, Shaughnessy notes that the surviving quotations from the Jizhong Zhoushu are unrelated to the received *Yi Zhou shu*. If the current edition does contain material from Jizhong, then it would seem to be limited in scope. See *Rewriting Early Chinese Texts*, 177–181.

14. See, for instance, *Yi Zhou shu huijiao jizhu*, 183–192, 447–448, 615–617.

15. As He and Nylan have noted, the term "preface" is something of a misnomer, since the document in question, like others of its ilk (referred to as *xu* 序), traditionally appears, when whole, as the last chapter in the series; see Ruyue He and Michael Nylan, "On a Han-Era Postface (*Xu* 序) to the Documents," *Harvard Journal of Asiatic Studies* 75, no. 2 (December 2015): 389–390. In fact, as of the late imperial period, not all received editions of the *Yi Zhou shu* included the preface as a separate chapter, and some of those that did not broke its line statements up and placed them with the relevant chapters, as was sometimes done with the *Shangshu*. See Huang Huaixin et al., *Yi Zhou shu huijiao jizhu*, 1117; on this practice see also Huang Peirong, "Zhou shu yanjiu," 20. I maintain the term "preface" throughout this work (as does McNeal, "The Body as Metaphor," 46 n. 1). Regardless of the position of the text within the collection, it serves a prefatory paratextual function (see Genette, *Paratexts: Thresholds of Interpretation*, 161, which treats postfaces under the same rubric as prefaces on these grounds).

16. A listing for a "Zhou shu" in the "Yiwen zhi" section of the *Han shu* specifies just the number of sections that the *Yi Zhou shu* preface indicates (seventy-one, i.e., seventy plus the preface itself), and later commentary quotes the Han bibliographer Liu Xiang, suggesting that he may have been aware of the work in something resembling the form in which the *Han shu* refers to it. See Shaughnessy, "I chou shu," 230–231.

17. See Huang Peirong, "Zhou shu yanjiu," 17–19; Chen Fengheng 陳逢衡, *Yi Zhou shu buzhu* 逸周書補注, Jiangdu Chen shi xiu mei shan guan, *Daoguang* 5 (1825), 22.19 (cited in Niu Hong'en, *Xin yi Yi Zhou shu*, 2 vols. [Taibei: Sanmin, 2015], 729); Shaughnessy, "I Chou shu," 230; He and Nylan, "On a Han-Era Postface," 423–424 (which includes a discussion of the possibility that the "Minor Preface" of the *Shangshu* was modeled after the *Yi Zhou shu* preface).

18. Niu Hong'en, *Xin yi Yi Zhou shu*, 738–739. Niu traces this viewpoint to Chen Mengjia 陳夢家, *Shangshu tonglun* 尚書通論 (Beijing: Zhonghua, 2005), though I am unsure whether Chen intended to suggest that Liu Xiang composed the preface (see Chen, 286–298).

19. Huang Peirong, "Zhou shu yanjiu," 17–19.

20. Throughout the sequence, the text of the original work follows Huang Huaixin et al., *Yi Zhou shu huijiao jizhu*, 1117–1125, unless otherwise noted. Citations of commentaries gathered in that work follow it as well, except where otherwise noted.

21. In the following sections, the translation has benefited greatly from the commentary of the Early China Reading Group at Indiana University. I have incorporated many of the members' suggestions; any errors remain my own.

22. Throughout this chapter, I translate the phrase *zuo* 作, where X is the title of an *Yi Zhou shu* chapter, in the passive. It is often, but not always, possible to read the subject of the preface lines forward into this clause (e.g., "he [King Wen] composed 'Du xun'"). In the interest of consistency, I have refrained from doing so.

23. Huang Huaixin, *Yi Zhou shu huijiao jizhu*, 1118–1119, notes that various editions carry a *mao* 冒 here in place of *xi* 習.

24. My reading of this clause is informed by Sun Yirang's analogy with the phrase *min san wu ji* 民散無紀, found in the preface entry for "Wen zhuo" 文酌; see Sun Yirang 孫詒讓, *Zhou shu jiaobu* 周書斠補, Sun Yirang, *Qing Guangxu gengzi* (1900), 4.20–21; *Yi Zhou shu huijiao jizhu*, 1118–1119.

25. Here I follow the viewpoint of, for example, Pan Zhen 潘振, that the *zhuo* of the chapter's title may be understood as *zhenzhuo* 斟酌, "to deliberate." As Chen Fengheng 陳逢衡 and Tang Dapei 唐大沛 both note, the extant chapter itself fits poorly with its description in the preface entry. See Chen Fengheng, *Yi Zhou shu buzhu*, 22.19b; Tang Dapei, *Yi Zhou shu fenbian jushi* 逸周書分編句釋 (Taibei: Taiwan xuesheng, 1969), cited in Huang Huaixin, *Yi Zhou shu huijiao jizhu*, 57.

26. *Shiji*, "Zhou ben ji," 116–119.

27. See Huang Huaixin et al., *Yi Zhou shu huijiao jizhu*, 72–84.

28. Notably, Huang Peirong does not include the "Di kuang" chapter in his proposed set of thirty-two "main body" (*zhuti* 主體) chapters that were likely composed or edited as a unit. See Huang, "Zhou shu yanjiu," 83–94.

29. By analogy with the use of *wei* and *huai* together in *Zuo zhuan*, Duke Xiang 4.2, *Shisanjing zhushu* (1933); as well as *Hou Han shu*, "Zheng Fan Chen Jia Zhang liezhuan," 1235.

30. The rendering "balance" follows Chen Fengheng's suggestion that *cheng* 稱 here can be understood as in *Sunzi*, "Jun xing," 4. See *Yi Zhou shu buzhu*, 3.1a; Huang Huaixin, *Yi Zhou shu huijiao jizhu*, 85; Wei Rulin, *Sunzi jin zhu jin yi* 孫子今註今譯 (Taibei: Taiwan shangwu, Minguo 73 [1984]), 109, 115–117; see also McNeal, *Conquer and Govern*, 99–101, which uses "scale."

31. Following Pan Zhen in understanding *de* as referring to people of virtue; see Huang Huaixin, *Yi Zhou shu huijiao jizhu*, 1120.

32. This rendering of the title of chapter 7 follows McNeal, *Conquer and Govern*, 106.

33. As pointed out in Huang Huaixin et al., *Yi Zhou shu huijiao jizhu*, 1121, scholars such as Lu Wenchao 盧文弨 and Zhu Youzeng 朱右曾 have questioned the format of this entry's attribution. See Zhu Youzeng, *Yi Zhou shu jixun jiaoshi*, 251; Lu Wenchao, *Yi Zhou shu*, 10.4a. I follow Huang Huaixin et al. in holding to the text as here rendered.

34. McNeal, *Conquer and Govern*, 134–135.

35. On this model see, for example, David Pankenier, "The Cosmo-Political Background of Heaven's Mandate," *Early China* 20 (1995): 130.

36. Besides the *Yi Zhou shu* itself, the earliest source mentioning this relationship with the Kunyi is *Mengzi* 孟子, "Liang Hui Wang xia" 梁惠王下, 10. See Ruan Yuan 阮元, ed., *Shisanjing zhushu* 十三經注疏 (Beijing: Zhonghua, 1980), 2674; see also *Zhushu jinian* and *Hou Han shu*, cited later. The population called the Xianyun is somewhat better attested; for a comprehensive overview, see Li Feng, *Landscape and Power in Early China: The Crisis and Fall of the Western Zhou, 1045–771 BC* (Cambridge: Cambridge University Press, 2006), 142–145.

37. Lin Chunpu 林春溥, *Zhushu jinian buzheng* 竹書紀年補證, 2.12, in Yang Jialuo 揚家駱, ed., *Zhushu jinian bazhong* 竹書紀年八種 (Taibei: Shijie, 1967).

38. Fan Ye 範曄, *Hou Han shu* 後漢書 (Beijing: Zhonghua, 1975 [1963]), 2870–2871.

39. As Li Feng, *Landscape and Power*, chapter 3, 141–192, shows, the Xianyun troubled the Zhou kings throughout the late Western Zhou period.

40. Here I adopt the inclusion of the additional character *zai* 災, which Huang Huaixin, *Yi Zhou shu huijiao jizhu*, 1121, notes as appearing in several editions but does not adopt in its own main text.

41. The application of the term "author" to any early Chinese text is of course problematic; for a recent and detailed treatment of the topic, see Hanmo Zhang, *Authorship and Text-Making in Early China* (Berlin: De Gruyter, 2018). Here I mean whatever confluence of creative interests, be they authors, editors, or copyists, were responsible for fixing the chapter in the form in which it appears in the received *Yi Zhou shu* collection. On the assignation of "Da kuang" to King Wen versus King Mu, see Huang Peirong, "Zhou shu yanjiu," 18–19; McNeal, "The Body as Metaphor," 50; Huang Huaixin et al., *Yi Zhou shu huijiao jizhu*, 1121.

42. Huang Huaixin et al., *Yi Zhou shu jiaobu jizhu*, 144.

43. In fact, the bronze record offers a small piece of evidence that this statement might refer to King Wen. The inscription of the Xiao Yu *ding* 小盂鼎, generally dated to the early Western Zhou, mentions the conduct of sacrifice to "the Zhou King, King Wu, and King Cheng" (周王, 武王, 成王). The natural assumption is to take the first figure in this sequence as King Wen, suggesting in turn that the phrase "Zhou king" in at least one early case referred to King Wen in particular. For the Xiao Yu *ding* inscription, see Zhongguo shehui kexueyuan kaogu yanjiusuo 中國社會科學院考古研究所, ed., *Yin Zhou jinwen jicheng* 殷周金文集成, 18 vols. (Beijing: Zhonghua, 1984–94), entry 2839.

44. See also Huang Peirong, "Zhou shu yanjiu," 18–19, which notes that King Wen and Wang Ji are both associated with Cheng, but not King Mu.

45. The chronology of King Wen's residence at Cheng in the *Bamboo Annals*, it should be noted, does not line up with the "three years" suggested here. However, the *Annals* do specify that the Shang king Di Xin—that is, Zhou of Shang—awarded King Wen the right of "independent campaigning" (*zhuan zheng fa* 專征伐) during his thirty-third year, and that King Wen relocated to Feng during

Di Xin's thirty-fifth year. If one imagines that King Wen's residence at Cheng was officially recognized only as part of the procedures conducted in year thirty-three, then the relocation during year thirty-five could indeed be interpreted as a three-year gap (inclusive). See Lin Chunpu 林春溥, *Zhushu jinian buzheng* 竹書紀年補證, 2.14–15. By highlighting such connections between the *Bamboo Annals* and the *Yi Zhou shu* preface, I do not mean to argue unequivocally for the authenticity of the received text of the former—only to note that it preserves some otherwise rare ideas about the biography of King Wen that were extant by the time the *Yi Zhou shu* preface took its present form.

46. On the role of the Jizhong find, from which the *Bamboo Annals* derived, in the textual history of the *Yi Zhou shu*, see Huang Peirong, "Zhou shu yanjiu," 45–82; Zhou Yuxiu, *"Yi Zhou shu" de yuyan tedian*, 52–64; Tang Yuanfa, *Yi Zhou shu cihui yanjiu*, 3–4; Shaughnessy, *Rewriting Early Chinese Texts*, 177–181, 183.

47. See Li Xueqin, ed., *Qinghua daxue cang Zhanguo zhujian* (1), 6–7, 47–54, 135–141.

48. Sima Qian 司馬遷, *Shiji*, 10 vols. (Beijing: Zhonghua, 1959), 116–118. This omission is of special note since Sima Qian himself apparently claimed descent from Chengbo Xiufu 程伯休父 ("Xiufu, Elder of Cheng"); see *Shiji*, 3285.

49. Sun Yirang's suggestion that an orthographic error may have converted "Zai cheng" into "Mu" represents one take on the former standpoint; see Sun, *Zhou shu jiaobu*, 1.9a, cited in McNeal, "The Body as Metaphor," 50 n. 12, as well as Huang Huaixin et al., *Yi Zhou shu huijiao jizhu*, 1121. Huang Peirong, on the other hand, sees this as part of a spectrum of disparities suggesting that the compilers of the preface and the collection itself were different people; see Huang, "Zhou shu yanjiu," 17–19.

50. See Kong Yingda 孔穎達 (Mao Heng 毛亨, Zheng Xuan 鄭玄), *Maoshi zhengyi* 毛詩正義, 6 vols. (Xianggang: Zhonghua, 1964), "Huang yi," 1381; Lu Wenchao, *Yi Zhou shu* 逸周書, *Sibu beiyao*, vols. 1109–1110 (Shanghai: Zhonghua, 1927), 10.4a; Huang Huaixin, *Yi Zhou shu huijiao jizhu*, 1121–1122.

51. These differences are reflected in the fact that Huang Peirong excluded "Da kuang," chapter 11, from his proposed list of thirty-two "core" chapters of the *Yi Zhou shu*; see Huang, "Zhou shu yanjiu," 83–94. If one accepts the idea that the "Cheng wu" text from the Tsinghua University bamboo slips is in fact a version of the lost chapter called by that name in the *Yi Zhou shu* preface (on which, see e.g., Li Xueqin, ed., *Qinghua daxue cang Zhanguo zhujian* [1], 135), then all three "Cheng texts" differed from each other in these respects.

52. Following the suggestions of Zhu Youzeng and Pan Zhen that 唯 be read as 惟; see Zhu Youzeng 朱右曾, *Yi Zhou shu jixun jiaoshi* 逸周書集訓校釋, ed. Yan Kejun 嚴可均 (Taibei: Shijie shuju, Minguo 56 [1967]), 251; Pan Zhen, *Zhoushu jieyi*, cited in Huang Huaixin, *Yi Zhou shu huijiao jizhu*, 1122 (as is Zhu).

53. I understand the title of this chapter, as contextualized by the preface, to refer to the use of capital punishment.

54. Here I follow Lu Wenchao, *Yi Zhou shu*, 10.4a (cited in Huang Huaixin, *Yi Zhou shu huijiao jizhu*, 1121, which also provides the textual history for this reading) in reading *kai* 開 in this position rather than the *jian* 間 that Huang maintains.

55. See Huang Huaixin, *Yi Zhou shu huijiao jizhu*, 183.

56. See Huang Huaixin, *Yi Zhou shu huijiao jizhu*, 1121–1122.

57. See the "Cheng dian" chapter in Huang Huaixin et al., *Yi Zhou shu huijiao jizhu*, 165–182. *Shiji*, "Zhou benji," goes to some lengths to explain, through the story of the reconciliation of the states of Yu and Rui, that King Wen's superior morality led to his recognition as the rightful lord of the realm; see *Shiji*, 117.

58. In this location I adopt the *ba*, "eight," that is, according to Huang Huaixin, *Yi Zhou shu huijiao jizhu*, 1123, common to various editions (rather than the *wen* 文 that Huang gives); see also Lu Wenchao, *Yi Zhou shu*, 10.4a, cited therein.

59. Huang Huaixin et al., *Yi Zhou shu huijiao jizhu*, 1123, gathers the various commentaries dealing with this issue.

60. See *Yi Zhou shu*, "Wen jing" and "Wen zhuan," *Yi Zhou shu huijiao jizhu*, 231–250, as well as *Qinghua 1*, "Bao xun" and "Cheng wu" (cited earlier). On "forewarning" (*jing* 儆, as in "Wen jing") as a textual framing in *Yi Zhou shu*, see Yegor Grebnev, "The *Yi Zhou shu* and the *Shangshu*: The Case of Texts with Speeches," in *Origins of Chinese Political Philosophy: Studies in the Composition and Thought of the "Shangshu" (Classic of Documents)*, ed. Martin Kern and Dirk Meyer (Leiden: Brill, 2017), 270.

61. On this event, see, for example, *Shiji*, "Zhou ben ji," 118.

62. Huang Peirong, "Zhou shu yanjiu," 17.

63. Huang Huaixin et al., *Yi Zhou shu huijiao jizhu*, 212–230; Li Xueqin, ed., *Qinghua 1*, 142–418.

64. Huang Huaixin et al., *Yi Zhou shu huijiao jizhu*, 231.

65. These include *Baoxun*, cited previously; *Shangshu*, "Gu ming" (*Shisanjing zhushu*, 237–241); *Yi Zhou shu*, "Zhai gong" (Huang Huaixin et al., *Yi Zhou shu huijiao jizhu*, 923–941), as well as the related manuscript in *Qinghua 1*, 22–25, 99–116, 173–179; and *Zheng Wengong wen Taibo* 鄭文公問太伯, in Li Xueqin, ed., *Qinghua daxue cang Zhanguo zhujian (liu)*, 2 vols. (Shanghai: Zhongxi, 2016), 10–13, 57–69, 118–126.

66. Huang Huaixin et al., *Yi Zhou shu huijiao jizhu*, 236–238. My understanding of the relevant portions of the chapter follows the emendations made by Lu Wenchao based on the quotation of a related passage in the *Taiping yulan*, as explained in *Yi Zhou shu huijiao jizhu*, 237. See also Lu Wenchao, *Yi Zhou shu*, 3.4b; Li Fang 李昉, *Taiping yulan* 太平禦藍, 4 vols. (Beijing: Zhonghua, 1995), 395.

67. Huang Huaixin, *Yi Zhou shu huijiao jizhu*, 1125.

11

Forging a "Meta-tradition"
The Distinctive Philosophy of the *Huainanzi*

Harold D. Roth

Introduction

The *Huainanzi* can be a daunting text to approach. It is the longest of all the pre-Han and early Han philosophical works and presents a rich and complex blending of the best ideas from the earlier lineages of thought and practice that, by then, were beginning to be given specific designations such as *rujia* 儒家 (Confucianism), *fajia* 法家 (Legalism), and so forth. This has led to considerable confusion about how to classify the *Huainanzi*: the Han historian Ban Gu 班固 (32–92 CE) called it *zajia* 雜家 (Eclecticism), while some recent scholars—myself included—have argued that it is an important work of "Daoist syncretism."[1] In the effort to make this important work more accessible to a wider audience interested in early Chinese thought and interested in doing serious scholarship on the *Huainanzi*, I have written this overview of the distinctive way in which this work was conceived, organized, and executed that I hope will provide some essential tools for the study of the philosophy and literary elegance of this important text. There is a depth of human experience—both culturally relative to second century BCE China and transcending its specific moment in time and location in space—that is captured in the rich and profound philosophy in this text. I commend it to thinkers everywhere as a major and still largely unexplored work that I consider to be the pinnacle of classical Daoism and for its attempt to establish what might most accurately be considered a Daoist-based "meta-tradition"—a tradition of thought and practice that transcends traditions.

The Text and Its Authorship

The entire twenty-one chapter work has traditionally been attributed to Liu An 劉安 (?180–122 BCE), the second king of Huainan and the grandson of Liu Bang 劉邦 (256–195 BCE), the founder of the Han dynasty. However, it is now generally recognized that, while he may have contributed to the writing of the work, it was a collaborative effort representing the work of eight scholars named in the Gao You 高誘 (ca. 168–212 CE) Preface, written around 212 CE. These scholars were part of a group of thinkers who assembled at the court of Liu An at Huainan 淮南 (in modern-day Anhui Province). Liu An's father, Liu Chang 劉長, angered that he had been passed over as successor to Liu Bang, was eventually sent into exile in 174 BCE for sedition against his half-brother, the Emperor Wen, and died en route. Liu An was subsequently enfeoffed with a part of his father's territory and, in 164 BCE, it was reestablished as the kingdom of Huainan, about one-third the territory of the same-named kingdom once ruled by his father. Within a decade Liu An had begun to establish an intellectual center at his court modeled after the Jixia intellectual center in Qi (that produced the *Guanzi* 管子 collection) and—to a lesser extent—the Qin court assembly of scholars that produced the *Lüshi chunqiu* 呂氏春秋. In the preface to his recension of the *Huainanzi*, the late Han commentator Gao You states that Liu An summoned scholars from a wide variety of earlier intellectual traditions to his court as well as practitioners of the various "esoteric arts" (*fangshu* 方術) that included astrology, pharmacology, demonology, alchemy, and medicine, many of which embraced the cosmology of the Yin and Yang and the Five Phases of *qi*.[2]

History records a rather extensive list of works created at the Huainan court, including collections of rhyme prose (*fu*), works of astrology and alchemy, and works of philosophy. The only work to have survived intact is the *Huainanzi*, initially referred to as the "inner book" (*neishu* 內書) in a trilogy that included "middle" and "outer" books (*zhong* 中 and *wai* 外). Qing dynasty scholars assembled surviving fragments of the "middle book" into several similar "reconstituted redactions" that show that the original work contained various sayings, stories, and formulae that appear to be part of the alchemical traditions of the esoteric arts. The "outer" book has not survived and little is known of it other than the cryptic comment by a Tang dynasty scholar Yan Shigu 顏師古 that it contained "eclectic theories" (*za shuo* 雜 說).³

Two other events stand out in the historical context of the *Huainanzi*. In 139 BCE, Liu An journeyed to the imperial court in Chang'an to visit his young nephew, the eventually powerful Emperor Wu (Han Wudi 漢武帝), who had succeeded to the throne in 141 BCE and who was still mulling over whether his government should be based on Confucian or Daoist principles. The emperor is said to have loved the work and secreted it away in his private collection for detailed perusal. In the end Wudi did not adapt the innovative Daoist syncretism of the *Huainanzi*; instead he chose to ally his government with the Confucian bureaucrats and their textual traditions.

Liu An, his philosophical positions rejected by his nephew (the emperor), saw the increasing centralization of power in the hands of the imperial government and out of the hands of the local enfeoffed kings of the Liu clan. Liu An realized that his opportunity to have a persuasive influence on the government of the empire was slipping away. According to the extant historical writings, he followed in his father's footsteps of plotting rebellion against the empire by sending a contingent of imperial troops to the Huainan capital of Shouchun in 122 BCE. During the ensuing events, Liu An and his entire family perished and his vibrant intellectual center was destroyed—its thinkers and its ideas scattered throughout the empire. This event can be seen as the final chapter in the development of the foundational or classical Daoist tradition and the beginning of almost three centuries of "underground" existence. It developed there outside the purview of the imperial historians, only to reemerge transformed into the two great millenarian rebellions of the latter half of the second century CE: the "Way of Great Peace" (*taiping dao* 太平道), in the northeastern part of the country; and the "Way of the Celestial Masters" (*tianshi dao* 天師道), in the West, in what is modern Sichuan.⁴

The Gao You Preface details not only the circumstances under which the text was originally written but also those circumstances in which Gao wrote his commentary, whose insights he humbly attributed to his teacher, Lu Zhi 盧植 (?–192 CE). Lu, who studied with the famous Old Text scholar Ma Rong 馬融 (77–166 CE), is known as the general who defeated the Taiping Dao Rebels under Zhang Jue 張角 in a series of battles in Hebei Province in 184 CE. There are two major extant commentaries on the work, one by Xu Shen 許慎 (58–148? CE), author of the *Shuowen jiezi* 說文解字, and the other by Gao You. While the Xu commentary originally circulated as a unique recension of the text, Gao lost eight chapters of his commentary and text before the final version was completed, so he supplemented his losses by copying from the Xu commentary and text. This conflated recension eventually became the sole surviving version of the text and all of the more than ninety editions are of this conflated recension. Some list Gao as the commentator; others list Xu. Because of the greater length of the Gao commentary, some redactions divided the text into twenty-eight chapters instead of the original twenty-one. This was accomplished by subdividing seven chapters into two parts, *shang* 上 and *xia* 下, as we find in the *Daozang jiyao* (DZJY) edition: chapters 1–5, 9, 13. The title of the Gao recension was originally *Huainan honglie jiejing* 淮南鴻烈解經 (The Vast and Luminous Book of Huainan, with Classical Explanations). The epithet *honglie* seems to have originated with the Xu recension and was borrowed by Gao when he conflated his work with Xu's. The phrase "Xu Shen *jishang*" (許慎記上) apparently means that, in the original Xu recension, his commentary was written above the text rather than as an interlinear commentary.[5]

The Structure, Purpose, and Central Topics of the Text

The *Huainanzi* is a collection of twenty-one distinctive essays on a wide range of topics including cosmology, cosmogony, astronomy, history, rulership, and the arts of war that are grounded in an intellectual perspective that is arguably described as "Daoist." Because it draws extensively upon earlier philosophical literature, in particular the *Laozi* and *Zhuangzi* as well as such works as the *Guanzi* and *Lüshi chunqiu* collections, the major historical writings such as the *Chunqiu* and *Zuo zhuan*, Confucian classics such as the *Changes*, and the *Odes*, and narrative collections such as the *Zhanguo ce*, the *Huainanzi* has been a challenge to categorize and has engendered a great deal of scholarly debate about its filiation. Despite the fact that it was initially classified as *zajia* ("eclectic traditions") in the "Bibliographical Monograph" of the *History of the Former Han* (*Han shu* "Yiwenzhi" 漢書藝文志) and despite its presentation of a broad range of ideas, a careful analysis of its philosophical positions demonstrates the priority given to a cosmology and method of self-cultivation that is found in the "Inward Training" (*neiye* 內業) text from *Guanzi*, the *Laozi*, and *Zhuangzi*. This strongly argues for its being not merely part of a classical Daoist tradition, but its most complex and sophisticated philosophical expression.⁶ Some scholars have further stated that the *Huainanzi* is a characteristic work of the "Huang-Lao" tradition, a later Warring States and early Han dynasty syncretic philosophy grounded in Daoist cosmology and self-cultivation but which incorporates the best ideas from earlier intellectual traditions.⁷

The twenty-one chapters of the *Huainanzi*, each of which is a distinct chapter with a principal theme or themes, are intended to provide a summa of all the ideas needed to govern effectively according to the authors. While we can no longer attribute the entire work to the hand of Liu An himself, since he did present the work to the emperor in person we can assume that he had a major hand in the planning and editing of the work. Gao You lists eight men who participated in the project of writing the *Huainanzi* and we have no way to identify who among them wrote which of the chapters. The variations in topics, literary forms, and personal writing style, as well as the specialized knowledge contained in at least some of the essays, do support the assumption that multiple hands were involved in its authorship. It is definitely *not* the work of one person. Moreover, the extensive amount of passages quoted or taken from earlier works further supports the historical record that Liu An had an extensive library, perhaps the rival of that in Chang'an. If we were able to attribute the authorship of any of these chapters to one specific person, it is most likely that it was Liu An who authored the final chapter, "An Overview of the Essentials" ("Yaolüe"). This chapter provides an explanation of the grand plan and the great purpose of the entire book, and is totally comprehensive. The chapter opens with the following claims:⁸

> We have created and composed these writings and discourses as a means to:
> Knot the net of the Way (Dao 道) and its Potency (De 德),
> and weave the web of humankind and its affairs,
> Above investigating them in Heaven,
> below examining them on Earth,
> And in the middle comprehending them through Nature's Patterns (*li* 理).
>
> Although they are not yet able to fully draw out the core of the Profound Mystery, they are abundantly sufficient to observe its ends and beginnings. If we [only] summarized the essentials or provided an overview and our words did not discriminate the

Pure, Uncarved Block and differentiate the Great Ancestor, then it would cause people in their confusion to fail to understand them.

Thus,
numerous are the words we have composed,
and extensive are the illustrations we have provided,
yet we still fear that people will depart from the root and follow the branches.
Thus,
if we speak of the Way but do not speak of affairs, there would be no means to shift with the times.
[Conversely], if we speak of affairs but do not speak of the Way, there would be no means to move with (the processes of) transformation.
Therefore, we composed the following twenty essays . . .⁹

夫作為書論者，所以紀綱道德，經緯人事，上考之天，下揆之地，中通諸理。雖未能抽引玄妙之中(才)〔哉〕，繁然足以觀終始矣。摠要舉凡，而語不剖判純樸，靡散大宗，則為人之惛惛然弗能知也；故多為之辭，博為之說，又恐人之離本就末也。故言道而不言事，則無以與世浮沉；言事而不言道，則無以與化遊息。故著二十篇。

The author then provides an analysis of the preceding chapters in the book from a number of different perspectives: detailed and poetic summaries of the twenty individual preceding chapters; explanations of how the chapters are linked together in an organizational chain, with each chapter specifically following on the one preceding it, much in the style of the *Yijing* 易經 appendix, "Discussion of the Trigrams" (*Shuogua* 說卦), which explains the specific order of the hexagrams in the received text.¹⁰ The chapter then concludes with a review of previous writings on related subjects, explaining how each is a product of its historical time, and then declares that the *Huainanzi* has surpassed them all. This review includes the writings of Confucius, Mozi, Guan Zhong (i.e., the *Guanzi*), and Shang Yang. The emphasis in this chapter is on the necessity of understanding both the profound nature and manifested activity of the Way and its Potency, but also on the great variety and detail of how these two foundational principles underlie both the natural and human worlds. While this chapter comes at the end of the entire work and thus constitutes a summary, it can also be read as an introduction to the work, providing an overview of its grand plan and a detailed précis of each of its twenty other constituent chapters.

In fact, Martin Kern has observed that the entire chapter is in the form of a "rhyme-prose" (*fu* 賦); therefore, it could very well have been recited to Emperor Wu to provide him with a succinct and artfully embellished summary of the entire text when Liu An presented the completed work to him at court in 139 BCE.[11]

While the *Huainanzi* does not traditionally contain any further internal divisions (like, for example, the *Zhuangzi* with its "inner-outer-mixed" structure), it is now generally understood that the first eight chapters constitute the "Basic Principles" of the entire work and that the second half is concerned with "Applications and Illustrations" (chapters 9–20).[12] Andrew Meyer and myself argue further that this division is in keeping with a "roots-branches" structure that provides a series of frameworks throughout the entire book, both in terms of its total organization and within many of its individual essays.[13] So, the first eight essays provide the basic philosophy and the remaining chapters contain a variety of detailed illustrations of how these basic philosophical principles work in the phenomenal world. In the root chapters, we find all the basic cosmology, cosmogony, epistemology, self-cultivation theory, and theories on history and politics that the authors regard as foundational; in the "branch chapters," we find illustrations of these foundations presented in a variety of literary styles: "precepts" (*cheng* 稱), "responses" (*ying* 應), "overviews" (*lüe* 略), "discourses" (*lun* 論), "sayings" (*yan* 言), and "persuasions" (*shui* 說). This is completely consistent with the grand plan of the work presented in chapter 21, which involves attaining a comprehensive balance between the cosmology of the Way and its Potency and the variety of its manifestations in the human world.

Summary of the Contents

The first eight of the twenty-one chapters of the *Huainanzi* are called the "root" chapters; and the first two of these provide the cosmological, cosmogonic, and self-cultivation foundations for the entire book. It is no accident that each of these chapters, "Originating in the Way" and "Activating the Genuine," borrows heavily from the *Laozi* and the *Zhuangzi*, respectively.

Chapter 1: Originating in the Way—"Yuandao" 原道

"Originating in the Way" opens with a poetic rhapsody (*fu* 賦) on the cosmology of the Way (Dao 道) and its Potency (De 德) in the tradition of the *Laozi* 老子. It is also reminiscent of the similarly entitled wisdom poem

"The Source That Is the Way" ("Daoyüan" 道原) that is among the five "silk manuscripts" found at Mawangdui.[14] The essay continues with a detailed examination of how the Way as the foundation of the cosmos is manifested within the phenomenal world and a detailed description of how sages are able to use their unique penetrating vision of these foundations, attained through a process of self-cultivation, to bring peace and harmony to the realm. It is only through the methods of self-cultivation advocated in the classical Daoist tradition that the *Huainanzi*'s ideal ruler may comprehend the inner workings of the cosmos and apply that wisdom to governing in harmony with them. Due to their self-cultivation, sage rulers are able to perceive the greater patterns (*li* 理) inherent in the cosmos and the innate natures (*xing* 性) characteristic of all things that govern their course of maturation and interactions with one another.[15] Thus, the *Huainanzi* states from the very beginning that it is not just a book about the Way nor is it a tract on how to govern; it is, rather, a deliberate combination of these two perspectives. Further, the opening chapter of the collection, "Originating in the Way," sets out general themes—such as cosmology, human psychology and self-cultivation, and political philosophy—that will be pursued in more detail in much of the remainder of the work. It cannot be overemphasized that the entire book is crucial for understanding the Daoist perspective and seeing it in a clearer light.[16]

CHAPTER 2: ACTIVATING THE GENUINE—"CHUZHEN" 俶真

Potency and human perfection are the principal themes of this chapter and, as such, they complement the principal themes in chapter 1 that explore the nature of the Way and how it operates in the world. These themes in chapter 2 include the nature of human perfection, its different categories, the methods to attain it, its role in rulership, especially in an ideal utopian past, and how implementing sage rulership relates to the opportunities or lack of them provided by *ming* 命 or "fate." The chapter begins with a famous passage that interprets the metaphorical infinite regress passage in *Zhuangzi* 2 ("There is a beginning; there is not yet begun having a beginning") in a very literal sense as a detailed cosmogony of the universe.[17] This essay introduces another major theme that infuses the entire book: that of human cultural history as the inevitable decline from an idyllic utopian condition, in which all people can spontaneously manifest their deepest natures and live in harmony, into an age of disorder and chaos in which only the most motivated and gifted of human beings can return to their foundation. The authors of "Activating the Genuine" further criticize the disciples of Confucius and those of Mozi, both of whom taught the techniques of Humaneness and Rightness yet cannot personally practice their own teachings. In contrast, when you attempt to break through to your own basic nature through the practice of apophatic inner cultivation, Humaneness and Rightness will spontaneously arise. This is another of the important and sophisticated examples of "syncretic Daoist" writing in the book.[18]

CHAPTERS 3: CELESTIAL PATTERNS—"Tianwen" 天文, 4: TERRESTRIAL FORMS—"Dixing" 地形, AND 5: SEASONAL RULES—"Shi ce" 時側

The first of these three "cosmological chapters" of the *Huainanzi*, "Celestial Patterns," opens with a cosmogonic passage that uses theories of *qi* and Yin and Yang to explain the origins of Heaven and Earth; this explanation is the basis for the chapter's presentation of the various astronomical structures and their movements throughout the year. Before Heaven and Earth was the Grand Beginning (*taishi* 太始), which generated the Nebulous Void (*xukuo* 虛霩), which generated space and time, which, in turn, generated Primal *Qi* (*yuanqi* 元氣), which then differentiated into Yin and Yang and, from them, eventually, the myriad things.

Thus, all phenomena are constituted by various forms of *qi*. Because of these origins, the principal argument of this chapter is that everything in the cosmos is interconnected, that human plans and intentions are subject to the influence of various cosmic cycles and correlations, and that such cycles and correlations must be understood and taken into account in the formulation of governmental policy.

Chapter 3, "Celestial Patterns," is followed by the two other most technical chapters: chapter 4, "Terrestrial Forms," which presents the geography of the known and imagined worlds and the creatures contained within it, much in the manner of the *Classics of Mountains and Oceans* (*Shanhaijing* 山海經), and chapter 5, "Seasonal Rules," which contains prescriptions and proscriptions for proper ritual clothing, behavior, and governmental actions in each of the five seasons ("Midsummer," the third month of the summer, is designated as its own season). Chapters 3, 4, and 5 form a distinctive subunit within the *Huainanzi*, a trilogy describing the cosmos, the earth, living creatures and other concrete phenomena (the "myriad things"), and the correlative influences of seasonal and monthly time. Deeply grounded in the "correlative" cosmology of Yin and Yang and the potency of each of the Five Phases (wood, fire, earth, metal, and water), these essays are all grounded in the cosmogony established at the beginning of chapter 3.[19]

CHAPTER 6: SURVEYING OBSCURITIES—"Lanming" 覽冥

Sharing the same correlative cosmology as the previous three chapters, "Surveying Obscurities" envisions a universe in which everything is intimately interconnected through being embedded in what might be called a "matrix of *qi*." This *qi* has an infinite variety of densities and textures and constitutes the basic substance of all things. It can be divided into two basic dimensions, Yin and Yang, and five major categories: earth, fire, metal, wood, and water. All worldly and otherworldly phenomena, all events that occur in spacetime, the many different aspects of all creatures—including the Five Orbs of vital energy and psychological states in human beings—are constituted of various combinations of these dimensions and categories of *qi*. Because of this, they interact and resonate (*ganying* 感應) with one another in ways determined by their particular types of *qi*. Perfected human beings who are grounded in the Way have developed a particularly rarefied type of *qi*, called *jing* 精 ("vital essence") and through this can influence events, persons, and phenomena across categories. In addition, individuals can also exert striking temporary influences upon the cosmic fabric in moments of extraordinary emotional intensity and energetic focus.[20] This chapter, "Surveying Obscurities," is filled with narratives that provide illustrative examples of how such people have influenced their environments. While implicit in chapters 3–5, what becomes explicit in chapter 6 is that the correlative cosmology of these chapters is in no way in conflict with the cosmology of the Way and its Potency, but, in reality, complements it.[21]

CHAPTER 7: THE QUINTESSENTIAL SPIRIT—"Jingshen" 精神

Huainanzi begins with a third cosmogonic passage that complements those in chapters 1 and 3. It presents the creation of the physical and the spiritual properties of the universe as the basis for an exploration of the origins and development of the various aspects of human beings, from body through mind and spirit. These properties are presented both in terms of various types and densities of *qi*, but also in terms of the intricate relationship between body and mind. The chapter also introduces the concept of the "Quintessential Spirit" (*jingshen*) as the force that animates the physical body and consciousness itself. This force is presented as a kind of specially refined form of *qi*, one that, like *qi* and *jing* (精 "vital essence"), shares properties of fluid motion and so could be considered an idea parallel to that of psychic energy in Western contexts.[22] This chapter also discusses the paragons of human perfection, that is, "Genuine Persons" (*zhenren* 真人), "Sages" (*shengren* 聖人), and "Perfected Persons" (*zhiren* 至人), who are characterized by, among other qualities, their ability to ignore external stimuli, to draw Potency from their source in the Way, and by their indifference to the exigencies of life and death. The qualities of human perfection are not cultivated through self-mortification but through an apophatic inner cultivation practice in which the adept empties the mind and body of passions, prejudices, and thoughts until realizing the unification of innate nature and the Way. These practices are referred to herein as the "Techniques of the Mind" (*xinshu* 心術) and they produce in the adept indifference to ordinary desires and the ability to respond spontaneously and harmoniously to whatever situation arises.[23] This is one of the most important qualities of perfected human beings throughout the classical Daoist tradition. In the political arena, such adepts are able to serve unerringly as ruler when the time is right, but they are not covetous of power, nor greedy for wealth or in the least bit concerned with self-aggrandizement. This is another of the most important Daoist chapters of the book and shares a basic conceptual vocabulary with *Guanzi*'s 管子 four "Techniques of the Mind" (*xinshu*) texts,[24] and with chapter 15 of the *Zhuangzi*, "Inveterate Ideas" ("Keyi" 刻意).[25]

Chapter 8: The Basic Warp—"Benjing" 本經

The government of sage rulers, taken from an historical perspective, is the main topic of the last of the root chapters. Chapter 8 begins with what might be called a kind of "cosmogony of government," which shows how it began in the ideal rulership of an imagined past and how it gradually degenerated until we reach the dissolute present age. It is the first of several similar degeneration narratives in the essay, all of which hearken back to an archaic time of agrarian primitivism when perfected human beings, embodying the Way and its Potency, could govern almost invisibly by means of Non-Action (*wuwei* 無為 or "effortless action"); both the human and the natural worlds responded resonantly to the superior qualities of an ideal ruler. But inevitably the world began to devolve from this archaic ideal. As the situation degenerated from primordial simplicity and unity, people became filled with desires, competition increased, disharmony arose, and, gradually, the institutions of social control took over. In such an era, when the human polity teeters on the brink of chaos, only the ruler—who knows how to embody the undifferentiated unity of the Grand One; how to align himself with the Way and its Potency; how to match his actions to the patterns and natures of the cosmos; and how to become imbued with spirit-illumination (*shenming* 神明) through the processes of inner cultivation—has the ability to govern the world and save it from chaos.

The narratives here seem to be an expansion of the arguments found in what A. C. Graham has called "The Primitivist" sections of the *Zhuangzi*, chapter 8 through the first part of chapter 11.[26]

CHAPTER 9: THE RULER'S TECHNIQUES—"Zhushu" 主術

Huainanzi 9 lays out in considerable detail the philosophy of government by the enlightened Daoist ruler and is the single longest chapter in the entire book, an indication of its significance; if there is any one chapter in the book that was intended by Liu An for his nephew, Emperor Wu, it is this one.

The advice begins with self-cultivation. The ruler must cultivate himself through the apophatic inner cultivation techniques well known in the Daoist tradition: reduction of thoughts, desires, emotions, and the gradual development of emptiness and tranquility. The ruler who accomplishes this is able to develop his Potency and perfect his Vital Essence (*zhi jing* 至精), and, as a result, he is able to penetrate and directly apprehend the essences of Heaven and Grand Unity (*Taiyi* 太一), in other words, the "Techniques of the Way" that were identified in chapter 7. This connects the ruler directly to the invisible cosmic web of the correlative cosmology of *qi* and its various types—Yin and Yang, Five Phases (*wuxing*), and Refinements (*jing*). With this connection through the types of resonance (*ganying*) detailed in chapter 6, the Daoist ruler can invisibly influence the course of events in the world and affairs among his subjects. This profound level of inner cultivation also enables the ruler to reduce desires to a minimum, to designate responsibilities within the government hierarchy in a totally impartial fashion, devoid of emotions, and, without hesitation, to spontaneously adapt to whatever situations arise. The essay is filled with various ideas on governing taken from earlier Confucian and Mohist traditions and other works, which has led some to conclude that it privileges no single intellectual position. While it is certainly the case that many earlier ideas are synthesized in the philosophy of rulership in this essay, it is clear that they are all trumped by a cosmology of the Way and a practice of inner cultivation taken directly from the Daoist tradition. Apophatic inner cultivation is now—and has always been—the root of good rule. The layered values and techniques drawn from other classical traditions (humaneness, rightness, ritual, music, standards, measures, rewards, punishments, etc.) are all the product of the spontaneous devolution from high antiquity, as described earlier in the text. Each technique became indispensable to human order in the age in which it spontaneously arose, just as cosmic phenomena, such as Heaven and Earth, became intrinsic to cosmic order at the point in the cosmogonic process in which they emerged. But, in order to function as a harmonious and organic whole, they must be prioritized correctly, in the order of their historical development and thus in the order of their normative distance from the undifferentiated "root" of good order (the Way). The argument of chapter 9 is that a ruler, in his own reign period, cannot rule without using the techniques of thinkers like Confucius, Mozi, Han Fei, among others, because human society has spontaneously evolved into a complex form that necessitates their employment. The basic perspective of the text remains Daoist, however, because it insists that only a ruler and ministers perfected through the Daoist program of apophatic self-cultivation will be able to employ these instruments of rule in a manner conducive to social and cosmic harmony. In this manner, this important chapter—the first in the "Branches" section of the text—brings together the principal insights from all the "Roots" section chapters into a careful synthesis of the best advice on sage rulership.[27]

CHAPTER 10: PROFOUND PRECEPTS—"Moucheng" 繆稱

This chapter is concerned with the inner emotional life of the sage ruler and speaks highly of the traditional Confucian virtues of Benevolence (*ren* 仁) and Rightness (*yi* 義). Yet, what marks sage rulers as perfected beyond the Confucian "Morally Superior Men" (*junzi* 君子) is that they have followed the apophatic inner cultivation practices outlined in the root chapters and attained a direct apprehension of the Way. Concomitant with this, they have been able to move their emotional lives beyond those of ordinary people though their cultivation of a highly refined inner "vital essence" (*jing*). It is through this vital essence that they are able to influence the people, through a resonance that works through the principles of correlative cosmology presented in the root chapters, particularly in chapter 6. This enables them to be completely and purely sincere and, hence, more efficacious in their emotional expressions.

Chapter 11: Integrating Customs—"Qisu" 齊俗

Like the previous chapter, "Qisu" is also concerned with the emotional lives of people; not of individuals, but, rather, of the various societies and groups of people who inhabit the far-flung empire of China in the middle of the second century BCE. This was precisely when the Han empire was consolidating its power and influence over these areas, many of which contained local peoples that the ruling Han considered to be "barbarians." The authors of this chapter argue that rituals and customs are constructed by sages in order to give full expression to the inner feelings of human beings, which, like all things in the universe, operate according to the correlative cosmology of *qi* and thus resonate within a greater context than just that of the individual. These constructions or patterns of human emotionality are to be assessed on the basis of the extent to which they allow, or inhibit, the free and spontaneous expression of human emotions, which directly arise from human nature and are th`ereby channeled and regulated by rituals and customs. Echoing the title and spirit of chapter 2 of the *Zhuangzi*, "Seeing Things as Equal" ("Qiwulun" 齊物論), this is the one par on which all are to be placed. Ultimately, both human nature and its emotional expression are grounded in the Way; and the suitable expression of emotion through the rites actually results in the manifestation of the Way in human experience. Thus, it is only the sages perfected through the apophatic inner cultivation techniques previously outlined who are best able to create the proper rituals and customs that will enable this kind of deep emotional expression. These rituals are neither fixed in the past nor associated with one region of the country, as they are for the Confucians.[28]

Chapter 12: Responses of the Way—"Daoying" 道應

This chapter contains fifty-six short narratives dedicated to illustrating various quotations from the *Laozi*, which the authors of the *Huainanzi* clearly regard as a major canonical source. These narratives are drawn from a wide variety of Daoist and non-Daoist sources, especially from the *Lüshi chunqiu* and *Zhuangzi*, which always conclude with a quotation from the *Laozi*, much as the seemingly Daoist-inspired chapter of the *Han Feizi*, chapter 21 "Illustrating Lao(zi)" ("Yü Lao" 喻老").[29] Each narrative can thus be read as an interpretation of the meaning of the phrase from the *Laozi* that ends it. Sarah Queen has identified three principal categories of these narratives: epistemological, featuring a Daoist blending of dualistic and nondualistic knowing; ethical, detailing the ways in which Daoist rulers nurture the governed through a kind of "moral potency"; and pragmatic, discussing ways in which rulers keep their positions through the ability to take advantage of the propensities of all things in the world and people in society and government (*shi* 勢).[30] These three categories well illustrate the unique form of "Syncretic" Daoism found in the *Huainanzi*. An additional value of this chapter consists in its recognition of the *Laozi* as a canonical source and its use of narratives to explain the author's distinctive understanding of the *Laozi*, which is a fascinating illustration of a hermeneutical genre that did not survive the early Han dynasty.[31] Larson Di Fiori has completed a thorough comparative analysis of this chapter and its similar precursors from the *Han Feizi*.[32]

Chapter 13: Discourses on the Boundless—"Fan Lun" 氾論

"Fan Lun" discusses the historical evolutions of sagely government and gives copious examples of how these perfected human beings, because of their being grounded in the Way, have been able to respond to the constantly shifting situations that arise because of the primacy of Change in the cosmos. Starting from a primitive Utopia, sages responded to the needs of their times and developed inventions that dealt with specific situations. However, in so doing, they unfortunately prolonged a degeneration from this primeval unity until the evils of Qin militarism arose and had to be defeated by the founder of the Han, Gaozu. Because they were attuned to the Way, sages enjoyed a unique capacity to assess (*lun*) the world around them in the context of the times in which they lived, in the circumstances arising in the moment, in the actions of other human beings, and in their own strengths and weaknesses. Thus, they were able to get rid of obsolete policies; discover the worthy; make use of timeliness and expediency to respond to changing circumstances; institute Rites and Music in accord with the times; and follow Humaneness and Rightness. Throughout the chapter, the Way is conceived of as the constant foundation from which sages continuously adjust their activities. When they do so, the people respond naturally, in accordance with the "matrix of *qi*" and the sympathetic resonance outlined by the text's discussion of correlative cosmology. It is through this sagely government—which established a harmony in the human polity that parallels the harmonies in the greater cosmos—that entire states attain Potency. Sages are able to do this because they cultivate the apophatic inner cultivation methods known throughout the book as the "Techniques of the Way." In addition to these, as a text, the *Huainanzi* has written, in its many words, the most important principles of sagely government that can be applied to create harmony in the current complex age.³³

Chapter 14: Explaining Sayings—"QuanyaN" 詮言

"Quanyan" begins with a comparatively abbreviated and general cosmogony—the fourth and last in the book—that emphasizes the origins of all things, from "The Grand Unity" (*Taiyi* 太一), which, in some passages in this text and other works of the classical Daoist tradition, is an alternate name for the Way and, in others, a principle of undifferentiated unity that is beyond even the Way itself.³⁴ This cosmogony provides the basis for the elaborations of the sayings this chapter contains on the nature of human perfection as the realization and embodiment of the Way and on governance by sages. The chapter is filled with "gnomic sayings," pithy statements of the important Daoist tenets of the *Huainanzi* that would have been familiar to most of the Huainan circle. These are followed by a series of explications of these sayings that bring out some of the most important themes and ideas from prior chapters in the book, in particular chapters 2 and 7, the other essays in the collection most influenced by the *Zhuangzi*. The chapter differentiates among concepts of human perfection, in particular: "Perfected Persons" (*zhiren*), "Sages" (*shengren*) and "Morally Superior Persons" (*junzi*). Using the "Techniques of the Way," the Perfected are adepts who are able to return to that primeval state of *Taiyi* from which both they themselves, and the universe itself, were born. Sages likewise cultivate themselves through these techniques but become rulers and apply them to governing. The Morally Superior also cultivate inner concentration and emptiness as the basis of acting ethically in the world.

Chapter 15: An Overview of the Military—"Binglüe" 兵略

Although greatly indebted to prior military works like the *Sunzi bingfa* 孫子兵法, "Binglüe" discusses military principles and affairs in a fashion generally in accordance with the overarching philosophy of the *Huainanzi*. As such "Binglüe" repeatedly sees military tactics and strategies in the context of their universal cosmological expressions and their being embedded in the correlative grand "matrix of *qi*." Moreover, there are morally correct uses of an army: to only attack a state in which the Way is ignored and to defend one's state from attack by others. To do otherwise is a violation of the cosmic harmony of the Way. Furthermore, generals of successful armies are successful only because they themselves have followed the apophatic inner cultivation practices that are commended to sage rulers throughout the book. Such generals are empty and formless and move in harmony with the Way. This gives them the extraordinary vision to see the overarching patterns of terrain and timely moment and to take positional advantage from them. Thus, the Daoist character of this material provides the greater context into which ideas from the prior military texts are situated.[35]

Chapters 16: A Mountain of Persuasions—"Shuishan" 說山, and 17: A Forest of Persuasions—"Shuilin" 說林

These two chapters are similar and include parallel collections of sayings and aphorisms to be used in persuasive arguments and disputations; the sayings and aphorisms probably served as talking points for use in discussions or to drive home conclusions in debate. As collections, they are similar to, but much shorter than, the two "Shuilin" 說林 chapters of the *Han Feizi*, chapters 22 and 23. Although these *Huainanzi* chapters do not contain many statements in common with earlier Daoist works, the former begins with a wonderful narrative in a *Zhuangzi*-style dialogue between the two souls believed to inhabit the body, the *po* 魄 (substantive soul, associated with *yin*) and the *hun* 魂 (ethereal soul, associated with *yang*). These two discuss how the Way could take on a physical form if it, itself, is Formless. The opening passage in chapter 17 argues for the timeliness of persuasions: one that works in a bygone era is not necessarily suitable for the present day. This applies another of the central tenets of sage governance, enunciated earlier in the text, to the area of verbal argumentation. Chapter 16 contains 162 of these sayings and chapter 17 contains 246.

Chapter 18: Among Others—"Renjian" 人閒

This essay is a masterpiece of a lost and highly structured prose form that incorporates narratives from a wide variety of sources, including the *Lüshi chunqiu* and the *Zhuangzi*, to illustrate various observations about the vagaries of fate and the necessity of inner cultivation to successfully respond to them. The ultimate point made by this chapter is that one must—through the apophatic inner cultivation practices enunciated in chapter 7—become a realized spirit or a sage; throughout the text, it is clear that one does this in order to distinguish the true motives of the people to whom one relates and to be able to assume a role of leadership "among others." The orientation of this chapter is thus recognizable as Daoist, although it draws from a wide variety of non-Daoist sources.

Chapter 19: Cultivating Effort—"Xiuwu" 修務

"Xiuwu" is another of the chapters with a sophisticated literary form, like chapters 14 and 18. Herein, we find seven distinct examples of oral philosophical debate of two basic types: one in which an initial philosophical claim is logically supported; and one in which such a claim is logically refuted. Within this structure, the overriding concern of the chapter centers on the necessity of putting effort into self-cultivation and sage rulership. In the first of these seven sections, the author asks how, if the Non-Action (*wuwei* or "effortless action") of the great sage rulers was grounded in emptiness and complete stillness, could they have achieved so much? Yet sagely government does not rest on taking Deliberate Action (*youwei* 有為) either, especially when it contradicts the propensity of things (*shi* 勢). The key to the practice of Non-Action is to have no selfish desires and personal ambitions and to comply with the natures, patterns, and propensities of things. Later sections argue against the notion that the natures of things are set in stone and incapable of being altered. The natures of people contain strengths and weaknesses, and effort is needed here as well, in order to transform the natures and propensities with which we are born.

Chapter 20: The Exalted Lineage—"Taizu" 太族

This chapter can be seen as a summation of what the compilers thought were the main philosophical tenets of the entire work, exemplified through historical narratives. Like many of the other chapters, "The Exalted Lineage" is concerned with sage rulership that is grounded in the personal realization of the empty and tranquil Way, through inner cultivation practices enunciated in chapters 2 and 7 and throughout the *Huainanzi*. Following these practices also leads to the development of further qualities needed for governing that are subsumed under the general category of developing Potency: the reduction of selfish desires; the ability to recognize and comply with the natures and active propensities of things and the patterns of their development and interaction; and the cultivation of the spirit, spirit-illumination, and the rarefied *qi* called "Vital Essence" (*jing*). Having developed Potency, the sage is then able to generate pure and completely sincere feelings that are communicated to the people through the "matrix of *qi*." It also empowers the sage to cultivate inner qualities such as a "Heavenly Heart" (*tianxin* 天心), Humaneness, Wisdom, and a sense of Rightness; these inner qualities must be supplemented by the external study of the accumulated wisdom of the past sages and their examples, as contained in historical narratives and poetry. Thus, sage rulership depends on the study of the chapters of this very text, the *Huainanzi*, combined with a profound practice of inner cultivation. Once again in this chapter, philosophical tenets from a wide variety of earlier traditions are synthesized within a framework that contains a universal cosmology of the Way and its Potency, a correlative cosmology of the "grand matrix of *qi*," a recognition of the natures, propensities, and patterns of all universal phenomena, and apophatic inner cultivation theory. As such, it constitutes an excellent statement of the overall scheme of this chapter and an accurate assessment of the entire book of Huainan.

CHAPTER 21: AN OVERVIEW OF THE ESSENTIALS—"Yaolüe" 要略

As we have seen earlier, "Yaolüe" 要略 contains a rationale, summary, and overview of the entire *Huainanzi*. It is precisely because it is such an important overview of the entire text and how it was conceived to cohere by its authors, especially Liu An himself, that I have included a description of it in my introductory section to this article. Sarah Queen and Judson Murray have made much of the following statement at the very end of this final chapter and, hence, at the end of the entire book:[36]

> In this book of the Liu clan . . .
> We have not
> followed a path made by a solitary footprint
> or adhered to instructions from a single corner (or perspective)
> or allowed us to be entrapped or fettered by things so that we would
> not advance or shift according to the age.
> Thus,
> situate [this book] in the narrowest of circumstances and nothing will obstruct it;
> extend it to the whole world and it will leave no empty space.[37]

若劉氏之書 . . .
. . . 非循一跡之路, 守一隅之指, 拘繫牽連於物, 而不與世推移也,
故置之尋常而不塞, (市)〔布〕之天下而不窕。38

Queen and Judson Murray contend that this florid ending to the entire book does much to establish the fact that the authors of the *Huainanzi* conceived of their "Book of the Liu Clan" as what Griet Vankeerberghen has called an "eclectic" work, one in which there are many ideas combined together on a relatively equal footing with none given priority.39 This is in contrast to a "syncretic" work, one in which many ideas may be put forth, but only certain ones that are emphasized provide an overarching foundation and framework for the entire work.

It should be clear by now what my position is on this. Chapter after chapter of this text demonstrate evidence that, despite the presence of a variety of ideas from other intellectual traditions—including the Ru and Mo and ideas from so-called "Legalist" works like the *Han Feizi*, or "Militarist" works like the *Sunzi bingfa*—the cosmological foundations and the self-cultivation processes of the "Tradition of the Dao" (Daojia), as defined by Sima Tan, dominate the *Huainanzi*; this is the case even in the chapters that could be regarded as otherwise focused on military affairs (chapter 15), or on the "Tradition of the Confucians ("Rujia" 儒家), ideas like human nature and moral potency (chapter 11). I would only add that to argue that the phrase "we have not followed a path made by a solitary footprint" does not at all necessarily imply that the work *does not* belong to a single tradition. For example, why could that tradition to which it belongs not regard *itself* as transcending any single viewpoint or tradition? Why could it not be a tradition of thought and practice that was deliberately syncretic, as we find advocated in the final chapter of the *Zhuangzi*, "Below in the Empire" ("Tianxia" 天下), which argues for the superiority of this syncretic perspective against the narrow perspectives of just a single tradition:40

> The whole world is (currently) in chaos, excellence and sagehood are not clarified, the Way and its Potency are not unified, *within the whole world there are many who take one narrow perspective to delight in.* This is akin to ears, eyes, nose, and mouth: each has something they clarify but we cannot exchange one for the other, just as the various specialties of the Hundred Traditions all have their strengths and at one time or another are useful.

However, none of them is inclusive, none is comprehensive: *these are scholars who each have their own single angle.* They split asunder the beauty of the Heavens and the Earth, chop up the Patterns of the myriad things, *and focus on one point in what the ancients considered a whole.* Few are those who are able to lay out the full beauty of the Heavens and the Earth and delineate the contents of Spirit-like Illumination. Because of this the Way to be inwardly a sage and outwardly a king is darkened and not clarified, becomes blocked up and not manifested, and *people throughout the whole world take what they prefer and turn it into their own distinctive method.* Sadly, if the Hundred Traditions set forth on this path and do not return, they will never again be united. And the students of later times unhappily fail to see the purity of the Heavens and the Earth, the grand embodiment of the ancients, the Techniques of the Way will be torn asunder through the whole world.[41]

天下大亂, 賢聖不明, 道德不一, 天下多得一察焉以自好. 譬如耳目鼻口, 皆有所明, 不能相通. 猶百家眾技也, 皆有所長, 時有所用. 雖然, 不該不偏, 一曲之士也. 判天地之美, 析萬物之理, 察古人之全, 寡能備於天地之美, 稱神明之容. 是故內聖外王之道, 闇而不明, 鬱而不發, 下之人各為其所欲焉以自為方. 夫, 百家往而不反, 必不合矣! 後世之學者, 不幸不見天地之純, 古人之大體, 道術將為天下裂.

There is a striking similarity between the *Huainanzi*'s phrase "we have not followed a path made by a solitary footprint or adhered to instructions from a single corner or perspective" (非循一跡之路, 守一隅之指) and the aforementioned concerns of the authors of this last chapter of the *Zhuangzi*, which are that, among the world's traditions of thought and practice, there are many who each have their own single angle (一曲之士也), who take one perspective to delight in, and who take what they prefer and turn it into their own distinctive method (各為其所欲焉以自為方), thereby tearing asunder the "grand embodiment of the ancients and the Techniques of the Way." Both texts use almost identical phrases to criticize the narrow-minded perspective of individual intellectual positions; both affirm the syncretic perspective that embraces all positions within the holistic vision of the Way and its distinctive methods of experiencing it. What the author of this ultimate chapter of the *Huainanzi* is affirming is that the entire project of creating the book is to present a Daoist tradition that embraces all prior perspectives, a "meta-traditional tradition," one that directly connects with the perspective advocated in the "Tianxia" chapter of the *Zhuangzi*. This is a syncretic perspective that combines the best ideas of the traditions that precede it to forge a perspective that professes to be much more comprehensive but, nonetheless, "Daoist" in preserving these essential techniques of the Way (*daoshu* 道術). This is also the perspective that is very clearly enunciated in Sima Tan's presentation of the essential teachings of the "Daojia" in his "Summary of the Six Traditions" in the *Historical Records*.[42]

It is no accident that the authors of the *Huainanzi* also conceive of their own tradition as following these distinctive "Techniques of the Way." There are eight passages in the text in chapters 2, 11, 12, 13, and 14 in which this characteristic phrase occurs.[43] For example:[44]

> For this reason, sages inwardly cultivate the Techniques of the Way and do not outwardly adorn themselves with Humaneness and Rightness. They are unaware of the demands of the eyes and ears and wander in the harmony of their Quintessence and Spirit.[45]

是故聖人內修道術, 而不外飾仁義, 不知耳目之 (宣) 〔宜〕, 而游于精神之和.

And:[46]

> Thus
> The Techniques of the Way cannot be used to advance and seek reputation
> but can be used to retreat and cultivate one's person.
> They cannot be used to obtain benefit
> but can be used to avoid harm.
> Thus sages
> do not utilize their conduct to seek a reputation,
> do not utilize their wisdom to demonstrate praiseworthiness.
> They model and comply with what is natural so that nothing interferes with them.[47]

故道術不可以進而求名, 而可以退而脩身; 不可以得利, 而可以離害. 故聖人不以行求名, 不以智見譽. 法 (脩) 〔循〕自然, 己無所與.

Conclusion

The "Techniques of the Way" in the *Huainanzi* refer to the apophatic self-cultivation practices called in other passages in this work and in a number of pre-Han Daoist works, the "Techniques of the Mind." The former term came to subsume the latter because these techniques—of emptying out the usual contents of consciousness through focused attention to the breath while sitting still—directly led to the experience of merging with the Way.[48] This is a characteristic practice referred to in many early sources of the inner cultivation tradition that form the evidence for a broad lineage of thought and practice that can be justifiably labeled "classical Daoism."[49]

Thus, the syncretism of the *Huainanzi* is not unique; it represents a deliberate continuation and elaboration of a perspective that is found in the last chapter of the *Zhuangzi*, which, I have elsewhere argued, was well known to the Huainan court because it was most likely compiled there. In the last analysis, one cannot understand the unique and original way in which the *Huainanzi* was written—with individual chapters on specific topics, incorporating ideas from a variety of earlier traditions of thought and practice within a grand synthesis intended to embrace and comprehend the entire cosmos—without understanding that its authors believed it to be grounded firmly in the cosmological and psychological principles of the tradition that Sima Tan called "Daojia" but also beyond any one specific tradition. In essence its authors saw it as establishing a Daoist-based "meta-tradition." The scope and grandeur of this comprehensive synthesis is best left in the words of the "Summary of the Essentials":[50]

> In this book of the Liu clan, (we have)
> observed the phenomena of the Heavens and the Earth,
> penetrated past and present discussions,
> weighed affairs and established regulations,
> measured forms and applied what is suitable,
> traced to its source the heart of the Way and its Potency,
> and united the customs of the Three Kings,
> collecting them and alloying them.
> At the core of the Profound Mystery
> the infinitesimal movements of the vital essence have been revealed.
> By casting aside limits and boundaries
> and by drawing on the pure and the tranquil,

(we have) thereby
unified the world,
brought order to the myriad things,
responded to alterations and transformations,
and comprehended their distinctions and categories . . .[51]

若劉氏之書，觀天地之象，通古今之論，權事而立制，度形而施宜，原道〔德〕之心，合三王之風，以儲與扈冶，玄眇之中，精搖靡覽，棄其畛挈，斟其淑靜，以統天下，理萬物，應變化，通殊類 . . .

It is not only this one book that was created: the authors of the *Huainanzi* had every intention of continuing the "meta-tradition" it reflects right into becoming the ruling ideology of the Chinese state. They had no idea that, within less than two decades, they and the entire intellectual center in the Huainan circle would be destroyed by order of the very emperor who had so doted on his aging uncle, Liu An, and who at first so loved the text that he put it into his private collection. They had no idea that their cherished *Huainanzi*, very much an intellectual blueprint for a sage government that transcended traditions and transcended, as Michael Puett has so aptly put it, history itself, would fall into ill repute because of the demise of its patron; Liu An was accused of treason and summarily executed, along with his entire family of several generations.[52] Yet one more reminder that history is written by the victors.

Notes

1. Harold D. Roth, "Daoist Inner Cultivation Thought and the Textual Structure of the *Huainanzi*," in *The Huainanzi and Textual Production in Early China*, ed. Sarah Queen and Michael Puett (Leiden: Brill, 2014), 40–82. For further discussion, see also Liu An, *The Huainanzi: A Guide to the Theory and Practice of Government in Early Han China*, ed. and trans. John S. Major, Sarah A. Queen, Andrew Seth Meyer, and Harold D. Roth (New York: Columbia University Press, 2010), abbreviated to Liu An, *The Huainanzi* in the following notes.

2. Harold D. Roth, *The Textual History of the Huai-nan Tzu* (Ann Arbor: AAS Monograph Series, 1992), 12–16.

3. Roth, *Textual History*, 17–18, 23–26.

4. Louis Komjathy, *The Daoist Tradition: An Introduction* (London: Bloomsbury, 2013), 22–24.

5. Roth, *Textual History*, 26–54.

6. Roth, "Daoist Inner Cultivation Thought," 40–82.
7. See, for example, Charles Le Blanc, "Huai nan tzu," in *Early Chinese Texts: A Bibliographical Guide*, ed. Michael Loewe, Early China Special Monograph, no. 2 (Berkeley: Society for the Study of Early China and the Institute for East Asian Studies, 1993), 189.
8. D. C. Lau, *Huainanzi zhuzi suoyin* 淮南子逐字索引, Institute for Chinese Studies Chinese Text Concordance Series (Hong Kong: Commercial Press, 1992), 223/21/21–24.
9. Liu An, *The Huainanzi*, 848–849, with slight modification.
10. *Yijing* "Shuogua."
11. Martin Kern, "Creating a Book and Performing It: The "Yao-lüe" Chapter of the *Huainanzi* as a Western Han *Fu*," in *The Huainanzi*, ed. Queen and Puett, 124–149.
12. Le Blanc, "Huai nan tzu," 189–190. See also the introduction in Major et al., in which the authors concur with this viewpoint about the first eight chapters constituting the foundations of the book (Liu An, *The Huainanzi*, 13–14).
13. Andrew Meyer, "Roots-Branches Structuralism in the *Huainanzi*," in *The Huainanzi*, ed. Queen and Puett, 23–39; Roth, "Daoist Inner Cultivation Thought," 40–82.
14. For a solid translation of "Daoyüan" and the four other texts from Mawangdui associated with the "Huang-Lao" tradition, see Robin D. S. Yates, *Five Lost Classics: Tao, Huang-lao, and Yin-yang in Han China*, Classics of Ancient China (New York: Ballantine, 1997).
15. For a detailed study of the significant role of the *Huainanzi* in the evolution of the classical Chinese concept of *li*, see Harold D. Roth, "The Classical Daoist Concept of *Li* and Early Chinese Cosmology," *Early China* 35/36 (2012–2013): 157–184.
16. For an analysis of the key ideas in this foundational chapter of the *Huainanzi*, see Harold D. Roth, "Nature and Self-Cultivation in *Huainanzi*'s 'Original Way,'" in *Polishing the Chinese Mirror: Essays in Honor of Henry Rosemont, Jr.*, ed. Marthe Chandler and Ronnie Littlejohn (New York: Global Scholarly, 2007), 270–292. For a different translation and analysis, see Roger T. Ames and D. C. Lau, trans., *Yuan Dao: Tracing Dao to Its Source*, Classics of Ancient China (New York: Ballantine Books, 1998).
17. Michael Puett provides a compelling analysis of this passage in his article "Violent Misreadings: The Hermeneutics of Cosmology in the *Huainanzi*," *Bulletin of the Museum of Far Eastern Antiquities* 72 (2000): 29–47.
18. For an analysis and theory of three phases of the classical Daoist tradition, see Harold D. Roth, "Psychology and Self-Cultivation in Early Taoistic Thought," *Harvard Journal of Asiatic Studies* 51(1991) 2: 599–650, and also Harold D. Roth, *Original Tao: Inward Training and the Foundations of Taoist Mysticism* (New York: Columbia University Press, 1999), especially 195–198.

19. For the definitive translation and analysis of these chapters, see John S. Major, *Heaven and Earth in Early Han Thought: Chapters Three, Four, and Five of the Huainanzi*, SUNY series in Chinese Philosophy and Culture (Albany: State University of New York Press, 1993).

20. A fascinating analysis of one example of this in chapter 6 is found in Anne Behnke Kinney, "Breaking through Heaven's Glass Ceiling: The Significance of the Commoner Woman of Qi in the 'Lan Ming' Chapter of the *Huainanzi*," in *The Huainanzi*, ed. Queen and Puett, 351–376.

21. For an alternative translation and important analysis of this chapter, see Charles Le Blanc, *Huai-nan Tzu: Philosophical Synthesis in Early Han Thought: The Idea of Resonance (Kan-ying) with a Translation and Analysis of Chapter Six* (Hong Kong: Hong Kong University Press, 1985).

22. For this analysis, see Harold D. Roth, "The Early Taoist Concept of *Shen*: A Ghost in the Machine?," in *Sagehood and Systematizing Thought in Warring States and Han China*, ed. Kidder Smith, John S. Major, Harold D Roth, and Donald Harper (Brunswick, ME: Bowdoin College, 1990), 11–32.

23. Lau, *Huainanzi zhuzi suoyin*, 7/60/9. See also 1/8/16 and 14/133/8.

24. These four texts are "Inward Training" ("Neiye"), "Techniques of the Mind," parts 1 and 2 ("Xinshu shang, xia" 心術上下), and "The Purified Mind" ("Baixin" 白心). For an analysis of these four texts and their place in the history of classical Daoism, see Harold D. Roth, "Daoism in the *Guanzi* 管子," in *Dao Companion to Daoist Philosophy*, ed. Liu Xiaogan (Berlin: Springer, 2014), 265–280.

25. For a partial translation and analysis of this chapter, see Claude Larre, *Le Traité VII du Houai Nan Tseu: Les ésprits légers et subtils animateurs de l'essence: Analyse des structures d'expression et traduction, avec notes et commentaires, de la partie doctrinale du traité VII du Houai Nan Tseu (HNT VII, 1a–7a)*, in *Variétés sinologiques*, vol. 67 (Taibei: Institut Ricci, 1982).

26. A. C. Graham, *Chuang-tzu: The Seven Inner Chapters and Other Writings from the Book of Chuang-tzu* (London: Allen and Unwin, 1981), 28, 197–217.

27. For an important and exhaustive translation and analysis of this chapter that arrives at a different conclusion about its intellectual affiliation, see Roger T. Ames, *The Art of Rulership: A Study of Ancient Chinese Political Thought* (Honolulu: University of Hawai'i Press, 1983; rpt. Albany: State University of New York Press, 1994).

28. For an accurate, if occasionally idiosyncratic translation and study of this chapter, see Benjamin E. Wallacker, *The Huai-nan-tzu, Book Eleven: Behavior, Culture and the Cosmos*, American Oriental Series, vol. 48 (New Haven, CT: American Oriental Society, 1962). This is a pioneering early English translation that, in 1962, was the first translation in the nearly three decades since Evan Morgan's flawed initial efforts: Evan S. Morgan, *Tao, the Great Luminant: Essays from Huai-nan Tzu* (1933 rpt.; Taibei: Cheng Wen, 1974), chapters 1, 2, 7, 8, 12, 13, 15, 19. Wallacker was a student of the brilliant Russian Sinologist, Peter Boodberg, and his translation

of HNZ 11 represents the most extensive application of Boodbergian translation principles that was ever published. That is both its strength and its weakness.

29. Sarah A. Queen has written a penetrating study that clearly distinguishes between the literary form of "Yü Lao," and *Han Feizi* chapter 20, "Jie Lao" 解溪 (Explicating Lao[zi]). Chapter 20 also includes embedded quotations that are now found in the received *Laozi*, but they are in the context of prose arguments rather than occurring at the end of illustrative narratives. See Sarah A. Queen, "*Han Feizi* and the Old Master: A Comparative Analysis and Translation of *Han Feizi* Chapter 20, 'Jie Lao,' and Chapter 21, 'Yu Lao,'" in *Dao Companion to the Philosophy of Hanfeizi*, ed. Paul R. Goldin (Dordrecht: Springer, 2012), 197–256. For a concise summary, see also Queen's introduction to her translation of the chapter in Liu An, *The Huainanzi*, 429–438.

30. For an insightful analysis of this chapter and its unique forms of argumentation, see Sarah A. Queen, "The Creation and Domestication of the Techniques of Lao-Zhuang: Anecdotal Narrative and Philosophical Argumentation in *Huainanzi* Chapter 12, 'Reponses of the Way' (Dao Ying 道應)," *Asia Major*, Third Series, 21 (2008) 1: 201–247.

31. Queen points out that the *Hanshi waijuan* 韓詩外傳 is another example of this soon to disappear hermeneutical genre. See Liu An, *The Huainanzi*, 437.

32. Larson Di Fiori, "Early Intertextual Uses of Parallels with the *Laozi* and Their Role as Sources of Authority," PhD dissertation, Brown University, May 2018.

33. Michael Puett has written a superb analysis of this chapter in his article "Sages, Creation, and the End of History in the *Huainanzi*," in *The Huainanzi*, ed. Queen and Puett, 269–290.

34. The idea of *Taiyi* as a cosmogonic unitive power, responsible for the generation of the differentiated universe of the heavens and the earth and the myriad things, dates back to the late Warring States period. Perhaps its earliest expression is in the excavated work from Guodian (ca. 300 BCE), the *Taiyi sheng shui* 太一生水. Sarah Allan wrote the first and most important study of the text, "The Great One, Water, and the *Laozi*: New Light from Guodian," *T'oung Pao* 89, no. 4/5 (December 2003): 237–285. For a recent incisive study, see Erica Brindley, "The *Taiyi shengshui* 太一生水: Cosmogony and Its Role in Early Chinese Thought," in *Dao Companion to the Excavated Guodian Bamboo Manuscripts*, ed. Shirley Chan (Cham: Springer, 2019), 153–162.

35. The best and most complete study and translation of this chapter and its parallels with other classical Chinese military texts is found in Andrew S. Meyer, *The Dao of the Military: Liu An's Art of War* (New York: Columbia University Press, 2012); Edmund Ryden, *Philosophy of Peace in Han China: A Study of the Huainanzi Ch. 15 on Military Strategy* (Taibei: Ricci Institute, 1998) is another important study of this chapter.

36. Sarah A. Queen, "Inventories of the Past: Re-Thinking the 'School' Affiliation of the *Huainanzi*," *Asia Major*, Third Series, 14 (2001) 1: 51–72; Judson

Murray, "A Study of 'Yaolüe' 要略, 'A Summary of the Essentials': Understanding the *Huainanzi* through the Point of View of the Author of the Postface," *Early China* 29 (2004): 45–110. While in each of these articles, their arguments are more complete, they both use this statement from the *Huainanzi* to offer final proof of the book not being the product of a single intellectual tradition.

37. Liu An, *The Huainanzi*, 867, modified by taking the translation of *yu* 隅 as "corner" from Puett, "Sages," 269.

38. D. C. Lau, *Huainanzi zhuzi suoyin*, 228/21/30–31.

39. Griet Vankeerberghen, *The Huainanzi and Liu An's Claim to Moral Authority* (Albany: State University of New York Press, 2001), 3–5.

40. D. C. Lau, *Zhuangzi zhuzi suoyin* 莊子逐字索引, Institute for Chinese Studies Chinese Text Concordance Series (Hong Kong: Commercial Press, 2000), 97/33/21–25.

41. Based on Graham, *Chuang-tzu*, 275, with substantial modifications.

42. For a more complete analysis of the Syncretic Daoism of the *Zhuangzi* and its relationship to the *Huainanzi*, see Harold D. Roth, "Who Compiled the *Chuang Tzu*?," in *Chinese Texts and Philosophical Contexts: Essays Dedicated to Angus C. Graham*, ed. Henry Rosemont Jr. (LaSalle, IL: Open Court Press, 1991), 79–128.

43. Lau, *Huainanzi zhuzi suoyin*, 2/11/25; 2/14/20; 11/102/10; 12/106/8 (2x); 13/130/7, 8; 14/135/16; and 14/137/18.

44. Lau, *Huainanzi zhuzi suoyin*, 2/14/20.

45. Liu An, *The Huainanzi*, 97 (modified).

46. Lau, *Huainanzi zhuzi suoyin*, 14/135/16.

47. Liu An, *The Huainanzi*, 548 (modified).

48. For more detailed arguments on these techniques of "inner cultivation," see Roth, *Original Tao*, 181–185, and Roth, "Daoist Inner Cultivation Thought," 43–50.

49. See Komjathy, *The Daoist Tradition*, 18–22.

50. Lau, *Huainanzi zhuzi suoyin*, 228/21/28–30.

51. Liu An, *The Huainanzi*, 867 (modified).

52. Puett, "Sages," the whole chapter, but especially 288–289.

Afterword

Harold D. Roth

In 1984 and 1985, I spent two wonderful years as a Canada Council Postdoctoral Fellow at the School of Oriental and African Studies (SOAS). There, during my first year, I formed enduring friendships and apprenticeships with three senior scholars: Angus Graham, Paul Thompson, and Sarah Allan. These turned out to be some of the most meaningful mentorships of my entire academic career.

We were rather like a "Gang of Four," spending the days reading texts together and the late afternoons and evenings in the bar in the basement of SOAS discussing Chinese thought and about everything else imaginable. The China section of what was then called "The Department of the Far East" seemed to regard a stop there after work as part of their daily schedule, and I most happily joined in. Being the junior member of this gang, I was always asking questions of my mentors, and often reaching home after the bar closed at 9 p.m. Struggling through the haze of alcohol consumption, I scribbled down my imperfect memory of what I had learned that day. These were some of the best conversations I ever had with scholars in my field, and I absorbed their ideas like a sponge hitting water for the first time.

SOAS in those days was a waning power in early China studies—and really all of the Asian languages and cultures. The Thatcher government, in the effort to save money by reducing government funding of higher education, devised some devious ways to reduce the size of the faculty at universities throughout the country. At SOAS their appointed Master, Jeremy Cowan, was weeding out SOAS faculty by enforcing retirement at age sixty-five and offering younger faculty lucrative incentives to retire early—with the caveat that their position would be made redundant. This shortsighted policy decimated the ranks of British scholars in all areas, but particularly African and Asian studies; it was eventually reversed less than a decade later but never succeeded in restoring the high levels of academic excellence of years past. By the time this government policy of reducing faculty rolls had been put into place, D. C. Lau—a towering figure of genteel brilliance who himself had mentored Sarah during her early days at SOAS—had already left and gone to an active retirement at the Chinese University of Hong Kong, one that would turn out to be of great benefit to our entire scholarly community via his creation and oversight of the CHANT concordance and critical text series.

On one particularly beautiful spring afternoon during my first year at SOAS, I attended the annual "Strawberry Social" to honor retiring faculty. To my great surprise, Angus, who was going into forced retirement at age sixty-five, showed up for the event in a jacket and tie reluctantly towed in by his wife Judy. It was the one and only time I ever saw Angus in such natty attire. He would often wear a decrepit old brown and pale-yellow wool sweater, covered in chalk dust from blackboards against which he'd leaned and had adorned with long threads of yarn hanging from the holes in the elbows. This time, despite being dressed in his finest, at the very moment SOAS Master Cowan began speaking, Angus muttered under his breath so only I could hear him, "If that man speaks, I am gone!" As I turned my head toward the front of the room to see Cowan, Angus bolted out of the room so quickly it was if he had disappeared into thin air. I had never seen him move that fast. Actually, even to this day, I have never seen *anybody* move that fast. If I hadn't realized it from prior conversations, it was abundantly clear to me then that Angus didn't suffer fools.

From that moment in his life, Angus literally abandoned his SOAS office and began the life of a peripatetic scholar, going to National University of Singapore, Chengchi University in Taiwan, and coming here to Brown for a most interesting semester. He finally seemed to find a home at the University of Hawai'i, where, under the auspices of his good friend, Roger Ames, he resided for two years and finally—at the very end of his career—felt respected as a philosopher. During that time, he would complete *Disputers of the Tao*, his monograph on correlative thinking, several important articles on Chinese thought, and his responses to the contributions to his Festschrift, which he completed shortly before his passing in the spring of 1991.[1]

Paul Thompson, who wrote the brilliant work of textual criticism *The Shen Tzu Fragments*[2] that was such an inspiration for my own first book on the textual history of the *Huainanzi*, was a person whose keen intellect was matched by his kind heart—he was a true *junzi*. At that time, he was getting more and more deeply involved in figuring out algorithms for computer speech recognition of Chinese, something that occupied him for most of the subsequent two decades. Despite this, Paul never lost his interest in textual criticism and could always be relied on for reflections on problems in this area. The last time I saw him in person was at the marvelous conference that Sarah organized on the Guodian *Laozi* at Dartmouth in May 1998. We spent an evening at the Hanover Inn with Wang Tao and Sarah going over the significance of the two different versions of chapter 64 that were part of the Guodian *Laozi* text.[3]

I learned about many things from Sarah, whose house at 6 Remington Street was the abode I inhabited during my first year at SOAS. I learned about the meaning of devoted commitment in marriage, hers to the brilliant but then unknown artist Nicol Allan. I learned how to cook and flip an omelet and learned about living in a house without many of the modern conveniences to which I——and most of the "first world"—had become accustomed, including television, microwaves, and central heating. I quickly learned the meaning of the term "Luddite," since Sarah had sworn off almost all modern devices save for a beat-up old table radio on which she listened faithfully every day to the BBC while she pecked away—a key at a time—on her giant old Remington manual typewriter. This left such a lasting impression on me that, to this day, I am still rather shocked when I receive an email from her, much less see her in a Zoom call or lecture.

More importantly for my academic career, I had many discussions with her about careful textual scholarship and about the courage to take intellectual risks by bringing important methodologies from outside the field into early China studies—as she did in her first book, *The Heir and the Sage*, and later in her brilliant use of George Lakoff and Mark Johnson's "metaphor theory" in her *The Way of Water and Sprouts of Virtue*.[4] I also learned about the many challenges faced by women working in a field like Chinese studies that was dominated by men who were often far from supportive, challenges that, regrettably, continue to this day. I was so pleased to see Sarah able to break through the "Glass Ceiling" at SOAS and finally be given the well-deserved endowed chair in Chinese studies at Dartmouth, where she continued to do groundbreaking and meticulously careful scholarship in many aspects of early China studies for more than an additional quarter century.

The depth and breadth of Sarah Allan's scholarship are so well demonstrated by these three volumes dedicated to her. They show her extensive influence on early China studies and the many friendships she created with scholars in China, the UK, Europe, and North America. They also demonstrate the considerable respect that she has garnered during her brilliant academic career. It will be a long time before we again see the likes of another such scholar, one who combines brilliantly meticulous attention to detail in research with extraordinary breadth of knowledge and who is willing to apply methodologies from vastly different fields to topics within the realm of early China studies. I am honored for now almost four decades to have called her my mentor and my friend.

Notes

1. Angus C. Graham, *Disputers of the Tao* (Lasalle, IL: Open Court Press, 1989); Henry Rosemont Jr., ed., *Chinese Texts and Philosophical Contexts: Essays Dedicated to Angus C. Graham* (Lasalle, IL: Open Court Press, 1991).

2. Paul Mulligan Thompson, *The Shen Tzu Fragments* (Oxford: Oxford University Press, 1979); Harold D. Roth, *The Textual History of the Huainanzi* (Ann Arbor: Association for Asian Studies Monograph No. 46, 1992).

3. Insights from this evening found their way into my article "Some Methodological Issues in the Guodian *Laozi* Parallels," in *The Guodian* Laozi: *Proceedings of the International Conference, Dartmouth College, May 1998*, ed. Sarah Allan and Crispin Williams, Early China Special Monograph Series no. 5, Society for the Study of Early China and the Institute of East Asian Studies (Berkeley: University of California Press, 2000), 71–89.

4. Sarah Allan, *The Heir and the Sage: Dynastic Legend in Early China*, revised and expanded edition (Albany: State University of New York Press, 2017); Allan, *The Way of Water and Sprouts of Virtue* (Albany: State University of New York Press, 1997).

Contributors

CUI Xiaojiao 崔曉姣 is Assistant Professor in the School of Philosophy at Beijing Normal University.

LI Boqian 李伯謙 is Emeritus Professor and Chair of the School of Archaeology and Museology at Peking University.

LI Feng 李峰 is Professor of Early Chinese History and Archaeology at Columbia University, and Director of the Tang Center for Early China.

Andrew MEYER is Professor of History at Brooklyn College, City University of New York.

Harold D. ROTH is Professor of Religious Studies at Brown University.

SHEN Jianhua 沈建華 is a research fellow at the Unearthed Manuscript Research and Protection Center, Tsinghua University.

Paul Nicholas VOGT is Assistant Professor of Early Chinese History in the School of Global and International Studies at Indiana University.

WANG Jinfeng 王進鋒 is Associate Professor of History at East China Normal University.

WANG Yunfei 王雲飛 is an assistant researcher in the Department of Philosophy at Hebei Social Sciences Research Institute.

Robin D. S. YATES is James McGill Professor of East Asian Studies and History and Classical Studies at McGill University.

ZHU Fenghan 朱鳳瀚 is Professor of History at Peking University and Director of the Peking University Unearthed Manuscript Research Institute.

Index

Allan, Sarah, ix–xiv, 212n4, 265n34, 267, 268, 269–70; on legends, 171–72, 184, 210; on Yi Yin, x, 1, 12
Ames, Roger, 268
An Jinhuai, 82, 83, 84
archaeology: and naming rules, 162, 164; and Nine Provinces, 90, 97, 114; of Xia dynasty, xi–xii, 77–87. *See also* bronze inscriptions; oracle-bone inscriptions
astronomy, 66, 80, 85, 242, 247

Bai Juyi, 147
Bao Biao, 140n15
Baoqing Kuaiji xuzhi, 41
Baoxun (Tsinghua University collection), 228
Beijing University. *See* Peking University bamboo-slip collection
Bin diviner group, 3–4, 22n20
Boodberg, Peter, 264n28
bronze inscriptions: on King Wen, 235n43; naming rules in, xii, 145–69; Nine Provinces in, 89–114, 116nn29–30; province names in, 107–13; on townships, 123, 125, 137; on tribute systems, 97–107; *zhou* in, 91–97

bronze inscriptions (named artifacts): Ban *gui*, 165; Bin Gong *xu*, 90, 97, 105, 114; Bo Junfu *ding*, 164, 165; Caihou Shen *pan*, 164; Chenhou *gui*, 150; Chensheng Que *gui*, 156; Da Yu *ding*, 97; Deng *gui* (4), 150; Fang Cheng *huan*, 123; First Year Shi X *gui*, 138n2; Geng *hu*, 111; Geng Ji *ding*, 125; Guo Bi *su*, 97; Guo Jiang *ding*, 153; Guozhong *li*, 162; Han Huangfu *ding*, 151; Han Huangfu *gui*, 155; He *zun*, 114; Huangzi *li*, 162–63; Jing *gui*, 165; Jin Jiang *ding*, 153; Ju Fu *xu*, 106; Ju Hou Xiaozi *gui*, 111; Ju Shu zhi Zhongzi Ping *zhong*, 111, 112; Ke *ding*, 116n30; Lai *pan*, 104, 105; Lu Bo Yufu *li*, 150; Lü Jiang *gui*, 153; Lu Ji *li*, 158; Mao Gong *ding*, 104, 105; Mian *fu*, 138n2; Mi Bo Shiji *gui*, 125; Pengbo *ding*, 151; Pengzhong *ding*, 150, 152; Qi Jiang *ding*, 158; Quanbo *ding*, 160; Rong zuo Zhou Gong *gui*, 97; Sanbo *gui*, 151; San Ji *ding*, 152; San Shi *pan*, 116n30; Shanfu Lübo *ding*, 152; Shangruo Gong *fu*, 159–60; Shi Dui *dun*, 116n30; Shi Hai *gui*, 156; Shi Huan *gui*, 105–6; Shi Xun *gui*,

bronze inscriptions (named artifacts) *(continued)*
  116n29; Shi You *gui*, 165; Shu Yi *bo*, 137; Shu Yi *zhong*, 92; Xiao Yu *ding*, 235n43; Xi Jia *pan*, 105; Xu Ji *li*, 152–53; Xun *gui*, 125; Xuzi Zhuang *fu*, 158–59; Yihou Ze *gui*, 164; Yuan *pan*, 152, 163; Zeng Bo X *fu*, 111; Zenghou *fu*, 158; Zewang *guigai*, 164; Zhai Ji *jue*, 158; Zheng Jiangbo *ding*, 164; Zhong Shengfu *li*, 152; Zhou Jisheng *gui*, 155; Zi *yi*, 164
Buddhism, 25, 35, 230

Cai Bian, 36, 37–38
Cai Jie, 65–66
Cai Jing, 38, 40
Cai Yong, 31, 50n52
calligraphy, 48n37, 48n40; and Cao E cult, 27, 31, 36, 38, 41, 43; of Kangxi Emperor, 51n66
Cao Cao, 31, 48n40
Cao E cult, 25–52; and Cao E as water/tide deity, 33, 38, 40–43; and Cao E river, 28, 32–33, 42, 46n18, 47n30; components of, 26–28; development of, 32–43; filial piety in, 27, 31, 33, 35, 38, 41–44; imperial recognition of, 38–39, 40–41, 42; male literati on, 26, 27–28, 38, 39, 42–44; origins of, 28–31; in Song dynasty, 27, 35–41, 43; stele inscription on, xi, 27–37, 42, 43, 49n48; temple of, 26, 27, 35–37, 38, 41–44, 47n30, 51n59
Cao E jiangzhi (Hu Fengdan), 27
Cao Gui, xiii, 171–95; contradictions in stories of, 174–78; fact and meaning in historiography of, 184–87; names of, 192n3; and Qi vs. Lu, 179–84

Cao jiang shiji, 27–28, 45n10
Cao jiang xiaonü miaozhi (Shen Zhili), 27, 30, 32, 35–39, 45n10
Cao Mie zhi zhen (The Battle Formations of Cao Mie; Shanghai Museum collection), 180–84, 193n20
Cao Mo zhi zhen (Shanghai Museum collection), 122
Cao Xu, 29, 47n27
Chan, Timothy, 47n27
chen (servitors, slaves), 92–97, 115n18
Chen, state of, 150
Chen Fengheng, 234n25, 234n30
Cheng Hao, 64, 65
Cheng Tang (Shang), xi, 2, 8, 19
Cheng wu (Tsinghua University collection), 223, 236n51
Cheng Yi, 62–68, 76n36
Chengzi yishu, 72, 76n36
Chen Hongshou, 38
Chen Jingzhong. *See* Gongzi Wan of Chen
Chen Mengjia, 95, 233n18
Chen Qun, 58
Chen Tianxiang, 67
Chen Wan. *See* Gongzi Wan of Chen
Chen Xiangdao, 63–64
Chen Zilong, 38
Chiang Kai-shek, 44
Chi jiu zhi je Tang zhi wu (Tsinghua University collection), xi
Chu, state of: and Cao Gui, 180, 182; in "Great King Leaving Bin," 199, 202, 208–9, 212, 213nn19–20, 214n21; naming rules in, 158, 159, 160, 161; townships in, 122, 126, 127, 128, 135, 138n3, 142n37
Chuci, 140n14
Chunqiu (Spring and Autumn Annals), 57, 191, 198
cities (*chengshi*), 128–32

Collingwood, R. G., xiii–xiv, 206–7
commentaries, xi. See also *Lunyu* 7.14
conceptual metaphor theory, ix, 269
Confucianism, 26, 230; and Cao E, 27, 33; and *Huainanzi*, 239, 241, 250, 251, 258
Confucius, 181, 182, 198; and *Huainanzi*, 244, 247, 251; *vs.* Mozi, 193n20; on Shao music in Qi, xi, 53–76; and Shun, 67–71, 73
Cong zheng (Shanghai Museum collection), 125
correlative cosmology, 247–48, 250–53, 254, 257, 268
Cui Zhu, 188–89, 190

Da Dai liji, 80
Dai Dachang, 72
Danfu, Duke. *See* Tai, King
Dan Qian, 76n30
dao (the Way): and Cao Gui, 179, 182, 186; in *Huainanzi*, 243, 244, 245–60
Daoism, 25, 35; classical, 240, 241, 242, 246, 249, 254, 261; of *Huainanzi*, 239–40, 242–43, 247, 249, 251, 254–56, 260; Huang-Lao, 210, 243; Neo- (*xuanxue*), 60; suppression of, 241, 262; syncretic, 239, 241, 247, 253, 260, 261. See also *Laozi*; *Zhuangzi*
daoshu (Techniques of the Way), xiii, 254, 260, 261
Dawenkou period, 111
de (virtue), 174–75, 179
deities/spirits: ancestral, 2, 3, 16–18, 22n18, 100, 174; anthropomorphization of, 8, 22n19; female, 25–26; imperial honors for, 40, 41, 52n77; of nature, 3, 8, 15, 18, 20, 22n19; Shang, 1–20, 99; water, 26–27, 33, 38, 40–43

Democratic Centralism (*minzhu jizhong zhi*), 161, 162
Deng, state of, 150
Di tribes, 199, 201–4, 206
divination: on sacrifices to Yi Yin, 2–23; tortoise shell, 200, 201. See also oracle-bone inscriptions
Donggu ji (Zheng Ruxie), 64
Donggu Yi yizhuan (Zheng Ruxie), 64
Dong Kai, 35, 50n57
Donglongshan culture (Shangzhou), 80
Dongxiafeng site, 78
Dunhuang manuscripts, 54–55
Du Shang, 29–30, 31, 33

Eastern Zhou period, 122, 148, 150. *See also* Spring and Autumn period; Warring States period
Eberhard, Wolfram, 26, 33
Eno, Robert, 116n30
Erlitou site (Yanshi), 78–85
Erya, 110, 112, 126

Fan, state of, 160
Fang Shao, 50n59
fangshu (esoteric arts), 240–41
Fang Xiaoru, 42
Fang Yanming, 82
Fan Ning, 59, 60, 62, 72
Fan Ye, 29
Fan Zuyu, 63
filial piety, 26, 27, 31, 33–35, 38, 41–44
Five Phase theory, 31, 240, 248, 250. *See also* correlative cosmology
Former Kings (*xianwang*), 8, 11, 15–18, 20
Former Lords (*xiangong*), 8–12, 15, 16, 18, 19, 20
Fu Yue zhi ming (Tsinghua University collection), 93–94

Gao Ming, 93

Gao You, 240, 241–42, 243
Gao Zhaozi, 54
Gaozu, Emperor (Han), 253
Genette, Gérard, 216
Ge Yinliang, 71
Gongzi Wan of Chen (Chen Wan, Chen Jingzhong), 54–56, 59, 64–68, 71, 75nn21–23
Goryeo, 38, 40
Goujian, King (Yue), 127
Graham, A. C., 250, 267, 268
"Great King Leaving Bin" narrative, 197–214; in *Shijing*, 198, 199–203, 207, 211; in *Zhou xun*, 199, 202, 203, 208–11
Guangya, 142n40
Guan Xiu, 34, 49n48
Guan Zhong, 57, 124, 137, 175–78, 179, 244
Guanzi, 193n19; on Cao Gui, 172, 175–78, 179, 180, 182, 183, 194n30; and *Huainanzi*, 242, 244, 249; and state of Qi, 240
Gu Jiegang, 118n67, 138n3
Gu Lun, 56, 58, 67
Guo Jiang, 153
Guo Moruo, 93, 96, 115n18
Guo Xiang, 59, 60, 62, 71, 72
Guoyu, 2–3, 77, 117n42, 121, 172, 193n20; on Nine Provinces, 95, 99, 103, 106; on townships, 124, 125, 126
Guxi wenbian, 123
Guxun huizuan, 141n17

Handan Chun, 31, 48n36, 48n40
Han dynasty, 31, 43; commentaries on *Lunyu* 7.14 from, 54–57, 71–72, 73; and *Huainanzi*, 240, 241, 245, 250, 252, 253; and *Yi Zhou shu*, 217
Han Feizi, 128, 251–53, 255, 258
Hangzhou Bay, 26, 28, 33, 46n13

Hansen, Valerie, 40
Hanshi waijuan, 265n31
Han shu (History of the Former Han), 242; on *Lunyu* 7.14, 54, 66, 68, 71, 72; and *Yi Zhou shu*, 232n9, 233n16
Hao Jing, 69, 70
He Bian, 59
Heir and the Sage, The (Allan), x, 1, 171, 174, 184, 269
Helü, King (Wu), 199, 202, 208, 212n7, 213nn19–20, 214n21
Hengshui site (Jiangxian, Shanxi), 151
Herodotus, 188, 189
He Yan, 58, 60
High Ancestors (*gaozu*), 8, 15, 16, 18, 19, 20, 22n18
historicity, 2, 80; of Cao E story, 29, 31; and meaning, 184–91; vs. myth, ix–xiii
Histories (Herodotus), 188, 189
historiography: and biography, 215–16, 229–30; bricolage, xiii, 184–87, 190, 191; of Cao Gui, xii–xiii, 171–95; Chinese vs. Western, 187–90, 197–99; fact and meaning in, 184–91; and paratext, 216, 217, 218, 233n15; of women, 26
Hou Ba, 30
Hou Han shu (History of the Later Han), 29, 31, 222
Huainan, kingdom of, 240–42
Huainanzi (Master of Huainan), 239–66; on Cao Gui, 172, 182, 183, 194n30; *Daozang jiyao* edition of, 242; on "Great King Leaving Bin," 198, 205, 209, 210, 211, 212n7, 213n21; history of, 240–42; literary styles in, 245; "Overview of the Essentials" (*Yaolüe*) in, 243–45, 257–58, 261–62; preface to, 240, 241–42; structure of, 242–45;

summary of, 245–60; as syncretic work, xiii, 258–60, 261, 262; works related to, 240–41
Huan, Duke of Qi, 175–78, 183
Huan, Emperor (Han), 31
Huang, state of, 159
Huang Huaixin, 234n23, 235n40
Huang Kan, 59, 60, 62, 66, 71, 72, 75n30
Huang Peirong, 218, 227, 232n11, 234n28, 235n44, 236n49, 236n51
Huang Shi (Huang Yin), 11, 22n20
Huang shi Lunyu yishu canding (Wu Qian), 72
Huan Maoyong, 72
Hu Bingwen, 67, 68
Hu Fengdan, 27, 45n10
Hu Guang, 70
Huichang persecution (845), 35
Huizong, Emperor (Song), 40
Hu Zhenheng, 49n48

"Identities of Taigong Wang in Zhou and Han Literature" (Allan), x

Jiang Hongzhen, 48n37
Jiang Xi, 59, 60, 62, 71, 72
Jiang Yong, 71
Jiao Hong, 70, 75n21
Jiao Xun, 124
Jie (Xia), 186, 187
Jin, state of, 122, 124, 135, 138nn3–4, 153
Jing, Duke of Qi, 137
Jingdian shiwen (Lu Deming), 61–62, 72
Jin Lüxiang, 66, 67
Jin Tingdong, 45n7
Jin Wen Gong ru yu Jin (Tsinghua University collection), 121
Jizhong guwen (Ancient Texts Recovered at Ji Mound), 81, 217, 233n13

Johnson, David, 33

Kern, Martin, 245
Kinney, Anne Behnke, 264n20
Knapp, Keith, 33
Kong Yingda, 112, 202–3
Kuaiji dianlu (Yu Yu), 29
Kuaiji zhi, 28

Laozi, 242, 245, 252, 253, 265n29
Lau, D. C., 268
Le, state of, 161
Lévi-Strauss, Claude, xii, 171–72, 184, 212n4
li (pattern), 243, 246
Li, King (Zhou), 105
Li, Wai-yee, 190–91
Liang Han Sanguo xuean (Tang Yan), 57
Liang Ji, 29, 31
Liang shu, 141n17
Li Bo, 34
Li Daoyuan, 34
Lienü houzhuan (Xiang Yuan), 29
Li Fang, 29
Liji, 3, 72, 95, 143n42
Li Ji, 78
Li Jiahao, 138n4
Li Ling, 108, 110, 112
Ling Shu, 71, 72
Lin Huan, 111
Lin Xin (Shang king), 109
literati: and Cao Gui, 174–75; and historiography, 187–90, 191; of Qi vs. Lu, 179–80
Liu An, 194n30, 240–42, 243, 245, 250, 257, 262
Liu Bang, 240
Liu Baonan, 73, 76n39
Liu Chang, 240
Liu Ji, 42, 52n82
Liu Qiyu, 114

Liu Xiang, 218, 232n9, 232n11, 233n16
Liu Xiaochuo, 34
Li Xian, 29
Li Xiaohong, 29
Li Xuanbo, 78
Longshan culture, 79, 80, 82–85
Lu, state of: and Cao Gui, 175–78; and marriage relations, 147, 166n3; vs. Qi, 179–84, 194n30, 195n39; Shao music from, 56, 67, 68, 69, 70
Lü, state of, 153
Lu Deming, 61–62, 72
Lu Lun, 56
Lü Nan, 70
Lunyu (Analects), xi; on Cao Gui, 179–80; editions of, 56–57; and Qi vs. Lu, 182; and townships, 91, 92, 143n42
Lunyu 7.14 (Shao performance in Qi), xi, 53–76; Han commentaries on, 54–57, 71–72, 73; issue of meat in, 62, 65, 66, 72; Ming commentaries on, 68, 69–71, 73; Qing commentaries on, 71–73; Six Dynasty commentaries on, 57–61, 66; Song commentaries on, 62–66, 67, 68, 72, 73; Tang commentaries on, 61–62; Yuan commentaries on, 66–68, 73. See also *Gu Lun*; *Lu Lun*; *Qi Lun*; *Yuelun*; *Zhang Hou Lun*
Lunyu guzhu jijian (Pan Weicheng), 71, 72
Lunyu ji (Huan Maoyong), 72
Lunyu jibian (Zhen Dexiu), 63
Lunyu jijie (He Yan), 58, 59
Lunyu jishuo (Cai Jie), 65
Lunyu xiangjie (Hao Jing), 69
Lunyu yishu (Huang Kan), 59, 62, 66, 71, 72

Lunyu yiyuan (Zheng Ruxie), 64
Lunyu zhengyi (Liu Baonan), 73
Lunyu zhushu (Xing Bing), 62
Lunyu zuanshu (Zhao Shunsun), 63
Luo Jiaxiang, 232n11, 232n13
Lu Shanji, 70–71
Lüshi chunqiu, 2, 172; on "Great King Leaving Bin," 198, 205, 210; and *Huainanzi*, 240, 242, 252, 255
Lu Wenchao, 224, 234n33, 237n66
Lu You, 41
Lu Yuanchong, 27
Lu Zhi, 241

Mao Qiling, 72
Mao Rong, 241
Maoshi zhengyi, 91, 92, 104, 141n18, 202, 224
marriage relations, 2, 94; and naming rules, xii, 145–50, 153, 155–61, 163, 164, 166n3
Master Chen of Xin'an, 70
Master Feng of Houzhai, 70, 75n18
Master Fu of Qingyuan, 70
Mawangdui manuscripts, 246
McNeal, Robin, 221, 230, 231
Mengzi (Mencius), 68, 93, 143n40, 230; on Cao Gui, 179–80, 186–87; on "Great King Leaving Bin," 198, 199, 202, 203–4, 205, 207–8, 211, 213n12; on *Lunyu* 7.14, 68
Meyer, Andrew, 245
Ming dynasty: Cao E cult in, 42, 43; commentaries on *Lunyu* 7.14 from, 68, 69–71, 73
Mohism, 250
Mozi, 93, 181–82, 244, 247, 251
Mu, King (Zhou), 103, 222, 223, 224
Murray, Judson, 257, 258
music: and Qi vs. Lu, 181–82, 193n20; and ritual, 251, 253; Shao, xi, 53–76

Index | 279

name differentiation, rules of, 145–69; explication of, 148–56, 160; and marriage relations, xii, 145–50, 153, 155–61, 163, 164, 166n3; for men, 153–56; Wu Zhenfeng on, 156–66
Nan Daji, 43
New Policies (Song dynasty), 38, 40
"Nine Provinces" (*jiu zhou*) model, xii, 89–119; province names in, 107–13; and Shang tribute system, 97–103; and Western Zhou tribute system, 103–7; *zhou* in, 90, 91–97, 107
Ni Shiyi, 67–68
Niu Hong'en, 218
Ni Yuanlu, 38

oracle-bone inscriptions: on Nine Provinces, xii, 89–114; province names in, 107–13; on sacrifices, 2–20; on tribute systems, 97–107; on Yi Yin, xi, 2–20; on *zhou*, 91–97
oral transmission: of dynastic legends, 172, 184; and *Huainanzi*, 256; and Nine Provinces, 90, 108
Orchid Pavilion Poems (*Lanting shi*; Sun Chuo), 60–61
Ouyang Xun, 29

Pan Weicheng, 71, 72, 76n35
Pan Zhen, 234n25, 234n31
Patterned Past, A (Schaberg), 190
Peking University bamboo-slip collection, xiii, 199, 202, 203, 208–11
Peng, state of, 150, 151
Peng Bangjiong, 113
Pengbo, 151
Pingdingshan site (Henan), 150
Plato, 197
poetry: on Cao E, 27–28, 34–35, 41, 42, 43, 49n48, 50n52, 50n58; in *Huainanzi*, 245–46, 257; and *Lunyu* 7.14, 60–61; and women's names, 145–48
political/state affairs: and Cao E cult, 35, 38, 39–40, 42; and eunuchs, 29–31; and "Great King Leaving Bin," 199, 203, 205–8, 210–11, 213n12; and historiography, xiii, 198; *Huainanzi* on, 246, 247, 249–51, 253–55, 256, 257, 262; and marriage relations, xii, 145–48, 149, 153, 154, 161; and Yi Yin, 3, 15, 18, 20. *See also* Cao Gui; "Nine Provinces" (*jiu zhou*) model; townships; tribute systems; Wen, King (Zhou)
Puett, Michael, 262
Pure Critics, 29–30, 31

qi, 61, 174; in *Huainanzi*, 240, 247–50, 252, 253, 254, 257
Qi, state of, 183, 193n19; and Cao Gui, 173–74, 175–78, 185–86; and *Guanzi*, 240; *vs.* Lu, 179–84, 194n30, 195n39; and marriage relations, 166n3; Shao music in, xi, 53–76; townships in, 122, 137, 138nn3–4; and "Traces of Yu," 90; version of *Lunyu* from, 56–57; women in, 145–47
Qi Lun, 56, 57, 58
Qin, state of, 90, 122, 138n3, 240, 253
Qing dynasty: Cao E cult in, 42–43; commentaries on *Lunyu* 7.14 from, 71–73
Qiong, state of, 158, 159
Qiu Xigui, 6, 101, 108
Queen, Sarah, 252–53, 257, 258, 265n31

ritual: and Cao E, 29, 39, 47n27; and *Huainanzi*, 247, 251–52; and music,

280 | Index

ritual *(continued)*
  54, 70, 181, 251, 253; and Nine Provinces, 99; and townships, 136. *See also* sacrifices
ritual propriety: and Cao Gui, 177–78, 181, 185–86; of Shao music in Qi, xi, 56
Rong Cheng shi (Shanghai Museum collection), 90, 107, 108, 110, 111, 112, 114
Ruan Ji, 61
Ruan Yuan, 45n7

sacrifices: calendar for, 8, 18–19; recipients of, 2–3, 8, 20; and Shang tribute system, 99–101; to Yi Yin, 1–20
sage kings, x, 3, 60, 171, 180. *See also* Shun; Tang
Schaberg, David, 190
self-cultivation, xiii, 226, 227, 242, 245, 246–60, 261
shamans, xi, 26, 29, 43
Shangdi, 18, 99
Shang dynasty: and Nine Provinces, 108, 114; sacrifices to Yi Yin in, 1–15, 18–19; tribute system of, xii, 90, 95, 96, 97–103, 104, 107, 111, 113, 114; and Xia, x, 2, 78–79, 80, 82, 83; in *Yi Zhou shu*, 219, 220, 222, 225–27, 229, 230, 235n45; *zhou* in, 91, 92–96, 97. *See also* oracle-bone inscriptions
Shanghai Museum bamboo-slip manuscripts, 90, 122–23, 125, 126, 172. See also *Cao Mie zhi zhen*; *Rong Cheng shi*
Shangshu (Venerated Documents), 80, 218, 233n15; on Nine Provinces, xii, 89–90, 93, 103, 107; on townships, 141n18, 143n40, 143n42
Shangshu dazhuan, 96

Shangshu zhengyi (Kong Yingda), 112
Shang Yang, 244
Shanhaijing (Classics of Mountains and Oceans), 247
Shao, Duke of, 155
Shaochai site (Gongyi), 80
Shaogong Shi, 226
Shao music, xi, 53–76
Shao Wangping, 97
Shaoxing cult. *See* Cao E cult
Shape of the Turtle, The: Myth, Art, and Cosmos in Early China (Allan), x
Shaughnessy, Edward, 218, 233n13
shenming (spirit illumination), 250, 256, 259
Shen Shouzheng, 71
Shen Zhili, 27, 45n10
Shenzi, 172, 182
Shiben, 77, 81
Shi Boxuan, 67
Shiji (Records of the Historian; Historical Records; Sima Qian), 1, 62, 213n19; on Cao Gui, 172, 183, 184, 194n30; on "Great King Leaving Bin," 198, 205, 209; on King Wen, 220, 223, 228–29, 230; on *Lunyu* 7.14, 54, 63, 68, 71, 72, 76n30; on Nine Provinces, 103; and Sima Tan, 260; on townships, 127, 137, 140n16, 141n18, 142n37; on Xia dynasty, 77, 81; and *Yi Zhou shu*, 237n57
Shijiahe site, 84
Shiji bianhuo, 72
Shijing (Classic of Poetry): on "Great King Leaving Bin," xiii, 198, 199–203, 207, 211; Mao commentary on, 91, 92, 104, 141n18, 202, 224; on Nine Provinces, 98; on tribute system, 104, 105; on women, 145–48; *zhou* in, 91, 92
Shiji yinyi (Xu Huang), 81

Shiji zhengyi (Zhang Shoujie), 81
Shiyijing wendui, 72
Shuijing zhu (Li Daoyuan), 34
Shun (sage-king), x, 171, 180; and Confucius, 67–71, 73; and Shao music, 54, 55, 59, 62, 64, 65, 68
Shuowen jiezi (Xu Shen), 242; on townships, 125, 126, 140nn15–17; and *Yi Zhou shu*, 232n9; *zhou* in, 91, 92
Shuoyuan: on "Great King Leaving Bin," 198, 205, 210; on *Lunyu* 7.14, 71, 72, 76n30
Siku quanshu, 63, 65
Sima Qian, 172, 236n48
Sima Tan, 258, 260, 261
Sima Zhen, 140n16
Sishu bianyi, 72
Sishu daiwen (Xiao Yi), 68
Sishu guanqie (Shi Boxuan), 67
Sishu guren dianlin (Jiang Yong), 71
Sishu Hunan jiang (Ge Yinliang), 71
Sishu jishi (Ni Shiyi), 67, 68
Sishu jizhu (Zhu Xi), 63
Sishu kaoyi (Zhai Hao), 72
Sishu tong (Hu Bingwen), 68
Sishu wenda (Dai Dachang), 72
Sishu yijie (Yuan Junweng), 68
Sishu yueshuo (Sun Zhaoxing), 71
Six Dynasty period, 57–61, 66
Song, state of, 137
Song dynasty: Cao E cult in, 27, 35–41, 43; commentaries on *Lunyu* 7.14 from, 62–66, 67, 68, 72, 73
"Song of Everlasting Sorrow" ("Chang hen ge"; Bai Juyi), 147
Song Yuan zizhi tongjian, 40
Song Zhiwen, 34
"Splendid Woman, A" (*Shijing*, "Airs of Wey"), 145–48
Spring and Autumn period, 158; Nine Provinces in, 90, 92, 110, 111–12; townships in, xii, 121, 122, 124, 125, 139n8. See also Cao Gui; Gongzi Wan of Chen
Sun Chuo, 60–61
Sun Qingwei, 84
Sun Yabing, 111
Sun Ying'ao, 70, 75n20
Sun Yirang, 234n24, 236n49
Sun Zhaoxing, 71
Sunzi bingfa, 172, 254, 258
Su Shi, 70, 71

Tai, King (Zhou; Duke Danfu), 199, 201–5, 207, 209, 212n5
Taigong Wang, 226
Tai Jia (Shang), 1, 2, 19
taiping dao (Way of Great Peace) rebellion, 241
Taiping yulan, 29, 80, 81, 237n66
Taiyi sheng shui (Guodian manuscript), 265n34
Tan, state of, 145–47
Tang (Shang sage-king), 1, 2, 186, 187, 189
Tang Dapei, 234n25
Tang dynasty: Cao E cult in, 34–35; commentaries on *Lunyu* 7.14 from, 61–62
Tang Yan, 57
Tao Zongyi, 50n59
Tengxian (Shandong), 150
Tertullian, 193n16
Thompson, Paul, 267, 268–69
tianshi dao (Way of the Celestial Masters) rebellion, 241
Tongjian dili tongshi (Wang Yinglin), 81
townships (*xian*), xii, 121–44; and cities (*chengshi*), 128–32, 133, 134, 135, 137; locations of, 122–25, 137; officials in, 132–34, 138; as settlements (*yi*), 134–37, 138; sizes of, 125–28, 137

tribute systems: Shang, xii, 90, 95, 96, 97–103, 104, 107, 111, 113, 114; Western Zhou, 90, 103–7

Tsinghua University bamboo-slip manuscript collection, xi, xii, xivn8, 93–94, 121, 223, 228, 231n2, 236n51. See also *Yue Gong qi shi*

Vankeerberghen, Griet, 258

Wadian site (Yuxian, Yuzhou), 80, 83
Waley, Arthur, 115n4, 117n35
Wallacker, Benjamin E., 264n28
Wang Anshi, 37–38, 64
Wang Bi, 60
Wangchenggang site (Dengfeng, Henan), 78, 80, 82, 83, 84, 85
Wang Guimin, 101, 103
Wang Guowei, 116n30
Wang Hunan, 67
Wang Niansun, 142n40
Wang Su, 58, 59, 62, 71–73, 76n30, 76n35, 76n39
Wang Xizhi, 27, 31, 48n37
Wang Yinglin, 81
Wang Yu, 27
Wang Yuanshan, 67
Wang Yun, 61
Warring States period: and Cao E, 26; Daoism in, 243, 265n34; King Wen in, 215, 217; Nine Provinces in, 89–90, 107, 111; townships in, 122, 139n8; Yi Yin in, x, xi, 18; and *Yi Zhou shu*, 217; *Zhou xun* from, 206, 210, 212n6. See also Cao Gui; *Yue Gong qi shi*
Wei, Prince of, 40
Wei (Wey), state of, 59, 60, 137, 145–47
Wei Lang, 31
Wei Zhao, 124, 126
Wen, Emperor (Han), 240
Wen, King (Teng), 203

Wen, King (Zhou), xiii, 70, 91, 155, 215–37; and "Great King Leaving Bin," 202–3
wen and *wu*, 174–75, 177
Wen Jiang, 147, 166n3
Wenxuan, 72, 218
Western philosophy: *vs.* Chinese, 187–90, 197–99; and history, 197–99
Western Zhou period: naming rules in, xii, 145–69; Nine Provinces in, 90, 96, 98, 111; townships in, 122, 124; tribute system in, 90, 103–7
Whitehead, Alfred North, 197
women, 11; chastity of, 42–43; as deities, 25–26; filial piety of, 33–34, 42; naming rules for, xii, 145–69. *See also* Cao E
Wu, Emperor (Han), 241, 245, 250
Wu, King (Zhou), 106, 111, 147, 186, 187, 189; in *Yi Zhou shu*, 226, 227–28
Wu, state of: in "Great King Leaving Bin," 199, 202, 208, 212n7, 213nn19–20, 214n21; naming rules in, 164–65; townships in, xii, 122, 126, 127, 128, 138n3, 142n37
Wu Changzong, 71
Wu Cheng, 67
Wu Ding, King (Shang), 94
Wu Qian, 72, 75n30
wuwei (non-action), 249, 256
Wu Xingzuo, 45n7
Wu Zhenfeng, xii, 156–66
Wu Zixu, 26, 29, 32–33, 213n19
Wu Zixu bianwen, 33

Xia dynasty, x, xii, 2, 77–87; capitals of, 78, 80–81, 84; classical references to, 77, 80–81, 85; dating of, 80–83; and Nine Provinces, 107–8, 114; and "Traces of Yu," 90
Xian, Duke of Qin, 212n6

Xia Nai, 79
Xiang, King (Zhou), 99
Xiang Yuan, 29
Xiao Yi, 67, 68
Xia-Shang-Zhou Chronology Project, xi–xii, 77–87
Xiaxu (Wastes of Xia) site (Henan), 78, 79
Xie Liangzuo, 62
Xin'an School of Principle, 67
Xing, state of, 145–47
Xing Bing, 62
Xinshu, 209, 211, 212n7, 213n20
xinshu (Techniques of the Mind), 249
Xinxu, 172
Xinyang Chu bamboo slips, 118n65
Xinzhai sites (Xinmi, Yuxian), 80, 82, 83, 84, 85
Xu, state of, 153, 159
Xuan, King of Qi, 186, 187, 189
Xuanren, Empress Dowager (Song), 38
xuanxue (esoteric arts, Neo-Daoism), 60
Xue, state of, 161
Xu Huang, 81
Xulu (Dan Qian), 76n30
Xu Shen, 232n9, 242
Xu Xusheng, 78, 79

Yan, state of, 122, 138n4
Yangjia site (Shaanxi), 104
Yangshao culture, 78, 79
Yang Shi, 62
Yang Xiu, 31
Yan Shigu, 140n16, 232n9, 241
Yan Ying, 137
Yanzi chunqiu, 137, 193nn19–20; on Cao Gui, 180, 181, 182
Yao (sage-king), x, 171, 180
Yijing (Changes), 57, 242, 244
Yili, 71
Yin and Yang, 31, 240, 247, 248, 250. See also correlative cosmology

Ying, state of, 150
Yin Gongcheng, 42
Yin Tun, 62
Yin Wei, 45n10
Yi Shi, 10–11
Yiwen leiju (Ouyang Xun), 29
Yi Yin, x–xi, 1–23; day-name (*riming*) of, 7, 19; and Former Lords (*xiangong*), 8–12; mythologization of, 11–12; as nature spirit, 12–18, 19–20; as shaman, xi
Yi zhi yi (Mawangdui manuscript), 142n40
Yi Zhou shu (Remnant Zhou Documents), xiii, 215–37; "Individual Instructions" section of, 225–27, 228; "Instructions and Models" sequence in, 219–20, 228; "Martial Endeavors" sequence in, 221–22, 228; preface to, 216, 217–31, 233n15; "Preparing a Legacy" section of, 227–28; "Residence at Cheng" sequence in, 222–24, 228; "Rule-Setting" section of, 224–25, 228; textual history of, 216–17; on townships, 140n16; on Xia dynasty, 77
Yi Zhou shu jixun jiaoshi (Zhu Youzeng), 140n16
Yongle dadian, 28
Youshen tribe, 2, 23n21
Yu (Xia ruler), 59, 80, 81, 84; and Nine Provinces, 89, 90, 91, 97–98, 103, 107
Yuan dynasty: Cao E cult in, 41–42; commentaries on *Lunyu* 7.14 from, 66–68, 73
Yuan Jie, 72
Yuan Junweng, 67, 68
Yue, state of, 26; cities (*chengshi*) in, 128–32; immigrants to, 129, 134–35, 138; townships in, xii, 121–44

Yue Gong qi shi (May the Lord of Yue Attend; Tsinghua University collection), xii, 121–44; on cities (*chengshi*), 128–32; on township officials, 132–34; on Yue townships, 122–28, 134–37
Yueji, 72
Yuelun (Ruan Ji), 61
"Yu gong" (Tribute of Yu; *Shangshu*), xii, 89–90, 96–98, 103, 106, 114; province names in, 107–13
Yuhuicun site (Shandong), 83–84
Yupian, 125, 141n17
Yu Xingwu, 101, 108–9, 119n80
Yu Yu, 29
Yu Yue, 143n42

Zai Wo, 57
Zang Wenzhong, 3
Ze, state of, 151, 152, 164, 167n10
Zeng, state of, 158, 159
Zeng Gongliang, 28
Zhai Hao, 72, 76n35
Zhang E, 45n10
Zhang Hou Lun (Marquis Zhang's Analects), 56, 57
Zhang Jue, 241
Zhang Shi, 62
Zhang Shoujie, 81
Zhanguoce, 172
Zhang Xiaobiao, 35
Zhang Yachu, 154
Zhang Yu, 56, 57, 74
Zhang Zhenglang, 22n21
Zhan Qin, 2, 3
Zhao, King (Chu), 199, 202, 208–9, 213nn19–20, 214n21
Zhao Gu/Jia, 35
Zhao Jianzi (Tsinghua University collection), 121
Zhao Ruji, 27
Zhao Shunsun, 63

Zhaowen, King (Zhou), 208, 210, 211, 212n6
Zhen Dexiu, 63
Zheng, state of: music of, 59, 60; naming rules in, 163–64; townships in, 136, 137
Zheng Qingzhi, 41, 52n76
Zheng Ruxie (Donggu Jushi), 64–65
Zheng Xuan, 54–56, 57, 58, 59, 74, 92, 141n18
Zheng Zijia sang (Shanghai Museum collection), 122–23, 126
Zhezong, Emperor (Song), 38
Zhi of Lu, Grand Preceptor, 67, 68, 69, 75n20
Zhong Kang eclipse, 80
zhou (province), 90, 91–97, 107
Zhou, Duke of, 147, 207, 226
Zhou, King (Shang), 186, 187, 219, 220, 235n45
Zhou Dunyi, 64
Zhou dynasty, x–xiii, 79, 80, 85; clans and lineages in, 145, 147–56, 167nn5–7; Ji clan of, 147, 149–53, 155, 156, 159, 161, 163–65, 167nn10–11; naming rules in, xii, 145–69; Nine Provinces in, 90, 96, 98, 108, 111, 114; townships in, 122, 124; tribute system in, 90, 103–7; Yi Yin in, 8, 11–12, 19; *zhou* in, 91, 97. *See also* Spring and Autumn period; Warring States period
Zhou li, 18, 109, 112, 124
Zhou Shenglie, 58, 59, 60, 62, 72, 73, 75n30, 76n39
Zhou shu, 232n9
Zhou Suping, 139n8
Zhou Tan, 50n52
Zhou xun (Zhou instructions; Peking University collection), xiii, 199, 202, 203, 208–11, 212n6

Zhu, state of, 150
Zhuang, Duke of Lu, 172–74, 176–78, 180, 186, 187
Zhuang, Duke of Qi, 188–89
Zhuangzi: on "Great King Leaving Bin," 198, 199, 202–5, 207–11, 213n12; and *Huainanzi*, 242, 245, 246, 249, 250, 252, 254, 255, 258–59, 260, 261
Zhu Di (Yongle emperor; Ming), 42
Zhu E, 35, 43
Zhu Fenghan, 118n55
Zhushu jinian (Bamboo Annals), 80, 81, 222, 223, 235n45; *Guben zhushu jinian*, 1, 19, 77

Zhu Wanli, 27, 43, 45n10
Zhu Xi, 54, 65, 66, 67, 68, 70; on *Lunyu* 7.14, 63–64, 75n21, 76n36
Zhu Youzeng, 140n16, 234n33
Zhuzi huowen, 72
Zifan Ziyu (Tsinghua University collection), 121
Zou Heng, 78, 79, 80
Zuo zhuan, 2, 20, 68, 121, 166n3; on Cao Gui, 172–74, 177–78, 179, 183, 184, 185–86, 187; fact and meaning in, 188–89; historiography of, 191, 195n42; on townships, 124, 126, 135–37; on tribute system, 106–7

Milton Keynes UK
Ingram Content Group UK Ltd.
UKHW021941270524
443198UK00003B/35